PLATONIC WRITINGS

EDITED BY CHARLES L. GRISWOLD, JR.

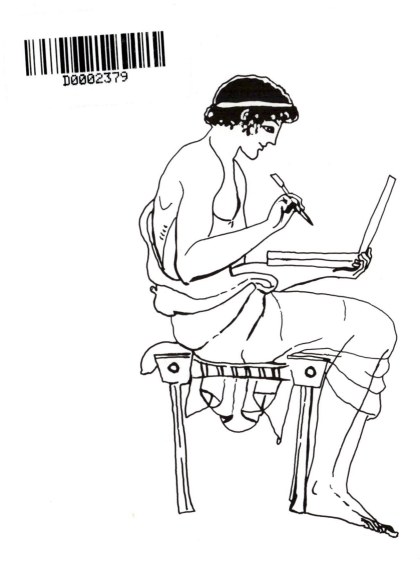

Platonic Writings,
Platonic Readings

PLATONIC READINGS

ROUTLEDGE   New York   London

First published in 1988 by

Routledge
an imprint of
Routledge, Chapman & Hall, Inc.
29 West 35 Street
New York, NY 10001

Published in Great Britain by

Routledge
11 New Fetter Lane
London EC4P 4EE

Library of Congress Cataloging-in-Publication Data

Platonic writings/Platonic readings.

  Bibliography: p
  Includes index.
  1. Plato. Dialogues. 2. Dialogue. I. Griswold,
Charles L., Jr., 1951-
B395.P54 1988 184   87-28635
ISBN 0-415-00186-2
ISBN 0-415-00187-0 (pbk.)

British Library Cataloguing in Publication Data

Platonic writings—Platonic readings.
  1. Plato
  I. Griswold, Charles L., Jr.
  184   B395

ISBN 0-415-00186-2
ISBN Pbk 0-415-00187-0

ὁ διάλογος κόσμος ἐστὶν καὶ ὁ κόσμος διάλογος
the dialogue is a cosmos and the cosmos a dialogue

ANONYMOUS COMMENTATOR ON PLATO

Contents

Acknowledgments

I am pleased to acknowledge the helpful criticisms of various drafts of the Introduction to this volume offered to me by Stephen Griswold, Mitchell Miller, Edward Regis, and David Roochnik. Katharine Fowle Griswold, Stephen Griswold and Dale Sinos made some valuable suggestions about the organization of the volume, for which I am also grateful. I would also like to thank Rémi Brague and Thomas Szlezák for reviewing the bibliography and for proposing several additions. My principal debt is to David Lachterman. His recommendations concerning both the Introduction and the other contributions to the volume were outstanding, and I adopted them all. None of these friends and colleagues, of course, is to be held responsible for any shortcomings this book may have.

I am greatly indebted to my editor at Routledge, Maureen Mac-Grogan, who did so much to make this book possible, and to Cecile R. Watters for her skillful editing of the final version of the MS. Jane Ashley Barr did a fine job in preparing the Index of Proper Names. I am also grateful to Sarah Fisher (Senior Painting Conservator at the National Gallery of Art, Washington, D.C.) for her help in arranging for the photographs used on the cover of this book. Finally, my thanks to the Graduate School of Arts and Sciences at Howard University for technical assistance in the preparation of the MS.

The text and translation of the quotation on the epigraph page are to be found on pp. 30–31 of L. G. Westerink's *Anonymous Prolegomena to Platonic Philosophy* (see the bibliography below). I note that with few exceptions only the first occurrences of Latin and transliterated Greek words in the present book are italicized, and that in almost all cases accents have been omitted from transliterated words.

Abbreviations

Alc. I, II	*Alcibiades* I, II
Apol.	*Apology*
Charm.	*Charmides*
Crat.	*Cratylus*
Epin.	*Epinomis*
Euthyd.	*Euthydemus*
Euth.	*Euthyphro*
Grg.	*Gorgias*
H. Maj.	*Hippias Major*
H. Min.	*Hippias Minor*
La.	*Laches*
Ly.	*Lysis*
Menex.	*Menexenus*
Parm.	*Parmenides*
Pho.	*Phaedo*
Phr.	*Phaedrus*
Phil.	*Philebus*
Prot.	*Protagoras*
Rep.	*Republic*
Soph.	*Sophist*
Pol.	*Statesman*
Symp.	*Symposium*
Theae.	*Theaetetus*
Tim.	*Timaeus*

Titles that are not abbreviated include *Crito*, *Ion*, *Laws*, *Letters*, *Meno*, as well as *Cleitophon*, *Critias*, *Erastai*, *Hipparchus*, *Minos*, and *Theages*.

Introduction

Charles L. Griswold, Jr.

Plato's influence on Western thought is assessed in Alfred North White-head's famous remark that "the safest general characterization of the European philosophical tradition is that it consists of a series of footnotes to Plato." Whitehead then explains his extraordinary judgment: "I do not mean the systematic scheme of thought which scholars have doubtfully extracted from his writings. I allude to the wealth of general ideas scattered through them. His personal endowments, his wide opportunities for experience at a great period of civilization, his inheritance of an intellectual tradition not yet stiffened by excessive systematization, have made his writings an inexhaustible mine of suggestion."[1] The resistance of Plato's writings to systematization, their ability to keep philosophizing alive, is surely inseparable from the kind of writings they are—namely, dialogues. Thus Plato's commitment to *dialogic* writing calls out for explanation.

This book responds by exploring two questions about Plato's dialogues: first, "why did Plato write dialogues?" and second, "how ought we to read Plato's dialogues?"

The focus of the first question is the rationale for Plato's exceptional rhetoric of inquiry. His dialogues stand apart from treatises on the one hand and, say, tragedies and comedies on the other. Plato is the only major philosopher in the Western tradition to have written dialogues almost exclusively (exclusively if none of the *Letters* is authentic). What underlies his dedication to this form of writing? The second question to be explored here is a special case of the hermeneutic problem of textual interpretation, and naturally leads to the following queries. What assumptions about the text do we make when we open a Platonic dialogue? What assumptions ought we to make? How do they illumine, and how do they conceal, the content of the dialogues? How would one go about defending them?

All the contributions to this volume deal principally with at least one of our two leading questions. Some of the essays discuss both why Plato wrote dialogues and how we ought to read Platonic writing, for the two are closely connected. Indeed, it could be argued that they are interdependent: if we are to explain on the basis of a given reading of the dialogues why Plato wrote dialogues, we would have to know how to interpret them. But to know how to interpret them is to know something about why Plato wrote as he did. For example, if we knew that Plato regarded all the "dramatic" aspects of his works (including the use of myths and imagery) as nothing more than entertaining decoration around a philosophic core of concepts best expressed in various technical arguments, then it would make sense to look through, or rather past the dramatic aspects to the dialogue's core meaning.

The interdependence of our two themes, however, need not prevent us from focusing first on one and then on the other. The issue of interpretation is the more easily accessible of the two. The general problem of interpreting texts has, to begin with, already been intensively discussed in a variety of fields. Therefore, the "how ought we interpret a Platonic dialogue" question will sound considerably more familiar to a broad spectrum of readers than the "why did Plato write dialogues" question (one that leads directly to central issues of Plato's metaphysics). The intended audience of this book includes not just Plato specialists but scholars working in areas such as the history of Greek thought, hermeneutics and literary theory, rhetoric, and the philosophy of literature.

Further, the surface form of Plato's dialogues gives us *some* clues as to how we might proceed in interpreting them, while providing little explanation about why Plato wrote as he did. Most obviously, these texts are not first-person monologues in which the author speaks directly to the reader; they are dialogues in which the author never speaks in propria persona. At least for the reader who begins without a clear thesis about Plato's reasons for writing dialogues, it seems prudent, for example, to exercise caution in reading the author's meaning from the utterances of the dramatis personae. For reasons such as these, each of the major sections of this volume ("Essays" and "Dialogues") focuses first on the "reading" question and then on the "writing" question. Within each of the sections, the movement of thought is from specific analyses of one or more Platonic texts to more general reflections on the principles of Platonic philosophy.

The questions explored in this book are far from new. In particular, the debate about how to categorize the Platonic writings—and so about how we are to read them—goes back to antiquity. In the third book of the *Republic* Plato himself provides the foundational discussion of genres. In the first book of the *Poetics* Aristotle explicitly takes up the issue of the *logoi Sokratikoi* (the "Socratic discourses"), remarking that "there is further an art which imitates by language alone, without harmony, in prose or in verse, and if in verse, either in some one or in a plurality of metres. This form of imitation is to this day without a name. We have no common name for a mime of Sophron or Xenarchus or a Socratic Conversation."[2] Alexandrian lecture notes on Plato,[3] Diogenes Laertius' report of conflicting characterizations of the Platonic dialogue (including of Thrasylus' arrangement of the dialogues into "dramatic" tetralogies),[4] and the recently found papyrus discussing both the "dramatic" dimension of the dialogues and the problem of determining which of Plato's characters (if any) "speaks" for him[5] confirm the venerable status of the question of the Platonic writings.

Nonetheless, in modern times the problem of interpreting Plato—and with it, the problem as to why Plato wrote dialogues—has not received the attention it deserves.[6] Scholars working on Plato tend to proceed in their work with insufficient reflection on their own assumptions concerning the two themes outlined above. They therefore tend either to ignore scholars making different assumptions or, when they do read them, to dismiss them as misguided or incompetent.[7] This is an odd situation in that, as already indicated, the general problem of textual interpretation has been discussed intensively in recent years by literary critics and some philosophers. It has become impossible to write successfully on any period of literature without a working knowledge of the whole problem of interpretation. Indeed, the importance of reflecting on the problem has impressed itself on philosophers of law and jurisprudence, and even on economists.[8] Of course, theologians and readers of Scripture have long since puzzled over hermeneutical issues. The time has now come for a full-fledged debate about the reading of Plato, and so also about the reasons for which Plato wrote dialogues. This book represents a step in that direction.[9]

This volume comprises two parts, "Essays" and "Dialogues." In each of them, the "how ought we to read Plato" question is explored first and the "why did Plato write dialogues" question second. These dialogues set into motion, as it were, the theses argued in the first section of the book. Each of these dialogues is structured by four elements: an important and recent book about Plato, a critical reading of the book in the light of one or another of our guiding themes, a reply by the book's author, and, of course, the reader's response to the entire exchange. Although all the dialogues in the present volume bring out the issues in a way that is of permanent value, a further word of explanation as to their inclusion in this book is in order.

In preparing this volume I solicited contributions from established scholars representing a wide variety of approaches to Plato. Given the scarcity of published debate about the problem of reading Plato, the deep disagreements between interpreters modern as well as ancient, and the genuine complexity of the issues involved, dialogues between the proponents of various positions seemed a particularly efficient way to bring out the essential characteristics and commitments, and indeed the strengths and weaknesses of these positions. Such debates help the reader to understand where the similarities and differences between standpoints lie and to evaluate their adequacy. The dialogues bring out the difficulties and objections that proponents of the various positions must address in order to be successful, at least in the eyes of other informed scholars. Even the junctures at which the participants in the exchanges seem unable to see each other's points are instructive for the reader, as are analogous junctures in Plato's dialogues at which dialogue falters. In all these ways, the exchanges contribute to the general discussion about Platonic writing that this volume as a whole is intended to encourage. Finally, in a book devoted to questions about dialogue, the inclusion of these debates is not inappropriate.

The guiding and unifying threads of the book are its two major questions, and the two parts of the book ("Essays" and "Dialogues") exhibit a parallel organization of the contributions around this pair of questions. I have already explained why the focus is first on "how to read Plato" and then on "why Plato wrote dialogues." The parallelism of the two sections goes still further. The movement of the essays as well as of the dialogues is from a focus on particular texts to a focus on broad questions about Platonic dialectic and writing. And in ways I shall adumbrate in a moment each essay leads to the next, and each dialogue to the next. It is my hope that the reader will feel encouraged by the book's internal unity to begin this "feast of discourses" (to borrow a phrase from Plato) at its beginning.

Our reflections on the problem of reading Plato begin with two essays on specific Platonic texts, the *Republic* and the *Gorgias*. Both essays outline competing theories of interpretation and argue that one of them better explains a Platonic text. These essays thus let us see how interpretive assumptions actually work in concrete situations, and so to understand what is at stake in the debate over reading Platonic writing. The "Dialogues" section of the book offers a similar start and a similar benefit.

The *Republic* has always been among the most widely read (perhaps simply *the* most widely read) and most bitterly disputed of Platonic dialogues. The history of criticism of its theses goes back to Aristotle's *Politics*. The Latin translations of the *Republic* in the Renaissance sparked a lively debate about Plato's political thought, a debate that explicitly touched on the problem of interpretation.[10] Philosophically minded statesmen such as Thomas Jefferson thought the *Republic* pernicious and in general its rhetoric sophistic,[11] a judgment also evident in Karl Popper's famous attack on Plato during the World War II years. The controversy about the dialogue has lost none of its vigor and continues to include debate about correct interpretive assumptions.[12] The *Republic* is thus an excellent place to raise the question as to how one ought to read Plato.

In his essay, Diskin Clay argues that we are warranted by inspection of Plato's use of the dialogue form in assuming certain basic principles of interpretation, such as respect for authorial anonymity and allowance for the possibility that views can be revised in the course of discussion. Clay goes on to argue that objections presented by characters other than Socrates are carefully planted by Plato to lead the reader to call into question Socrates' own theses propounded earlier in the discussion. In the light of those points Clay argues that interpretations of the *Republic* such as Popper's are untenable. Clay's reflections illustrate "the difficulties of interpreting the *Republic* without coming to terms with the distinctive character of Platonic writing in the *Republic*." In the course of his discussion he offers a number of valuable observations about the dialogue, as well as an interpretation to the effect that the *Republic*'s *kallipolis* ("beautiful city") is neither a blueprint for a totalitarian state (Popper) nor a utopia that we are meant to try to institute in practice. The *Republic* is, Clay argues, an "open dialogue" that constantly challenges its readers to reexamine its own theses. This challenge is evident, Clay maintains, in the various paradoxes and tensions Plato embedded in the *Republic*, such as the paradox of the philosopher king and the tension between the good of the individual's soul and the good of the *polis* that supposedly represents the soul writ large.

Clay's reading of the *Republic* suggests that deficiencies, paradoxes, tensions, and even fallacies in a Platonic dialogue ought to be taken not as signaling Plato's inability to reason well but as intentionally designed invitations to the reader to sort through the topic at hand himself. The design of Plato's rhetoric reflects both Plato's understanding of the truth of the topic and his understanding of the pedagogical tropes best suited for conducting a reader to the truth. This line of reasoning is taken up by Richard McKim in his essay on the *Gorgias*. He does so in connection with the theme of the good of the individual's soul, a theme with which the preceding essay by Clay concludes and that is crucial in the *Gorgias*.

McKim begins with a criticism of both the "analytically trained commentators" who read the Platonic dialogues as though they were treatises and the "speculative excesses" to which writers who stress Plato's "dramatic irony" and supposed "unwritten teaching" are prone. McKim argues that a middle way is possible and indeed that his discussion of the *Gorgias* illustrates it. While McKim argues for a certain way of reading Plato, his study also offers an explanation as to why the *Gorgias* is a *dialogue* and more broadly as to why Plato adhered to the dialogue form of writing.

McKim distinguishes between the dialogue carried on "within" Plato's text and that which Plato carries on with the reader of the text. Although the interlocutors within the text may not be able to understand the fallaciousness or real purpose of an argument, the reader of the text may be expected to do so. That is, the reader is a participant in a conversation with Plato (and the latter is assumed to know what he is doing). Platonic reading thus takes on a characteristic of Platonic writing. According to McKim, Plato has Socrates defend his axiom that virtue "is always supremely beneficial to the moral agent himself" not so much in a "logical" as a "psychological" way, and this for a very strong philosophical reason: at heart there is no "logical proof" of the axiom. Rather, the evidence for it depends in good part on beliefs or intuitions we all hold, however much we might wish to avoid acknowledging them (and "sophistical debaters" are precisely those who do avoid acknowledging them). In the crucial phenomenon of "shame," McKim finds evidence that Plato believed that there exists truth that is beyond the pale of argument. Nevertheless, argument can help dispose us to "face up to the moral consequences of our sense of shame." McKim's thesis about the philosophical status of shame and moral insight provides powerful support for his reading of a Platonic dialogue, and indeed for reading them *as* dialogues in their literary/philosophical integrity.

At this point the reader is likely to want to know more about the history of the competing schools of interpretation referred to by both Clay and McKim, as well as to want a more detailed exposition of a theory of interpretation. Both are provided in Alan C. Bowen's essay, the next chapter. Bowen discusses Eugene Tigerstedt's seminal but neglected *Interpreting Plato*, a book that traces in detail the history of Plato interpretation. Bowen believes that an examination of this history resolves the present debate about the matter. According to Bowen, the antagonists in this debate—including Tigerstedt—assume a pivotal hermeneutic principle inherited from their predecessors—namely, that the meaning of a text consists in what the author meant by it. Bowen argues that authorial intention ought not to serve as the criterion for understanding Plato, and that once it is rejected, the old debates about whether Plato was a dogmatist or a skeptic, whether his thought developed or not, or whether he was an esotericist or not, all disappear. The dialogues ought first to be understood "philologically," with an eye to discerning what the text (not the author) means. This task would require the reader to take seriously the dramatic dimension of the text: "one cannot isolate the logical and dialectical structure of the argumentation in a dialogue without paying heed to humor and irony at the dramatic level. Nor can one simply proceed by analyzing passages culled from different dialogues, the 'scissors and paste' method that is so common today." Thus prompted by the text, the reader may also, Bowen argues, reflect on the dialogues philosophically, with an eye to determining the truth of their theses. The first process is not, he says, dependent on the second. The distinction between philological and philosophical levels of the Platonic text is analogous to the distinction between the two levels of dialogue (one within the text, the other between Plato and reader) suggested by McKim.

Appraising the philological level of the dialogue involves many difficulties, of course. The status of Plato's myths has always been among the greatest of them. These myths confront the reader with the "literary" question head on, and any theory of reading the dialogues ought to tell us something about their interpretation. It would be difficult to achieve this end without also saying something about the philosophic importance of myth—once again, reflection on the "how to read Plato" question leads to the "why did Plato write as he did" issue. For instance, interpreters who dismiss the myths as not worth serious study assume a conception of philosophical logos. Jean-François Mattéi's essay, which succeeds Bowen's piece, examines the role of myth in the dialogues. He offers us reason to read them as serious, indeed indispensable, elements of the dialogues, and gives examples of such readings.

Mattéi first focuses on the dialogues as drama. After pointing out how alien they are in that respect from the now traditional rhetoric of philosophical reasoning, he suggests that reflection on Plato's use of myth both helps explain the theatrical dimension of Plato's dialogues and serves as a radical provocation to our understanding of what it means to do philosophy. Mattéi goes on to argue that the Platonic dialogue form, and still more strikingly Platonic myth, are in fact indispensable to philosophy as *Plato* understands that enterprise. Both the dialogue form and myth dramatize theory; both thus suggest that in some sense imagery is the context or, better, the "theater," that orients theorizing. As Mattéi puts one of his central points: "*Logos* is capable of elaborating a *theory of knowledge* at the conclusion of dialectical conversations only after *muthos* has oriented the philosopher with a *knowledge of theory*. The latter engenders the natural movement of the soul that enables it to see the theater of Ideas. It seems to me unfruitful to oppose in Plato's works the muthos to the logos, as one might an unprovable speech to a provable one, with the sole object of concluding that one is *logically* superior to the other. Rather, the mythical language serves another purpose: it offers from a unique standpoint a picture of the world through which dialectic must progress step by step." In arguing for an interdependence of muthos and logos, image and insight, drama and dialectic, Mattéi can insist that the interpreter of Plato grant Platonic myth a "serious" function. Mattéi then offers a reading of a number of Plato's myths and images (such as that of the "puppet theater" in the *Republic*'s simile of the cave). The style of his essay may reflect his subject matter and may thus offer an example of the "self-illustration" discussed in Robert Brumbaugh's essay. The reader is again prompted to wonder what sort of writing about Plato is Platonic.

Mattéi closes his essay with a reference to the *Seventh Letter,* the text that provides the focus of Brumbaugh's piece which follows it. The themes of insight or vision, as well as the question as to how we should read those examples of Platonic writing that seem more like monologues than like dialogues, lead naturally to the *Seventh Letter.* This document has often been offered as a counterexample to the thesis that Plato thought that philosophy cannot be expressed in nondialogical fashion or that Plato insisted on "authorial anonymity." If, however, the *Letter* possesses the characteristics Brumbaugh attributes to it, then its literary dimension is far more important than is usually thought, and its force as a counterexample is thereby weakened. Brumbaugh argues that the *Seventh Letter* employs the devices of "digression" and of "self-illustration" typical of many of Plato's dialogues (for example, the *Phaedrus'* palinode exhibits the "art of rhetoric" outlined later in the dialogue). In order to demonstrate this (a side benefit of which would be, Brumbaugh claims, evidence of the *Seventh Letter's* authenticity) he examines how these literary techniques operate in several of Plato's dialogues. He thus supplies us as well with some suggestions about reading the dialogues. In examining the question as to how we are to read the *Seventh Letter*—quite possibly a genuinely Platonic text—Brumbaugh expands the scope of our reflections on Platonic writing.

Brumbaugh's reflections lead us to a puzzle: given that the dialogues and the *Letter* exhibit similar dramatic devices, is there any real difference between reading a dialogue and reading a document written in the fashion of the *Letter*? If not, why did Plato write dialogues? This question is pressed on us by the author of the *Letter* when he writes that "no work of mine exists on such topics, and none ever will, for there is no way of putting them into words like other studies" (341c4–6), and that "no intelligent person will ever risk putting what he really understands into language, especially not in fixed form as is the lot of written characters" (343a1–4; Kenneth M. Sayre's translation, in the essay that follows Brumbaugh's piece). Brumbaugh closes his essay by raising the important question of the substantive ties between the *Letter's* statements about writing and the dialogue form. Sayre makes this question his primary focus, thus bringing us squarely to the second major question this book addresses: why did Plato write dialogues?

Sayre argues that even if the *Letter* is not authentic it nevertheless yields substantial clues as to why Plato wrote dialogues and, consequently, as to how we are to interpret them. To begin with, the *Letter* does not, according to Sayre, suggest that oral discourse can articulate the truth, whereas written discourse cannot. All discourse (including names, descriptions, and scientific knowledge) suffers from the same fundamental deficiency, namely, its involvement in sense experience. Consequently, logos is incapable of fully articulating philosophical insight or vision. According to Sayre, the "nonverbal nature of philosophic understanding" that eludes speech and writing is also represented in the *Phaedrus, Symposium,* and *Republic.* The *Letter*'s description of the experience of coming to an insight, moreover, helps explain why, in spite of the weakness of discourse, Plato wrote dialogues. The process of question and answer, of repeated exploration of one's opinions as well as those of others, serves to remove false views and prepare the soul for the true. Sayre argues that this notion of dialectical discourse as preparing the soul for insight is the core meaning of the *Meno*'s doctrine of "recollection" (*anamnesis*). It is intrinsic to anamnesis that the learner not be *told* the truth, but rather bring himself to undergo the insight into the truth. Hence the aporetic or seemingly inconclusive character of so many of the early and middle dialogues exhibits the *Seventh Letter*'s teaching about the relationship between discourse and insight, a relationship that could be accounted for in terms of the notion of recollection. Although that notion seems not to have persisted in the later dialogues, Sayre argues that the core view of philosophy "as a non-discursive grasp of reality" remains present. Just as that view explains why Socrates would have preferred dialectical exchanges to monologues, so it explains why Plato wrote dialogues. Philosophical insight cannot be expressed discursively, but dialogue—whether written or spoken—is virtually indispensable if a mind is to be recalled to insight.

Sayre's essay naturally stimulates us to want to hear more about the all-pervasive "weakness of discourse." In the essay following Sayre's, Rosemary Desjardins takes up that issue. Starting once again from the *Seventh Letter*, she agrees that the deficiency of logos holds as much for oral as for written discourse. Her analysis of this deficiency leads her to the important notions of "interpretation" and "ambiguity." For Desjardins, once we see that discourse is inherently ambiguous, we also see that to understand a logos is to interpret it. We are then in a position to appreciate three levels of the Platonic dialogue. The first concerns Socrates' interpretation of his own tradition, a key component of which is the *elenchus*, or cross-examination. Desjardins argues that for Socrates prephilosophic opinions are rarely altogether false. Rather, they are false under a certain interpretation, and a function of Socratic elenchus is to bring out the respect in which opinions are true. Socrates' hermeneutic investigations led to his being charged with corrupting the young, for the Athenians interpreted him as rejecting rather than as trying to understand their tradition. Acknowledging the unavoidability of interpretation in any effort to understand, Desjardins argues, is crucial to defending Socrates against such charges.

For Desjardins, the dialogue form of writing is central to Plato's interpretation of Socrates and the Socratic tradition, and thus constitutes a second level of the issue. Socrates did not leave his tradition unchanged, and by writing—indeed, writing dialogues in which Socrates is fictionalized—Plato too changes the very tradition that he is appropriating. Desjardins further argues that the dramatic dimension of the dialogues—including the interplay between word and deed in them—is crucial in Plato's view to overcoming the ambiguity intrinsic to discourse and in presenting a correct interpretation of Socratic philosophizing. Plato's decision to write *dialogues* thus reflects his awareness of the very same weaknesses of discourse and the importance of interpretation that guided Socrates' decision to philosophize through dialectic. Plato's dialogue with the Socratic tradition is directed in part to an audience Socrates did not have, namely, the readers of Plato's texts. This audience must also engage in a process of understanding, interpretation, and dialogue—with written dialogues that now constitute the basis of their own tradition. Therein lies, for Desjardins, the third level of the matter.

The crucial role of interpretation for Plato not only sheds light on why he wrote dialogues and on how we should read his writings but also brings Plato into the current debate about hermeneutics. Desjardins argues that Plato's position on "what it means to understand" is quite close to that of Hans-Georg Gadamer, a position that she views as offering a middle way between a naive "objectivism," which takes linguistic utterances as simply clear and certain, and "subjectivism" or "relativism," which hold that words (and texts) mean whatever an interpreter feels they mean. The middle way combines acceptance with interrogation, respect with critique. It admits both that philosophy has a nature and that philosophizing is open-ended, and so implies that philosophizing is fundamentally dialogical.

But might not the association of dialogue with philosophy be *merely* a part of *a* tradition rather than part of the "nature" of philosophy? In order to answer this question, Jürgen Mittelstrass spells out both the theoretical and the existential dimensions of dialogical knowing implicit in the preceding essay by Desjardins. Without a detailed analysis of how dialogue leads to philosophical knowledge, we would be unable to answer the above question, and would therefore be unable to refer to the nature of philosophy by way of explaining why Plato wrote *dialogues*. Mittelstrass develops his analysis through consideration of seven propositions about Socratic/Platonic dialogue, in the course of which he ties together the notions of dialogue, recollection, elenchus, maieutics, and philosophy understood as a "way of life" and "disposition of the soul." Mittelstrass's argument suggests that dialogue implies substantive metaphysical theses and that dialogue ought not to be understood as a method or technique that might on occasion be useful to philosophers for solving problems. Like Sayre, he argues that although Plato is not an esotericist in the sense of possessing a "secret teaching" that can be articulated in the medium of the spoken word alone, Plato does believe that insight cannot be "proven" discursively or presented the way propositions in some branches of knowledge can be.

For Mittelstrass the dialogue form of writing—thanks in part to its literary character—is perfectly suited to the demands of philosophizing so understood. The dialogue form "is capable of partially suspending its own textual character" by drawing the reader not just into a theoretical investigation but also into adopting a certain stance toward the world (for example, the reader is called upon to identify through imagination with certain of the characters in the drama, but not with others). Plato's dialogue form represents philosophy as "argumentative action" and copes effectively with our natural tendency to dogmatism. Mittelstrass's argument has important implications for our interpretation of Plato's texts, such as the requirements that we take with utmost seriousness his use of myth, irony, intentional fallacies and gaps in the argument, authorial anonymity, and the like.

In the seventh and final section of this chapter Mittelstrass argues that philosophical reason cannot be "demonstrated" to someone who does not possess it. Rather, it has to be "developed" and undergone in order to show itself as the "right" way of approaching questions. Mittelstrass contrasts the Platonic commitment to dialogical reason with the subsequent tradition of "Platonism" in the history of philosophy and science that emphasizes monological and systematic thinking. In suggesting that dialogue is not an optional characteristic of philosophizing properly understood, Mittelstrass points to a strong rationale for Plato's decision to write *dialogues*.

At this juncture the reader may well wonder whether a strong identification of dialogue with philosophical reason can really be sustained. Even if one grants that philosophy rests fundamentally on the individual's *insight* into the truth, that discourse requires interpretation in order that its intrinsic ambiguities be met, and that philosophy is a way of leading one's life, why could not a philosopher communicate effectively, and even "dramatically," in a nondialogical fashion?

In the final chapter of this section of the book, I argue that for a very good philosophical reason, philosophers cannot defend their own activity— and so their way of life—nondialogically. The reason is that any monological defense of philosophy against the radical critiques of the varied poets, skeptics, sophists, politicians, and other nonphilosophers portrayed in Plato's dialogues, would be circular and so unconvincing to the philosopher himself. Plato's decision to write *dialogues* stems from his deep awareness of the intrinsic difficulty of justifying philosophical reason, of showing that it is legitimate, indeed good and worthwhile, to philosophize. To be a philosopher is to make certain kinds of claims about oneself and the world—for example, the claims that one ought to know what one is talking about and that to possess knowledge is to be able to give a logos of a certain sort. I try to show why these are not claims that can be sustained nondialogically in the face of sufficiently clever opponents (namely, those who do not claim to have a [philosophical] *position* to the effect that philosophy is impossible). I also try to show that Plato's dialogues supply plenty of evidence, by virtue of both their form as dialogues and their content, that Plato understood the objections of such opponents and that he wished to meet them, that is, to make a case for the superiority of philosophy. The "ancient quarrel between philosophy and poetry" really is a basic dispute for Plato.

As an effort to reflect philosophically on philosophy, the argument is metaphilosophical in character. Kant's "critical" project can be understood in part as one of a long series of efforts to reform philosophy by reflecting metaphilosophically on its "grounds" and "conditions," and so to determine "prior" to philosophizing about this or that topic what it would mean to be successful in claiming to know something. Judged by the standard of philosophical self-consciousness thus characterized, Plato's dialogues seem hopelessly naive, unsystematic, and unreflexive. But the Kantian project assumes too much, and as Hegel immediately demonstrated, reason's "critique" of itself is either question begging or leads to an infinite regress. I argue that Plato shares that Hegelian objection to any Kantian effort to secure the "foundations" of philosophy.

Can dialectical philosophy—the supposed alternative to the Kantian critique—establish *its* own metaphilosophy without succumbing to the same objections? That question brings us again to the fundamental dispute, which lies not between proponents of dialectic and those of nondialectical epistemology but between dialecticians and the critics of reason giving as such. I argue that those critics—including Nietzsche, Rorty, and Derrida—are justified in accusing Hegelian dialectic of begging the question. But Platonic dialogue as exhibited in his dialogues is not susceptible to that criticism, precisely by virtue of their literary character. Plato *shows* us, phenomenologically as it were, how critics of philosophy fail on *their* own grounds to sustain their critique, and how their pronouncing opinions about this or that topic commits them to giving reasons for their opinions. Plato does all this while retaining his anonymity as author, thus avoiding the accusation that he is begging the question. That is, Plato *has* to write the sort of dialogues he did write in order to refute successfully the critics of philosophy. Platonic dialogue is necessarily reactive, pedagogic, unstructured, crucially dependent on the philosopher's "erotic *techne.*" It does not follow that Platonic dialogue is without ontological implications, and I try to show how reflection on the *experience* of philosophical dialogue leads to doctrines of a positive nature.

As is already evident, I develop my analysis of Plato's reasons for writing dialogues by means of contrasts between Plato and other figures in the recent history of philosophy. The Platonic dialogue is thus brought into the current debate about the limits of rhetoric, philosophy, and self-reflexivity.

The second part of this book consists of dialogues about the issues raised in the first part. Some of the dialogues illustrate vividly and concretely what several of the authors in the "Essays" section discuss in a theoretical way. Indeed, the reader will find a number of the observations offered in Bowen's essay relevant in evaluating the debate. All the dialogues under "Readings" bring out explicitly and in detail various theories about interpretation and their application to Plato. Just as the first part began with an analysis of the much disputed *Republic,* the second part begins with a discussion of one of Plato's best known "political" writings, namely, the *Crito.* Are the reasons Socrates gives there for refusing to flee prison sound? Is the implied theory of political obligation reconcilable with Socrates' own statements in the *Apology*? The exchange between Clifford Orwin and Richard Kraut illuminates clearly the ways in which one's answer to such questions is connected to one's assumptions about interpretation. For example, Kraut denies that just because a philosophical work is presented as a dialogue that it is not also a treatise. One Platonic text may be importantly dialogical, whereas another—such as the *Crito*—may perhaps be profitably read as though it were a monologue and so without complicating considerations of its dramatic or rhetorical structure.

McKim's contrast between analytical and contextual approaches to interpretation is strikingly exhibited by the next dialogue, that between Terence Irwin and David Roochnik. Irwin is author of one of the most widely read and discussed books on Plato published in English in recent years. His lively exchange with Roochnik spells out in detail—for the first time so far as I know—the basic interpretive assumptions underlying his approach to Plato. As was the case in the exchange between Orwin and Kraut, Roochnik and Irwin disagree at a fundamental level about what it means to read Plato.

In contrast, the succeeding dialogues between Ronald Polansky and Paul Woodruff, and between Joachim Dalfen and Kenneth Dorter, illustrate with reference to specific Platonic texts how readers who claim to agree about the basics of interpretation can nevertheless disagree deeply about how a specific text should be read. These exchanges are particularly useful in helping us to flesh out what "taking the drama seriously" might mean. A key problem is distinguishing between reading what the text says and reading into the text what we think it should say. The problem is especially acute when the interpreter claims that the text doesn't mean what it says—that it is ironic. The *Phaedo*'s famous "proofs" for the immortality of the soul present a crucial test case in this regard, as the disagreement between Dorter and Dalfen shows. I note that their debate as to how best to read the *Phaedo* exemplifies some of the conflicts discussed in Mattéi's essay.

The book concludes with two exchanges focusing on why Plato wrote dialogues. Kenneth M. Sayre's explanation of the connection between the theory of recollection and the dialogue form is examined critically in his debate with Jon Moline. A key issue in their dialogue is whether the rationale for Plato's decision to write dialogues depends on Plato's continued acceptance of the "theory of recollection," and whether that theory is present in, or at least is compatible with, his later dialogues. Several of Moline's comments about the meaning of "recollection" echo Mittelstrass's interpretation of the same notion.

The final dialogue in this book presents us with the first published response by Hans-Georg Gadamer to an evaluation of his approach to Plato by an interpreter influenced by what we might loosely call (following several contributors to the present book) "analytical" philosophy. Nicholas P. White and Gadamer take us through several issues that lie at the heart of Platonic philosophy, issues that were discussed in various ways by Sayre, Desjardins, Mittelstrass, and myself earlier in the book. In particular, White and Gadamer discuss the sense in which Plato was committed to the view that our knowledge of things is imperfect and fallible, and the sense in which Plato felt that dialogue is the appropriate response to the human condition. Since, as Gadamer points out, he and White seem at times to be addressing different questions to Plato, we are led to wonder which readings are and which are not truly measured by Plato's writings. Reflection on the problem of Platonic writing has here brought us full circle to the problem of reading Plato.

The efforts of the interlocutors in part II to respond to each others' writings and readings seem to bear out Desjardins's observations about the inseparability of understanding and interpretation and about the ambiguity intrinsic to discourse. I leave it to the reader to ponder the self-reflexive questions playfully implied by the title of this book.

Although the contributors to this volume represent a broad spectrum of approaches to the issue of the Platonic dialogue, the further discussion the book is intended to provoke might profitably include two approaches to Plato interpretation that were repeatedly discussed in passing in the essays and exchanges. One is that of the "Tübingen school" represented by K. Gaiser and H. J. Krämer. In its extreme form this view holds that no serious Platonic teaching is to be found in the dialogues except in the mode of allusion to the "unwritten teachings." John Findlay has argued along similar lines.[13] The other approach is that inaugurated by Jacques Derrida. Both are readily available in print and have been extensively discussed in the secondary literature.[14]

To the best of my knowledge, a volume such as this one is unprecedented in the area of Plato studies. The presupposition of this book is that serious consideration of the twin problems of interpretation and of Plato's reasons for writing dialogues is essential to a successful understanding of his work. Of course, the issues are also philosophically worthwhile in their own right. The presupposition of the dialogues included in this volume is a Platonic one: a philosopher cannot be confident of the truth of his own views until he has subjected himself to the objections of his rivals. This volume represents an initial effort to stimulate, as well as to exhibit, the dialogical thinking Socrates and Plato made fundamental to philosophy.

Although this is a book on Plato, the quandaries it evinces haunt the history of philosophical composition and interpretation after Plato as well. Even in the era of "deconstruction," surprisingly little has been done in the way of detailed readings of the texts of, among many others, Aristotle, Descartes, Spinoza, and Hegel in their *literary* integrity. A good deal of work about the connection between the philosophical and literary dimension of works such as these remains to be done. Both of the themes guiding the present book could be usefully pursued in the study of other philosophers. In deciding how best to read, say, Spinoza's *Ethics,* we ought to ask why Spinoza cast his thoughts in the form that he did. And we are entitled to wonder not just whether dialogues by authors other than Plato are dramas in an important sense but whether ironies, silences, misdirections, metaphors—in short, the rhetorical devices frequently deprecated by philosophers—are inseparable from even the most systematic or architectonic works. How authoritative or final is the apparent divorce of philosophy from rhetoric and poetics? Are philosophical texts really autonomous in the way that many philosophers suppose, or do they retain traces of dialogue (in particular, dialogue between the author and his readers, the author and the "secondary literature")? If they are not autonomous, might the tension between exotericism and esotericism, traditionally associated with the problem of reading Plato, represent a deeply philosophical phenomenon?[15] Questions of this sort, so insistently raised by the genre defined by Plato's dialogues, cut to the core of the meaning of *philosophy* itself.

Part I

Essays

1

Reading the *Republic*

Diskin Clay

The Open Dialogue and Its Enemies

At times it seems that the city of Plato's *Republic,* which bears the proud name of Kallipolis (7.527c), is not the city he intended to found in theory, unified as if it were a single body tending to a single end which is the cohesion and happiness of the whole (cf. 4.442e). It seems rather a number of cities, and then not a city at all, but a projected image of the human soul. The more one reads the *Republic* and the more one reads on the *Republic,* the more Kallipolis comes to answer to that striking image Leibniz offered in his *Monadology* of a city viewed from its walls by a number of individuals, each of whom sees a private city unified only in the mind of God.[1] In the case of the *Republic,* this unity might be said to derive from the mind of the divine and plastic artist who created it (ὁ θεὸς πλάττων of *Republic* 3.415a). Yet it can also be said that this same plastic god is responsible for some of the stasis and controversy that have surrounded the interpretation of his *Republic,* especially since World War II.

The *Republic* proclaims for all to hear that it is a work of theory and artistry, and the product of an imagination that moves toward daydreaming as Socrates stirs up the three waves of paradox in Book 5.[2] The deep note of pessimism over the possibility of a Kallipolis ruled by a philosopher king or a king become a philosopher leads finally to the conclusion of Book 9, where Socrates declares himself the citizen of a city established within his own soul according to a pattern laid up in heaven. The stark idealism of this conclusion has led readers of the *Republic* to an otherworldly, utopian, and Christian reading of Plato's project, a reading reflected in Aristotle's view of the *Republic* as a state established "as one would wish" (κατ᾽ εὐχήν; *Politics* 2.1260b29) and the interpretation implicit in St. Thomas

More's *Utopia*.[3] The "utopian" reading of the *Republic* is the charitable reading, and it is one encouraged by the *Republic* itself. Inevitably, and especially in the last generation of Platonic criticism, Plato has been taken at Socrates' word, and the utopia of an earlier age has come to be sternly viewed as a "blueprint" for a totalitarian state. I need only to recall the wartime protest of Karl Popper in the first volume of *The Open Society and Its Enemies* (begun on the day of the Nazi invasion of Austria and finished in 1943). For Popper, as for others of his generation, Plato's *Republic* was a totalitarian document, one that endorsed the Big Lie, advocated eugenics and infanticide, encouraged "racialism," and brutally subordinated the integrity of the individual, and the integrity of Truth herself, to the unwholesome Whole of a closed and dictatorial state.[4]

In fairness to Karl Popper, I think there can be no question but that the social system of the *Republic* is a "closed society"; but it must be added that the closed society of the *Republic* is not the only society of the *Republic*. The artisan and ruling classes enjoy a freedom the guardian class does not, although these classes too must abide by the natural division of labor on which this new state is founded.[5] But in fairness to Plato, it must be said that to make the society of Kallipolis a "totalitarian state" and to view its only project as political is to occlude from view the theme with which the *Republic* opens and closes. This is the justice of the individual.

Yet the status of that class which guarantees the unity of the *Republic* poses a problem; it did for Adeimantus within the *Republic* (*Rep.* 4.419a–420a), as it did for Aristotle (*Politics* 1.1264b6–25), and as it has for others. It is natural to identify the society of Kallipolis with its middle class, since the artisans, once introduced, are virtually left out of the account and since the ruling class shimmers like a mirage on the far horizons of the dialogue.[6] And since the focus of the dialogue is most precise in the delineation of this class, the closed society it represents comes to represent the society of Kallipolis as a whole. To begin with, the guardian, or auxiliary class is treated as livestock from the beginning of the dialogue (*Rep.* 2.375e),[7] and any culture that is not conducive to the spirited and discerning qualities needed in the guardians is not admitted into the polis. The guardians have no personal possessions; they live in a community in which the distinctions of persons, family, and even personal pronouns are obliterated (see *Rep.* 5.462c). They are raised amid salutary propaganda and civic hymns sung in praise of the virtues of the class to which they belong.[8] They are not free to travel of their own choice (*Rep.* 4.420a), and their natural instincts for love and procreation are regulated with great religious trumpery. And in that society which so closely resembles the military caste system of Crete and Sparta, we hear nothing of popular assemblies in which the guardians can exercise the intelligence cultivated in them by the state. This class is further narrowed by the practice of eugenics and infanticide.[9] Finally we come to contemplate in the exile of all citizens over the age of ten the grimmest of the proposals for the means to bring the city of Kallipolis into existence (*Rep.* 7.540d).[10]

Yet this closed, austere, guarded, and blinkered society of the guardian caste exists in a context that appears wide open to development, to challenge, to reconsideration, and to doubt. And Plato's reader is forced to ask if he has understood Plato in his attempt to understand the proposals of Socrates. Aristotle was capable of distinguishing Plato from the Socrates of the *Republic*,[11] and the bitter controversies over the meaning of the *Republic* illustrate one of the fundamental problems of Platonic interpretation: that of Platonic anonymity. Despite the title of Paul Shorey's book, it is impossible finally to determine from the language of a single character within a Platonic dialogue "what Plato said." In his dialogues, at least, Plato said nothing directly and in his own person. And so far as the "inner dialogue" within the *Republic* is concerned, it is difficult to think of another Platonic dialogue in which what Socrates says is challenged as often as it is by the very *structure* of the dialogue in which he speaks. That is, the *Republic* is the only Platonic dialogue that displays *within itself* the possible dialogues the argument of any Platonic dialogue can and should provoke.

Consider Book 1 of the *Republic*. In Germany, where Plato was not immune from the analysis and corrosive doubt that had dissolved the epics of Homer, Book 1, which Dümmler had titled the "Thrasymachos," came to be seen as an early and aporetic dialogue in search of the definition of a single virtue—like, say, the *Euthyphro, Laches,* or *Charmides*.[12] In it, Socrates would have shaken the opinion of Polemarchus that justice consists of giving each his due and reduced his next interlocutor not to assent but to weary and sour acquiescence. Its ending is not only aporia but Thrasymachus' decision to give Socrates his way: "Feast on your argument with good relish. I am not going to oppose you. I don't want to attract the anger of any of your companions here" (352b; cf. 354a). There is no conclusion to this dialogue, and it is Socrates who finally confesses his own disappointment with a dialogue that ends as does the "Thrasymachos": "So far as I am concerned, the result of our present discussion is that I know nothing" (354c). There are parallels to this inconclusive conclusion to a dialogue, but other Platonic dialogues can afford nothing like the opening of Book 2: "When I had said this, I thought that I was finished with the argument" (357a). What could have ended as a closed and aporetic dialogue continues with vigorous challenges which Glaukon and Adeimantus put to Socrates.

The reopening of the problem of justice and injustice in Book 2 demonstrates that Plato has taken care not to leave the argument at a standstill and in bafflement. The fraternal speeches that renew the argument of the *Republic* at the beginning of Book 2 are not primarily designed to lay bare the inadequacies of Thrasymachus' case for the understanding of justice as the interest of the stronger (*Rep.* 2.367c); and what the brothers say by way of engaging Socrates in his sustained defense of justice as a way of life is perhaps not so important for understanding the *Republic* as is the fact that Plato has, in the closure of Book 1 and the opening of Book 2, suggested that any claim for the closure of such a discussion must be illusory. Within the *Republic* there are still other examples of how the closure of positions taken by the speakers within the dialogue is challenged by a dialogue that refuses to conclude.

The vigorous but short-lived challenge that Adeimantus puts to Socrates' characterization of the guardian class at the opening of Book 4 shows not only a natural uneasiness with the conditions of the guardians of Socrates' new state; it shows that even when we find a character like Glaukon in strong agreement with the principles governing the life of the guardian class (as in *Rep.* 3.417b), another interlocutor, or Plato's reader outside the dialogue, might disagree and thus open an "outer" dialogue. The difference between the *Republic* and the early, aporetic dialogues is that this question is made explicit within the dialogue itself by one of its personae: "What would you say in your defense, Socrates, if someone were to say that you don't make these men very happy?" (419a). In this case, and within the dialogue itself, Adeimantus is easily satisfied by Socrates' defense (*Rep.* 4.421c7). Other readers have not been, and Plato's script for Adeimantus suggests that he did not count on the easy assent of his readers. One could say that, by adopting this rhetorical tactic of anticipating objections on the part of his readers, Plato anticipates hostile objections to his theory on his own terms in order to quell dissent on his own terms. But it could be that such moments of overture within the *Republic* are the expression of Plato's intent to bring his reader to interrogate the adequacy of the arguments of the inner dialogue held within the house of Cephalus.

This inner dialogue is itself complicated because it is polyphonic. There are ten characters present in the house of Cephalus and, of these, seven speak, if briefly. The agreement of any one of these characters does not guarantee the assent of the others and it is not meant to prompt assent in Plato's reader. This becomes clear for the last time in the dialogue at the moment when Socrates turns from the city he, Glaukon, and Adeimantus have founded "in words" to consider the types of polity that are inferior to it and that, along with their citizens, fall short of its perfections. This seems to be the next step in an orderly discourse (*Rep.* 5.449b; cf. 8.543c). But Socrates is thrown off course by a disturbance in the room as Polemarchus draws Adeimantus to him and asks: "Shall we let him go on, or what?" It is this interruption, unexpected by Socrates, but planned by Plato, that introduces the more difficult themes of the *Republic,* which we associate with the three waves of paradox that bring in their wake the possibilities of an equality of the sexes, a community of wives and children, and the rule of the philosopher king or king become a philosopher. Without this dramatic interruption, and without these three books (5–7), there would have been no proper discussion of the controlling element of the soul and the controlling element of the state, and no discussion of philosophy. And the dominant note of pessimism about the possibility of Kallipolis would never have entered the dialogue; nor would the dialogue have turned to recognize the antagonism between the values of philosophy and the philosopher and those of contemporary Greek society.[13]

To be sure, Polemarchus' concern is not with the neglect of philosophy in the new foundation of Socrates, Glaukon, and Adeimantus. His curiosity was aroused by Socrates' seemingly offhanded application of the proverb "common are the possessions of friends" to the women and children of the guardian class (*Rep.* 5.449c, which takes us back to 4.423e). It is curious that it should be Adeimantus who gives audible voice to Polemarchus' whispered doubts. He was the character in the dialogue who was so strongly in agreement with Socrates when he made precisely this suggestion (Ὀρθότατα γάρ, ἔφη, γίγνοιτ᾽ ἄν; *Rep.* 4.424a2).

These challenges within the *Republic* should shake our confidence in the closure of any Socratic argument in the *Republic*. One wonders if they were meant to. At the very least, the reader of Plato is brought to ask why the *Republic* stands unique among the Platonic dialogues in its capacity to include within itself an outer dialogue that seems, as if by the merest accident, to radically qualify a discourse that could have been self-content and self-contained. The reader of the *Republic* is forced to consider the interpretation of a *Republic* of one book, the aporetic "Thrasymachos," or *On Justice*. He is then brought to consider an interpretation of a *Republic* of three books (1–3), and of six (1–4, 8–9)[14] and finally he is brought to ask just how self-contained a *Republic* of ten books is. The opening of the *Republic* adds its stimulus to this question, for Socrates' words are addressed to an audience outside the *Republic*.

By opening new frontiers of argument, and reopening arguments that had seemed settled by the agreement of the characters within the dialogue, the *Republic* is an open dialogue. Although it describes as an ideal the closed society of its caste of guardians, the *Republic* seems to challenge its reader to engage it from without, as do Glaukon, Adeimantus, and Polemarchus within. The discourse of this dialogue suggests a series of concentric rings: innermost is the discourse of Socrates and his companions within the house of Cephalus in the Peiraeus. The characters of this inner dialogue are not only interlocutors; they are capable of reopening an argument when it had seemed closed. Beyond these characters and outside the house of Cephalus is the group Socrates addressed, presumably in Athens, with the words: "Yesterday, I went down to the Peiraeus with

Glaukon." And outermost is the group of readers Plato addresses through the argument, action, and structure of the *Republic.*

The Foundations of Kallipolis

Plato's most overt challenge to the reader of the *Republic* comes with the very foundation of a new state Socrates calls Kallipolis, the fair and noble city (*Rep.* 7.527c). Kallipolis is the result of the long search for the meaning of justice and injustice and thus a decision about the life that offers the greatest happiness for the individual, as for the state. Already in Book 1 and the conversation with Thrasymachus, Socrates had brought the state into association with the justice or the individual (*Rep.* 1.347d and 351c), but it is Socrates' decision to project the individual soul onto the large screen of the state, where its justice and injustice can presumably be seen "writ large," that introduces the political dimension into a discussion that had until then turned on the individual and the choice of a life.[15] It also introduces a serious problem in interpreting the *Republic* and, indeed, a series of problems: "Now we are not very clever, in my opinion, in carrying out a search of this kind. Imagine that someone were to tell people with poor eyesight to read tiny letters at a distance and then that someone were to notice that this same text could be found elsewhere, in larger letters and a larger format. This would come as a godsend, for they could first read these larger letters and then examine the smaller letters in their light to determine if they are the same" (*Rep.* 2.368d).

One problem with this model for inquiry is that the state might not prove to be an adequate representation of the human soul writ large.[16] Another is that the static character of this model does not cohere with Socrates' attempt to discover the origins of justice and injustice in describing the genesis of a city (*Rep.* 2.369a). That is, Socrates is seeking to determine the moment when justice is produced in a state as it develops and not a static "text" in which justice can be read. The two foundations of Kallipolis are not on a level: the striking model or metaphor of the state as a projection of the individual soul and the attempt to discover justice and injustice in the evolution of society are related in their objective, but are very dissimilar as methods. For our purposes the second of Socrates' enterprises is the more interesting, since it involves the question of Platonic interpretation rather than Platonic argumentation. Socrates' question to Adeimantus is the first version of a question Plato poses for his reader: "Were we to discover the city as it came into being in discourse [λόγῳ], would we then be able to observe its justice and injustice in their genesis?" (*Rep.* 2.369a). Adeimantus' response is only "perhaps." In the end, neither Adeimantus nor Glaukon is able to discover the moment either justice or injustice enters Socrates' emerging city and it is left to Plato's readers to discover that Kallipolis is founded on an act of injustice.

In what follows in Book 2, Socrates brings three cities into existence. First is the healthy city, a city that is the expression of fundamental human needs and a city that can be termed one of absolute essentials and the true city (*Rep.* 2.369d and 372d). The city that evolves from this city is one that has grown beyond the limits of the fulfillment of essential human needs; it is the product of the appetite for gain and self-aggrandizement and also of human delusions; in it we discover the mimetic arts, musicians, actors, beauticians, barbers, and with the new regime, doctors (*Rep.* 2.373b–c) Although they are not mentioned by Socrates here, it would seem that philosophers are also required to care for the soul as the doctors care for the inflamed body of this new city.[17] Socrates' third city is Kallipolis, the city of the *Republic.*

In the long argument that is initiated here and continues through Book 9 (and in the discussion of mimesis in Book 10) there seem to emerge two questions. Socrates insists on them, and this is reason enough to keep them in mind. First is the relation between the large and the small, the state, that is, and the individual; second, and strictly connected with this, is the question of the nature of justice and injustice, first as it appears in the state and then as it is manifest in the individual.

In his description of the genesis of the healthy city, Socrates addresses Adeimantus; in his history of the "inflamed" city, he addresses Glaukon. Neither of the brothers seems able to respond to his challenge to discover the moment justice and injustice enter the city, despite Socrates' urging. When he has finished his sketch of the origins of the first city, he asks Adeimantus: "Now where is justice and injustice in our city; and with what in all we have considered did it come into being?" (*Rep.* 2.371e). Adeimantus has no ready answer, and his answer, such as it is, is often mistranslated: "I cannot think of what, Socrates, unless it comes about in one of the dealings of these very citizens among themselves" (*Rep.* 2.372a).[18] The answer could apply to the genesis of justice in the first city or to the genesis of injustice. Socrates is not sure that Adeimantus has answered his question, but at this point he does not press him. There is, indeed, a form of justice adumbrated in Socrates' primitive city; it is to be discovered in the principle of a natural division of labor by which each citizen performs the task to which he is suited already adumbrated in the question "should he not trouble himself in his association with others but perform his own task himself relying on himself?" ([δεῖ] μὴ ἄλλοις κοινωνοῦντα πράγματα ἔχειν, ἀλλ᾽ αὐτὸν δι᾽ αὐτὸν τὰ αὑτοῦ πράττειν; *Rep.* 2.370a). Yet, this new conception of justice does not seem to be what Adeimantus had vaguely in mind.

As for injustice, which is almost always paired with justice in descriptions of the quest of the *Republic,* it would seem that it is nowhere to be discovered in this city, except implicitly in Socrates' statement that the citizen, in his association with others, should not cause them trouble, but pursue his own tasks as an individual and by himself. The citizens of Socrates' first city satisfy their essential needs by a division of the labor necessary to satisfy these needs. They also exhibit a virtue absent from the unhealthy city. This is piety, and to this is coupled prudence. Once their work is done, they stretch out on beds of bryony and myrtle and feast with their children, drinking wine, singing anthems to the gods, and taking care to avoid both war and poverty by not increasing beyond what their land can sustain (*Rep.* 2.372b). Their prudence adumbrates one of the virtues of Kallipolis, and this is the concern for the preservation of the stability of a society, as well as its unity: "And living their lives in this way in peace and in health they come, in the course of nature, to the end of their days in old age and they will pass on a life just such as theirs to their descendants" (*Rep.* 2.372d).[19]

As the city of luxury develops, the question of the origins of justice and injustice is posed once again. Socrates' response to Glaukon's characterization of his healthy city as a city of pigs reminds us of the object of all this inquiry: "So it appears that we are seeking not only how a city comes into being, but how a city of luxury comes into being. And this might be just as well, since in studying such a city we could possibly catch sight of how it is that justice and injustice will arise in cities" (*Rep.* 2.373e). Socrates does not pause, as he had with Adeimantus, to ask at what point justice and injustice arise in his second city, and Glaukon is not concerned with this question. But Plato has left it to his reader to detect the moment the serpent enters Eden. The passage describing the origin of injustice in Socrates' second city deserves quotation for it suggests that an initial act of injustice lies at the foundations of Kallipolis, and it leads to the question of how it is that political philosophy is possible only in an unjust society (*Rep.* 2.373d–e):

Socrates: "Now the land, I suppose, which was once capable of supporting the men of that time will prove small where once it was sufficient. Or what shall we say of it?"

Glaukon: "That is right."

Socrates: "Will it not be necessary to cut off land from the territory of our neighbors, if we want to have sufficient land for pasture and for plowing? And will they not need to do the same to ours, should they too abandon themselves to the pursuit of possessions without limit, once they have gone beyond the boundary of what is necessary?"

Glaukon: "There is no avoiding it, Socrates."

Socrates: "And let us not make any comment yet as to whether war
produces ill or good, but let us rather restrict ourselves to the
fact that we have now discovered *as well* [αὖ] the origin of
war, from which, more than from any other cause, ills come
about, and when it occurs it affects both cities and individuals."

Glaukon: "That is quite true."

"As well" (αὖ) is an interesting word. It registers the fact that Socrates
and his two companions have discovered the origins of war as well as the
origins of human communities and it reminds us that we are still in search
of the origins of something else, justice and injustice. We are reminded of
this again as Socrates discusses the qualities needed in the class of guardians
who have become necessary to protect the city from the consequences of
its initial act of injustice (*Rep.* 2.376d). Plato has challenged his readers
to discover the origins of injustice at precisely this moment in the development and aggrandizement of Socrates' second city, and with this discovery comes still another: Kallipolis has its foundation in an act of injustice. It is this act of aggrandizement and the warfare it provokes that makes
the guardian caste necessary to Socrates' fully evolved city, and it is with
this caste that Kallipolis is so naturally identified. About this, Socrates,
Glaukon, and Adeimantus are silent, precisely where Plato is not.

It is only in Book 4, when their city seems to have been founded, that
Socrates and Glaukon catch sight of the quarry that had eluded them in
Book 2 as the caste of guardians became a necessary part of the second
city (*Rep.* 4.427c). At this point, Socrates asks for a light to reveal justice
and injustice. Once he has examined the virtues of his newly founded state
(with the exception of piety), he can offer a conjecture: "I think that your
city, if, indeed, it has been properly founded, is completely virtuous" (*Rep.*
4.427e). And here at long last the founders of this virtuous city can close
in on the object of their long search: "Well, Glaukon, now is the moment
for us to surround it, like hunters around a thicket, and to keep a careful
watch to make sure that justice does not escape us and vanish without a
trace" (*Rep.* 4.432b). The quarry they have trapped at last is the definition
of justice as each individual in the state doing his proper job (*Rep.* 4.433d),
precisely the definition that had been within sight as Socrates first described
the origins of the healthy city (*Rep.* 2.370a). And its reverse, *polypragmosyne,* falls into place as the definition of injustice.[20] And a more conventional form of injustice, which is consonant with this new conception,
had been sighted in that act of aggrandizement which involves the unhealthy
city in war with its neighboring states (*Rep.* 2.373d).

The question that emerges as the objective of the *Republic* as followed
through its first four books is this: did Plato fail to recognize that the state
described at such length was founded in an initial act of injustice? For,

without injustice and the dominance of one social appetite over the controlling element of society, there would be no need for a guardian class (Books 2–4) or for philosophers (Books 5–7). Or did Plato leave the discovery of the weakness of the foundations of Kallipolis to the readers outside his dialogue, whom he challenges to respond to Socrates' challenge, as Adeimantus and Glaukon fail to?

This is the question and I think it is plain that Plato resolved to force upon his readers the discovery that injustice is at the origin of the guardian class of the city that evolves, with the introduction of philosophy, into Kallipolis. He forces upon us the reflection that all civilization rests on injustice and the uncontrolled need of the lowest and most passionate element of the soul to violate the frontiers of what is necessary to life for what is thought to be necessary to the good life (*Rep.* 4.423b and 436b). As the Cretan puts it in the *Laws:* "All men are both publicly and privately the enemies of all, and individually each man is his own enemy as well" (after Bury's translation, 1.626d).[21] Glaukon's second city is the unhealthy city, and philosophy is to spiritual disease what medicine is to physical malady. And here is the consolation, if it can be seen as that, of the viciousness of the foundations of Kallipolis; without the distemper, which is at the origin of the guardian class, the city would have no need for philosophy: *felix culpa.*[22]

It is odd, and a significant oddity, that as Socrates persues the paradoxes of Book 5 and as he approaches the conception of the philosopher king, he complains that he and his companions must keep their search for justice and its opposite in mind; for he sees this search as having brought them to the pass of contemplating Socrates' third wave of paradox and the prospect of the philosopher king (*Rep.* 5.472b). How can Socrates have forgotten that he has already discovered the nature of justice, properly understood, as he says, "but if we could discover the nature of justice . . ."? Does Plato seem "to overlook the fact that the search was virtually completed in the fourth book"?[23] Plato is not one of "our forgetful authors." Nor has he forgotten the search of Books 2 through 4 as he confronts the problems of the relation of philosophy and the polis. Rather, I would argue that he would reopen the entire question of justice and injustice in the *Republic*, even as Socrates has penned its guardians into their closed society.

It is with the third wave and the prospect of the philosopher king that a cloud of pessimism comes to cast its shadow over the project of Plato's *Republic*. A *Republic* without these books—the *Republic* contemplated by Socrates—would not be a *Republic* at all; it would have none of the comedy of these books and none of the tragedy that emerges as the shadow of Socrates' death is cast against the wall of the cave in Book 7 (517a). Socrates' initial project of seeing in the state an enlarged image of the soul would have been frustrated, for there would have been no discussion of the controlling or ruling element of the soul to balance the long treatment of the class that represents the middle element of the soul. And, without these books, Book 9 could not end as it does with the initial optimism of the founding fathers of Kallipolis restricted to the prospect of founding a just polity within the soul of the individual who had contemplated the pattern of justice "laid down in heaven" (592a, a passage returned to below). With these central and seemingly accidental books, our confidence in the possibility of Kallipolis is irrevocably shaken and our attention turns both to the antagonism between philosophy and contemporary societies (as in *Rep.* 6.487b–500b) and to the choice of the individual who must live in such societies.

None of this is recognized by the enemies of Kallipolis, who reckon neither with the problems of Platonic anonymity nor with the meaning of the structure of the *Republic* nor with the abiding presence of the individual and his choice of life within the dialogue. As for Kallipolis, Socrates casts himself, Glaukon, and Adeimantus as the founders of a new Greek city and anticipates the role of the Cretan, Kleinias, in the *Laws*, who was to be the *oikistes* of the new Knossian colony of Magnesia.[24] By the conclusion to Book 4, Socrates can say that the "dream" (ἐνύπνιον) of his new state is complete and that it reveals the principle and essential outline of justice (*Rep.* 4.443b). But the sudden and oblique introduction of the theme of the philosopher into the dialogue, and the two waves of paradox that precede it in Book 5, shake our confidence in the foundations of this city. As the question of the possibility of Socrates' new state becomes more acute, Socrates comes to describe his full project as a kind of daydreaming (εὐχή). And the founding fathers of this state are cast increasingly in the role of artists in their attempt to render an ideal, whether or not such an ideal actually exists.[25] Again, Plato has thrown his dialogue open to doubt, and Socrates' new language describing his project and the project of the *Republic* makes it difficult to characterize the *Republic* as offering a "blueprint" for social revolution or for a "totalitarian" state. And these reflections illustrate not the true character of Plato's intentions in the *Republic* but the difficulties of interpreting the *Republic* without coming to terms with the distinctive character of Platonic writing in the *Republic*.

The State Writ Small

As the theme of philosophy comes to dominate the argument of the *Republic*, the philosopher and the perfect polity he would direct come into conflict with actual societies, with a remarkable result: the individual reasserts his claim on our attention. In Books 2–4 he had been submerged in a characterization of the class to which he belongs, in this case, the class of guardians; and in Books 8–9 the project of the dialogue comes to center on types of states and the type of individual that corresponds to their distinctive polities. And even though the professed topic of Books 5–7 is the class of the philosopher (τὸ φιλόσοφον γένος; *Rep.* 6.501e), there is a striking shift in this long discussion away from the generic to the individuals who in their careers illustrate the virtual impossibility of a philosopher developing his full potential in a corrupt society. There had been something like this in Book 1, where Socrates names four tyrants (Periander, Perdiccas, Xerxes, and Ismenias of Thebes; *Rep.* 1.336a), two of whom were his contemporaries. But in Book 6 the world of Socrates returns to the dialogue as Socrates gives a description of the careers of Alcibiades (494a–495a) and Theages (496b), and even touches on his own career (496c), and in a moment of Platonic and dramatic irony intimates his own fate (496d), just as he does when he comes to the end of his illustration of the cave in Book 7 (517a).

In Kallipolis the philosopher would be king; but in Athens he would be corrupted by the mob and his kinsfolk (the case of Alcibiades), or be kept from politics by a lack of physical stamina—the "bridle of Theages," or be put to death, as in the case of Socrates, whose "divine sign" (*Rep.* 6.496c) could keep him from a political career but not execution by the prisoners in the cave. When Socrates says that in such a society there is no ally to join a philosopher in his championship of justice and assure his survival (496c–d), we are reminded that the entire project of creating Kallipolis is subordinated to the search for justice in the human soul and the individual's choice of life. The long discussion begins with an old man's fears that he might not have paid his debts to the gods as he faces death (*Rep.* 1.331a–c). And the individual is present throughout the dialogue in the person of Socrates, who has, as Adeimantus describes him, devoted his entire life to the pursuit of an understanding of justice and its opposite (*Rep.* 2.376d–e).

The entire purpose of creating Kallipolis "in discourse" is to see the justice or injustice of the individual soul writ large (*Rep.* 2. 268c–d). In Books 2–4, the individual and the condition of his soul are occulted in the larger image of a single class of Socrates' new state; but he makes an appearance, briefly, in Socrates' exposition of the three elements out of which the human soul is compounded (in *Rep.* 4.439e–441e). When Socrates illustrates his separation of the soul into three elements by speaking of the "factional strife" (στάσις) within, he has, in fact, reversed the model he had created for an understanding of justice in the soul of the individual (*Rep.* 4.440b and e). From this point of the dialogue, the soul of the individual can be seen as a polity writ small.

It is almost inevitable that the underlying question concerning the justice of the individual should arise as Socrates returns to the origins of his search for justice and, in Book 5, urges his claim that there can be no end to the evils of societies unless a philosopher becomes king or the king a philosopher: "If we discover the nature of justice, let me ask, will we demand that the *just man* should differ from that standard of justice in the abstract in no respect but should conform to it completely, or will we be content if he comes to approach it as closely as possible and possesses more of it than any other men?" (*Rep.* 5.472b). We have seen how the individual—not as a generic concept, but as a contemporary reality—is engaged in Socrates' discussion as Socrates' theme of philosophy brings to the fore the antagonism between Socratic philosophy and contemporary Athens (in Books 5–7).

Once the "digression" (see *Rep.* 8.543c) of these three central books that radically alter our earlier conception of an ideal society is over, the connection between the individual and the state is reaffirmed, as the constitution of a state is matched with the constitution of an individual type. In Books 8–9, which would have followed Book 4 if Polemarchus had not interrupted Socrates' program to reveal Plato's plan, the discussion of the variety of types of human character and the corresponding variety of constitutions brings Socrates to the basest type of state and individual—the tyrant. And here we return to Socrates' description of the *pleonexia* of the unjust man (and *Rep.* 1.349c) and the foundations of Kallipolis. In Socrates' delineation of the psychology of the tyrant we have a explanation of that moment when the unhealthy city came to aggrandize itself at the expense of its neighbors, for the tyrant is in fact a slave to the lowest and worst part of his soul and is actuated only by his passion for gain (*Rep.* 9.591d–e). And in describing the character of the tyrant's soul, Socrates returns to the metaphor of the "polity," or constitution within the individual soul (see *Rep.* 9.591e).

Now the state is projected as an image of the human soul. Glaukon responds to this metaphor of the polity within the soul by observing of the philosopher: "If this [inner harmony] is his deepest concern, he will not willingly become involved in politics" (*Rep.* 9.592a):

Socrates: "Yes, so I take an oath by the dog, this will certainly be the case in his own city; yet perhaps this will not be the case in his own country [πατρίδι], unless some providential accident intervenes."

Glaukon: "I understand. You are speaking of the city which we have been founding in our conversation, the one founded in speech, since I think that it exists nowhere on earth."

Socrates: "Yet perhaps there is a pattern for this laid up in heaven for the man who wants to observe it and, holding it in his sight,

> to found this city within himself [ἑαυτὸν κατοικίζειν] (italics
> added). It makes no difference whether it exists now or ever
> will. It is in the life of this city that he would be active and in
> no other."

Glaukon: "That seems likely."

This inner polity is the foundation of the foundation of Kallipolis, and its development is perhaps the overriding purpose of the *Republic*. Without the third wave of paradox that Socrates confronts in *Republic* 5, and without the deep sense of pessimism about the possibility of founding Kallipolis in anything but speech that this wave bears with it, the project of the *Republic* would have been very different. But the recognition of the antagonism between philosophy and society that Socrates voices in Books 5–7, and finally at the end of 9, forces attention away from society back to the individual. It is not true that "in the field of politics, the individual is to Plato the Evil One himself."[26] In the *Republic,* the growing pessimism over the possibility of a society governed by philosophy is qualified by an emergent hope for the perfection of the individual soul. The argument of the *Republic* begins with Cephalus' fears concerning the afterlife and it ends with an individual's choice of a life in the afterlife. In the myth of Er, Odysseus has the last choice of life:

> By chance, the soul of Odysseus received the last lot of all and went
> forward to take it up. And the memory of its former hardships had cured
> it of all ambition. Wandering about for a long time, it sought out the life
> of an ordinary citizen who minds his own business, a life he could discover
> only with difficulty in some place where others had passed it by. And
> when it caught sight of this life it said that it would have made exactly
> the same choice, had it had first choice, and would have chosen it gladly.
> (*Rep.* 10.620c)

This is an odd note on which to end a dialogue entitled the *Republic*. Victor Ehrenberg must be right about Odysseus' choice of the life of an individual who minds his own business (βίον ἀνδρὸς ἰδιώτου ἀπράγμονος): "it seems justifiable to see in it a deeper and wider meaning."[27] Whatever its meaning, however, Plato's choice of such a conclusion for the myth of Er and his *Republic* cannot be read out of this significant detail alone. The career of the theme of the individual in the *Republic* carries a great deal of Plato's meaning, but this theme itself cannot be understood in isolation from the other themes of the dialogue, one of which is philosophy. One of the many paradoxes of the *Republic* is that the society it elaborates with such care and at such length is based on two foundations. One is that of the soul of the individual as this is projected onto the state; and the other is Socrates' attempt to discover justice by offering a genetic account of the evolution of human societies. In the very genesis of the guardian class of Kallipolis is to be discovered a primordial act of injustice. And this has its spring in a state of soul that is fully described only in *Republic* 9. As for the metaphor of individual and state, Socrates can complete his version of the correspondence between states of mind and states of society only by giving a full account of the ruling element of the soul and society in the discussion launched by his paradox of the philosopher king. As he does, he virtually destroys our confidence in the possibility of his project for Kallipolis by introducing into the dialogue a reflection of the actual conflict between philosophy and society in contemporary Athens.

And as he enters into this conflict, Plato reminds us of his own fate. The reflection that leads finally but inconclusively to Odysseus' choice of life comes from an awareness of this very real antagonism and, it would seem, a premonition of Socrates' own fate. As he speaks of himself and the divine sign that kept him from engaging in the political life of Athens, Socrates reveals his own choice of life—a choice that led to his death:

> And those who have joined this small company [of philosophers] know how sweet and blessed a thing it is to possess, and have as well seen enough of the madness of the many and are aware that no one succeeds in any action that is healthy—so to speak [and here Socrates has shifted his attention from the few to the one]. And they know that a person will not even have an ally to help him survive as he goes out to fight in the cause of justice; but like the man who has fallen into a den of wild beasts, he would refuse to join the party of injustice and would not be strong enough as a single individual to defend himself from these wild animals, but rather he would die an untimely death before he could help either his city or friends and would prove to be of no use to himself or to others. Well, these would be his reflections and he will keep his own counsel and keep to his own proper task [ἡσυχίαν ἔχων καὶ τὰ αὑτοῦ πράττων], as if he were to stand apart under the protection of a wall in a storm of a sudden squall of wind and rain; and he will be content if, as he sees others filled with lawlessness, he can live his life on earth somehow pure of the taint of injustice and unholy actions and depart from this life with good hope, content and serene. (*Rep.* 6.496c–e)

In Kallipolis, Socrates would be king, perhaps; but in Athens he is at least the ruler over the polity within his soul.

2

Shame and Truth in Plato's *Gorgias*

Richard McKim

The dominance of analytical philosophy has blinded the bulk of Anglo-American scholarship in this century to the interpretive challenge posed by Plato's choice of the dramatic form of the dialogue as the vehicle for his thought. Analytically trained commentators tend to assume that Plato must have been trying to do the kind of philosophy they have been trained to evaluate—namely, mount proofs and disproofs of propositions in accord with the standards of logic. Thus they tend to read the arguments he has his protagonist, Socrates, address to fellow characters as if the dramatist were a treatise writer addressing them in his own voice to his readers. Since logical analysis reveals that these arguments are usually full of holes, the analyst feels called upon to patronize Plato by supplying the excuse that, great philosopher though he was and try as he might to be logical, he labored in the benighted infancy of his discipline. We are to rest assured that, had he not been born too soon to enjoy the blessings of Aristotelian and modern symbolic logic, he would have done much better.

By treating Socrates as Plato's mouthpiece, the analyst collapses the critical distance between the author and what his characters say, a distance we take for granted in any other great or even competent dramatist and that distinguishes the drama from the treatise as an implicit rather than an explicit form of communication between author and audience. I propose to interpret the *Gorgias* as a drama so as to show that, rather than urging Socrates' arguments upon us as his own, Plato dramatizes them in order to communicate implicitly with us *about* them, and in particular about the method of Socratic dialectic, or elenchus by which he has his protagonist construct them. It will turn out that Plato presents Socrates as not even *trying* to meet the standards of logical proof and, even more dismaying from an analytic perspective, that he presents the elenchus as a far more formidable weapon for defending Socratic morality than if it were designed to meet them. My reading restores to Plato the critical distance essential to his dramatic craft by establishing a distinction between the dramatist's implicit objective with respect to his audience (to get us to reflect upon the principles of Socratic method) and the protagonist's explicit objective with respect to his fellow characters (to ply that method upon them).

This approach should point the way toward a plausible and satisfying answer as to why the *Gorgias* is a dialogue, and in general as to why Plato adhered to the dialogue form.[1] In trying to come to grips with Plato as a dramatist, however, many non- and antianalytic interpretations have proven no less liable to viewing him through the distorting lenses of their own philosophical assumptions. Further, although the arbitrary logical expectations of the analysts often run counter to Plato's dramatic objectives, the disciplined rigor of their approach to the texts should by rights provide a check upon the arbitrary speculative excesses to which concepts like dramatic irony and Plato's alleged "unwritten philosophy" tempt us. It should become clear that my own attempt to advance beyond the analytic reading of the *Gorgias* is very much grounded in the analysts' own methods and results.

Plato generates the central dramatic tension of the *Gorgias* by having two of the sophist's protégés, Polus and Callicles, challenge the conviction that lies at the foundation of Socratic morality—namely, that the virtuous life is a better and happier life than one of vice. For Socrates, virtue is always supremely beneficial *to the moral agent himself* as well as to those toward whom he acts virtuously, whereas vice, in addition to the material harm it inflicts on others, is always supremely harmful to the agent, being bad for the health of his soul. We may refer to this belief as the Socratic Axiom that virtue is always beneficial and vice harmful. Polus denies the Axiom by asserting that injustice is more beneficial than justice, and Callicles denies it by asserting that intemperance is more beneficial than temperance.

In the inconclusive, or aporetic group of early dialogues, Socrates restricts himself to refuting the beliefs of his fellow characters or answerers,[2] exposing their ignorance while professing his own as well. In the *Gorgias*, on the other hand, he defends his Axiom as a positive alternative to their beliefs, as if he possessed knowledge that they lack. Thus the Socrates of the *Gorgias* has traditionally been read as more "Platonic" and less "Socratic" than before, as if Plato were beginning to transform him from an agnostic into the dogmatist of the middle dialogues, and to apply the elenchus to constructive ends alien to the strictures of its "Socratic" role as a method of refutation. Socrates, however, continues to profess ignorance in the *Gorgias* despite the passion with which he defends his beliefs (509a4–7). Moreover, as Irwin and others have noted, although his earlier professions are never merely ironical, they never preclude positive moral convictions.[3] He appeals from the first to a number of his own beliefs as criteria of truth, including above all the Axiom. His more important aporetic refutations frequently rest on his answerers' acknowledgment that they share his belief in the Axiom so deeply that they will reject any belief that can be shown to conflict with it, requiring no further proof as to which of the two is false. Thus the awareness of ignorance that Socrates seeks to share with his answerers never involves any doubt about the Axiom. On the contrary, it requires a heightened awareness that the Axiom must be true. For Socrates' wisdom, as Plato presents it, consists in the discovery that virtue must be knowledge, but of a kind we do not yet possess—namely, the knowledge of good and evil. And we discover this only once we see that "the knowledge of good and evil" is the only definition of virtue that satisfies the Axiom by defining it as something that is always beneficial to the agent.[4]

Neither Socrates nor Plato, then, has suffered any increase—or decrease—in dogmatism between the earlier dialogues and the *Gorgias*. Whether implicitly or explicitly (for example, in the *Apology* and *Crito*), the former are just as dogmatic as the latter about the Axiom and its consequences for moral life. The difference is that the answerers in the former always accept the Axiom as a criterion, so that Socrates need not defend it, whereas in the *Gorgias* they refuse to, so that he must. Plato uses the aporetic works to dramatize how Socratic dialectic can reveal our moral ignorance so long as its Axiom is granted. But he assigns to the *Gorgias* the complementary function of dramatizing how that same method defends its Axiom if it is *not* granted. The defense is vital not just to Socrates' methodology but to his way of life. For, just as the Socratic life follows from the Axiom that virtue is more beneficial than vice, so the anti-Socratic life espoused by Polus and Callicles follows from their axiom that vice is more beneficial than virtue. If he failed to defend his Axiom against theirs, he would be powerless to defend his way of life against theirs. Thus Socrates twice proclaims in the *Gorgias* that what is at stake is how best to live our lives (472cd, 500c).

The analytic interpreter would assume that the defense must consist of attempts to prove by logic that the Axiom is true. My central thesis, in contrast, is that Socrates tries to demonstrate instead that *everybody already believes* that it is true. He is convinced that we all share the Axiom by nature as our deepest moral belief. If he is correct (and Plato presents him as correct), then even the likes of Polus and Callicles, who think they disbelieve it, already believe in it more deeply than they could in any argument "proving" it to be true. Thus, if Socrates can demonstrate that even they already believe the Axiom as deeply as he does, he feels that he has provided the strongest possible defense of it.[5] His method is there-tore psychological, not logical—not to argue them into believing it but to maneuver them into acknowledging that, deep down, they have believed it all along. Whether or not he plays by the rules of logic is determined by whether they are the most effective psychological means of dredging up in a given answerer that suppressed belief. His chief weapon in this psychological warfare is not logic but *shame*. We shall find that, against Callicles, logic plays a merely subservient role to shame and that, against Polus, the very features of Socrates' argument that are logically objectionable are precisely those that render it psychologically telling.[6]

Polus' thesis is that to commit injustice is preferable to suffering it. In other words, he denies the Axiom by asserting that the injustice is more beneficial to the agent than justice, especially when justice requires us to let others treat us unjustly. Socrates admits that he would prefer to avoid both committing injustice *and* suffering it if possible, but declares that when suffering it can be avoided only by committing it, then the former is to be preferred—in other words, that to be just is *always* more in our own interest than to be unjust (469b8–c2). The ensuing argument, however, concerns not whether the just life is preferable in fact, but whether *everybody already believes* that it is preferable. Thus Socrates states the position that he will defend as follows: "I believe that you and I *and all men* consider doing injustice to be worse than suffering it" (474b2–5). And Polus responds with the contrary thesis: "But I believe that neither you nor I *nor anyone else* believes that" (b6–7; italics added).[7] In case we miss it the first time, Plato has both characters immediately repeat their stands on the issue at stake. Polus asks, "Would *you* prefer suffering injustice to doing it?" Socrates replies that not only would *he* prefer it, "but you as well *and everybody else*." And Polus counters, "Far from it: neither you nor I *nor anyone else* would prefer it"(b8–10, italics added). Well, Socrates says, answer my questions (c1), and the refutation immediately ensues.

In this passage Plato virtually beats us over the head with the point that his characters are arguing about whether all men already believe what Socrates says they do or what Polus says they do. To proceed, as so many have done, to analyze Socrates' argument as if it purported to be a logical proof of the preferability of suffering injustice, rather than as a demonstration that Polus and everybody else already believes it to be preferable, is to exhibit a rather impenetrable insensitivity to Plato's dramatic signals. Socrates does not deny that men often in fact choose injustice over justice; thus his argument *is* designed to encourage Polus to choose justice instead. But this encouragement consists of a psychological demonstration that it is *already* the choice that Polus and everyone else would always make, even at the expense of suffering injustice, *if they followed their own better judgment* as to their best interests. Before demonstrating this account of the argument with Polus in detail, it will be helpful to look ahead to the confrontation with Callicles, where Plato more explicitly dramatizes the role of shame in Socrates' method for revealing what people really believe. We can then return to the Polus argument and see the same method implicitly at work.

Callicles expounds the view that neither justice nor temperance is a virtue "by nature" (*phusis*) but only "by convention" (*nomos*).[8] He identifies the good with pleasure, primarily the pleasures of the body, and advocates an indiscriminate hedonism whereby the best life is one devoted to the immediate and insatiable gratification of any and every desire. He invokes the ideal of a "superior" man with a larger appetite for pleasure and greater powers of gratification than his inferiors possess, declaring that by natural, as opposed to conventional, justice such a man has the right to indulge himself to the maximum. Intemperance is therefore a virtue by nature, being the superior man's exercise of this right, whereas temperance is by nature a vice since it inhibits his will to pleasure, making him "worse" by depriving him of "goodness." Inferior men agree among themselves to praise temperance as just and to decry intemperance as unjust, not because they really believe in these conventional values but rather because they want to shame their superior into curbing his appetites. For they know that in a state of nature he would take advantage of his prerogative by hogging all the pleasure that he could at their expense. Socrates sides with conventional morality against Callicles in that he defends temperance as a virtue and attacks intemperance as a vice, and in that he considers Callicles' "natural justice" to be unjust, although of course Plato presents his protagonist's morality as far more profound than society's.[9] Thus in Socratic as well as conventional terms Callicles advocates the thesis that vice is more beneficial to the superior man than virtue, contrary to the Socratic Axiom that virtue is always more beneficial for everyone.

Shame, then, according to Callicles, is an unnatural feeling induced by conventional morality in order to make people suppress their natural belief in the benefits of vice and pay lip service to virtue instead. He applies this theory of shame to a critique (482ce) of Socrates' previous arguments against Polus and Gorgias. When Polus asserted the thesis that committing injustice is preferable to suffering it, he was, according to Callicles, voicing his real belief. Socrates then induced him to concede that committing it is nevertheless more shameful and refuted his thesis, as we shall see, by arguing that it is incompatible with this concession. But Callicles objects that in conceding unjust acts to be shameful Polus was merely yielding to conventional morality, afraid of what others might think of him if he voiced his "real" belief in the "natural" truth that justice is the more shameful as well as the less desirable way of life (483a7–b4). Similarly, Callicles thinks that Gorgias gave in too easily to shame. Gorgias first claimed that, as a teacher of rhetoric, he was not responsible for ensuring that his pupils practiced rhetoric justly. But Socrates quickly shamed him into saying that, after all, if a pupil came to him ignorant of justice he would feel obliged to make him just before teaching him rhetoric (459c–460a). Callicles objects, as Polus had before him (461b4–c1), that Gorgias made the latter concession "merely" out of shame—that is, because he was afraid of offending conventional morality (482d2–3).

Callicles accuses Socrates of practicing a characteristic trick in both cases: if his answerer's thesis represents a "natural" belief, Socrates refutes it by shaming him into granting premises that hold merely by convention, whereas if the thesis holds merely by convention, he refutes it using premises the answerer grants because they represent what he really believes by nature (482e–483a). Since, for Callicles, natural and conventional values are always at odds, he admits that Socrates can always refute any thesis by playing them off against each other in this way. But such refutations are phony in his view because they do not expose any inconsistency within the system of natural beliefs itself.

Now E. R. Dodds speaks for all commentators in supposing that Plato endorses this critique, committing him to Callicles' theory of what men really believe.[10] But that is a radical misinterpretation that completely skews our understanding of what is going on in the *Gorgias*. In fact, as I shall argue, Socrates' implicit view of the relationship between shame and belief is the exact opposite of Callicles'. Whereas shame is for Callicles an unnatural feeling that inhibits our real preference for vice, Socrates believes to the contrary, on my reading, that our shame about vice is a natural sign that deep down we really prefer virtue. What Callicles calls our "natural" beliefs represent for Socrates the artificial values imposed upon us from without by such corrupting influences as a Gorgianic rhetorical education.

On the other hand, what Callicles dismisses as society's merely conventional values represent for Socrates what men believe by nature—values we continue to hold deep down despite the fact that society tempts us toward vice. Although society officially encourages us to be ashamed about vice, it also places an unofficial premium on wealth and power as absolute goods. For Plato, it thereby corrupts us into paying the likes of Gorgias to teach us how to attain these goods without regard for morality and tempts us to envy those who attain them through vice without getting caught. Hence Polus defends the preferability of injustice by pointing to the wealth and power of the evil tyrant Archelaus (471ad). Nevertheless, on the Socratic view, by officially reinforcing our natural sense of shame about vice, society helps us maintain our lifeline to our deep-down belief that, for all its material rewards, vice is nevertheless far worse for us than virtue, whatever material suffering virtue may bring.

Thus, although Callicles may be right that anticonventional morality is internally consistent, Plato presents him as wrong to think that it is illegitimate for Socrates to refute it by appeal to the "conventional" beliefs dictated by shame. Socrates does not purport to expose inconsistencies within anticonventional morality but rather exploits our sense of shame to reveal that we do not really believe in it, despite the fact that we may say or even think we do. In short, although he agrees with Callicles that whatever all men believe by nature must be true, the two take opposite views of what that is. Whereas Callicles says that men assert out of shame what they really believe to be false, Socrates thinks that men assert out of shame what they really believe to be true; and whereas Callicles says that men are ashamed to assert what they really believe to be true, Socrates thinks that they are ashamed to assert what they really believe to be false.[11]

He compliments Callicles several times on his "frankness" (*parresia*) in expounding anticonventional ideas (487a3, d5–7, 492d1–3), and Callicles seizes on the compliment (491e7–8), imagining himself to be impervious to the shame that keeps other people from voicing their real beliefs. In Dodds's phrase, he boasts that unlike them he has "the courage of his convictions."[12] Once again Dodds voices a consensus in assuming that Plato agrees with Callicles' self-assessment and in taking Socrates seriously when he plays along with it. Plato, however, makes it dramatically clear that Socrates' praise of Callicles for frankness is highly ironical.

Indeed, in response to Callicles' opening harangue, Socrates praises him for three qualities, the other two being knowledge and goodwill toward Socrates himself (487a2–3). That his praise of Callicles' "knowledge" is ironical needs no demonstration from me. As for goodwill, the reason he gives for accepting Callicles' claim to be "fairly friendly" toward him (485e3)[13] is that Callicles confides the same view of philosophy to his closest friends as he has just voiced to Socrates (487b7–d4). But, of course, this view is that philosophy is a childish and slavish waste of time.[14] In this "friendly" spirit, Callicles has declared that anyone who pursues philosophy into adulthood "deserves a beating" (485c2). When he caps his profession of goodwill with the warning that, unless Socrates abandons philosophy for rhetoric, he can be clubbed on the head with impunity since he will be unpersuasive in court (486b4–c3), Plato clearly invites us to reflect that Callicles and his friends are of the ilk most prone to philosopher-bashing and that this must be as obvious to Socrates as it is to us. It should be our natural suspicion, then, that Socrates is being just as ironical about frankness as he is about knowledge and goodwill.[15]

Now Socrates always insists as a matter of elenchic principle that his answerers be frank about what they believe. Plato repeatedly confronts him with answerers predisposed to approach the elenchus as a sophistic debate in which their objective is to protect their thesis, true or false, from refutation in order to avoid "losing." Thus they are tempted to answer Socrates' questions contrary to their beliefs if they feel that an honest answer might enable him to refute their thesis and "win." Socrates wants them to approach dialectic instead as a cooperative inquiry in which each partner is grateful to the other for disabusing him of false beliefs. He therefore insists that his answerer must always say what he really believes even (or especially) if it will lead to refutation, since if he lies to avoid "losing" he blocks their progress from false beliefs toward truth.[16] This principle is especially crucial in defending the Axiom. For Socrates' objective is to show that an answerer who denies it really believes it. He must therefore show that the answerer currently holds beliefs he could not possibly hold unless he already believes it, and success depends on the answerer's good faith in being frank about those other beliefs.

Plato dramatizes Callicles, however, as the most anti-Socratic of answerers in violating this principle, just as he is the most anti-Socratic in his professed view of the good life. For all his boasting about his freedom from shame, he turns out to be just as ashamed of his thesis as Gorgias and Polus were of theirs, and just as certain deep down that it must therefore be false. But, so far from exhibiting "the courage of his convictions," he is far less frank than they were, for his fear of "losing" the argument makes him too cowardly to admit his sense of shame even after his claim to believe in his thesis has become blatantly dishonest. Socrates' strategy for combating this refusal to be frank is to draw from indiscriminate hedonism a series of shameful consequences, each more so than the last, and in the process to tease Callicles about his boasts of frankness, until he breaks down and confesses that his thesis is too shameful to be true.

The first of these consequences is that, if pleasure is the good, then a life of scratching itches must be happy, and Socrates ironically admonishes him not to "shy away out of shame" from accepting it (494c). Callicles blusters that the argument is sheer demagoguery (d1), although to maintain his thesis he must go along with it. "Surely," Socrates persists (494d2–4), "you are not going to be struck down by shame as I struck down and shamed Gorgias and Polus—for *you* are courageous!" The reader is meant to see, of course, that if Callicles really had "the courage of his convictions" he would confess to his feeling that a life of scratching itches would be shameful and that the hedonism that entails commending it must be false. Instead, however, he protects his thesis by pretending to believe that the scratcher would live happily ever after (d6–8).[17]

And so Socrates draws an even more shameful consequence—namely, that the life of the catamite is happy (494e). Here, with a nice touch of dramatic irony, Plato has Callicles exclaim, "Aren't you ashamed to force such subjects into the discussion?" (e7). Obviously, it is Callicles' thesis that has "forced" its consequences upon them, and by calling Socrates shameless he is only trying to avoid a frank admission that he cannot really believe in such a shameful thesis.[18] But this time he admits that he will call the catamite happy only "in order that my position [logos] should not be inconsistent" (495a5–6). This is tantamount to admitting that he no longer claims really to believe in his thesis, and Socrates now scolds him for answering contrary to his beliefs (495a7–9). Callicles tries to save face by asserting that such consequences are shameful only "in your opinion" (495b7). But his previous expostulation—"Aren't you ashamed?"—serves as Plato's dramatic proof positive that Callicles feels them to be shameful as well.

Shame has him teetering on the brink of frankness at last. Socrates, however, now tries to push him over it by an argument whose conclusion is not that hedonism is shameful but merely that it is logically impossible. Pleasure, it runs, cannot be the good because the pair of opposites, pleasure and pain, cannot be identical with the pair of good and evil (495e–497d). Callicles' response to the conclusion of this argument is silence (497d8). The dramatic significance of his silence is twofold. First, it shows that he can find no logical flaw in the argument (whether or not there is any), as does his helpless earlier outburst against it as a lot of sophistic nonsense (497a6–c2).[19] But, second, his silence shows that logic alone is not enough to make him admit that his thesis must be false. The contrast between his silence here and his irrepressible "Aren't you ashamed?" in response to the last shame-argument is Plato's way of dramatizing that shame and not mere logic is the weapon that Socrates needs to deliver the coup de grace that will finally force Callicles to be frank.

Accordingly, Socrates immediately reverts to his shame-series and draws from Callicles' hedonism the consequences that the coward enjoys just as much goodness as, or even more than, the brave man, since the pleasure (the good) that the former enjoys in running away from danger is at least as intense as the latter's pleasure in facing it (497d–499b). Now Callicles may be anti-Socratic in other respects, but he is just as sure as Socrates that the courageous man is better—possesses more of the good— than the coward. Indeed, courage is the "natural" virtue that he admires and covets most,[20] in ironic contrast to his own fear of frankness in dialectic. That his thesis should commit him to a moral equivalence between courage and cowardice, then, is a consequence that even Callicles finds too morally shameful to stomach. He openly repudiates his hedonism at last, admitting that all along he has believed "as everyone else does" that some pleasures are bad (499b4–8).[21]

Notice how Plato focuses at this climactic juncture not directly on the truth of Socratic values but on the question of what everyone really believes. No one could believe that some pleasures are bad for us, as Callicles now admits that he and everyone else does, without also believing like Socrates that temperance, the self-restraint that enables us to resist harmful pleasures, is more beneficial than intemperance, the impulse that encourages us to indulge in them. By his own admission, then, Callicles has all along believed that temperance is preferable to intemperance, contrary to his professed disbelief in Socrates' Axiom, and that everyone else prefers it too, contrary to his theory about what people believe by nature. Now that his shame has burst the dam, he quickly concedes that the techne of sorting out bad pleasures from good is essential to the good life (499c–500a).[22]

By forcing him to acknowledge his real beliefs both to himself and to the others present, Socrates has fulfilled his announced objective to make "Callicles agree with Callicles" and "see himself aright" (482bc, 495e)—that is, to make what Callicles *says* he believes correspond to what he really believes deep down. He may not at first have been fully aware of his real beliefs, but we have seen how the shaming pressure of the elenchus has gradually forced the realization upon him and how he tried to hide them nevertheless. Hence Socrates rebukes him twice more for answering contrary to his beliefs (499bc, 500b), saying that this is something a friend would never do (499bc2–4). So much for Callicles' goodwill as well as his frankness, then. Here Socrates ironically attributes to himself an error in judgment as to Callicles' character, but he has obviously known all along that it is no more frank than friendly.

We can now explain why Socrates hails him at the outset as his "touch-stone" of truth (487e1–3). He propounds such an extremely anti-Socratic morality, and his false pride in being impervious to shame makes him, by comparison to Polus and Gorgias, so obstinate in withstanding elenchic pressure, that if Socrates can show that *even Callicles* believes in the Axiom at heart, then he feels that he has shown a fortiori that all men do and that it must therefore be true. Thus he says that Callicles' agreement with him will represent the telos of truth (487e7). When Socrates proceeds to spin out the predictable moral consequences of the Axiom as it applies to temperance, Callicles repeatedly tries to disassociate himself from them by refusing to cooperate any further as an answerer (for example, 501c, 505cd, 510a). But Plato presents him as conclusive proof despite himself for the validity of Socrates' appeal to shame as a sign of what everyone really believes and hence of the truth of Socratic morality. And so Socrates triumphantly declares that what Gorgias and Polus agreed to out of shame has proven true (508b7–c3).

We are now in a position to interpret the argument with Polus, whose denial of the Axiom takes, as we saw, the form of what I will call his Harm-Thesis:

(HT) Suffering injustice is more harmful to the sufferer than committing it is to the agent.

Like Callicles, Polus thinks that everyone else agrees with his anti-Socratic view, citing in his favor the fact that everyone would dismiss Socrates' professed preference for suffering injustice as a laughable outrage against common sense. Socrates insists that he cares nothing about what everybody else says as a mob, but only about what Polus says in elenchus as an individual answerer. What people in general may think or say they believe before they have been subjected to the one-on-one shaming pressure of the elenchus is of no value for Socrates as evidence for whether they really do.[23] His strategy, as with Callicles, is to exploit Polus' sense of shame in order to make him "see himself aright" and, by extension, everyone else aright as well.

He first gets Polus to acknowledge his belief in what I will call his Shame-Thesis:

(ST) Committing injustice is more shameful than suffering it (474c7–8).[24]

Then his refutation runs as follows:

(A)   Whatever is admirable (*kalon*) is so on account of being either pleasant (*hedu*) or beneficial (*chresimon, ophelimon*) or both (474d3–475a4).

(B)   The opposite of admirable is shameful (*aischron*), and the opposites of pleasant and beneficial are painful (*luperon*) and harmful (*kakon*) (475a4–5).

(C)   Therefore, whatever is shameful is so on account of being either painful or harmful (475a5–b2).

(D)   But committing injustice is certainly not more painful than suffering it (475b3–c4).

(E)   Therefore, since it is more shameful by ST, it must be so on account of being more harmful, contrary to HT (475c4–9).

(F)   Therefore, nobody would prefer to commit injustice rather than suffer it (475d1–e6).

If Socrates were trying to prove F by a logical disproof of HT, this argument would be flagrantly indefensible for reasons soon to be discussed. But Socrates' goal is rather to prove F by showing that Polus and everyone else already disbelieve HT. To do so, he must circumvent both Polus' illusion of belief in it and his wariness as a would-be sophist about any admissions, true or false, that might result in refutation. Accordingly, steps A to E represent not a series of logical inferences from ST but a roundabout psychological strategy using Polus' genuine belief in ST to expose his disbelief in HT, while concealing this objective from Polus until it is too late for him to foil it. And the psychological validity of the demonstration resides precisely in its logical invalidity. For it shows how irresistibly the sense of shame expressed in ST compels Polus to acknowledge his Socratic preference for suffering injustice despite the fact that he is obviously under no logical compunction.

Socrates begins in A with his division of the admirable into what is pleasant and/or beneficial for two reasons. First, he intuits (correctly, as Plato presents him) that this is what everyone really does admire so that Polus will consider A self-evident. The division seems to some too utilitarian or hedonistic to be Socratic, so that Socrates seems to be arguing from a premise he deems false.[25] But his examples of the admirable—art, laws and customs, and knowledge (474d3–475a2)—show that he is thinking of nonmaterial pleasures and benefits such as those of good laws to society or of knowledge to the soul. Interpreted in this way, A is impeccably Socratic—what *else* does Socrates admire? The significance of Polus' assent to A in the sense evoked by these examples will shortly appear.

Second, Socrates begins with A because, although he has in mind a simple map of how to get from there to an admission of disbelief in HT, A is sufficiently far removed from HT that to someone like Polus, who lacks such a map of the interconnections between his beliefs, it seems an admission he can safely make without exposing HT to refutation. After all, HT concerns the relative harmfulness of committing and suffering injustice, and here is Socrates asking him out of the blue about the apparently irrelevant concept of admirability. This epitomizes the genius that Plato ascribes to his protagonist as a psychological strategist: to pick as his first premise an uncontroversial common belief that provides the shortest possible route to a refutation of his answerer's thesis, but that appears so remote from the thesis that it triggers no resistance.

The most notorious point of analytic attack, thanks to G. Vlastos,[26] concerns Socrates' opposition between "pleasant and/or beneficial" and "painful and/or harmful" in moving from A to B. When Polus grants in A that the admirable may be pleasant, Vlastos supposes that he means pleasant to a beholder, in accord with Socrates' first example of works of art. Thus, when he grants in C that the shameful may be painful, the same restriction logically applies. Now, in order to trap Polus into the admission (E) that committing injustice must be more shameful than suffering it by virtue of being more harmful, he must induce him first in D to reject the alternative "more painful." But he does so by asking whether the agent or the victim of injustice suffers more pain. Polus considers it obvious that the victim does and that therefore committing injustice is definitely not more painful. Vlastos protests that logic demands the question "Which is more painful *to the beholder* of an unjust act?" not the question of who suffers more, its agent or victim.[27] He passes over the fact that Socrates' other examples of the admirable do not give pleasure only to a beholder.[28]

Still, it remains logically open for Polus to posit that committing injustice is shameful by virtue of being painful to a beholder, just as an act might be admirable by virtue of being pleasant to one. Since a shameful act need only be painful *or* harmful, not necessarily both, he could thus have denied that committing injustice is harmful.

An analogous objection, missed by Vlastos, may be added concerning "beneficial" and "harmful." For Socrates' examples of the admirable evoke a variety of types of beneficiary, and yet he assumes that the harm done by a shameful act must be harm to the agent.[29] Hence, even if Polus felt compelled to choose harm rather than pain as the reason committing injustice is shameful, he could still have insisted that, although it must be harmful to someone or other, it is not necessarily so to the agent. "Had Polus been on the *qui vive*," in Vlastos's words, he could have taken advantage of the logical loopholes provided by these ambiguities and avoided his "abject capitulation."[30]

Here Vlastos expresses the fond wish of most analysts that Socrates' answerers would seize on every logical opportunity to escape refutation. But this is to wish that they would violate the cardinal principle of elenchus by answering in such a way as to avoid "losing" rather than in accord with what they really believe. When, like Polus, they fail to challenge a logically vulnerable move on Socrates' part, commentators fail to consider that Plato may be presenting the answerer as already believing in the assumptions required by the move. If so, it is from the Socratic point of view a dialectical virtue for him to concede it rather than obstructing the elenchic path to truth by trying to "win" with an objection that, although logically possible, conceals his real beliefs. Instead of exploring this dramatic hypothesis, the analyst patronizingly assumes that Plato himself is unaware of the logical possibilities. Plato, however, demonstrates repeatedly throughout his career the capacity to bring fallacies of this elementary sort to our attention by making one of his characters point them out.[31] He therefore deserves the respect of our following this rule of thumb: if a fallacy seems obvious to us, that is because the dramatist has *made* it obvious for some dramatic purpose. And if he has his characters pass over it in silence, this is because he wants us to think about *why* they do.[32] Here, he wants us to ask what it shows us about Polus that Socrates can so easily induce him, without even trying to exert logical coercion, to repudiate HT by admitting that injustice is harmful to the agent. And what it shows, of course, is that Polus already believes this and hence does not need to be argued into it. The "necessity" (*ananke*) that he feels in the argument (475a5, b2, b8) is psychological, not logical. And, unlike Callicles, Polus is frank enough about his real beliefs to yield to that necessity wherever it might lead.[33]

Although Socrates' examples of the admirable lump together various types of beneficiary, we have already noted the salient characteristic that holds them together as a set—namely, that they all confer nonmaterial benefits in contrast to the wealth and power conferred by unjust acts. Socrates is trying to wean Polus away from his preoccupation with these material benefits, as expressed in his envious paean to Archelaus, by reminding him that he already recognizes nonmaterial kinds and already admires those who enjoy and confer them. In this way, when the argument shifts to the harm done by shameful acts, Polus has been subtly primed to think in terms of another category familiar to but neglected by him, nonmaterial harm.

Now Socrates, of course, believes that committing injustice is shameful by virtue of being *both* painful and harmful, since he thinks in terms of the agent's soul, whereas Polus rejects "more painful" in D because injustice obviously causes *material* pain to the sufferer, not to the agent. Thus "painful" is ambiguous in yet another respect which vitiates the argument as logic.[34] But what matters in a shame-argument is how Polus understands the premises, not how Socrates does or what the logical possibilities are. What D shows about Polus is that he feels committing injustice to be shameful for the agent (ST), that is, to belong to the class of things that are painful and/or harmful to him (C), despite his belief that it is "painful" only to the sufferer. He must, then, feel it to be "harmful" to the agent in some sense other than the material damage he inflicts upon his victim—in other words, that it causes the agent *non*material damage. In Socratic terms, Polus already believes that it is detrimental to the health of the agent's soul—*and* that such soul-harm outweighs the material benefits of committing injustice, since otherwise he would feel it to be admirable by virtue of being on balance beneficial.

Polus himself unwittingly confirms that, deep down, he has harbored these beliefs all along. For a little later he volunteers, without being argued into it and as if it were no news to him, that committing injustice engenders sickness of soul and that this is far more shameful than poverty or bodily sickness (477bc).[35] A brief reprise of steps A to E has him quickly agreeing that soul-sickness is by far the most shameful sort of sickness by virtue of being by far the most harmful (477ce). Clearly, he can never really have believed that committing injustice, with its harm to our soul-health, is preferable to the merely material ills of suffering it. The effect of these free admissions is that of the cat springing out of the bag. Once Socrates has wakened Polus' sense of shame from its Gorgianic slumbers, his real beliefs begin to burst forth of their own accord. Plato thereby dramatizes the idea that our shame at the thought of committing injustice is rooted in a natural intuition that we would be harming ourselves far more than others.[36] If we really believed that injustice would benefit us as agents, then we would envy the likes of Archelaus as Polus thinks he does. But deep down, Plato implies, neither Polus nor anyone else really envies such a man, for we are sure that the harm he did to his soul so far outweighed his material rewards that he was, as Socrates says, not enviable but miserable (469a, 478e–479a).

By making the logical weakness of Socrates' argument obvious, Plato invites us to take the logical way out of it for ourselves. But this invitation is really a challenge: *can* we take the logical way out, any more than Polus could, if we are honest with ourselves about what we really believe? If we demand a logical proof that shameful acts are harmful to their agents, instead of acknowledging, as Polus must in the end, that we feel them to be shameful because we already believe this, we lower ourselves in Plato's view to the level of sophistic debaters, refusing to admit what we really believe in order to "win" the argument regardless of the truth. We might prove ourselves cleverer logicians than Polus (a dubious distinction)—but, more important from Plato's point of view, we would prove ourselves no more frank than Callicles, and just as dishonest with ourselves in refusing to face up to the moral consequences of our sense of shame. Thus Plato throws down his gauntlet: *of course* you can detect logical flaws in the argument—I, Plato, planted them there for detection—but can you honestly contend that you *need* logical demonstrations for Socrates' beliefs? Can you honestly deny that, like his answerers, you already share them so deeply that they beggar the power of logic? Like his protagonist, Plato is certain that we cannot, and he deploys his dramatic powers to imbue us with his belief that Socratic morality is grounded so deeply within us that its truth is beyond argument.

3

On Interpreting Plato

Alan C. Bowen

> When you are considering the philosophy of an epoch, do not chiefly direct your
> attention to those intellectual positions which its exponents feel it necessary ex-
> plicitly to defend. There will be some fundamental assumptions which adherents
> of all the variant systems within the epoch unconsciously presuppose.
>
> A. N. Whitehead, *Science and the Modern World*

For all the talent and skill of individual students of Platonic thought, it is
curious that our discipline as a whole is unreflective, that there is little
critical recognition of the historical roots of the assumptions and techniques
we use that divide us so sharply into schools. There are, of course, an-
notated bibliographies by Cherniss, Rosenmeyer, McKirahan, Manasse,
and Brisson, to mention a few.[1] But these and the many more lists found
in monographs, journals, and series like *L'année philologique,* invaluable
as they are, serve a different purpose: they assemble a small part of the
relevant data not to facilitate the study of scholarship itself but to promote
scholarship by reporting the state of research on particular issues. It seems,
then, that as students of Plato in the twentieth century we risk becoming
prisoners of the more recent past by unwittingly and pointlessly rehearsing
old debates. To avoid this danger, we need more actively to pursue the
history of our field in order to understand its projects, its methods, and
its results. So it is that I commend Eugène Tigerstedt's *Interpreting Plato*
(1976),[2] a brief but useful study in English of how Plato has been interpreted
in the past two hundred years. Flawed though it may be, this is an important
and provocative book that rewards attention.

Let me explain. There are two questions that strike the reader of what
Plato wrote and of the secondary literature about it: "What did Plato
think?" and "Why do scholars differ so extremely in their accounts of
this?" According to Tigerstedt, the proximate answer to the second ques-

tion lies in the history of Platonic studies, in particular, that of late eighteenth- and early nineteenth-century Germany.[3] For at this time in Germany, the study of Plato was set on its present course because of two convictions: that the Neoplatonic interpretation was not acceptable, and that philosophy as rational thought is by its nature systematic (Brucker, Tennemann, Hermann, pp. 66–69). The first entailed that scholars return to the *ipsissima verba* of Plato to establish their interpretations. But this return to the text as witness to what Plato thought conflicted with a consequence of the second: if all philosophical thought is systematic, that is, a hierarchy of principles with those that are ultimate, subordinate, and coordinate, and with a fixed technical terminology, Platonic thought must be systematic, too, because Plato was a philosopher. The conflict emerged when scholars actually examined the corpus and attempted to discern Plato's views on a given topic by collocating all the relevant passages: instead of a system they found a tantalizing series of propositions characterized by gaps, ambiguities, and contradictions. So they were forced to ask: how is one to deal with Plato's words when they are so unsystematic (and, hence, apparently unphilosophical) in matters of philosophical importance? But this question immediately raised another: which writings of Plato are authentic? And this was in turn connected with a third: what is the chronology of the authentic texts? All three questions came to be known as *die platonische Frage* in the German literature.

Tigerstedt maps out the response to this "Platonic question" ahistorically; that is, he concentrates more on the major strategies employed than on the proponents and their personal histories: individuals are mentioned and discussed only as representatives of attitudes and opinions that many share (p.110 n.1). This approach does falsify history, at least to the extent that the individuals named did in fact occasionally combine strategies (for example, Zeller, pp. 16–17, 67, 78, 84, 98; Robin, pp. 59–61; Hermann, pp. 27–30, 40–44, 67–69) or even change them during their careers (Jaeger, pp. 50–51, 74; Hoffmann, pp. 56–58); but perhaps we should take Tigerstedt's identification of scholars with particular schools of interpretation as his assessment of the historical impact of their work. Nevertheless, the resultant ahistorical taxonomy of "positions" is a useful starting point in understanding the history of Platonic interpretation.[4]

It is useful for two reasons. Without the sort of critical structure Tigerstedt supplies, the data of past scholarship are unmanageable and the study of this data becomes both antiquarian and blind. Moreover, without such an accounting, it becomes difficult (if not impossible) to transcend the trench-warfare characteristic of professional exchanges today and to attempt a further-reaching philosophical criticism of contemporary work. Yet what Tigerstedt writes is still only a starting point. His exposition of the basic questions motivating Platonic studies and his classification of the competing answers have to be tested further against the historical data and revised in light of it, if the philosophical understanding and criticism of recent work is to be cogent. (Such revision may prove quite extensive, as Szlezák indicates:[5] Tigerstedt's account of the interpretations offered by certain scholars misses the mark, and it is not clear that he has properly canvassed all the major contributions.) In addition, *Interpreting Plato* needs to be supplemented. For there are other ways of looking at the last two centuries of Platonic interpretation and these are equally necessary: classical scholars too readily see themselves as working alone in ancient gardens; seldom do they admit that the history of their studies is one of institutions and individuals as well as one of ideas, that interpretations once developed must be transmitted if they are to have any life.[6] Thus, inasmuch as Tigerstedt does not deal with questions of transmission and academic sociology, there is need for the sort of historical *Forschungsbericht* which Holger Thesleff has recently disparaged:[7] tracing the history of similar views and mapping their communication and evolution would serve to control Tigerstedt's account, to connect old assumptions and opinions now "fossilized into facts" with the questions and strategies that inspired them, and so to drive home the philosophical criticism of our field.

In what follows, I propose to develop as a challenge the thesis that much of today's scholarship and its polemic consists only in the blind application of clever answers to a bad question. To begin, I must pass over the question of the historical veracity of Tigerstedt's account: my subject on this occasion is the taxonomy of Platonic interpretation Tigerstedt presents, a taxonomy that is of considerable philosophical interest in its own right. Thus, I will first distill Tigerstedt's analysis of the basic questions and assumptions governing Platonic scholarship and briefly consider his solution to the problem of interpreting Plato. Only then will I undertake to state an alternative solution and thereby establish the criticism just declared. I recognize, of course, that my remarks and my alternative solution are preliminary, just as are Tigerstedt's history and proposal. Yet there seems no other way to proceed. In that this chapter is part of a collection devoted to the problem of interpreting Plato and, especially, of why he wrote dialogues, it is appropriate to examine the question of interpretation itself and to consider the conditions under which it and the more specific question of the dialogue form may be answered. But the question of interpretation is very much a matter of history (at the least, because history is a source of our tacit assumptions), and the history of Platonic scholarship is only partly written; so the best one can do is offer hypotheses that, if they are successful, will motivate the historical and philosophical reflection on current Platonic interpretation we so manifestly need.

A History of Platonic Study

If one supposes Plato's thought to be systematic because it is philosophical, the Platonic question is a challenge to determine how the written works express this system. According to Schleiermacher, Plato was possessed of his system from the very start but chose to present it gradually and from different viewpoints in the dialogues (pp. 25, 85: cf. Hoffmann, pp. 56–59). Eduard Zeller, a pupil of Hegel, endeavored to argue the same, but his difficulty in expounding the system as it appears in the dialogues and his disapproval of Plato's using myth—it was bad enough that Plato did not present his views systematically—brought him to entertain seriously the possibility that Plato was not a philosopher at all, that the inconsistencies, obscurities, and omissions in the dialogues preclude a systematic underpinning (pp. 16–17). The a priori systematic unitarianism that Schleiermacher proclaimed and Zeller sought renders the contradictions and so on in Plato's writings merely apparent: they are attributed to the fact that the system is at any point exposed only partially.

The difficulties in ordering the dialogues chronologically and unifying them by reference to an unchanging system or doctrine were obvious to all. Friedrich Ast among others proposed to simplify the matter by the expedient of athetesis—that is, by denying that dialogues recalcitrant to systematization are authentic. In principle this was nothing new; even the ancients considered certain of the works that have come to us in Plato's name as spurious, and many scholars before and after Ast have been moved to reject what they did not understand or could not encompass. But in practice these critics devastated the *corpus Platonicum:* at one point, only nine dialogues were considered genuine.[8] Such radical surgery is a tactic of desperation and it is to be regretted that not even the stylometric analyses of Campbell and Ritter, for example—analyses that reinstated most of the traditional corpus in the face of the atheticist attack and that constitute one of the real contributions of nineteenth-century philology to Platonic studies—have been sufficient to prevent the resurgence of atheticism in the last forty years by those whose criterion of authenticity amounts to no more than agreement with their intuition of Plato's meaning (pp. 19–21).[9]

The stylometric reply to extreme atheticism was connected historically with a broader and earlier attack on a priori systematic unitarianism. The main thesis of this attack was that the unity or coherence of the Platonic writings was to be found not in some unchanging system but in the continuous evolution of Plato's thought to a system.[10] Thus, the geneticists granted the reality of the problems in systematizing Plato's thought as evidenced in his writings, but viewed the inconsistencies, omissions, and ambiguities as signs of intellectual progress. Given the assumption that language mirrors thought, it is not surprising that they endorsed the statistical demonstration that Plato's language and style show considerable change throughout the dialogues (pp. 25–26).[11]

There are many species of geneticism. Dialectical geneticists argued that the evolution of Plato's thought was purely philosophical, that it was only an unfolding of the potentialities of certain initial and constant assumptions (Susemihl, Ribbing: pp. 26–27). Others, however, viewed this evolution as being due to nonphilosophical factors. One of the important nondialectical geneticists was Karl Friedrich Hermann, who held that Plato's thought is a summation of previous philosophy which is a product of his personality (*Persönlichkeit*) and milieu, and that this summation is unified not by a system but by Plato's distinctive personal character (pp. 27–30: but cf. pp. 67–69). Many members of the nondialectical school of geneticists were less influenced by the assumption that literary work expresses its author's mind, spirit, and personality, and that the author's mind is an ultimate determinant of the work's content and artistic unity; they took a harder line by emphasizing the nonintellectual (for example, milieu) at the expense of the intellectual factors (*Persönlichkeit, Geist*), and the boldest simply attributed the evolution of Plato's thought to purely nonintellectual influences. Thus, for example, after classifying Platonic philosophy as essentially political, the social positivists identified Plato's socioeconomic status as determinative of his personality and so of his thought (pp. 30–33), whereas the psychological positivists concentrated on his (homo)sexuality (Kelsen: pp. 33–36). Still others chose to view Plato's intellectual development as the manifestation of his life and personal experiences, and espoused what may be called biographical positivism (Wilamowitz: pp. 40–48), or else they identified Plato with his work and attempted to interpret the texts by referring to the inner form and law of the personality that is reconstructed from their intuitive insight into each text (George: pp. 48).[12]

The geneticist attack on a priori systematic unitarianism and the popular success of geneticism in Germany did not go unnoticed. Paul Shorey responded by reaffirming the constant unity of Plato's thought and argued that it could not be reduced to matters of biography (pp. 47–48). This reaffirmation of the unity of Plato's thought also cut against Schleiermacher and Zeller because Shorey did not think it to be that of a philosophical system. Rather he viewed it as the profession of certain general ideas or a worldview and declared this compatible with the contradictions one finds in the dialogues. In short, Shorey's a priori nonsystematic or rhetorical unitarianism treats Plato not as a philosopher but as a moral teacher who understood the limits of philosophy and the subordinate role of metaphysics and logic (pp. 52–56). Other unitarians took a different tack and effectively prepared the way for esotericism and the Tübingen school (Gaiser, Krämer). Unlike Shorey, Léon Robin, for instance, continued to insist that

Plato is a systematic thinker or philosopher. But unlike Schleiermacher and Zeller, Robin constructed this system by turning to the indirect or oral tradition, that is, to the fragmentary accounts of Plato's lectures and views found in works by Plato's disciples and in Aristotle's treatises; moreover, Robin saw the system as undergoing development and modification. For him, behind the debates depicted in the written works stands the oral tradition and behind this, the living system (pp. 59–61: cf. Gomperz, pp. 61–62).

The genetic reading of Plato's works, the most popular then and now, was developed by way of attack on Schleiermacher's a priori systematic unitarianism, which was itself in part a response to the esotericism of Tennemann (pp. 66–67: cf. Hermann, pp. 67–69, 85). Esotericists admit the extreme difficulty, if not the impossibility, of discovering a system behind or in the dialogues. Still, they suppose there is a system (but see Oehler, pp. 87–88). To reconstruct it and so solve the problem of Platonic interpretation, they distinguish the dialogues (which are marked by variation and change) from the oral tradition and maintain that this tradition alone provides the key to Plato's system (pp. 63–64). Now recourse to this secondary or indirect tradition is hardly new in scholarship; many proponents of the other schools allow its validity and rely on it in their reconstructions (for example, von Stein, Zeller, Rosen—pp. 77–79 with n. 142 and 82; Wilpert, Ross, Taylor, Burnet—pp. 84–85 with n. 185: cf. pp. 64–66). What sets the esotericists apart is their utter depreciation of the dialogues; for various reasons (none unchallenged), they ignore Plato's writings and turn instead to the few, slender, and often inconsistent reports of his doctrine, which are scattered in the ancient literature (pp. 69–85). Esotericists like Krämer and Gaiser find a system that is expressly Neoplatonic. Others like Philip Merlan are more cautious: he tries to uphold the value of the oral tradition against Cherniss's attack (cf. pp. 79–83) and notes the Neoplatonic character of Platonism, but refrains from claiming that the tradition accurately represents Plato's philosophy (pp. 63, 84).[13]

If Tigerstedt is critical of esotericism and the other schools of interpretation I have mentioned, he is equally opposed to the skepticism of George Grote (pp. 17–18) and the evolutionism of Richard Robinson (pp. 22–23: cf. Bocheński, pp. 23–24). For Tigerstedt, the contradictions and so on that one encounters on any "sincere" reading of the dialogues (p. 82) are real; still they do not warrant Grote's despair of finding a coherent interpretation of what Plato wrote. Nor do they mandate Robinson's view that they occur because Plato was writing at a time when logical theory lacked nomenclature for fallacies and thus he often fell victim to sophistries which he deployed on other occasions so adroitly. As Tigerstedt sees it, then, the problem of the inconsistencies, omissions, and obscurities in the dialogues has brought scholars to a false dilemma of dogmatism and skepticism: they misread the text either by supposing a closed system of doctrine or by emphasizing its aporetic, tentative character to the exclusion of doctrine. On the first horn, we have the unitarians, the atheticists, the evolutionists, the geneticists, and the esotericists (pp. 92–93); on the second, the skeptics and all who would reduce Platonic philosophy to empty "philosophizing" (pp. 102–5).[14]

Tigerstedt's Proposal

To pass between these horns, Tigerstedt announces three necessary conditions of interpretation: (1) there is a Platonic philosophy and it cannot be reduced to nonphilosophical factors; (2) this philosophy is found in Plato's writings *alone*; and (3) Plato was intelligent (p. 93). He then describes what he takes to be the data, that is, what is readily apparent to any intelligent first reader of the Platonic corpus:

- Plato wrote some thirty items of prose.
- These texts are not systematic treatises—they are letters or they are dialogues; the latter represent a speech or series of speeches to some audience or they portray (directly or indirectly) conversations between two or more persons.[15]
- Each text stands by itself; very few contain cross-references and these do not entail that understanding one requires reading the other (pp. 54, 99).
- Plato is anonymous; that is, he does not claim authorship and he neither addresses the reader directly nor enters the conversation portrayed— the two occurrences of his name in the corpus are incidental (pp. 14–15, 93–95).
- These texts challenge the reader.

Tigerstedt makes some acute remarks about this data, for example, that Plato's anonymity or dissociation from the dialogues marks his debt to Socrates and the conviction that philosophy is not found in books or lectures but in dialectical conversations between particular individuals (pp. 96–97). Indeed, on the strength of a credible reading of the *Phaedrus* and *Letter 7* (pp. 44–47, 69–70, 73–74), Tigerstedt vigorously maintains that the process of question and answer is essential to all the dialogues, that to ignore it is to falsify our evidence (pp. 97–98). This contention is, I think, double for Tigerstedt, since, as he says, the dialogues are double. On one hand, the reader is obliged to attend a conversation or speech to which he is a silent listener and in which he has no part; yet, on the other, he is challenged to reflect on this conversation and to address its questions. The first dialogue occurs between the interlocutors in a given text; the second takes place between Plato and the reader (pp. 98–99) or, less figuratively, within the reader as he reflects on the text. So, it follows for Tigerstedt, I presume, that one cannot ignore the process of question and answer at either level, that is, either in the interchanges of the interlocutors or in reflecting on these interchanges.

Unfortunately, it is difficult to say exactly how Tigerstedt expects to avoid the dilemma of dogmatism and skepticism or, for that matter, what he makes of the real contradictions he allows are in the dialogues: the closing pages of his book are cryptic, elliptical, and unfocused—this is, in my estimation, the most disappointing part of his book. He praises Luigi Stefanini and characterizes Plato's thought as inquiry (*skepsis*), which confronts and approximates ever more closely an objective reality that is already known in some sense, although he objects to Stefanini's assumption that this objective truth is to be found in Christianity (pp. 105–7). The upshot is that, for Tigerstedt, Platonic philosophy is an inseparable unity of doubt and assertion, of question and answer (p. 107). But there is a problem here that Tigerstedt seems not to recognize.

In Tigerstedt's view, Plato's thought cannot be abstracted from the interchange of question and answer such as the dialogues represent; it is not a discursive system or dogma awaiting codification but an inquiry. Yet neither is it mere philosophizing without intrinsic philosophical content, since at any point the answers constitute an approximation to an objective truth. Now what holds of Plato's thought must also hold of its interpretation: given what Tigerstedt writes (especially pp. 105–8), it follows that each reader is guided by critical reflection on the dialogues, that is, by question and answer, to a conception of Plato's philosophical inquiry and that this conception is not a mere reproduction but the reader's own creation and approximation (pp. 99–101: cf. pp. 20–21). Accordingly, neither Plato's thought nor its interpretation is to admit of dogmatism or skepticism: both are a union of doubt and assertion, of inquiry and solution or approximation. It would remain to add that, although Plato's inquiry and its interpretation must be irreducible if Platonism is to have its own content, they do in fact have the same ultimate goal—that objective reality and truth that is dimly known *ab initio* by all—assuming that the interpretation is likewise philosophical. Consequently, although philosophical interpretation of the Platonic inquiry manifested in the dialogues is very much a function of the interpreter, there are still limits to its variety, since both Plato's inquiry and the reality ultimately inquired about in it are objective data for the interpreter. This may help explain Tigerstedt's final words: his admission that there is no easy method for solving the problem of Platonic interpretation, and his assertion that interpretation is in part transformation which is bound to produce disagreement that is limited by the rules of historical and philological criticism (pp. 107–8: cf. pp. 20–21).

If this is Tigerstedt's response to the problem of interpreting Plato, it is disquieting to find at the close that all the rival methodologies he attacks are reinstated, to realize that Tigerstedt has unwittingly recast the problem so as to invite the same old solutions and that his hope of tempering scholarly debate is futile. Tigerstedt insists that the dialogues are self-contained units and infers that the question of an overall system is a secondary issue: for him, the first problem is to interpret each dialogue and to deal with its contradictions, ambiguities, and gaps (p. 99). But, if so, how is the reader to view the relation between Plato's inquiry in a given dialogue and the text? Does Plato report or gradually disclose in the dialogue an inquiry that is already completed? Or does the dialogue reveal an inquiry that is in progress and evolving? Do the contradictions indicate blunders in Plato's study of an issue? Or do they really show that there is no sustained inquiry underlying the dialogue? Tigerstedt would undoubtedly find such questions obnoxious, since his solution aims to avoid skepticism and dogmatism in all its various competing forms. But, so far as I can tell, he is liable to them. For, in fact, he has only substituted his notion of Platonic philosophy or thought as inquiry and approximation for the previous notion of it as system, and this means that he has opened the door for skepticism and suitably modified versions of the unitarian, evolutionist, geneticist, and esotericist interpretive strategies. In sum, Tigerstedt's solution to the dilemma of dogmatism and skepticism simply reinstates it.

There is much to agree with in Tigerstedt's response to the problem of Platonic interpretation, particularly, his emphasis on the centrality of question and answer to Plato's writings and how one is to understand them, and his general account of the corpus. Yet his proposal ultimately fails, I think, in precisely the same way as the solutions he criticizes. In the final analysis, there is little to choose between reading the text as evidence of its author's systematic philosophical thought and as evidence of his philosophical thinking or inquiry. The fundamental assumption made in either case is that the text is evidence of something other than itself, its author. (See Tigerstedt's requirements 1 and 2, above.) This assumption is the root of modern scholarship and its polemic; in accepting it, Tigerstedt misdiagnoses why the dilemma of dogmatism and skepticism is false.

An Alternative: The Text as Evidence of Itself

Readers of Plato's dialogues have from ancient times asked, "What did Plato think?" But not all have meant this question in the same way. Ancient intellectual historiography and interpretation differ very much from the modern in purpose and criteria of success. Aristotle and the Neoplatonists, for example, aimed to determine what Plato was really trying to say, always in contexts determined by their own immediate philosophical purposes; they very clearly felt no obligation to render Plato's thought as he thought it, that is, to defend by reference to the text their accounts as ones to which Plato would have assented or to connect these accounts closely with the letter of the text. Nor were they always concerned to relate a coherent statement of this real meaning. In general, when they are not uncritical compilers of doxographies, the Platonic and Aristotelian commentators ascribe to Plato positions that are defined in some dialectical construct that is alien to Plato's writings themselves: the focus is not on the text per se but on what Plato is perceived as really trying to say and how this bears on certain questions of the day. Matters of accuracy in reporting the problems to which a dialogue is addressed and how they are dealt with are beside the point.[16] In contrast to this dialectical search for the essence of Platonism stands the work of Brucker, Tennemann, Schleiermacher, Hermann, and so on. These modern interpreters take the question "What did Plato think?" to mean how is one to discern a systematic philosophy in a corpus of (authentic) dialogues, when collocating the passages relevant to a given topic brings to light all manner of contradiction, obscurity, and omission? In Tigerstedt's hands, the problem becomes one of ascertaining the philosophical inquiry manifest in each dialogue.

At issue is how one reads texts and their status as evidence. By and large, the moderns take certain Platonic texts (letters, dialogues, and/or the oral tradition) as indicating their author's philosophical thought; they propose to construct and verify their conception of his thought by reference to these texts. The ancients, however, proceed differently. They make no evidentiary distinction between Plato's esoteric and exoteric teaching (pp. 64–66), and seem undisturbed by the contradictions the moderns find in the texts. Moreover, when they refer to a passage in a dialogue, the ancients either cite it as authority for some opinion, list it in a doxography, use it as a point of departure for their own speculation, or connect it with some predetermined and obviously alien position; they do not offer it as the basis of an interpretation and the means by which this interpretation is to be tested.

Consequently, the question Tigerstedt finds at the heart of modern thought is not, I think, perennial; it is but a creature of German Critical Philosophy and Idealism (the thesis that philosophy must be systematic), German Romanticism (the view that a text expresses and is determined by the mind, spirit, and personality of its author), and the rejection of Neoplatonic interpretation.[17] But, if so, we should perhaps inquire whether those dogmatists who initiated the modern era of Platonic interpretation were right to suppose that the question "What did Plato think?" necessitates reading the corpus as the record of its author's systematic thought. Is the question as they took it reasonable or well put?

I suspect it is not. First, there is no compelling reason to require that philosophy be systematic, as the history of philosophy in the last two hundred years amply demonstrates. So there is no reason to suppose that Platonic philosophy is systematic. Second, only the Platonic corpus may serve as evidence of Plato's philosophical thought. Given the ancient form of intellectual historiography and its inadequacy from our standpoint in matters of fidelity, ancient reports of Plato's philosophy (whether based on his dialogues or on some oral tradition) cannot serve as independent evidence of what Plato actually thought; one can use these reports only if they are known to be accurate, but to know this requires prior and independent interpretation of the direct evidence we have—Plato's writings. So far I follow Tigerstedt. But this brings me to the third and most important point and introduces my disagreement with him: the dialogues themselves are not witness to Plato's philosophical thought; they are not to be used as a means for constructing and verifying some conception of Plato's philosophy. There is nothing in the corpus itself that demands it be used this way, as the ancient literature surely shows. But the romantic view of texts as unified expressions of the author's intellect or mind (Geist) is a pretty conceit and it dies hard. Even the neoromantic critics or positivists acknowledge it: their contribution is simply to deny the integrity and autonomy of this mind, to regard it as itself the expression or product of nonintellectual factors. There may, of course, be literature that should be read as a manifestation of its author's thought: the question is whether this is true in the case of what Plato wrote.

As Tigerstedt observes, the Platonic corpus comprises mostly dialogues that dramatically portray particular speeches to some audience or conversations between two or more persons; Plato neither addresses the reader directly nor enters the conversation he depicts. One consequence of this is that no speaker in any dialogue is Plato's spokesman or mouthpiece, since each speaker addresses not the reader but his audience or interlocutors. (Alternatively, if one speaker is to be Plato's mouthpiece, they *all* are and equally so, and what Plato says through each to the reader is not what the speaker actually says to his dramatic listeners or respondents—if one can tolerate such use of *mouthpiece*.) The point is that the dialogues are double: there is the conversation or speech portrayed to which the reader is a silent listener and there is a different conversation between the reader and Plato—that is, there is the reader's reflection on the conversation presented.[18] It is here that I depart from Tigerstedt. In denying the assumption that the dialogues show us something of Plato's thought, an assumption Tigerstedt makes in common with those he criticizes, I propose instead that interpreting a dialogue marries two disciplines.

The first is devoted to the dramatic conversation depicted and, for want of a better term, I shall call it philology (one should recognize that such usage, although not unfounded, is perhaps controversial, given the variety of activities now termed philological). The second concerns the process of reflection on this conversation and is philosophy. Neither involves interpreting Plato's philosophical thought: philologists interpret Plato's texts and philosophers think with the text as a guide.

Let me elaborate. Given the double nature of the dialogues, to interpret them requires first the study of each as intellectual drama, a study that includes consideration of its language, style, and authenticity, as well as examination of the logical and dialectical structure of the speech or conversation constituting the action of the dialogue. There is no intrinsic difference between such analysis of a Platonic dialogue and that of a tragedy by Euripides or a comedy by Aristophanes. In each case what is written is evidence of itself, by which I mean that the analyses (here termed philological) are of the written text, not of its author or his thought, and that these analyses are verified by looking at this text.[19] In other words, the ultimate object of philological concern is the literary artifact taken by itself and in abstraction from all its historical accidents: the philologist argues from the written word, about the written word, to the written word. Now it may be objected that this is not true when the philologist speaks to the significance or meaning of his text, that the significance of Euripides' *Hippolytus* (its tragic view and so on) is what Euripides thinks; and, thus, that as in the case of drama where a text may be evidence of what its author thinks, so the dialogues may be evidence of Plato's thought.

I doubt that it is either fruitful or necessary to regard claims about the meaning of particular dramas as claims about the author's thought. Granted, it *seems* reasonable to assume that Euripides intended to convey in the *Hippolytus* his own view of man and the sources of human misery, and to allow that the tragedy does indeed convey this vision. But what seems reasonable is not always advisable. We should distinguish the author's views that inform and unify his writing of a text from the meaning or significance of this text: the former are prior and that of which the text is an expression, whereas the latter is derivative and dependent insofar as it requires the interaction of text and reader. Thus, when the philologist construes the *Hippolytus* as an independent literary artifact and remarks on its meaning, he is not commenting on the thought or intention that has produced the text but on the thought that the text effects in the reader. (Let us pass over the question as to whether the thought effected is universal or particular, that is, whether there is ultimately one meaning for all readers of the drama or as many meanings as there are readers.) Given that these two thoughts are not necessarily the same, that we must distinguish them for the most part in practice (unless we are prepared to hold that anyone may fully grasp the author's intention or views after one reading), and that we may identify them only if Euripides tells us directly how to understand the drama (which he does not—and were he to, would we be obliged to agree?), it is simpler by far to say that the meaning of the tragedy is determined solely by the text. Thus, references to Euripides' views or thoughts are, for the philologist, merely a shorthand for talking about the text alone. But not only is it simpler; it is, I think, necessary. As Cherniss says and Tigerstedt would agree, philologists must uphold the integrity and independence of literary works of art: if such works are important to people as people (and not just to biographers, historians, psychoanalysts, and so on), philologists must maintain that the artistic qualities by which we discern meaning are contained in the text; that these qualities not only make possible a diversity of interpretation, but limit it; and that such accessibility to different readers of different ages is possible only if the text is independent of the accidents of its producer and production.[20] Be this as it may for drama and its significance, we should examine the objection further in the case of the Platonic dialogue: the reason that there is no purely philological study of Plato's intellectual drama is because so far as the philologist endeavors to lay out the meaning of a dialogue he must engage in philosophy.

The speeches and conversations Plato depicts have little significance or meaning in the way that the *Hippolytus* does, since the reader's interaction with the text is of a very different order. It is, as Tigerstedt aptly terms it, a second dialogue. In other words, whereas the meaning of a drama is picture, attitude, or thesis, the meaning or significance of a dialogue is a series of questions by answering which the reader comes to think about justice and the value of the just life, for example. The *Hippolytus* challenges its reader and audience to experience and reflect on some truth; a Platonic dialogue invites the reader to observe carefully and to begin a course of guided inquiry. Such reflective inquiry uses the text as a starting point and should advance to the most abstract of philosophical issues. Unlike philology, which takes the written word as the ultimate and only object of concern, philosophy—or more precisely, the philosophical study of Plato's writings—seeks to answer the questions these writings raise and thus moves from the text toward solution of general problems.

Initially, this process of inquiry is focused by the chief interlocutor, who not only sets the topic but also indicates how it is to be addressed. For instance, in the early dialogues, Socrates typically asks what some virtue or excellence is and stipulates that the answer is to disclose an *eidos*, or essence, which makes all particular instances of that virtue what they are and which is the means of discriminating these instances.[21] As the conversation proceeds, the reader is further directed in several ways; I shall mention only three.

First, he is tempted to identify himself with one or other of the interlocutors, to test the cogency of the arguments given at any point, and to determine their viability more generally. This is a natural response to the dialogue form and, indeed, it dominates the recent secondary literature. Unfortunately, this literature usually couples this response with the assumption that the object of interpretation is Plato's thought; consequently, this type of criticism all too often results in poor philosophy and worse philology. On one hand, it answers the challenge to think with doctrine — theses are accepted or overthrown on the strength of the soundness of Plato's dramatic depiction of a particular conversation and their consiliance with antecedent convictions; on the other, it presumes to study literary art by editing it. There are, of course, several checks on such extremism, not least of which is that the reader is never addressed directly—he is to pay attention but not to intervene. More important, though, is the fact that reflection on a dialogue need not be limited to the logical form of the arguments uttered by the dramatis personae: once one has tested the validity of the particular arguments given, it still remains to consider their logical and dramatic position in the conversation as a whole, for the course of the conversation or speech portrayed typically falls into stages and each stage may be viewed as an attempt to answer an implicit question, a question that further indicates how the central problem may be analyzed. This is a second way in which Plato's text guides the reader. For example, if one considers the function of the several sections of the preamble to the image of the Sun in the *Republic,* one finds they point to general issues pertaining to the characterization of any summum bonum in moral theory,[22] issues that must also be investigated if one is to decide whether the just life is indeed better than a life of injustice. Related to this is a third way in which Plato's writings direct the reader. As all readers quickly notice, the dramatic conversations and speeches regularly introduce a great number of diverse philosophical topics: this means that in attending to the logical progress of the speeches or of the interchanges and how the central problem is to be dealt with, the reader is also brought to realize that tackling the central problem entails thinking about matters that initially seemed quite independent.

Such metaconversational hints, however, do not constitute doctrine. They guide the reader but do not restrain him: in that the reader discerns them by way of questions asked of the text, in particular, questions that bear on the central problem and how to solve it, he is forced to question the validity and worth of these hints as well. But in doing this, he thinks for himself; he does not discover what Plato thinks. Unlike the works of Aristotle and later philosophers, Plato's text does not require the reader to sit in Plato's school and learn his philosophy; it demands instead that the reader become a philosopher in his own right.[23] And, of course, there will be a great divergence in what each of us thinks. Not only do we differ in interest and ability; we will choose to discover and evaluate differently the hints in the text.

Still these hints, rooted as they are in what Plato has written, do provide a general framework for philosophical study. And this is true, I think, whether one eventually comes to accept or reject them, so long as this acceptance or rejection is the result of sustained critical reflection and not the mere adoption of unexamined dogma. If to interpret a Platonic dialogue philosophically is to think for oneself, there is no intrinsic restriction in the theses one affirms or denies. But if this philosophical interpretation is really a response to what Plato has written, that is, if it is predicated on sound philology and advances by a continuous series of questions and answers to the solution of the general problem of the text, then it will be limited and stand out as Platonic by virtue of its form, its focus, and its history. Thus, whereas Tigerstedt hopes to avoid dogmatism and skepticism by taking Platonic thought as inquiry that approximates an objective reality, I propose that the philosophical interpretation of what Plato has written consists in one's own thinking about the central problem of a given text, when this thinking advances by a process of question and answer that is guided by the text.

Philosophy and Philology

This account of the second dialogue is admittedly brief. But since the only way to present it properly would be by interpreting a particular dialogue, it will have to do for now.[24] I have tried to argue on the strength of Tigerstedt's history that today's academic interpretation of Plato is a response to a bad question since it subscribes to the late eighteenth-century German assumption that the Platonic text is the means by which we are to contruct and verify our views of Plato's philosophical thought.[25] My contention is that we should prescind from trying to read the text as evidence of anything but itself: the study of Platonic texts is not mental archaeology. Accordingly, I maintain that the polemic and lack of any consensus among contemporary schools of interpretation is due in large part to an attendant confusion of two distinct activities that are necessarily involved in interpreting the Platonic corpus. In assuming that scholars interpret Plato's philosophy in light of what he has written, we mistake and confound philology, which interprets the text as an autonomous literary work, with philosophy, which is guided by the text in the pursuit of knowledge. As a result, not only do we lose the objective control there may be in philology, but we leave ourselves with more to dispute and fewer respectable means of adjudication. Of course, abandoning the critical supposition that the dialogues are evidence of Plato's philosophy will not obviate scholarly differences. But by distinguishing the philological and philosophical responses and their different criteria for success, we can temper it and reintroduce some measure of real agreement. Or failing that, we can at least state our disagreement in a way that others consider relevant.

I have indicated why the philological study of the dialogues is necessarily propaedeutic to the philosophical. At the same time, I should say that, given the ways in which Plato's text guides its reader, the philosophical response to a dialogue must be predicated on a sound philology *if* it is to be guided by the text. This has consequences. It means, for instance, that one cannot isolate the logical and dialectical structure of the argumentation in a dialogue without paying heed to humor and irony at the dramatic level. Nor can one simply proceed by analyzing passages culled from different dialogues, the "scissors and paste" method that is so common today. Both the philologist and the philosopher are primarily concerned with single dialogues: the former, because passages have their meaning essentially in their context and because each dialogue is a literary unit; the latter, because his inquiry is to be guided by what Plato has written and because the dialogues are presented as philosophically independent—there are no footnotes or cross-references that make the arguments interdependent. (I do not deny that philosophical reflection on more than one dialogue at once is desirable, but I doubt that it should occur first or that it involves comparing passages rather than philosophical interpretations: in short, such comparison belongs to a stage of inquiry far beyond the text.)

Further, since the Platonic philosophy I have described is neither a doctrine Plato held nor idle philosophizing but the reader's thinking by way of question and answer as directed by what Plato writes, its touchstone is not the text itself: this is the criterion of philology. Rather, in criticizing philosophical claims, we should assess both the importance of the questions they answer and whether the answers are successful. Accordingly, although we may find theories about the nature and extent of the world of Forms interesting, insightful, or useful, and believe that they illuminate the text of Plato, that is, that they help our own reflection on the text, we should not test them by recourse to the text; such theories are to be evaluated in the same way we evaluate Plotinus' metaphysics or Aristotle's.

Finally, let me emphasize that philosophical theories are no warrant for philological conclusions. A thesis about what soul is and whether it is one or many which is reached by critical reflection on the *Symposium, Phaedo, Republic,* and *Phaedrus* is not grounds for arguing the authenticity or chronology of these dialogues. Indeed, one of the advantages to this distinction between philology and philosophy, based as it is both on the integrity of each dialogue as an artistic unit independent of its author and the circumstances of its production and on the view that each dialogue is a double conversation, is the fact that our data becomes more stable. Again, in proscribing philosophical conclusions about authenticity and chronology, we are also armed to reject any interpretation of meaning that involves making or supposing argument from or to some proposition about the unity or development of Plato's thought. The unitarian, geneticist, evolutionist, esotericist, and skeptic hypotheses about Plato's philosophy as well as the interpretative strategies they entail are irrelevant in both the philological and philosophical studies of the dialogues, once the texts are no longer read as means for building and testing accounts of Plato's views. In short, the dilemma of dogmatism and skepticism that rules the recent history of Platonic interpretation is not to be met as Tigerstedt wishes: it is to be denied not because it mistakes philosophy for system rather than inquiry but because it takes the text as evidence of its author's thought.

If the proof of a good book is the attention given it and the constructive discussion it provokes, then I trust the reader will take interest in the questions Tigerstedt's work raises about the history of Platonic scholarship and about the proper goals and criteria of this scholarship. Such tribute to an author now deceased is not only seemly, especially when scholars are assembled to consider why Plato wrote dialogues; it is necessary. As Tigerstedt says in the opening pages, "No scholar who in any way, be it ever so limited, is dealing with Plato and Platonism, can escape from making up his mind about the vexatious problem of interpreting Plato. He cannot simply leave it to the 'experts,' . . . for they disagree deeply" (p. 13).

4

The Theater of Myth in Plato

Jean-François Mattéi

τοὺς τῆς ἀληθείας . . . φιλοθεάμονας
Plato, *Rep.*, 5.475e

The inspired speech of myth/begotten of the Daimon/reveals that the world/
is the theater/of the periodic revolution of soul.

Myth

Tradition has long acknowledged that the dramatic form of Plato's dialogues makes them unique and memorable. The suspicion that the dialogues are marginally philosophical precisely because of their dramatic cast is at least as venerable. Even in the prologues of his texts, Plato stages a whole gallery of picturesque characters who, as the elaborate plot unfolds in a familiar setting, slowly weave together the threads of a philosophical drama the images of which will remain long after the fall of the curtain. One may forget Parmenides' dialectical argument from his third hypothesis about the One, but one will remember the concerted movement of the chorus in the *Protagoras,* under Callias' porch, as well as Phaedrus and Socrates walking in hot summer weather to the shade of a plane tree alive with the music of cicadas. Even the "metaphysical" works in which the roles of conversation and action are considerably reduced compared with the earlier dialogues display an implicit dramatic structure, as Stanley Rosen has recently emphasized with respect to the *Sophist.*[1] It is very tempting then, for those who come after the curtain falls to want the play reenacted. Agathon's symposium already imitated, unbeknown to those present, the symposium of the gods celebrating the birth of Aphrodite. In the same way the ten Florentine scholars summoned by Lorenzo de' Medici in Careggi in November 1474 played anew the primeval scene so as to celebrate the anniversary of Eros' birth together with that of Plato's death.[2] The dramatic aspect so characteristic of Plato's art, illustrated by his use of the "coup de théâtre" (Socrates suddenly appearing to Alcibiades' eyes) as well as of the deus ex machina (Zeus' final intervention at the end of Critias' tale) seems rather alien to the traditional rigor of the philosopher. Therefore in order to "save" dramatic "appearances," interpreters have usually ascribed them to the requirements of the dialogue form, and have explained that Plato chose the dialogue form in order to portray his characters on the road to dialectic. Plato's works are then said to recognize in human speech the origin of the dramatic conflicts that are later played out in the dialogues as on a stage. And conversely these works are also said to emphasize in turn the theatrical play of human relationships that occur when people live out the judgments implicit in their day-to-day discourse.

Yet while shedding light on the dramatization of theory made effective in the dialogues, the preceding line of thought leaves in the dark the entirely different dramatic art present in the other Platonic speech, namely muthos. With the exception of the Neoplatonists, interpreters have paid very little attention to myth, for the most part reducing it to a minor form of knowledge, if not merely dismissing it from Platonism altogether. The reason is easy to understand: myth is a tale that falls within the moving domain of opinion and belongs to poetic imitation or blind tradition. Unreliable and unverifiable as it is, such a semblance of truth could never be allowed to block the road of pure knowledge. Whether considered with Couturat as an illusory speech revealing the false instead of the true,[3] or with Brochard as the expression of probability which Plato ascribes to the notion of destiny,[4] myth is always judged in comparison with a logical standard of knowledge previously formulated by the interpreter. We read in a recent study, one that nevertheless shows some sympathy for the Platonic function of the myth: "Si Platon s'intéresse tant au mythe, c'est qu'il veut en briser le monopole pour imposer le type de discours qu'il entend développer, c'est-à-dire le discours philosophique à qui il reconnaît un statut supérieur."[5]

Obviously such a rationalistic interpretation could not be accepted until we substitute an ideal Platonism coined on the same pattern as logico-mathematic knowledge for the real Platonism at work in the discussions actually portrayed in the dialogues. Admittedly one finds in Plato many a passage in which the dialectician, acting as both judge and plaintiff in the conflict, seems to choose logos at the expense of muthos—muthos he then gives up to poetic inspiration (as is ironically noted by Socrates at *Phaedo* 61b). Yet it remains the case that Plato's criticism of myth, if we are to take it at its own words, bears only on the myths of his predecessors. Indeed, the *Phaedo* ends with a myth, not with a demonstration of the immortality of the soul. One cannot therefore avoid the following question:

if myth, fallacious and deceptive as it was for Couturat, is to be banned from the ideal city along with the other lies of the poets, why does Plato reintroduce it regularly in a serious contemplative mood at every decisive stage of his reflections?

I would like to point out here that in the works of Plato *such as we have them,* in dialogue form—and not as the interpreters try to reconstruct them in the form of a system—it is the mythic language of "representation" (to use the Hegelian vocabulary) that is at the origin of the theoretical language of "speculation." Logos is capable of elaborating a *theory of knowledge* at the conclusion of dialectical conversations only after muthos has oriented the philosopher with a *knowledge of theory.* The latter engenders the natural movement of the soul that enables it to see the theater of Ideas. It seems to me unfruitful to oppose in Plato's works the muthos to the logos, as one might an unprovable speech to a provable one, with the sole object of concluding that one is *logically* superior to the other. Rather, the mythical language serves another purpose: it offers from a unique standpoint a picture of the world through which dialectic must progress step by step. Let us then contrast logos and muthos on five basic criteria which reveal their complementary aspects:

LOGOS	Criteria	MUTHOS
1. dialogue	*form*	1′ monologue
2. argumentation	*process*	2′ narrative
3. concept	*mediation*	3′ image
4. verification	*finality*	4′ truth
5. thing (λόγος τινὸς)	*reference*	5′ world (μῦθος κόσμου)

Platonic myth may thus be roughly defined as a tale of various episodes reported by the voice of one narrator only, usually Socrates,[6] which tries to reveal in iconic form the initial truth of the world. The synoptic function of the myth whose circular structure duplicates that of the cosmos enables it to integrate in one vision the manifold experiences acquired by men through contact with things. As in a theater the representation of the invisible takes shape and puts rhythm into space. At the center of the enclosure built in the hill and opened on the outer world, the drama that holds together the lives of men with those of gods, as well as the forces of heaven with those of earth, enacts the meeting point of all the perspectives to which it communicates its primal unity. At the beginning of the myth of the cave, Socrates makes Glaucon "see" in one instant (ἰδὲ) the "images" (εἰκόνα, 514a3–4) of the prisoners confined in their underground dwellings. This imperious word which is repeated on four occasions (ἴδε, 514b5; ὅρα, 514b9; σκόπει, 515c4; ἐννόησον, 516e3), makes of the listener a *seer* addicted to contemplating the truth. Whereas logical argumentation calls for active step-by-step verification of the theory in question, mythic *theoria* delivers the soul right away to the free expanse of the truth. Critias justifies in this manner the words he is about to say to his companions at the beginning of the *Timaeus*: "Listen Socrates to a story that is very odd [λόγου μάλα μὲν ἀτόπου] but perfectly true [παντάπασί γε μὴν ἀληθοῦς], just as it was told once by Solon, the wisest of the seven wise men" (20d–e).

The narrative form of Platonic myth, dense and sustained, its ending made conspicuous by its remoteness in the past, conjures up a regular chain of dramatic episodes that the listener, in being subjected to the magic of the word, starts to imagine as if he were the spectator of an invisible show. Listening to this atopic speech, strange and out of its place, is the first condition of the mythic perspective, as is evident from the infernal myth of the *Republic*. The judges ask Er to listen to (ἀκούειν) and look at (θεᾶσθαι, 614d4) what is going on in the field where the last judgment is held. And as Glaucon is silently listening to Socrates repeating Er's words, the latter listens to the stories told by the souls at the end of their long journey. In Platonic muthos it is not the eye that listens but the ear that sees. And since it escapes from the eye of the body the myth gives the impression that it makes visible the hidden things capable of arousing and awakening the eye of the soul. As if in an enclosed field mythic narrative conjures up a series of images in the soul which contemplates their theory, all in order to make apparent to the soul the five classes of beings of which is made, according to Socrates, the secret matter of the myth: gods, daimons, heroes, Hades' inhabitants, and men (*Rep.* 392a). When the myth starts to speak and to tell its iconic tale, Socrates, the lover of ancient legends (*Phr.* 229c–230a), enters and draws in the visible the shape itself of the invisible.

Daimon

In truth Socrates almost always maintains a distance from the strange stories he tells his audience. Whereas he unreservedly launches into dialogues in spite of his professed ignorance, he withdraws from myths at their beginning and lets the impersonal, neutral voice of a stranger speak on his behalf. At the close of the narrative only unanswering silence echoes the myth, as at the end of the *Republic* or *Gorgias*. With the exceptions of the myths of the *Protagoras* (which alone of the myths is attributed to a sophist) and that of the cave (which refers to the narrator himself), all the Platonic myths are placed under the aegis of gods, priests, wise men, poets, or venerable customs. But whatever the inspiration, myth reveals at once its mysterious character with that voice from beyond which reduces the listener to passivity and arouses in him the sense of being both bewitched and awed by the feeling of immeasurable distance. The voice speaking through Socrates as if he were but a puppet pulled by his master, a ventriloquist from the beyond world, is the daimon's voice whose presence is more atopic than that of Phaedrus' companion. If the daimonic figure belongs to the myth of which it is one of the five topics, the myth in turn reveals itself as thoroughly daimonic as soon as it involves all the forms of mediation between the soul and the world.

The prophetic inspiration repeatedly claimed by Socrates (*Ion* 534c–d; *Meno* 81a–b; *Phr.* 235b, 244a; *Theae.* 152a, 156a; *Phil.* 16c, and so on) stands for the positive manifestation—luminous, as it were—of the daimon whose actions, in the shade of the philosopher, are usually negative. Just as myth puts an end to conversation and cuts short dialectic progression, so the daimon suddenly interrupts Socrates and suspends the movement he had engaged in. Since early childhood the daimon appears to Socrates as a "voice" (*Apol.* 31d; *Phr.* 242c) and a "divine sign" (*Apol.* 40b; *Phr.* 242b; *Euthyd.* 272e) which turn him away from what he was about to achieve. Thus Socrates will stand stock-still under the porch of Agathon's neighbors in the middle of the meal in the same way as he had remained motionless one day and one night, during the campaign at Potideia. Such is the sentence of the daimon: it prevents Socrates from following his first impulse and, for instance, forbids him to cross the river in order to flee Lysias' admirer; on the contrary it compels him to stay within its own *limits*. Whenever Socrates runs the risk of offending the "divine" form of his soul (*Phr.* 242c) in his words as well as in his actions—for instance, when he goes to a symposium to face the sophists' disciples and especially the speech of the very Agathon who will fling on him the Gorgon head of Gorgias (*Symp.* 198c)—precisely at that point the daimon interrupts him at once "right in the middle of what [he was] saying" (*Apol.*, 40b). So the daimon does too when Socrates follows Phaedrus' urgent request, and even goes so far as to deliver an impious speech about Eros. The power of the daimon leaves Socrates speechless and replaces the voice of the philosopher with a more primeval one, the voice of the soul. In that sense the daimon is not Socrates' *double,* the disquieting semblance which, as in a mirror, would reflect the philosopher's image and live in his body as well as in his own house (*H. Maj.* 304d); it is rather *simply* Socrates, the constant witness of the original purity of a soul prey to the natural "duplicity" of language (*Crat.* 408a–c).

Keeping Socrates in suspense equally distant from a soul that returns to him and from an unfinished action, the daimonic power prepares Socrates to turn his thoughts toward the origin. The suspension of human action is the necessary condition of contemplation. Thus the daimonic silence of Socrates and the Socratic speech of the daimon both attest to the profound feeling of distance experienced by each soul when it casts a glance at its inner theater. Therein lies the source of the synoptic vision of myth from which knowledge stems and where it ends, a vision that dialectic will later attempt to reconstruct. Such reserve toward the divine part of the soul, apparent in Socrates' withdrawal behind myth, is called αἰδώς, "modesty" or "respect," in Plato. The myth of Protagoras bestows the gifts of modesty and justice to the "divine lot" granted by Zeus and equally divided among men (322c). Modesty is the first sign of the simple look which the soul has been casting on the world since early childhood and which reminds it of the "theory" of forms it has previously contemplated. One understands that the daimon must be the essential figure of Platonic pedagogy and psychagogy, both of which demand the mediation of myth. Hegel was therefore right when he remarked about Plato that "the myth belongs to the pedagogic stage of the human race" and that myth is "always a mode of presentation which, as belonging to an earlier stage, introduces sensuous images, which are directed to imagination, not to thought." But if one is to admit from a Hegelian viewpoint that "when the Notion attains its full development, it has no more need of the myth,"[7] one will also acknowledge the fact that for Plato the soul that is "related to" the Ideas (*Pho.* 79d) always remains in infancy compared to the Ideas. The parallels tirelessly made by Plato between myths and old wives' tales (*Grg.* 527a; *Rep.* 350e, 377a–c, 381e; *Laws* 887d) or children's games (*Soph.* 242c; *Pol.* 268e) have no other purpose than that. The presence of myth in the inmost recesses of the Platonic search demonstrates that the pedagogy of the soul is eternal, as eternal as philosophy itself. Philosophers will never reach the shores of absolute knowledge. Thus Plato is led to acknowledge that the soul could not go beyond the teaching of myth which lays out its own limits. Dialectic starts its journey within an enclosed yet boundless world offered to the periodic revolutions of the soul even before it was born.

The most obvious illustration of all this can be found in Book 7 of the *Republic,* where the nature of man considered with regard to both education and lack of education (514a2) is first made visible (ἰδὲ, ὅρα, σκόπει) through the image of the cave. This occurs before the dialogue between Socrates and Glaucon—dialogue guided by myth—embarks on the gradual path to knowledge which leads to the supreme science of dialectic. One perceives here the true nature of the daimon: it is nothing but the principle of the circular movement of the soul, the origin of the liberation and conversion (518c–d) of the prisoner leading him to "the contemplation [θεωμένη] of the most luminous part of the being" (518c9–10). Along the journey that draws the soul out of the cave and leads it back to its native place, with *anabasis* and *katabasis* marking the rhythm of exile and return, the soul of the prisoner remains constantly bound to the invisible figure of the daimon. The latter not only stops the bad impulses of the soul, as Socrates often recalls in his *dialogues* with partners, but also puts the philosopher's soul back on the right track, as Socrates again attests, this time through *myths*. The daimon and the daimon alone is the origin of Socrates' palinode in the *Phaedrus,* as it is the cause of the turning around of the prisoner who on earth and under heaven is always acting contrarily, standing up toward the light when in the shade and turned back toward the shade when in the light.

The wrenching of the bonds is done instantaneously (ἐξαίφνης; 515c7) in the same way as is the first look cast toward the solar heights (516a3) and the second look cast on the underground shadows (516e5) at the time of return. Each one of the sudden turnings of the prisoner is ordered by the daimon, which exhibits here all the power of the ἐξαίφνης later defined by Parmenides as "the starting-point of two opposite changes" (*Parm.* 156d). Socrates' daimon represents the mythic form of this passage from motion to stillness and from stillness to motion situated in the in-between of opposites, even as Parmenides' ἐξαίφνης is the logical formulation of it. In both one can see the origin of the circular movement of the soul of which knowledge is properly made. At each turn the soul is set in motion, or more precisely "animated," by this instantaneous principle. That principle remains unseen by the soul that has inherited it, unseen both in the dialectical reversals of the third hypothesis between the One which is *and* is not, as well as in the turnabouts of the prisoner from darkness to light *and* from light to darkness. We are then led to conclude that the daimon is the blind spot on which the vision of the soul is founded, a unique standpoint that commands the logical evidence required by dialectic and, at the same time, the metaphysical ordeal enacted on the broad stage of the world even before the curtain has risen on existence. The end of the myth of Er testifies to this: Fate orders the soul to choose freely the daimon that is to accompany it in its future life; then Lachesis, the Moira who sings of the past, gives the soul this guardian of its existence. The daimon then leads the soul to Clotho who weaves the spindle of the present, and last to Atropos who will cut the thread of the future. On the following night in the plain of Lethe, just when Heaven and Earth embrace, the daimon makes the soul ascend in a single bolt of lightning (ἐξαπίνης, 621b3) toward the superior world of birth. As for Er, he suddenly (ἐξαίφνης, 621b6) opens his eyes at the dawn of a new life, even as he is lying on his funeral pyre. Here the Platonic narrative teaches us two things: the genealogy of the soul the daimon begets, thus binding the soul to all the things it will come to know, and the origin of the myth itself. Since the daimon is the true creator of myth, only myth can make us see the invisible face of the daimon.

World

The speech of the myth, prompted in Socrates by that primeval imperious and absent voice which is proper to daimonic inspiration, dons the circular shape of the world from which it stems. When the logos bounded by opposing forces in the interplay of questions and answers is suspended by the intervention of the daimon, the muthos reconciles all the beings and the perspectives in the unity of the whole. Like traditional myths, the Platonic narrative takes its audience back to the origin of the world, situates the events it records in an indefinite past, and is introduced by the characteristic "once upon a time" (ἦν ποτε; *Prot.* 320c8; *Phr.* 259b6) or simply "once" (ποτέ; *Rep.* 359d1; 614b4). Thus it goes back to the initial period from which time comes and to which it will return according to the law of cosmic cycles: "Once upon a time there was and there will be once more" (ἦν τοίνυν καὶ ἔτι ἔσται; *Pol.* 268e7).

If we attempt to situate that voice from beyond that time and again discloses the topography of the myth, we shall discover that it speaks from above (ἄνω) and particularly from the center (ἐν μέσῳ), exactly where being takes place. Whether Plato has priests, wise men, or poets speak, or places himself under the control of tradition and the patronage of gods, it is always from the center of the world between earth and heaven that the daimonic messenger brings the wills of the gods to the men and the prayers of the men to the gods. In order to prepare the sophist for the myth of the last judgment which occurs at the end of the *Gorgias,* Socrates conjures up for Callicles the theater of the world: "Heaven and Earth, Gods and Men are held together by a community made of friendship and order, of wisdom and spirit of justice, and that, my friend, is the reason why [the wise men] called this whole cosmos or order, not disorder or licentiousness" (*Grg.,* 508a).

As an actor engaged on the stage of politics, the sophist remains blind to the *geometric equality* holding the whole together, and he does not see the cosmos any more than he hears in Socrates' speech the words of the wise Pythagoreans. Thus the final myth of the *Gorgias* sheds light on the divisions of the world and reveals its justice. To prevent the judges from being deceived by the disguises still donned by the dead in the world beyond, Zeus decides that the soul of each judge will have to look at (θεωροῦντα) the soul of the dead man directly (ἐξαίφνης, 523e4) in the center of the Meadow where his three sons are sitting. Minos, Aeacus, and Rhadamanthus pass their sentences "at the crossing of two roads, one leading to the Isles of the Blessed, the other to Tartarus"; the souls meet at the intersection of two other roads, some coming from Asia to be judged by Rhadamanthus, the others from Europe to be judged by Aeacus (524a). The topography of this Nekuia of the judges, with its four cardinal dimensions laid in regular order around the center of the world, can be found a second time in infernal form in the eschatologic myth of the *Phaedo*. Each one of the dead is led by his daimon to some place (εἰς δή τινα τόπον; 107d8) whence the souls set out for their journey to Hades' abode once they have been judged. Among the numerous underground streams leading them to their final residence, Socrates isolates a certain group of four rivers, the Ocean and the Acheron, the Pyriphlegethon and the Cocytus. They are opposed in pairs around Lake Acherousias "where the souls of most dead finally arrive" and which looks like the very center of Hell (113a). Yet at the opposite of this center seen by the souls, there is in Hades the unseen center of the Tartarus, an abyss running right through the earth, the starting point of the diverging streams of all the rivers and conversely the point at which they all converge (112a).

In Uranian form this time, the myth of Er repeats with more fullness the tetradic distribution of space oriented around one center. "In a daimonic place" (τόπον τινὰ δαιμόνιον, 614c2), where the souls come to be judged, two adjoining terrestrial apertures are facing two similar celestial apertures between which (μεταξὺ) judges are sitting. There, in the center of the world—compared once more to a meadow (614e3, 616b3), as in the analogous myths of the *Gorgias* (524a3) and *Phaedrus* (248b8)—lies the crossing of the two roads that join Earth and Heaven. The two on the right ascend from Hell to the Meadow and from the Meadow to Heaven and are beneficent, whereas the two on the left that descend from Heaven to the Meadow and from the Meadow to Hell are maleficent. The similar structure of the three Nekuias in the *Gorgias, Phaedo,* and *Republic* have been remarkably pointed out by Proclus in his *Commentary on the Republic*. Proclus considers as identical the words *daimonic place, crossroads,* and *meadow*: "according to Plato, [they] are nothing but the middle [τὸ μέσον] of the whole Heaven."[8] However this myth introduces a fundamental novelty about the filiation of the soul and world: the disposition of the four celestial and terrestrial apertures draws the four crossed branches of an X articulated at the junction where the judges are sitting. Proclus rightfully notes the likeness of this chiasma to the X figure of the *Timaeus* (36b–c) resulting from the intersection of the two harmonic branches of the soul patterned after the double tetractus. Moreover, according to Porphyry the Egyptians might have known such a sign "where the X was surrounded by a circle symbolically representing the soul of the world."[9] But I shall not emphasize this aspect any longer, having dealt with it at length in my previous works.[10] For my present purpose I shall retain only the constant assimilation in the three narratives of the *daimonic place* from which the myth stems to the *center of the world* which enables the soul to circulate. The cross-shaped figure of the four roads starting from a single center to which they eternally converge links the microcosm of the soul to the macrocosm of Heaven and Earth, of Men and Gods, in order to ensure the harmony of the whole. Callicles remains forever hostile to this universal law of analogy binding the world as if with iron or steel bonds, or as if with a shining column of light.

Let us now approach closer to the mysterious nature of the daimon by considering the genealogy of Eros that Diotima teaches Socrates. The revelation of the priestess on the double nature of love takes place during a slow progression marked by four essential stages: (1) the first dialogue between Diotima and Socrates on the daimonic nature of Eros (201e–203a); (2) the first myth about the birth of Eros (203a–204c); (3) the resumption of the dialogue about the benefits of love and the desire of immortality (204c–209e); and (4) the return to the myth with the tale of the initiation in the Mysteries of Eros (209e–212c). Using mythical sounding dialectical arguments, Diotima demonstrates first that the daimon is "intermediate between the god and the mortal man" (μεταξύ ἐστι θεοῦ τε καί θνητοῦ; 202e1). Consequently Eros, the "great daimon" (δαίμων μέγας), is in charge of conveying the prayers and sacrifices of men to the gods and the orders and favors of the gods to men. Halfway (ἐν μέσῳ; 202e5–6) between gods and men, the philosopher Eros is also halfway (ἐν μέσῳ; 203e6) between knowledge and ignorance. The world of Eros reconstructs in a slightly different way the cosmic community of the *Gorgias* centered around equal geometry: "men" and "gods" will eternally form the first pair of beings whose destiny has been sealed once and for all. Yet the residences to which they have been appointed are called not "Heaven" and "Earth" but "knowledge" and "ignorance" so that the *philo*sopher's speech can directly express its amorous mediation. Eros embodies the living bonds, indissolubly sensual and spiritual, which were previously attributed to geometric equality in the form of the cosmic bond of community (συνέχειν; *Grg.* 508a1). They allow the gap to be filled between the four determinations so that Eros is truly "the bond which holds the whole together with itself" (202e7).

The genealogy of Eros later expressed in the myth of Poros and Penia justifies its double nature: as the son of a god and a mortal woman, Love is halfway between the two worlds inhabited by its parents, lying on the ground and sleeping in the open. A restlessly wandering vagabond, this mobile and elusive center paradoxically finds the place of its atopy which assembles and separates the human and the divine. Therefore the philosopher's amorous daimon embodies the highest cosmic mediation holding knowledge and ignorance together: an analogy that discourse *accords*—in the double sense of "grants to" and "puts in harmony with"—the basic measures of the world. After the discordant performance of Aristophanes, who underlined the divorce between gods and men in a dramatic and burlesque comedy by mutilating each body in "the symbol of man" (191d5), the final initiation of Diotima recovers the major accord of Earth and Heaven, men and gods, and develops all their harmonics in the theater of the Beautiful. The curtain rises on the five acts of "ultimate mysteries and revelations" (τὰ δὲ τέλεα καὶ ἐποπτικά; 210a1): the right path to the love matters progressively raises the initiate, as if by degrees, (1) "from one beautiful body to two," (2) "and from two to all," (3) "from beautiful bodies to beautiful morals," (4) "and from beautiful morals to beautiful sciences," until it finally reaches, in a "sudden" revelation (ἐξαίφνης; 210e4), (5) "some beauty of a wonderful nature," not to be compared with any living being "on earth or in heaven" (210b1). Tearing again the sacred speech of the myth, the ἐξαίφνης occurs like a coup de théâtre which in a flash gives the soul the recognition of Supreme Beauty and justifies all the looks formerly cast on the numerous beauties (θεάσασθαι, 210c3; θεωρῶν, 210d5; θεώμενος, 210e3; θεωμένῳ, 211d2; θεᾶσθαι, 211d7; θεωμένου, 212a2). At the time of its ultimate *act,* the final word of the theater of love is no longer "action" but rather "contemplation."

Theater

In its older and more universal practices such as dance, mime, puppet show or shadow show, the theatrical form tends to express itself in the world of the eye rather than in the world of the ear and to favor the experience of space over that of time. Whether Greek drama stems from the cyclic dances connected with certain Dionysian worships in the dithyramb, and with the processions of peasants dressed up as satyrs in the drama, or whether its origin is still more obscure, it nevertheless takes the essentially visual form of a series of animated scenes in which the chorus' entrance and departure through the side entrances, the circular evolutions of the chorus on the orchestra, and the concerted movements of the protagonists on the proscenium submit the spectators to the continuous tension of the performance. The rhythmic movements of the bodies organize space on the stage and make for the appearance of speech. When faraway looks are cast on the outlines of the beings whose unity is reinforced by a distant stylization, then the world can take place.

The Platonic approach that considers the soul under its various aspects—ontological, ethical, and political—deserves indeed the beautiful name of a "theory" inasmuch as it shows the circular journey of souls contemplating the truth. It is against the mythic background of the procession of the soul toward supreme forms that the legitimacy of dialectical thought will be established by the hypothesis of recollection. And as science naturally originates in the theater of the soul, Platonic epistemology in turn takes its place in the theater of myth. The strict *choreia* of the circular

trips of the soul within the cosmos clearly demonstrates that Plato draws
his inspiration here from the theatrical model. Around Dionysus' *thumele*
(altar) the primitive chorus led by its visible daimon, the chorus master,
makes its rounds on the orchestra (a scene that haunts many images in
Plotinus' works; *Enneads* IV, 3, 17; VI, 9, 8). In Platonic dramatic art
myth somehow plays the part of the cyclic chorus whose movements give
birth to drama—that is, to the action of the Ideas. We can see it first at
work in the Nekuia of the *Republic*. Er has been able to tell what he had
seen there because when he had reached the Meadow the judges had
relieved him from the common sentence and ordered him to "carefully
listen and watch everything happening in that place" (ἀκούειν τε καὶ
θεᾶσθαι πάντα τὰ ἐν τῷ τόπῳ; 614d4). Before acting as the messenger of gods (614d3, 619b2), Er is the spectator of the drama enacted
in the center of the world where the souls from the Earth meet the souls
from Heaven "as in the Panegyrics" (614e3). The theatrical aspect of the
narrative is emphasized by the sequence of various episodes which Ar-
menius' son always contemplates with the same distance (θέας, 615a3;
ἐθεασάμεθα, 615d5; θεαμάτων, 615d6; τὴν θέαν, 619e7); episodes
such as the judgment in the Meadow; the dreadful spectacle of the sentences
(the great Ardiaeus); the spindle of Necessity and the cosmic revolutions;
the choice of the destinies of the souls; and finally the return of the souls
to life. The rhythm of all these scenes is generated by the continuous
movements of the souls whose theory is first vertical (from Hell to Heaven
and from Heaven to Hell), then horizontal (the four days' journey to the
light which connects Heaven and Earth as an iridescent column and the
one-day trip to the spindle; the search for the various destinies displayed
on the ground as goods in the marketplace), and then vertical again with
the final incarnation of souls carried upward to the superior world at the
speed of a shooting star.

The finest illustration of the cosmic procession of souls can be found
in the *Phaedrus* when Socrates, having explained the myth of the winged
team, presents the spectacle of the world with incomparable fullness. Following Plato's usual approach (*Tim.* 34b, 36e–37a; *Laws* X, 895b–c, 896a),
Socrates first defines the soul as the thing "that moves itself" (αὐτοκίνητον,
245c6; cf. 245c–246a), before stating that it travels in "the entire heaven"
when it is perfect and winged in order to govern "the whole world" (246b–
c). After these preliminaries, Socrates makes us contemplate the celestial
procession of the souls guided by Zeus and his host of gods and fiends
organized in eleven sections; like the thumele (altar) standing still in the
middle of the orchestra, Hestia remains alone in the house of the gods.
Surrounding her the eleven divine choruses move in concentric circles
according to their ranks: "blissful are the spectacles played on the inside
of heaven" (μακάριαι θέαι; 247a4). Once they have reached the top of

the canopy of heaven the immortal souls heave themselves onto its roof
and let themselves be carried—motionless now—by the divine merry-go-
round which makes them contemplate (θεωροῦσι; 247c1) the supracelestial
place. This is the reverse of the scene in the *Phaedo* in which Socrates
imagined that men, endowed with wings, "could see from above" the real
earth (ἄνωθεν θεῷτο; 110b6) like a many-colored dodecahedron, "a show
worthy of blessed spectators" (θέαμα εὐδαιμόνων θεατῶν; 111a2–3).
In the *Phaedrus*, by contrast, those blessed spectators, gods and superior
souls, contemplate from below the truths external to heaven. There lies
the "Plain of Truth" (τὸ ἀληθείας πεδίον, 248b7) and its Meadow
inhabited by the intelligible forms with which the winged souls nourish
their plumage. This cosmic picture displays a twofold theatrical structure:
listening to the myth we are the spectators both watching from the concentric *cavea* the divine choruses dancing in a circle on the orchestra and
also contemplating, on the other side of the upper edge of the *skene*, this
scene of pure light where the drama of Ideas is enacted. Henceforth the
very life of the soul becomes engrossed in contemplation (θεατὴ, 247c8;
θεωροῦσα, 247d4; θεασαμένη, 247e4; θέας, 248b5; τεθέαται, 249e6;
θεῶνται, 250b5, θέαν, 250b7; πολυθεάμων, 251a2) and is thereby initiated in the highest mysteries.

The theater of shadows in the *Republic*'s cave is the reversed figure
of this theater of light. Designed after the double pattern of the shadow
plays and puppet shows, the spectacle offered by this myth—the oddest
of all the Platonic myths—may seem base when compared to that of the
Phaedrus. Yet it exhibits an even more intricate mechanism. We have
indeed here four theaters linked together: (1) *the inferior theater of sem-
blances* made up of the shadows of puppets and confusing echoes that the
cave's wall reflects back to the prisoners; (2) *the intermediary puppet theater*
of which the prisoners are not aware; this is a show by itself with its little
wall across the road and its unconscious puppeteers carrying objects that
show above the wall; (3) *the superior theater of realities,* which the prisoner
discovers when he comes up to the surface of the earth: shadows, images,
things, celestial bodies, and heaven itself; and (4) *the theater of the myth
in its entirety*, which is external to the three other ones and which Glaucon
is made to contemplate by Socrates. Socrates' companion is able to see
the three joined theaters without being aware of the theater of which he
is a part. I would like to remark in passing that the situation of Socrates'
audience—contrary to what he says ("they [the prisoners] look like us";
515a5)—is not comparable to that of the spectators doomed to the underground shadows, since the latter cannot maintain any distance from the
show, whereas the former are able to view the inferior theater from a triple
perspective. The status of the myth, however, remains unaltered; although
it teaches all that philosophy has to know on the upper and the lower

worlds, it remains obdurately silent about itself. Like the world, Platonic myth is a speech that always comes first and evades all dialectical speculation in which every word reflects another word. If the eye looking at another eye sees itself reflected on the pupil (*Alc.* I, 132e–133b), the myth is not an eye or the mirror of the soul but a light: it suddenly bathes the scenery and reveals all that is, except itself. Also, in listening to Socrates, Glaucon rediscovers himself paradoxically situated in the world; he is both between the three theaters of the cave and out of the world, in the blind spot that cannot be apprehended and yet holds together the remotest regions of Heaven and Earth.

The existence of myth allows us to distinguish two sorts of spectacle lovers. The first are the crowd and the sophists who unreservedly dedicate themselves to the sensible beauty of colors, forms, and voices. As Socrates puts it to Glaucon: "those who love to watch" (φιλοθεάμονες) and "those who love to listen" (φιλήκοοι; *Rep.*, 475d2) remain the prisoners of appearances even if they show an unconscious desire for a higher kind of knowledge. In front of them, "those who love to know"—the philosophers—are in search of the luminous theater of truth beyond the shadow play. Like the pure souls released from their bodies and contemplating the vast plain of Truth, and like the initiate in Eros' mysteries contemplating the boundless ocean of the Beautiful, "the genuine philosophers are those who are in love with the spectacle of the truth" (*Rep.*, 475e).

Soul

Related to intelligible forms as seen in the myth of the recollection, and arranged in circular order from the center to the uttermost ends of Heaven as shown by the composition of the Soul of the world, the soul remains constantly linked in Plato's work—whether muthos or logos—to the mythic cipher of the cosmos, the number five or "pentad." I do not intend here to repeat the conclusions of my book about the symbolic function of the nuptial pentad (πέντε γάμος) which governs not only Plato's ontology and theory of the knowledge but also his religious, ethical, and political analyses, and discloses the hierogamy of Heaven and Earth in the cosmic order.[11] I should like to prove the soundness of these conclusions by looking at several of Plato's works and by showing how the pentad, which in its cyclic nature[12] recalls the circular movement of the soul as well as the spheric disposition of the cosmos, is associated with both myth and theater. In the first part of this chapter I pointed out that myth is explicitly defined, in the longest analysis made by Plato of the matter, by the five essential topics of its speech: Gods, Daimons, Heroes, Hades' inhabitants, and Men, that is to say the five forms of superior souls (*Rep.* 376e–392c; summed up at 392a 4–8). Thus the topography of the eschatological myths of the *Gorgias, Phaedo,* and *Republic*—to say nothing of the genealogical myth of Atlantis in the *Critias*[13]—draws naturally the pentadic structure of the world—four directions and one center—and discloses the suitable place for the evolutions of the soul.

The fact that the drama of the world is unraveled in five acts on five different stages is foreshadowed by Homer's teaching to which Plato refers twice. In the fifteenth canto of the *Iliad* Poseidon justifies the partition of the cosmos between Cronos' sons as follows: "The world has been divided into three parts: each one of us has got his apanage. By the drawing of lots I have received the white Sea to inhabit forever. Hades' lot has been the foggy Darkness and Zeus' the boundless Heaven amidst the clouds. And we share between us the Earth and high Olympus" (187–93).

This division of the cosmos into five sections—recalled in yet another way by the five plates of Achilles' shield which, according to Heraclitus the rhetor, correspond to the five zones of the world[14]—appears at the beginning of the myth of the *Gorgias* (523a4–5) just before Socrates mentions the crossing of the four roads around the Meadow. Then it is again emphasized by Critias in the dialogue of the same name (109b, 113b–c) when he is about to explain how Poseidon, in the island of Atlantis, builds a wall made of five wheels of earth and sea around the acropolis where he will give birth to five male twins. Yet the pentadic division appears particularly powerful in the theater of the *Phaedrus.* While the soul has indeed a triadic structure (the two horses of the winged team and their charioteer) just as in the analyses of the *Republic,* the cosmic contemplation in which the soul is engrossed during her revolutions is tied to the number five. For when the immortal souls led by the gods stand bedazzled on top of the heavenly dome in order to contemplate the Plain of Truth, they are looking at the true realities, of which Plato mentions only one group of five: "True Knowledge" (τὸ τῆς ἀληθοῦς ἐπιστήμης, 247c7–d1; cf. 247e3), "Justice" (δικαιοσύνην, 247d7), "Wisdom" (σωφροσύνην, 247d7), "Beauty" (κάλλος, 250b5), and finally "Thought" (φρόνησις, 250d4). Similarly in a much discussed passage in the *Phaedo* (75c8–9), only five "realities in themselves" (αὐτὸ ὃ ἔστι) are presented by Socrates as examples of Ideas: the "Equal" (τοῦ ἴσου), the "Beautiful" (τοῦ καλοῦ), the "Good" (τοῦ ἀγαθοῦ), the "Rightful" (δικαίου), and the "Sacred" (ὁσίου). In both texts Plato selects five forms from the range of forms without justifying a choice that seems accidental.

The same thing occurs again in two conclusive passages of the *Phaedrus.* When the souls come to be initiated in the mysteries of Ideas, which are the sources of later recollections, the objects of initiation are characterized by five essential features: "integrity, simplicity, immutability, bliss, and unveiled apparitions" (ὁλόκληρα δὲ καὶ ἁπλᾶ καὶ ἀτρεμῆ καὶ εὐδαίμονα φάσματα μυούμενοι τε καὶ ἐποπτεύοντες; 250c2–4). Moreover, the complete initiation of the soul depends on its faithfulness to a god whose cosmic pageant it follows. Among the eleven gods followed by their daimons and the army of souls, Plato chooses to describe the procession of the first five. On the circular theater of the world Zeus' chorus goes first (252c4), followed by Ares (252c6), then Dionysus (253a6),[15] Hera (253a8), and Apollo (253b2); inside each chorus every soul which is the "follower" of the divinity (χορευτής; 252d2) performs its heavenly evolution. The astral revolution of myth thus imitates the form of the dances of the chorus—which is composed of fifteen choristers for tragedy and fifty for dithyramb—on the circular orchestra of Greek theater.

When Plato classifies the general forms of the soul or defines its specific qualities, he constantly associates the soul with the number five. The *Timaeus* organizes the physical bodies in five elementary polyhedrons (tetrahedron, octahedron, icosahedron, cube, and dodecahedron; 53c–54d) which are assigned in the *Epinomis* to the five elements (fire, ether, air, water, earth) and to the five living bodies (heavenly bodies, daimons of the ether, air and water, men; 981a–985c). It also singles out five kinds of souls: the Soul of the world stretching from the center of the cosmos to its uttermost ends (34b–37c), the immortal soul of man (thought), the mortal souls of courage and desire (69c–70e), and last the mortal soul of reproduction (91a–b). "Is the world itself unique," asks the philosopher from Locri, "or are we to think that five of them have been created?" (55d2). The infernal world of the *Phaedo* considers in turn five categories among the souls of the dead (113d–114c), according to the respective degree of their guilt, and five ornaments of the soul (temperance, justice, courage, liberty, truth; 114e–115a).

Similarly the Athenian Stranger of the *Laws* credits the soul with five specific qualities (judgment, anticipation, intelligence, art, law; 892b), five activities (to want, to examine, to provide, to debate, to judge; 897a), and five causes for crime (sorrow, pleasure, common ignorance, illusion of knowledge in the strong, illusion of knowledge in the weak; 862b–864c). We also learn in the *Protagoras* that the soul has five virtues (prudence, moderation, courage, justice and devotion; 349b–d, 359a–b). Courage itself appears under five aspects in the *Laws* (632e–633c): meals taken in common and gymnasium exercises preparing for the war, hunting and endurance in front of pain, and then the ordeal of the *crupteia* (a sort of endurance test). Following a first "swarm" of five or six virtues—those of men, women, children, and old men whether free or in bondage (71e)—the *Meno* proposes a new list of five virtues: justice, courage, wisdom, prudence, and liberality (73e–74a). Finally, all the ethical and political considerations in the *Republic* are based upon a classification in five political systems of government (monarchy, timocracy, oligarchy, democracy, and tyranny) and in five corresponding human temperaments so that "if there are five systems of government, there must be at the same time five forms of soul in the individuals" (544e4–5; cf, 445c–d). Therefore one understands that when the gods pull the strings of the human puppet on the theater of the world (*Laws*, 644c–645a) they will play with the five cords of the soul: pain, pleasure, confidence, fear, and reason which is the fifth and last string entirely made of gold.

The pentadic number—a mythical cipher of the soul, of circular revolution, and of the world—also affects the dialectic and ontologic analyses belonging to the authority of the logos. There may be found the most obvious clue to the hidden bond that joins the logical and mythical forms of speech in the works of Plato. Corresponding to the five components of Good reached by dialectical research in the *Philebus* (62a–64a)—beauty, proportion, truth, sciences, pure pleasures—we find not only the final classification of five forms of Good (measure, proportion, intellect, sciences, pure pleasures of the soul; 66a–c), but also five hegemonic sciences—two metretic and two arithmetic ones, inferior and superior, the four of them being commanded by dialectic (57d–58d). Let us not forget that there are five supreme forms in the same dialogue, at least if we are to trust Protarchus' remark (23d9) when he asks Socrates for a "fifth discriminative" species (πέμπτον διάκρισίν; cf. 23e1 πέμπτον) besides unlimitedness, limit, mingling, and cause. Let us point out here the most disquieting analogy to be found in the *Sophist* when the Eleatic Stranger forms in a dialectic way the independent group of "the five kinds of being"— change, rest, same, other, and being—whose "number it is impossible to reduce below the one which has been previously obtained" (256d).[16] After the interpretations of Proclus and Damascius, it would be useless to emphasize again the influence of the pentad over the logical constitution of the first five hypotheses in the *Parmenides* organized around the hypothesis of the ἐξαίφνης, (the instantaneous). These interpretations have been revived today by such commentators as Jean Trouillard and Joseph Combès who have definitively explained how the chiasmatic structure of the pentad in the positive hypotheses about the One discloses the self-constitution of the soul and the movement of knowledge.[17] I shall only recall by way of conclusion Plato's teaching in the *Seventh Letter:* "the soul," he writes (342c), must discover in itself the first four factors of knowledge—name, definition, image, knowledge (342a–343d)—before it is able to approach "in the fifth place" what its true object really is. Is it only accidental, then, that this fundamental speech (τούτῳ δὴ τῷ μύθῳ; 344d4) in which the soul ascends through the stages of reality indicates on *five occasions* that there are only *five* roads leading to knowledge (342a8: πέμπτον; 342d2: πέμπτου; 342e2: πέμπτου; 343a7: πέμπτῳ; 343d3: πέμπτον)?

Identified with his immortal soul, the "lover of wisdom" is thus not only a "friend of myth," as Aristotle will later admit, but a "lover of spectacles" as Socrates acknowledges. But already he to whom we owe the very word *philosopher* was right about this natural privilege granted to the look. If we follow Pythagoras' testimony, says Diogenes Laertius, there are three types of men: those who go to the Panegyrics in order to fight, those who go there in order to trade, and finally those who are content with tasting from a distance the beauty of the spectacles. This is quite necessary if one is to recognize at each turn the path to the theater.[18]

5

Digression and Dialogue: The *Seventh Letter* and Plato's Literary Form

Robert S. Brumbaugh

The purpose of this chapter is to show that two devices typical of Plato's dialogues also occur in the *Seventh Letter*.[1] The first of these is the use made of a so-called digression to introduce a relevant, but more abstract, philosophical consideration. This is a matter of style that has an air of paradox about it, when the supposed deviation is really the central consideration; although I suppose a forger *could* imitate it, I think that much less likely than its showing Platonic authorship.

The second consideration is more central, and the argument much stronger. This second point rests on the fact that Plato's middle and earlier late dialogues have a literary form that involves methodological self-illustration. I mean more by this than the evident fact that the characters are chosen to personify and instantiate the theme under discussion. Over and beyond this, when there is a key passage central to a dialogue discussing some method abstractly (dialectic, philosophical, rhetoric, the technique of division), the contextual dialogue itself often uses and illustrates the method in question. (Since the point is not generally recognized, although it has sometimes been suggested, one of my first steps will be to establish its validity.)

Now, the relevance of this observation is that the same device of illustrating a method in the context of an abstract discussion of it occurs in the "philosophical digression" of the *Seventh Letter*. Here the self-applying organization is at once far too systematic to be accidental and more informal than an imitator or literal admirer of a late Platonic logical technique would have made it.

These two comparisons with the dialogue form, transposed here into a dialogue with the reader, seem important evidence bearing on the *Letter*'s authenticity, which have not been given sufficient attention.[2]

The metaphor of digression, of straying from a fixed or direct path, held a wide set of associations by Plato's time. Much earlier, there are the paths of the planets—called "wanderers" by shepherds and primitive observers, but revealed as patterned singers and dancers to wise men "able to calculate." On the other hand, wandering was not always only a matter of appearance, part of a larger, nonrandom plan. Parmenides, probably with Heraclitus in his sights, reproaches "fools, two-minded, wandering on a back-turning path."[3]

Here and elsewhere the background idea of digression carries with it the historic notions both of hidden harmony and of unresolved discord and deviation. Plato takes advantage of both associations, as his literal descriptions suggest the latter (unresolved deviation), but the contextual structural organization in fact leads the so-called deviation to a resolution (the outcome of a hidden harmony).

One case can illustrate what is typical of many. In the *Theaetetus*, according to one widely accepted reading, the philosophic issue seems to be what happens if one tried to define *knowledge* without reference to Platonic Forms. Theaetetus tries out one model after another equating knowing with sensation, perception, and opinion. But each time, quietly standing by, there is someone present in the dialogue itself who has a kind of "knowledge" that his sophistically affiliated models cannot explain. Ironically, and with the point made backward—in terms of mathematical error, not proof—the models cannot account for mathematics, which seems not reducible to mad aviary, blank tablet, or storage cans full of sorted impressions.[4] Equally to the point, the models cannot account for the kind of knowledge a philosopher has, in contrast to the "knowledge" of the lawyer.

To the "man is the measure" view of Protagoras, Socrates contrasts the wisdom of the free soul able to use another measure. The philosopher is not limited by convention and sensation, but has another kind of wisdom. Socrates shows us what that other kind of wisdom is. In the text, this demonstration of Socratic knowledge is referred to repeatedly as a "digression."[5] But in fact it is not: it is rather a presentation of another kind of knowledge in addition to the mathematical, which, apart from Platonic Forms, cannot be defined or explained. (This structural central role of the digression fits beautifully with the observations of Wyller and of Klein that usually the main topic and point of a dialogue is to be found at its center of symmetry, its quantitative center. When we apply this insight to the *Theaetetus*, the central line comes at our so-called philosophical digression. I think this supports my view rather than constituting an objection to the canon.)[6]

Other cases come to mind where a longer way proves better than a shortcut. The entire central section of the *Republic* is presented in this way; the longer schema of division in the *Statesman* is another case, albeit less spectacular.[7] Thus, a digression may digress to a higher dialectical level, from which one better understands the original lower level.

At this point, we might look again at the *Theaetetus'* digression with the *Seventh Letter* in mind. The digression in the *Letter* contrasts Plato, the philosopher, with Dionysius II, the vain and pretentious dictator. The contrast raises to a higher philosophical level the explanation of the Sicilian venture which the *Letter* as a whole recounts.[8]

Thus this labeling of the passage we are to analyze as a digression has substantial precedents in the Platonic dialogues and seems to function here in context as it does there.

This need not, perhaps, be an argument *for* the authenticity of the section in question (although I rather think it is), but certainly it does not tell *against* it. In particular, it certainly suggests a better alternative than the proposal that this philosophical section is somehow an extrinsic discussion, forcibly inserted in a way that interrupts the running historical narrative of the contextual *Letter*.

The second point is the *Letter's* self-illustrating organization. As I have said, Plato tends in the middle and late dialogues not only to discuss various methods he is using, but to embed those discussions in larger contexts that employ and illustrate the very methods that are topics of discussion.[9] For instance, the *Phaedrus* itself, through the great myth, is an example of the philosophical rhetoric that Socrates at one point explicitly defines. (That is, art recognizes which kind of soul the speaker is addressing and which kind of speech will instruct it. Given what we know of Phaedrus, both from the *Symposium* and from the opening of the present dialogue, it is clear that Socrates has chosen exactly the right style of speech to educate him.) The *Republic*, I have argued, is itself an example of the mysterious method of dialectic prescribed for higher education in its Book 7.[10] Thus we can read the argument as running from ordinary opinions through three alternative hypothetical-deductive models of human nature and conduct. The three must be seen synoptically; once this is done, we have a more adequate view of the self and society. Books 8 and 9 use this for a new account of kinds of states and individuals. More explicit than the *Republic* is the *Statesman*, which announces itself as concerned mainly with "the method of division." The *Sophist* and *Statesman* both offer the reader extensive examples of the method, as the context for an abstract discussion of it.[11]

This is a device other classical philosophers do not use; it is almost as distinctively Platonic as a fingerprint or trademark.[12] When I demonstrate that the *Seventh Letter* also has this structural property, however, this will still leave open a number of important questions. For example, it will not tell us whether Plato thought his objection to "writing" could be circumvented by presenting shared "investigation" (*tribe*) in dialogue form. It will not tell us how close Plato thought a new colonial city could come to duplicating the curriculum of his own Athenian Academy. Nor will it even untangle the relative dates of composition of what seem readjusted drafts and sections of projected late dialogues.[13] But it *will*, I think, add some important internal evidence in favor of the authenticity of the *Seventh Letter*.

Let me cite two more cases of self-referential devices of style. Somewhat more subtle than the examples cited, and considerably less generally appreciated, is the relation, in the *Meno*, of methods as subject of discussion and methods in operation in the discussion itself. The teaching methods that Meno recognizes—namely, precept and example—certainly fail to teach virtue. But Plato shows us a third method—the Socratic method—in action and its effect on Meno, as he improves in virtue. Unfortunately, the effect of the single conversation is only temporary, and Meno goes on to campaign in Persia.[14]

Another case, brief and amusing, of action illustrating argument occurs in the *Hippias Minor*. The argument is Socrates' thesis that a voluntary liar is better than an involuntary one. When, as the dialogue opens, Socrates ironically salutes Hippias as wise and Hippias soberly accepts the compliment, we have the action opening with a voluntary versus an involuntary lie.[15]

Now, the digression in the *Seventh Letter* is an account of a method for teaching by means of language, particularly language as written.[16] The author says that it is a statement he has already made but will now repeat.[17] The main points are two. First, there is a brief technical summary of the tools by which symbolic communication is carried on: these are name, definition, and image or example. Second, there is a sharp statement of the limitations of such symbols—at least as written in textbooks—to communicate effectively about the "highest matters" of metaphysics or ethics (which was what Plato understood the book of Dionysius II claimed to do).[18] An author's written works, "whether they be laws or anything else," are not his most serious thoughts if he himself is serious.[19]

That the name-formula-instance scheme is Platonic is clear from the use made of it in *Laws X*; from the insistence on examples as aids to learning in the *Statesman*; and from the insistence on the definition as well as the name in *Laws XII*.[20] That Plato distrusted writing had been clear from the *Phaedrus* on.[21] But how far he intended this distrust to extend to philosophy in dialogue form, as opposed to textbooks, statutes, and set speeches, is an open question.

Thus it is not entirely clear how far the criticism of thoughts immobilized in writing (*ametakineton*) in the *Seventh Letter* would apply to shared investigation presented in other literary forms. The reference to "laws" suggests that the author of the *Letter* does not see Plato's *Laws* as serious dialectical investigation. But Plato himself can hardly have thought his detailed legal code an example of shared dialectical inquiry, "with friendly questions and refutations devoid of envy." (And, besides, although he claims to have discussed philosophy with Dionysius II only once, in the *Eighth Letter* it turns out that Plato and Dion may have had further discussions of laws, their appropriate prologues, and legislation with the young dictator. That, of course, still would not make Dionysius II a serious student of Plato.)[22]

In context, the digression has as its specific target Dionysius II's textbook presentation of philosophy—including the highest principles. This will be particularly annoying for Plato when he recognizes that the work will be taken by some readers as a summary of his own thought and by others as the work of a dissatisfied student going beyond his teacher.

But let us turn to the second point: that the new account of method uses that method itself for its presentation.[23]

There is a true logos, Plato says—namely, that "there are three tools by use of which knowledge comes to be: knowledge itself is a fourth thing; and as a fifth, there is the thing itself, knowable and real." The first of the three means for acquiring knowledge is the *name*, and Plato's next statement gives the names of his three tools: "One of these is the *name*, second the *formula*, the third is the *image*, while the fourth is *knowledge*."

The next passage turns to the *image* moment and gives a specific image of each of the three things that have just been named: "Take a single case and learn from it." The case chosen is a "circle," which we introduce by its name: "There is a thing called 'circle,' the *name* of which is what we have just now said." Next, we are given the specific illustration of a formula: "The formula is 'that of which the extremes lie everywhere equally removed from the center.' And this is the *formula* of what we call 'round' and 'spherical' and 'circle.' " (Note that the one formula extends over three names in this example.) This definition seems a standard one in early Greek geometry; it is used in Plato's *Parmenides* as a standard definition of "circle" at 137e2. Now the account turns to the image moment, giving us specific examples of images: "And third are those [circles] that are drawn and erased, and [spheres] that are turned and deformed." A note is interpolated here to remind us that this last list is not to be confused or identified with the *real* circle or sphere, for "the circle itself does not undergo these changes" (of drawing, erasure, turning, and so on).

The author now goes on to *knowledge*. This continues the contrast between the thing itself and the specific images, and locates knowledge both in relation to name and image and to the circle itself. The text then, on the level of knowledge, offers a general account of the N-F-I method: "The same account holds of (1) straight and curved shape, and color; (2)

the good, the beautiful, and the right; (3) and bodies, whether (a) artificial or (b) generated in nature—fire, water, and all such things; (4) and all animals, and habits in souls; (5) and being acted on and acting in general." This knowledge section is closely related to the *Parmenides*. It seems to give Plato's answer to the question, left undecided in that dialogue, of the *extent* of the domain of Forms. There Socrates, as a young man, agreed that there were Forms of structural concepts (one, many, same, other); and he was certain that there were forms of "the good, the beautiful, and the right." He was undecided, however, about Forms of man or animals or natural elements. And some trivial compounds (such as "mud and hair") seemed to him not to deserve Forms at all. (The present extension of the domain is partly anticipated in the *Theaetetus*, where Socrates takes the formula defining "mud" as an example of proper definition.) The section closes with a summarizing remark that applies both to it and to the preceding three sections: "unless one somehow gets these four, there will never be sharing [*metochos*] in complete knowledge of the fifth."

Predictably, the lesson continues by moving to another level and contrasting the thing itself to each of the tools used as means to the acquisition of knowledge of it. "But we must learn again from what has been said."

The first "learning again" takes up the image (the circle of the earlier account) and contrasts such images to the thing itself: "Every circle drawn or turned is full of the opposite of the fifth: for it touches the straight everywhere. But the circle itself has neither less nor more of its opposite in its nature." It seems that in the present passage the circles of geometry (drawn in the mathematical disciplines) are subject to the same criticism (in their role as images) that applies to sensible circles and physical spheres. (When the latter are mentioned, the reader may have been expected to remember Protagoras' sarcastic discussion "Of the Contact Between a Hoop and a Beam." That contact is not at a point at all, but the hoop is flattened so that it is rather a straight line.)[24] The notion that the circles drawn by the mathematician are included here is certainly correct: the present section is organized to develop the contrast of "the fifth" to "knowledge."

The critique now turns from the image to the name. The name is in no way stable; it is merely conventional. We could exchange the meanings of *round* and *straight* and "the names would serve equally well in their reversed sense." The formula, too, is unstable, "because it is composed of [names, namely] nouns and verbs." Finally, knowledge and the three tools for its acquisition alike offer the soul "qualities" that distract it from the "thing itself" which it tries to know.

The passage thus has the following topic outline:

I.   The means to knowledge, and knowledge itself
    A.   The "true logos" now repeated: there are three means by which knowledge is acquired, and knowledge is itself a fourth.

B.   The names of these are
1.   Name
2.   Image
3.   Formula (definition)
4.   Knowledge
C.   Images. A specific example will give an example; the instance chosen is a "circle."
1.   Example of a name: there is a figure called "circle."
2.   Example of a definition: "that of which the extremes lie everywhere equally distant from the center" is the definition of "circle" and "round" and "spherical." (Note that while definition includes all circles, it is wider in extension, since it also defines "round" and "spherical.")
3.   Example of the example:
a.   Examples are the circles that are drawn and erased; and
b.   The spheres that are turned and deformed.
D.   Knowledge
1.   The circle itself differs from its examples, since it does not undergo their changes.
2.   Knowledge differs both from the name and example, and also from the circle itself.
3.   The range of knowledge is a wide one: "The same account holds of":
a.   Straight and curved shape, and color; and
b.   The good, the beautiful and the right; and
c.   Bodies, either:
i.   Artificial, or
ii. Natural: fire, water, and the like; and
d.   All animals, and habits in souls;* and
e.   Being acted on and acting in general.
II.   The contrast of these three means, and of knowledge, to the thing itself.
A.   Contrast of the thing itself and its images: a return to the circle: "The images, drawn and turned, are everywhere in contact with the straight, but the circle itself has neither less nor more straightness."

---

*The outline would make its point more sharply, I think, if the outline were understood here as: (d) all animals and (e) habits in souls and (f) being acted on and acting in general.

B. Contrast of the thing itself and its name: names are conventional—for example, " 'straight' and 'circular' could have their meanings exchanged and still function equally well; but the thing itself is stable."

C. Contrast of the thing itself and its definition: "Since the logos is composed of names (for example, of the two kinds, 'names' and 'verbs' needed to construct definitions) and names are unstable, the logos is also unstable, while the thing itself is not."

D. Contrast of the thing itself to knowledge, as well as to the means for acquisition of it. Finally, knowledge and the three means used to acquire it "each offer the soul some quality [*poion*] which distracts it from the thing itself [*to ti*] which it wants to know."

III. The negative implications of this analysis for the writing of philosophy are next developed.

As the topic, the application to writing, is developed, the conclusion follows that the project of Dionysius II was a mistake which showed his ignorance both of metaphysics in general and of Plato's philosophy in particular.

I think my case—that the discussion of method here is self-referential—has been established; and that characteristic also comes close to certainty in establishing the *Letter*'s authenticity.

Another interesting matter of style is the variation in the order in which the same topics occur in different sections of the outline. This is good Platonic style, and indeed good classical rhetorical or dialectical style. Plato prefers, given a clear set of topics running from 1 to 4, to vary the order. Thus the four accounts of the Good in *Republic* 6–7, evidently matching the levels of the Divided Line, come in the order 1-2-4-3, not 1-2-3-4. The projected *Republic—Timaeus—Critias—Hermocrates* tetralogy (also a projection of the levels of the Line), would have represented the same 1-2-4-3 order. (Aristotle, discussing style in the *Rhetoric*, suggests that where there is an obvious linear order, the good speaker will vary it. This makes the result more interesting and more surprising.) Two other cases of varied order in Plato occur in the *Theaetetus* and the *Parmenides*. In the former, the kinds of knowing are presented (and personified) in a 4-2-1-3 pattern. In the latter, when Parmenides asks young Socrates about the range of the latter's world of Forms, he follows the Divided Line segments, but in 2-1-3-4 order.

Now, a later Platonist who admires Platonic metaphysics and method is not likely to deviate from a standard linear order in his or her outline. For example, my own Ph.D. dissertation applied the method of the *Seventh*

Letter to the discussion of mathematics, in absolutely rigid, repetitive, linear order.

Unfortunately, my present considerations of outline and style do not decide the central question the *Letter* raises. That question is the extent to which the critique of writing applies: for example, how far it does or does not apply to Plato's own work prior and perhaps subsequent to the *Seventh Letter*. The supposed *Second Letter* with its total disclaimer of *any* serious authorship on "Plato's" part, is obviously a misreading of the *Seventh Letter*.

6

Plato's Dialogues in Light of the *Seventh Letter*

Kenneth M. Sayre

I

There are several signs from antiquity that Plato did not commit his philosophy to writing. One is the tantalizing Lecture on the Good, in which Plato mystified both his audience and his subsequent commentators with the summary pronouncement that the Good is Unity. Another indication is Aristotle's *Metaphysics*, burdened with remarks about Platonic philosophy that are equally at odds with anything found in the dialogues. As if to clinch it all, Plato himself announces categorically in the *Seventh Letter* that he never has and never will commit his philosophy to writing, for such matters cannot be verbalized like other studies. But how are we to retrieve Plato's philosophy if it is not written in the dialogues? And why did Plato *write* dialogues if not to convey his philosophy?

The seriousness of such problems is indicated by the extreme solutions that have been offered in attempts to resolve them. At one extreme we find the "esoteric" position, defended by the German scholars Gaiser and Krämer, among others, to the effect that Plato reserved his true philosophy for oral presentation within the Academy, and that our primary access to this philosophy is through the writings of Aristotle. At the opposite extreme is the position so meticulously argued by Cherniss, insisting that Aristotle himself relied primarily upon the dialogues in his attempts to understand Plato's teaching, and that the discrepancies between the dialogues and his remarks about Plato are due to nothing more mysterious than Aristotle's obtuseness. On the first count the student of Plato is encouraged to set aside the dialogues and to take up the *Metaphysics*, somehow coming to terms with Aristotle's poor reputation as an objective reporter of his predecessor's views. On the second count Aristotle is doubly culpable. Not only did he fail to grasp the content of Plato's writing, but moreover he neglected to take advantage of repeated opportunities to set his mind straight in conversation with the author.

A more credible alternative is made available by rejecting the assumption, shared by Cherniss and his adversaries alike, that the Platonic principles reported by Aristotle cannot be found in the dialogues. In *Plato's Late Ontology* I have argued that the views attributed to Plato in the *Metaphysics* can be found in the *Philebus*, with terminological changes illuminated by the later Greek commentators. Since the themes of the Lecture on the Good can be identified point by point with Plato's philosophy according to Aristotle, the alleged discrepancies that fueled the controversy in effect disappear.

But even if this middle ground has been secured, and we may remain confident that there is no major discrepancy between the views expressed orally in Plato's lecture and those recorded in the late *Philebus*, a substantial problem remains of what to make of the *Seventh Letter*. For there the author states explicitly that his philosophic teachings have never been expressed in written form and that they never shall be, and moreover that they never could be so expressed by their very nature. What is at issue is not only the degree of overlap between Plato's oral and written teachings but more fundamentally the possibility of extracting a properly Platonic philosophy from any of the written dialogues at all. One neat expedient, which many historians and commentators appear to find attractive, is to deny the authenticity of the *Seventh Letter* and in effect to proceed as if it did not exist. Although the authorship of this document remains a matter of scholarly disagreement, this expedient has less appeal than at first might appear. For one thing, if the letter was not written by Plato, it was at least written during his lifetime; and whatever motives might have underlain forgery would have ruled out disclosure in the form of gross misrepresentation. For another, the same reservations about writing as a philosophic medium can be found as well in certain of the unquestionably authentic dialogues, as defenders of the "unwritten teachings" have been quick to point out.

If the considerations to be laid out in this chapter can be trusted, however, there is an even more important reason for taking the *Seventh Letter* seriously. For it can be seen upon due reflection not only that the strictures of that document do not rule in favor of oral over written discourse as a philosophic medium, but moreover that the *Seventh Letter* yields substantial hints about how the dialogues are to be understood in that capacity.

It remains a stubborn fact that Plato never speaks within the dialogues in propria persona and moreover that there are no characters in the dialogues that may be assumed reliably and consistently to represent the views of the author. This provides one obvious sense in which Plato in fact did not commit his philosophy to writing—he did not commit himself to any views expressed in the dialogues. But it does not follow that Plato's philosophy is not communicated by his writings. If the *Seventh Letter* can help us see how that might be accomplished, this is reason in itself for taking it seriously.

II

At 341c4–6, the writer of the *Seventh Letter* states unambiguously that "no work of mine exists on such (philosophic) topics, and none ever will, for there is no way of putting them into words like other studies." This blanket disqualification of written language for philosophic purposes is reinforced at 343a1–4, where it is affirmed that "this being so, no intelligent person will ever risk putting what he really understands into language, especially not in fixed form as is the lot of written characters." Armed with these passages (and some similar advice from the *Phaedrus*), as noted above, advocates of the unwritten teachings are ready to set aside the dialogues as possible repositories of Platonic philosophy and to project instead an esoteric doctrine presented orally within the confines of the Academy.[1]

A shortcoming of this manner of dealing with the *Seventh Letter* is that it passes too lightly over several important passages. A full reading of these passages indicates that the author's complaint is not confined to written discourse alone. Although writing is most starkly deficient in this respect, *all* language of an ordinary sort (written or oral) is criticized for being too much bound up with sensible imagery to be adequate for the expression of true philosophy. The advice of passage 343a1–3 quoted above, for instance, is that no intelligent person would risk putting what he understands into language—into language (logos) of *any* sort—although written language is cited as particularly unreliable. But the full generality of this criticism does not appear until 343b–c, where the author explains what it is about language that makes it unfit for philosophic purposes. Before this, at 342a–b, there are listed three classes of objects involved in our scientific conceptualization of "what is truly understandable and real" (342b1)—in order, the name (*onoma*), the description or definition (logos), and the physical instantiation (*eidolon*)—with the scientific concept itself as fourth in the series. The fourth listing is further expanded at 342c4–5 to include "scientific concepts, understanding, and true judgment" (ἐπιστήμη καὶ νοῦς ἀληθής τε δόξα), which collectively are characterized as residing "neither in sounds nor in physical shapes but rather in minds" (342c6–7). Although each of the three is mental in character, *nous* (understanding, intelligence) is distinguished from *episteme* at 342d1–2 as more closely approaching the truly real in "kinship and likeness." Another reason for translating *episteme* in this context as *scientific concept* (rather than *knowledge* in a general and unqualified sense) is that each of these four levels is contrasted with knowledge of a yet higher sort—a "knowledge that the mind seeks" (343c2) of true being rather than of particular qualities. Diverse as the four levels are among themselves, nonetheless, they are alike in contrast to the fifth entity, which is truly understandable and real. The respect in which the first four are all alike, and therein deficient in relation to the fifth, is that each admits characteristics that are opposed to that true reality. Names, to begin with, are "in no way firm" (343b1), since nothing precludes calling straight what is now called circular, and vice versa. The same may be said of definitions, since they are composed of names and verbs—which is "not at all sufficient grounding to provide security" (343b6). Indeed, the author goes on to say, although there are thousands of reasons why each of the four is uncertain (343b7), the essential fault is that "each of the four presents the soul with words and actions" (343c2–3) that are always subject to "easy refutation by the senses" (343c4). As a consequence, anyone who undertakes "to speak or to write or to respond" (343d5–6) in an enquiry regarding the fifth entity is easily made to appear ignorant by someone skilled in refutation. What is sometimes not realized, the author concludes, is that in such cases it is "not the soul of the writer or speaker that is refuted, but rather the character of the four, each being naturally defective" (343d8–9). Names, descriptions, physical instances, scientific knowledge: each is naturally unqualified to represent true being because of its involvement with sense experience.

Hence there is no way of putting philosophy into words like other studies. In the case of philosophy, what happens instead is that "from frequent conversations about and living with the matter itself, it is suddenly generated in the soul like a torch light kindled by a leaping flame, and straightway becomes self-sustaining" (341c6–d2). "Living with the matter itself" is a discipline imposing severe requirements, including a "constant cleaving to philosophy" (340d3) and a "natural affinity" (340c2, 344a3) for the topic. It also requires a "well-ordered regimen" (340e2) and a great deal of hard work (340c, e). The image of the fulfillment that follows this discipline as an incandescent state of the soul is repeated at 344b, where the author warns that "wisdom and intelligence" (344b7–8) in matters of virtue and vice come only after much "thrashing together of names, descriptions and sense perceptions" (344b4–5), and much toil in noncontentious question and answer—but then, with this patient preparation, "shine forth with an intensity almost beyond human power to endure" (344b7–c1).

Sections 341–344 of the *Seventh Letter* are aimed primarily at discrediting the reputed attempts of the tyrant Dionysius to compose a handbook of philosophy, and they contain repeated warnings against written language as a vehicle for philosophic understanding. There is, however, no endorsement of spoken language as a more suitable vehicle. The contention instead is that neither oral nor written language is capable of expressing the grasp of being that stands at the end of philosophic inquiry. Although linguistic exercises of various sorts (questions and answers, comparison of names and definitions with sense perceptions) are involved in preparing a receptive soul for the comprehension of being, this comprehension comes like a flash of insight that cannot be expressed in linguistic form.

III

The argument to this point is merely that the *Seventh Letter* will not support the contention that Plato reserved an esoteric doctrine for oral presentation to his more intimate students, and that in fact a careful reading of this document runs contrary to that contention. Since the authenticity of the *Seventh Letter* probably will never be established beyond reasonable doubt, however, it is worth considering what some of the unquestionably authentic dialogues have to say on the topic.

Proponents of the unwritten teachings typically pair the *Seventh Letter* with the story of the Theban king toward the end of the *Phaedrus,* which is comparably unappreciative of written language. The king complains that writing encourages forgetfulness. And not only that, says Socrates picking up on the story, but there is something strange about written words that makes them similar to paintings. Although they stand before us as if alive, they remain silently aloof to questioning. They just go on "signifying the same thing forever" (275d9). Moreover, "when something is put into writing once and for all, the whole composition circulates all over the place" (275d9–e1), not knowing whom to address and with whom to remain silent. In short, the problem with writing is not only that it serves as a crutch to memory (the king's problem) but also that it soon passes beyond the control of its original author (Socrates' problem). In this connection, it is relevant to recall that the dialogue begins with Phaedrus reading a rather scurrilous speech composed by Lysias, the manuscript of which had been hidden beneath this cloak. Subtleties of context aside, Socrates' problem is one that would attend the recitation of a memorized speech as well. Thoughts when verbalized become fixed and unresponsive. Words "just go on signifying the same thing forever," whether committed to writing or to an uncomprehending memory. A fact commonly overlooked by the esoterics is that the comparison with painting at 275d is not restricted to language in the form of writing. What 275d7 says literally, in applying the compar-

ison, is that "it is the same with verbal utterance (speech, language)."
While standing before us as if intelligent, it is verbal discourse generally
that remains unresponsive to questioning.

Nonetheless, says Socrates, "can we not discern another kind of discourse (logos), a legitimate brother of the former" (276a1–2), and see
"how far it exceeds the other in fittingness and power?" (276a2–3). To
this Phaedrus responds: "You mean the discourse of those with mental
perception, a living and vital discourse of which it may justly be said that
written speech is the merest image?" (276a8–9). Socrates allows that he
meant just that, and concludes the dialogue with the observation that
didactic speeches like those of Lysias, whether "spoken or written" (277d2),
serve at best as reminders, while discourses (logous, 278a5) of a form that
is really worthy are "written in the soul concerned with justice, goodness
and honor" (278a3–4). Far from extolling vocal over written speech, the
primary burden of these passages in the *Phaedrus,* like those of the *Seventh
Letter* examined previously, is to draw attention to a kind of intellectual
awareness that eludes expression in speech and writing.

A more elaborate treatment of the nonverbal nature of philosophic
understanding can be found in the *Symposium,* where Socrates recounts
his introduction to the love of wisdom. Love, says his teacher, the priestess
Diotima, is begetting upon the beautiful in body and spirit. But the highest
fruits of love are those brought forth within the soul, in particular the social
virtues that accompany wisdom. Although Diotima is confident Socrates
will be able to understand such mysteries as these, she is not at all sure
that he is capable of the final revelation. Nonetheless, she undertakes to
initiate him to the ladder of love. Beauties of bodies come first, and then
those of institutions and of knowledge, leading finally to the point at which
the initiate is strong enough to "catch sight of a certain assuredly singular
understanding" (κατίδη τινὰ ἐπιστήμην μίαν τοιαύτην: 210d7–8) of
the Beautiful itself. To someone who has achieved this final revelation,
Diotima continues, this beauty will not take the appearance of a face, or
hands, or anything bodily, nor again that of discourse (211a7) or knowledge
211a8) or something dependent upon something else, "but in itself, by
itself and with itself will exist uniformly forever" (211b1–2). When this
beauty dawns upon the candidate's inward sight (*kathoran,* 211b7; also
210e4), when he finally "attains vision of Beauty itself" (*theomeno auto
to kalon,* 211d2–3), then he will have "beauty itself uniformly within his
visual grasp" (211e3–4). Returning finally to the theme of virtue as companion to wisdom, Diotima ends her speech by remarking that only when
the philosopher views beauty itself through what makes it visible (212a3–
4) will he be enlivened with the true and not a seeming virtue, and that
only such a man gains immortality so far as any man can.

This extensive use of visual imagery[2] in the depiction of philosophic understanding easily moves one's thoughts to the vivid images at the heart of the *Republic,* dominated by the analogy between the sun and the Good. As the sun is the source of both the generation and the visibility of sensible objects, so the Good in the realm of eternal Forms is source of both being and intelligibility. The comparison of the intelligible and the visible is further articulated in the figure of the Divided Line, while the stepwise progression from the lower level of the visible to the higher level of the intelligible is luminously portrayed in the allegory of the cave. The sense of philosophic understanding as some form of mental vision remains close to the surface of both the sun and the cave imagery. The Divided Line, however, has been considered by some to be a locus classicus of a discursive view of philosophy.[3] Although such an interpretation is not clearly ruled out by the text, a careful reading points toward a "nondiscursive" view instead. At the very least, the latter reading eliminates several problems that remain recalcitrant under the discursive view.

Now there is one explicitly methodological passage in the dialogues that clearly invites a discursive view of philosophic knowledge. This passage occurs toward the end of the *Phaedo,* and in fact makes up the core of Socrates' last philosophic remarks before taking the hemlock. The philosophic method there described is one having recourse to propositions.[4] Its first stage is to lay down (*hypothemenos,* 100a3) a proposition from which the "truth of the things" (τῶν ὄντων τὴν ἀλήθειαν: 99e6) in question can be deduced, and to test the proposition for consistency among its consequences. If inconsistent, the proposition is rejected and another laid down. If consistent, the proposition is supported by deduction from a more general proposition, which in turn must be subjected to a consistency test. This procedure continues by iteration, as it were, until a general proposition is reached that (1) is consistent, (2) is sufficiently self-sustaining within the context to require no further justification, and (3) yields the truth to be shown as a deductive consequence. Commentary has established that this so-called method of hypothesis was probably suggested by the geometrical method of analysis; and a major shortcoming of this procedure as a *philosophic* method is precisely that it is indistinguishable from a method that is clearly mathematical.

The obvious improvement over the method of the *Phaedo* found in that of the Divided Line is that the procedure of philosophy in the latter context is sharply distinguished from that of mathematics. In the context of the Line, these two procedures together are opposed to those of imagining and opining, being occupied with the intelligible instead of the sensible. But mathematical procedure nonetheless differs from that of philosophy in (1) its employment of sensible diagrams and (2) its reliance on hypothetical starting points. By contrast, philosophy deals with forms, eschewing images, and begins with principles that are not hypothetical (*an-*

hypothetou, 510b7). Given this apparently clear-cut distinction between mathematics and philosophy, it has seemed natural simply to graft the account of the *Republic* onto that of the *Phaedo.* The result is to think of philosophic method for Plato as a matter of inferring less general from more general propositions, with the provisos (1) that no use be made of pictures or images and (2) that the propositions of highest generality be somehow self-evident or beyond need of justification. In a nutshell, the truths of philosophy like those of mathematics are propositional in character, but are secured beyond doubt in apodictic first principles.

This conception of the philosophic undertaking, however, belies the actual text of the Divided Line passage in several important respects. For one, the methodological complaint against the mathematicians at 510c is not that they begin with hypotheses in the sense of axioms or postulates, the truth of which is simply taken as given. Their shortcoming, rather, is that they begin by assuming (*hypothemenoi,* 510c3–4) the odd and even (for arithmetic) and figures and angles (for geometry) as if these were known (*eidotes,* 510c6), and "make them foundations" (*hypotheses,* 510c6–7), and moreover take them as evident (*phaneron,* 510d1), not requiring any kind of account (*logon,* 510c7). In other words, the complaint is not that the mathematicians proceed by deduction from propositions the truth of which is only assumed (which presumably they do) but that they posit a subject matter which they proceed to treat as if it required no further clarification. The problem is not in the way they treat their propositions, but in their mental grasp of the objects about which they reason.

In the dialectic of the philosopher, in contrast, the soul (*psyche,* 510b5) advances from what is laid down (*hypotheseos,* 510b7) as a beginning to a "nonhypothetical principle" (*archen anhypotheton,* 510b7, 511b6–7), by a "method relying on Forms alone" (510b8–9). The second problem faced by the discursive interpretation of the Line is that there is little in this description of philosophic method that would suggest such an interpretation to someone not previously committed to it. For one thing, the method is explicitly described as relying on Forms alone, a restriction further detailed at 511b9–c2 as "making no use of anything sensible at all, but proceeding through Forms by means of Forms and with Forms as conclusions." Not only is there no apparent sense in which Forms might be thought of as statements or propositions, but moreover the only uses of the term *logos* in its propositional sense[5] occur in the description of imagistic thinking (510d5, 7) which is explicitly excluded from philosophic reasoning. For another thing, although the principle to which the philosopher advances is characterized as being nonhypothetical, there is no reason in the text to think of this principle as a self-evident and singularly general proposition. The sense, that is to say, is not that of a nonhypothetical proposition, but of a nonpropositional principle that is uniquely intelligible.

This leads to a further difficulty for the discursive interpretation, having to do with the relationship between the nonhypothetical principle and the Good which is the source of being and intelligibility. Although the text does not establish the point conclusively, it is a reasonable assumption that Plato intended to characterize one and the same fundamental principle by the two descriptions. Inasmuch as the Divided Line is explicitly presented as an explication of the contrast between the visible and the intelligible domains introduced in the sun analogy, the natural presumption is that the superlative principle of one context corresponds to that of the other. When Socrates returns to the topic of the Line toward the middle of Book 7, moreover, he provides two characterizations of dialectic that together provide strong support for the identification of these principles. At 532a–b, dialectic is described as a process "prescinding all things sensible" (532a6) through which one sets out to discover the essence of each entity, and does not desist until one has "grasped by reason . . . the essence of the Good itself" (*dia tou logou . . . auto ho estin agathon*; 532a7–b1), and thereby "arrives at the limit of the intelligible" (*ep' auto gignetai to tou noetou telei*, 532b2). Dialectic next is described at 533c–d as a method that "does away with hypotheses" (533c10), and proceeds "to the principle itself in which it finds certainty" (533c10–d1), and thereby leads "the eye of the soul" (533d2) upward to a view of reality. According to the latter description, the upward movement of dialectic terminates in "the principle itself," which seems obviously to be the nonhypothetical principle of 510b7 and 511b6–7. According to the former, dialectic terminates with "the Good itself . . . at the limit of the intelligible." Short of saying so explicitly, the text could not have indicated much more clearly that the Good *is* the nonhypothetical principle at which dialectic aims. If so, however, then it makes little sense to think of that principle as propositional in character. For the Good also is the source of being and intelligibility, a role surely beyond the capacity of linguistic entities.

In upshot, the philosophic method of the *Republic* differs from that of the *Phaedo* not only in its stress upon nonhypothetical principles, but more basically in its departure from the conception of philosophy as dealing with systems of statements or propositions in the first place. Like the *Symposium* and the *Phaedrus*—where this stance might seem less surprising—the *Republic* appears to agree with the *Seventh Letter* in setting philosophic understanding somehow beyond what can be adequately expressed in language.

IV

If the *Seventh Letter* is to be taken at face value, and if Plato in fact never did commit his properly philosophic thoughts to writing, what is to be made of the written dialogues? Why did Plato go to the bother of writing about philosophic topics in the first place if he was so convinced that language is incapable of expressing philosophic understanding? More important, what hope is left for readers of later generations—whose primary access to Plato's thoughts is through his writings—of ever recapturing his basic teachings?

A key can be found within the *Seventh Letter* itself. While being explicit in its insistence that philosophy cannot be put into words like other subjects, it is equally explicit in its description of how philosophy does come into fruition. What happens in the case of philosophy, the author says at 341c–d (quoted above), is that it is generated "in the soul" from "frequent conversations" (*sunousias* at 341c7 can also mean association with a teacher, as at *Statesman* 285c8) and from "living with the matter itself." When philosophic understanding comes upon a soul, moreover, it comes suddenly "like a torch light kindled by a leaping flame, and straightway becomes self-sustaining." Brilliant imagery aside, three factors appear essential in this description. One is that such understanding comes about as the result of thorough immersion in ("living with") a topic in the course of frequent conversations with a teacher. The seemingly unmistakable allusion here is to Socratic conversations of the sort recorded in the early and middle dialogues. Another crucial factor is that philosophy comes to fruition in the soul of the student—not in the form of conclusions to written or spoken arguments but in a flamelike flash of illumination not dependent upon discourse or other sensible phenomena. This brings to mind the so-called legitimate discourse of *Phaedrus* 276a, which, although akin to linguistic discourse, is written in the soul of those who have understanding. A mark of this interior discourse of the *Phaedrus* is that it is able to defend itself, knowing when to speak and when to remain silent, which corresponds to the third crucial factor of philosophic understanding identified in the *Seventh Letter*—that when kindled in the soul it becomes self-sustaining.

Once we have broken with the misleading notion that the *Seventh Letter* advocates spoken over written discourse for philosophic purposes, the description of philosophic learning there offered to the companions of Dion appears to fit the notion of learning as recollection that figures in the *Meno,* the *Phaedo,* and the *Phaedrus.* In barest outline, this notion is based upon the theory that "the truth about reality (*tōn ontōn*) is always in our souls" (*Meno* 86b1–2), but that association with the body and its passions has beguiled the soul into the opinion that the only true things are those that can be touched and seen and used for gratification (*Phaedo,* 81b). Given this background, the soul can be returned to its original grasp of the truth by refutation of that false opinion, for which purpose frequent conversation with Socrates was particularly well suited. After "being examined many times in many ways on a given topic" (*Meno* 85c10–11), the pupil would come "to understand as consummately as any person" (*akribos epistesetai peri touton*, 85d1). In this fashion his or her understanding becomes self-sustaining. Learning thus is a process of recollecting truths previously grasped by an unencumbered psyche.

Teachers and commentators frequently draw attention to the inconclusive character of the early and middle dialogues, pointing out that the basic questions posed by Socrates in his conversations typically do not receive positive answers before the conversation terminates. What is usually overlooked in this connection is that, if the theory of learning as recollection is to be taken seriously, there is no need for Socrates to articulate the proper responses to his questioning. If the office of removing false opinion has been successfully carried out, then the soul of the respondent is already well on its way toward recovering the truth previously within its grasp. If the admonition of the *Seventh Letter* and the *Phaedrus* are to be taken seriously, moreover, it would be distinctly inappropriate for Socrates in *oral* communication to attempt a verbal formulation of the truths awakened in the soul of his respondent. Exactly the same considerations apply in the *written* communication between Plato and his reader. On the one hand, linguistic discourse—whether oral or written—is inadequate for the expression of philosophic understanding. On the other, written questioning—as well as oral—can serve in the removal of false opinion.

A provisional answer to the question of why Plato wrote dialogues follows directly from these considerations. Given the view that philosophic understanding is a kind of intellectual discernment that cannot be adequately expressed in language, the goal of philosophic instruction would be to bring about this state in the mind of the student. And given the view that learning is a matter of regaining a grasp of the truth through judicious refutation of false opinion, one manner of bringing about such a mental state is exposure to the process of Socratic elenchus. For those who are unable to converse with Socrates directly—a class of persons including the readership of Plato's dialogues—there is no better alternative than to be exposed to *recorded* Socratic conversations with persons who exhibit approximately the same confusions and misapprehensions as are likely to beset the typical reader. Seen from this perspective, the Socratic dialogues serve the purpose both of recording typical applications of elenchus by Socrates himself (presumably in artistically purified form) and at the same time of providing an intellectual exercise that (if diligently pursued) will bring the reader to the point of recapturing in explicit awareness truths incipient within his or her psyche. It should be carefully noted that the restrictions against language in the *Seventh Letter* no more rule out Plato's use of written language for the guidance of his readers than Socrates' use of spoken language for the guidance of his listeners.

The reason this answer can be only provisional is that the theory of recollection is a factor in only three dialogues and does not appear to have persisted into the later period. There are reasons to suspect that it was a Socratic view that Plato saw fit to represent more or less at face value in certain dialogues directly concerned with Socratic practice (the *Meno,* the *Phaedo,* and the *Phaedrus*), but which was quietly set aside as Plato began to grapple in his own terms with questions of philosophic methodology in the *Republic* and the later dialogues.[6] At *Phaedrus* 249c, where the theory of recollection last appears, in fact, it is rather pointedly reinterpreted in terms of collection and division; and it is conspicuously absent in the *Theaetetus* where Plato turns for the first time to an explicit consideration of the nature of knowledge.

But we should be careful to distinguish one aspect of the theory of recollection that appears to have been retained in Plato's later writings. Gone is the mythical component of the soul's preexistence, which figured prominently as a premise in one of the major arguments for immortality developed in the *Phaedo.* Gone also is the nativist extravagance of attributing knowledge to the soul at birth, and with it any basis for confidence that refutation alone is sufficient for achieving a state of philosophic understanding. But what apparently is not jettisoned is the view of philosophic understanding as a mental discernment of true existence. Textual evidence has already been examined to the effect that this view prevailed through the middle period. Although Plato's approach to problems of knowledge changed significantly with the *Theaetetus* and the *Sophist,* there are indications that his view of philosophy as a nondiscursive grasp of reality remained intact through the later period as well.

A critical text for this issue is *Sophist* 253c–264b, beginning with the chance encounter with "the science of dialectic" (253d2–3), otherwise described as the "free man's knowledge" (see *Theaetetus,* 172d, for the significance of "free man"). What dialectic amounts to is just "dividing according to kinds" (*to kata gene diaireisthai,* 253d1) with due attention to sameness and difference. The one who can do that—the philosopher—is able thereby to perceive distinctly (*diaisthanetai,* 253d7) which kinds combine and which do not, and to perform collections and divisions on the basis of this discernment. Inasmuch as collection and division exhibit necessary and sufficient conditions, respectively,[7] the philosopher's distinct perception enables the formulation of definitions such as those actually accomplished in the *Sophist* itself (the *logoi,* that is to say, of the angler, the "sophist of noble lineage," and the authentic sophist, undertaken at 218e, 226b, and 218c, respectively). In this fashion, dialectic is a guide for discourse (literally, provides "right expectancy for proceedings by means of discourse" as foreshadowed at 253b11.

The philosopher's knowledge provides a *guide* for discourse of the sort illustrated in the logoi of the angler and the sophist. But from this it does not follow that the philosopher's knowledge itself can be *expressed* in a clear logos. There is a relatively straightforward way of reading the *Theaetetus* and the *Sophist*, in fact, which shows why philosophic knowledge cannot be so expressed. This can be indicated (although of course not fully defended) by a brief review of relevant passages.

Discourse of the sort illustrated by the three successful definitions worked out in the *Sophist* stands in contrast with the "bewitched discourse" (234c5) of the sophist himself, in that the former is true while the latter is false. Consideration of the latter provides occasion for reintroducing the problem of false judgment left unresolved in the *Theaetetus*, which out of deference to Parmenides is formulated in the *Sophist* as one of making sense of how "what *is not*" (falsehood) nonetheless can *exist* in speech. The problem purportedly is resolved in the course of the dialogue by the development of a conception of the Form Not-Being, which epitomizes the manner in which Forms or kinds might fail to blend with each other. Not-Being then is shown capable of blending with logos, which makes way for a distinction between true and false discourse. Whereas true discourse says of things-that-are that they are, false discourse says this of things-that-are-not.[8] With this characterization of false discourse the prohibition of Parmenides (237a, 258d) is overcome, and the definition of the sophist proceeds quickly to its conclusion.

As the Stranger is quite careful to make explicit, however, the examination of Not-Being shows also that it blends with *doxa* (judgment), making possible a characterization of false judgment as well. The cases of doxa and logos are the same in that both involve affirmation and denial (264a). Their point of difference is that, whereas discourse is vocal (μετὰ φθόγγου, 263e8), judgment is the conclusion of thinking (*dianoia*), where thinking is "a conversation in the soul without sound" (263e4). When the soul concludes its conversation with itself by representing things-that-are *as* they are it has reached true judgment, whereas false judgment represents things-that-are-not as things that are.

This characterization of judgment as the conclusion of nonverbalized thought is practically identical to that in the middle section of the *Theaetetus*, where Socrates examines the hypothesis equating knowledge with true judgment and finds it wanting. Not only is the hypothesis subject to mundane counterexamples (for example, jurors who reach true judgment not based on evidence), but moreover there appears to be no available conception of truth and falsehood in judgment that applies to abstract as well as sensible objects. When Theaetetus attempts to remedy the former defect by proposing that true judgment might become knowledge with the addition of logos and then joins Socrates in rejecting four senses of logos that rather obviously will not turn the trick, the whole enterprise is beset with an air of futility. For even if they were to hit upon an adequate sense of logos, the concept of true judgment remains unclear. With the development in the *Sophist* of a conception of truth and falsehood that is not limited to judgments about sensible objects, however, the hypothesis identifying knowledge as true judgment accompanied by logos takes on new interest.

Commentators have been too quick to interpret failure of each of the four senses of logos proposed at the end of the *Theaetetus* to make the difference between knowledge and true judgment as failure *tout court* of this definition of knowledge. In fact, this definition is never refuted in the dialogue.[9] To the contrary, Socrates expresses confidence in the definition at 202d, even while preparing to explain his dissatisfaction with the "dream theory" of logos. The question at 202d6–7 is obviously rhetorical: what *"might* knowledge (episteme) be apart from logos and true judgment?" There are several senses of logos more promising than those actually tested, and a properly inquisitive reader might be expected to try out a few on his own. An obvious candidate is the logos illustrated by the three definitions accomplished in the *Sophist* (angler, "sophist of noble lineage," authentic sophist)—a formula expressing necessary and sufficient conditions. In fact, the reader of the *Theaetetus* should have this sense freshly in mind, inasmuch as the explicit task of that dialogue is to find "a single logos that applies to the many kinds of knowledge" (148d6–7) as illustrated by the definition of the surds at the start of the dialogue. Perhaps knowledge is true judgment accompanied by definitional logos.

This seems not entirely wrong. If one has formed the true judgment that angling is an acquisitive art and is able to back this judgment up with a definition identifying angling as the art of stealthy and forceful acquisition of living water animals by fishing techniques involving striking from below during daylight (*Soph.* 219a–221c), then that judgment would seem to represent a kind of knowledge. But there are several difficulties with this conception that prevent it from being generalized. For one, the logos of the angler *itself* constitutes knowledge; and this knowledge surely cannot be adequately characterized as true judgment accompanied by the logos itself. For another, unless the logos itself has been established as accurate, its addition to true judgment cannot amount to knowledge in a strict sense. As with the case of the mathematicians on the Divided Line, mere deduction from an hypothesized logos does not produce knowledge from true judgment. Moreover, this conception fails to capture the "free man's knowledge"—the dialectic that *guides* the way of discourse. The knowledge that guides the formulation of a definition is more than true judgment accompanied by the definition itself.

Like each of the several logoi examined and found wanting at the end of the *Theaetetus,* the logos of definition pertains to language. Suppose one were to look for a sense of logos not necessarily involved with speaking and writing [10] A sense that immediately comes to mind is that of the "legitimate" kind of discourse identified at *Phaedrus* 276a8—"the logos of those with mental perception." The sense in question must be like the logos of *Republic,* 532a7, that "seeks out the essence of each thing, the Good included." Looking ahead to the *Philebus,* we must view it as something like the "dialectical reasoning" (17a4–5) that takes as its business to discern (*katidē,* 16d8) "the entire number between the unlimited and the one" (16d8–e1). The sense of this passage[11] takes us back to the *Sophist,* where philosophic knowledge is identified as the ability "to discern kind by kind how each is able and not able to combine" (253e1–2). A parallel passage occurs at *Sophist* 254a8–9, where the near-synonym *logismos* is used to allude to "reason constantly applied to the Form of Being" (*te tou ontos aei dia logismon proskeimenos idea*). A similar use occurs at *Meno* 98a4, where "reasoning about causes" (*aitias logismo*) is identified as recollection. Although these passages range chronologically from the relatively early to the very late dialogues, a point advanced by each is that the logos attending knowledge is in some fashion an intellectual grasp of being. Suppose the logos in question were a grasp of being, that enables judgment to distinguish correctly between what is and what is not. Such a logos is not discursive, being instead the "free man's knowledge" by which discourse is guided.

Suppose that Plato thought of the philosopher's knowledge as an intellectual grasp of being; as logos of a sort that is not added to true judgment, but rather that carries true judgment within its train. Suppose, however, that he intended his attentive readers to hit upon this sense of logos in something like the fashion in which it was hit upon above. Suppose these things, not as a hypothesis to be defended, but as a conjecture to help illustrate the concluding points of this chapter.

1. Knowledge can occur in the form of a true judgment accompanied by logos in the sense of definition, as illustrated by the three successful definitions of the *Sophist* and the definition of the surds at the beginning of the *Theaetetus.* Unless the logos itself is known in some other sense, however, knowledge of this sort corresponds to the scientific conception described in the *Seventh Letter* as falling short of the "knowledge that the mind seeks" (343c2) of true being itself—a failure that is "due to the inadequacy of discourse" (343a1).

2. The "knowledge that the mind seeks" is a nondiscursive grasp of being, illustrated by the allusions cited above in dialogues as far apart as the *Meno* and the *Philebus.* It is like the dialectic described in the *Sophist* as a guide for logos; but, being nondiscursive, it cannot be formulated in logos itself. Perhaps knowledge of this character—the so-called "free man's knowledge" of the *Sophist*—is the εἰδέναι (341c2) that the writer of the *Seventh Letter* claims cannot be put in words like other subjects.

3. Granting that the nature of this "knowledge that the mind seeks" cannot be formulated discursively, we must admit that its nature nonetheless has been conveyed by the written dialogues. Up to the series of suppositions directly above, the argument of this discussion has been closely tied to the texts. Our understanding of Plato's conception of philosophic understanding has been stimulated by his writings, although that conception itself was never formulated in words.

V

With this, we are ready to propose a less provisional answer to the question of why Plato wrote dialogues. Although knowledge worthy of philosophy cannot be expressed discursively, it does not follow that language has no role to play in the philosopher's quest for understanding. Skillfully conducted conversation can be next to indispensable in preparing the mind for that intellectual grasp of reality that constitutes philosophic knowledge. For those of us not fortunate enough to be able to engage in conversation with a master teacher like Socrates, an alternative is to become actively involved in recorded conversations between Socrates and other persons who exhibit approximately the same confusions and misapprehensions as we ourselves are prone to experience. More accurately—since Socrates does not figure in several of the later dialogues—the alternative is to become actively involved in conversations artfully composed to provide the same sort of intellectual stimulation to the properly attentive reader as conversations with Socrates could provide the fifth-century Athenian.

Active involvement in any case is entirely essential. For understanding does not come from mere acquiescence to arguments, nor from unwitting submission to clever refutation. The later dialogues were not shaped by a theory of learning postulating innate states of knowledge that could be recovered by elimination of false opinion. If the dialogues of Plato's maturity were shaped by any specific view of learning at all, it would have to be a view like that stressed by Parmenides in his namesake dialogue with the youthful Socrates. Even with the great passion for argument that you exhibit, says the master philosopher to the talented neophyte, "the truth will escape you" (135d6) unless you exert yourself and submit to a "more rigorous discipline" (135d4). Whatever else this discipline amounts to, Parmenides makes clear by his illustration that it involves a thorough examination of the thing in question, in all respects and from all viewpoints, both positive and negative. Translated to the case of the reader, active involvement of this sort requires being attentive to the dramatic significance as well as to the soundness of Plato's arguments. For there is probably no argument placed by Plato in a dialogic setting that is not constructed for its rhetorical as well as its logical consequences. Active involvement also requires maintaining a firm fix on the issues behind a given conversation, for there are few dialogues whose main concerns are with their "officially announced" topics. But above all, it requires incessant exploration of the paths along which the dialogue leads us.[12] For even though Plato had reasons for never committing his truths to writing, these reasons did not prevent his composing conversations that are capable of leading actively involved readers to discover these truths for themselves.

For these purposes, the recorded conversation is not inferior to its oral counterpart, inasmuch as one can probe a written dialogue time and again with new questions in mind. But when one has done this often enough and persistently enough, and in company with other active inquirers, one may experience a growing capacity to divide Forms "according to objective articulations" (*Phr.* 265e)—or "to perceive distinctly which kinds combine and which do not" (*Soph.* 253d–e)—or "to discern the entire number between the unlimited and the one" (*Phil.* 16d–e), as the case might be. And then at some point this capacity will come into fruition—suddenly, "like a torch light kindled by a leaping flame" (*Seventh Letter,* 341d)— and one will have secured grasp of the very lineaments of being. When this happens, one will have, beyond mere correct judgment, "a living and vital logos" (*Phr.* 276a) of the thing in question. One will have arrived, that is to say, at philosophic understanding.

The esoterics are right in maintaining that the dialogues do not contain an explicit doctrine of philosophic principles. But they are wrong in conjecturing, on the basis of the *Seventh Letter,* that he presented an oral doctrine of philosophic principles within the Academy. Neither oral nor written discourse can express such teachings, for philosophy cannot be put in language like other subjects. What the dialogues *can* do—and as far as we know can do as well as oral conversation—is guide the apt student along a path of enquiry that might lead to understanding as Plato conceived it. For on this account the culmination of philosophy is a state of the psyche, which can be fostered by language but never formulated discursively.

7

Why Dialogues? Plato's Serious Play

Rosemary Desjardins

Problems involved in reading the Platonic dialogues are many and complex. This chapter will focus on one difficulty, which might be cast in the form of a dilemma. If, on the one hand (in accordance with Plato's own warning), the dialogues are not to be taken seriously, then why did he spend so much time and effort to bequeath them to us? If, on the other hand, the dialogues *are* to be taken seriously, then how do they defend Socrates against the joint charge of rejecting the traditional gods and corrupting the youth? In seeking a solution to this dilemma, this chapter will develop a thesis about the role of interpretation in the dialogues.

Even on a first reading it must surely seem odd that, whereas on the one hand we have Plato's notorious strictures against all written works, on the other he has himself bequeathed to us a voluminous literary legacy.[1] What are we to make of this? How can it be that Plato apparently worked and painstakingly reworked his dialogues[2]—and yet at the same time maintained that every serious person in dealing with really serious subjects carefully avoids writing (*Letter VII* 344c1–7; *Phr.* 277e5–8)?

And lest we were tempted to see the puzzle as applying only to the writings of others, but not to Plato's own work, there is his quite extraordinary claim that "there does not exist, nor will there ever exist, any treatise

This chapter derives in part from work on language and interpretation in Plato's dialogues that was made possible by a grant from the National Endowment for the Humanities—for which I am grateful. Earlier versions of the chapter were given at Vassar College and the University of Sydney. I should like to thank my colleagues for comments and suggestions offered on those occasions—and also, in particular, Charles Griswold for his generous and helpful criticism.

[*sungrammu*] of mine dealing with my philosophy. For it does not at all admit of verbal expression [*rheton gar oudamos estin*] like other studies" (*Letter VII* 341c4–6).[3] In fact, "he who thinks . . . that *anything* written [*oukoun ho technen . . . en grammasi*] will be clear and certain would be an utterly simple person" (*Phr.* 275c5–7). But, again, lest we suppose it is simply the written word that is the target of attack, it becomes increasingly clear that the problem leads from written to spoken language—and so eventually to language as such.[4] Thus, the very same criticism that in the *Phaedrus* is brought to bear against the *written* word is in the *Protagoras, Theaetetus,* and *Sophist* brought to bear against the *spoken* word—and this, moreover, in terms that seem deliberately designed to echo each other. Thus while written words, "like painted images, seem to be intelligent," they really exhibit only "the appearance of wisdom," thereby masking the grossest ignorance (*Phr.* 275a6–b2); but so too "spoken images" (*eidola legomena*) that likewise "seem to be true" can also exhibit an "appearance of wisdom" that merely masks the sophistic ignorance beneath (*Soph.* 234c2–7). As in the *Phaedrus,* where Socrates compares written words to dumb paintings which respond to questions by simply repeating the same words over and over again (*Phr.* 275d4–9), so too in the *Protagoras,* he compares the spoken words of the rhetoricians to dumb books which can neither ask nor answer questions but which, like the reverberation of a gong, keep booming out the same sound until silenced (*Prot.* 329a2–6).

The problem seems, in both cases, to derive from an inability to explain and defend, an inability to offer intelligent *interpretation.* Hence, for the written word, the *Phaedrus* suggests the metaphor of author as parent who needs to protect and defend his writing as though it were a helpless child (*Phr.* 275e3–5). What is striking, however, is that when in the *Theaetetus* Socrates criticizes their spoken account of Protagoras' doctrine, he resorts to exactly the same metaphor of fatherless offspring who need protection and defense (*Theae.* 164e3–5).

Both written and spoken words are thus seen to be vulnerable in similar ways: both present themselves as images, apparently true or intelligent; yet both need the defense of supportive interpretation. The problem thus seems to lie in the very nature of language itself—which is just what Plato suggests in the *Seventh Letter* when he warns of "the weakness inherent in language" (343a1). But if this be the case, then the problem must analoguously affect not only Plato's own writing but even the Socratic conversations themselves. To understand the dialogues would in that case call for reflective interpretation both of what Plato himself is doing in *writing* the dialogues and of what his protagonist Socrates is saying *within* the dialogues.[5]

Setting out from this recognition that for Plato, language—at least language about a society's most important concepts and values—requires interpretation, this chapter will develop a triple analogy in the course of which I believe our original dilemma will be resolved. At a first level, reflecting on how Socrates interprets his own tradition, we will come to see that the dialogues do defend Socrates against those charges; this will lead to a second level where, reflecting on how Plato interprets Socrates and the Socratic tradition, we will come to understand the appropriateness of his reservations about writing; this in turn will lead to a third level where, reflecting on how we ourselves might interpret Plato and the Platonic tradition, we will perhaps find a more fruitful way to read the dialogues.

The plan of the chapter, then, is relatively straightforward. It will argue, first, that the problem of ambiguity and consequent need for interpretation, already present in the earlier tradition, is absolutely central to the Platonic dialogues; second, that in the dialogues this problem of interpretation is resolved—for Socrates as protagonist *within* the dialogues, for Plato as author *of* the dialogues, and for us as inheritors of the dialogues; and third, that the way in which the dialogues structure and resolve this problem of interpretation brings Plato as a genuine participant into the current conversation about hermeneutics.

Ambiguity

Arguing that the central concepts and values of a tradition do indeed call for interpretation, Plato has Socrates put the problem simply. In some areas, communication is clear and agreement easy; in others, not so. Thus, "when one says 'iron' or 'silver', we all understand the same thing, do we not? But what if one says 'justice' or 'goodness'? Do we not part company, and disagree with each other and with ourselves? . . . Let us call the latter the class of the doubtful [literally, 'those in which we wander': *en hois planometha*]"(*Phr.* 263a2–b5).[6] It is not, however, only individual terms that prove to be thus unreliable. Since statements are in turn made up of the interweaving of verbs and nouns (*Soph.* 262c4–6; *Theae.* 202b2–5), they too (whether written or spoken) will likewise be brushed by a kind of ambiguity. Hence the recognition that "logos, inasmuch as it is compounded of nouns and verbs, is in no case established with sufficient stability" (*Letter VII* 343b4–6). For Plato, consequently (it is my contention), there is for logoi seldom a simple true or false, but rather true or false always *under an interpretation*. This perception, which we will find played on throughout the dialogues, is indeed not new with Plato; rather, it is inherited through a long tradition.

The tradition Plato inherits

As with Newton, so too with Plato: what makes possible the scope of his own complex vision is the fact that he stands on the giant shoulders of his predecessors. One of the difficulties, however, as Plato has Socrates put it, is that "the ancients . . . *concealed* their meaning from the multitude by their poetry" (*Theae.* 180c8–d1).[7] He is, of course, right: it is not simply that the pre Socratics often wrote in poetry, but that the power of their communication moves deliberately through the indirection of imagery, metaphor, and the whole gamut of symbolic expression. When Socrates talks of Protagoras revealing "the hidden meaning" of his doctrine "in secret" to an inner circle of disciples (*Theae.* 152c8–10, 155d9–e1), he seems to be assuming a traditionally recognized distinction between surface and deep-level meaning—the latter often reserved only for initiates. What I am arguing here is a twofold assertion about the ancients' "concealment" of meaning: first, that teaching seems not to have been automatically, nor even primarily, via straightforward statements of plain language but frequently through modes of indirect discourse; second (and as corollary of the first), that meaning often proves to be multileveled, yielding layers of interpretation normally requiring (as in so many cultures other than Greek) that one be *led* from one level of understanding to another. In other words, to be able—even correctly—to report beliefs or recite doctrines is not sufficient for understanding. This, presumably, is why we find Aristotle reduced to mere speculation as to what even known Pythagorean teaching might really mean (*Met.* 990a8–29); similarly, with reference to Parmenides' spheres and sun maidens Plato was led to acknowledge: "I am afraid we may not understand his words, and may be still further from understanding what he meant by them" (*Theae.* 184a13);[8] and as for Heracleitus, there was said to be a familiar warning: "Do not be in too great a hurry to get to the end of Heracleitus the Ephesian's book; the path is hard to travel. Gloom is there, and darkness devoid of light. But, if an initiate be your guide, the path shines brighter than sunlight."[9]

My point here is simply to reiterate the fact that this need for interpretation, for distinguishing levels of meaning beneath the surface, thus seems to have been already woven through the cultural fabric as Plato inherited it. It was his genius to adapt this inheritance to his purpose, weaving into the fabric of his own dialogues an analogous pattern of ambiguity and interpretation.

The need for interpretation

Everybody is, for example, familiar with Socrates' jesting comparison between Euthyphro's statements and the statues of Daedalus that refuse to stay where they are put (*Euth.* 11b9–e1, 15b7–c1). What is important to recognize, however, is that it is less a question of words themselves being incorrect than of just *how* various statements are to be interpreted. Thus, in response to Euthyphro's next proposal—that piety is service or care of the gods—Socrates will quite simply acknowledge, "What you say seems fine, Euthyphro—except that I don't quite understand exactly what you mean by 'care' " (*Euth.* 12e5–13a2), the ambiguities of which then turn out to be Euthyphro's undoing. When, again, Charmides suggests that *sophrosyne* might be "minding one's own business," they confront an analogous challenge to discover what the formula might *mean*. As Socrates explains, "I shall be surprised if we can find out how it stands, for it looks like a kind of riddle [*ainigmati*] . . . for the speaker of the words presumably did not mean them quite as he spoke them" (*Charm.* 161c8–d2). And sure enough, after brief cross-examination, Charmides too will admit: "so that person was riddling after all [*einitteto*]. . . . it is perfectly certain, in my opinion, that he propounded it as a riddle [*ainigma*] in view of the difficulty of understanding what 'minding one's own business' can mean" (*Charm.* 162a10–b6).

Although sometimes it is in terms of a riddle or enigma that Plato thus communicates a sense of basic ambiguity, at others he points up the sudden realization that even the right words are insufficient and unreliable (for example, *Meno* 77b2–4, 80b2–4). Sometimes, again, there is acknowledgment of meaning hidden beneath the surface and revealed only to some inner group—as in the case of Protagoras' "dark saying" in the *Theaetetus* (152c9). Later in the same dialogue, the statement of "the sophisticates" will require a kind of "initiation" in order for Theaetetus to understand its true meaning (*Theae.* 155d9–156a3).

Although much in language will prove on examination to be unclear or uncertain, it is two categories of statement in particular that will be the focus of attention in the dialogues. First of all, there are the traditional texts or formulas inherited from the poets and philosophers; these are, in a variety of contexts, shown to be susceptible of various interpretations— some true, some false. Thus, Critias' inadequate interpretation of the cryptic formula "minding one's own business" is elsewhere countered by a rich interpretation that vindicates it as an account of virtue.[10] So too Polemarchus' trivializing interpretation of Simonides' "riddling account of justice . . . given after the manner of the poets" (*einizato . . . poietikos; Rep.* 332b9–c1) is found wanting and is rejected; but note that instead of discarding Simonides, Socrates by contrast concludes that "it is then something *other* than this that Simonides must, as it seems, mean by saying that to render what is due is just" (*Rep.* 332a7–8). This alternative interpretation they then go on at length to develop (for example, *Rep.* 433a1–6, 433e6–434a1, 441d12–e2, 443c9–e6). Meanwhile, statements of the philosophers fare no better; they likewise lend themselves to widely differing interpretations—whether it be Anaxagoras' assertions about nous,[11] Heracleitean doctrine of flux,[12] Protagorean claims about man the measure,[13] or Parmenides' teaching about being and nonbeing.[14] So pervasive is the problem of ambiguity, that not even the words of the god himself escape this kind of testing and analysis. Thus, whereas Critias' efforts to defend the Delphic inscription, "know thyself," succeed only in pointing up the falseness of the formula *under the interpretation that Critias puts on it* (*Charm.*, 165b3–4, 166e5 et seq.), the *Republic* elsewhere directs our attention to a different interpretation.[15] Meanwhile, even the oracle's judgment of Socrates' wisdom—that superficially simple but deeply "enigmatic" statement (*ainittetai*)—needs likewise to be pruned of false interpretation (*Apol.* 21b2–7).

But this leads us to a second category of ambiguous language. For if it is true that the statements of ordinary participants in the dialogues, the sayings of the poets, the doctrines of philosophers, and even the words of the gods must all be subjected to purification in order that false interpretations might be cast away and the true preserved (cf. *Soph.* 226d5–7)—then what about Plato's own statements and doctrines themselves?[16] Might we not expect *them* to be in some especially privileged position? But, as I understand him, Plato seems always to be aware of the burden of ambiguity that must threaten any mere statement of doctrine—*including his own*. It is not, of course, that such statements, accounts, or definitions are not necessary; it should by now be clear that they are. It is simply that to think we ever have—or ever could have—significant truth literally and unambiguously wrapped up in any logos is to be "an utterly simple person" (*Phr.* 275c7). It is his preoccupation with this basic vulnerability in language (*Letter* VII 343a1) that drives Plato on the one hand to downplay the importance of his own writing, yet on the other seriously to cross-examine interpretations of his own doctrines; for "cross-questioning is the greatest and most efficacious of all purification, and he who is not cross-questioned, even though he be the Great King, has not been purified of the greatest taints" (*Soph.* 230d6–e1). As Socrates puts it at one point, he finds himself pressed by the need "to investigate the meaning of my own words—from a fear of carelessly supposing at any moment that I knew something while I knew it not" (*Charm.* 166c8–d2).

This is why characteristic Platonic doctrines are themselves subjected to cross-examination and *under certain interpretations* suffer elenchus. Thus Meno's understanding of the Platonic claim that virtue is knowledge is shown to be indefensible, Theaetetus' understanding of the Platonic doctrine that knowledge involves true opinion and logos is shown to be inadequate, and young Socrates' understanding of the doctrine of forms is shown to be fragile under the cross-examination of Parmenides. This is also why Plato was outraged that Dionysius should so casually "claim to know many of the most important doctrines"—and should then in his presumption go on to publish these doctrines in a neat little treatise (*Letter VII* 341b1–5). If, for Plato, statements of doctrine will be true or false only under an interpretation, then it would seem that any mere presentation of basic statements of doctrine—by a past, present, *or* future writer (*Letter VII*, 341b7–c1)—not only would be self-defeating but would at the same time reveal the philosophical ignorance of such a disciple-turned-author.

Ambiguity and Elenchus

Given the problem of ambiguity in language, and the need to move from surface to deep-level meaning, it is hardly surprising that the first step in a dialogue's development usually requires that one be shaken from a complacent kind of satisfaction with the surface of language and forced to recognize that language does not transparently and unequivocally *mean*, just like that. This process—in which one is made to realize that to come up with even the right words is not enough, that one's unquestioned assumptions are often really obstacles to true understanding—constitutes the familiar pattern that we know as elenchus; it is carried out, so the *Sophist* tells us, for the positive purpose of purification (230b4–e3).

Sometimes it takes a rude shock to jolt someone into this kind of recognition: one remembers how Meno found the shock comparable to the paralysis induced by the torpedo fish (*Meno* 80a2–b4).[17] This stage of shock—when it is first discovered that words do not simply *mean*, that language is indeed beset with what Plato regards as a basic "weakness" that is due to obscurity, uncertainty, or instability (*Letter VII* 342e2–343a1, 343b4–c5, 343d3–e1), and, consequently, that one does not know what one thought one knew—produces a state of perplexity, or aporia, and usually constitutes an important phase of Platonic inquiry. This is true not only in early dialogues like the *Lysis* (for example, 216c4–6) or *Laches* (194c2–4) but equally in later dialogues like the *Theaetetus* where Socrates frankly admits that he "drives men to distraction" (149a8–9) or the *Sophist* where the heart of the discussion is marked by aporia (for example, 236e2–3, 237e7–238a2, 238d1–7, 241b4–6, 243b9–10, 249d9–10, 250d7–e7).

This kind of aporia—meaning literally "no passage," "no way out," "no exit"— is intended, of course, not as an end but rather as a beginning, for as Protarchus, "storm-tossed in the puzzling cross-currents of the discussion" in the *Philebus*, explains: "Let us not imagine that the end of our . . . discussion is a mere puzzling of us all [*aporian*]" (19e4–20a4; cf. 29b1–2). This, presumably, is why a later dialogue like the *Sophist* (230b4–e3) will reinforce the *Meno*'s earlier insistence that aporia is in fact a crucial phase of inquiry. Not only is it useful in a negative sense, in hastening the discovery that "besides not knowing, one does not think he knows," but it is also fruitful in a positive sense, in actually "giving assistance toward finding out the truth of the matter" (*Meno* 84a3–b11). But how or why is this the case? What kind of assistance, and why through elenchus and aporia? Because (Socrates goes on to explain), "he who does not *know* about something or other may yet have *true opinion* about that same thing about which he *knows* nothing" (*Meno* 85c6–7). This assertion will prove to be important, because it turns out that true opinion is in fact essential to knowledge: as Socrates explains to Meno, it is the securing or grounding of true opinion with causal reasoning (*aitia logismos*) that will engender knowledge (*Meno* 97e6–98a4); as he puts it to Theaetetus, "what knowledge *could* there be apart from logos and true opinion?" (*Theae.* 202d6–7).

But if this approach to language reflects Plato's attitude correctly, then certain implications seem to follow for our reading of the argument of the dialogues. And this brings me to the core of my thesis. For I believe that a major goal of the dialogues (both for the Platonic Socrates as heroic protagonist within the dialogues and for Plato himself as author of the dialogues) is precisely to address this problem of how best to interpret one's tradition. For it will be only through pursuit of this task of trying to understand the tradition that makes us to be who we are that the youth of Athens (or Plato, or we ourselves as in turn inheritors of that tradition) can begin to grow in self-knowledge.

Given then this challenge of ambiguity and the need for interpretation, Plato sets out deliberately to lead us from surface to deep-level meaning— and this through a twofold mode of presentation. He speaks and he points: his characters both argue and act. The dialogues, in short, communicate through words *and* deeds; what is more (and more subtle) they communicate through the actual interplay of these two aspects, which constitute, respectively, the discursive and dramatic elements of a dialogue. Although it will be doing violence to the organic unity of Plato's art, for the sake of clarity I should like to look separately at the way he exploits these two modes of interpretation that the Greeks distinguish as logos and ergon— words and deeds.[18]

Interpretation

Logos: the discursive dimension of the dialogues

Sometimes Plato's dialogues are seen as presenting a series of attempts at definition, attempts successively attacked and rejected. But if one takes seriously the view of language being proposed here, then what is being rejected in cross-examination will seldom be a particular logos as such but rather various inadequate (and to that extent "false") interpretations of what the logos in question really means. In other words, it is seldom a question of rejection but rather one of purification, precisely because, as we just heard Socrates explain, it is possible to have an opinion about something, for the opinion to be actually true, and yet for us not to *know* it to be true (*Meno* 85c6–7). According to this reading, then, the goal of a dialogue is not to reject such true opinion; rather, starting with this ability to come up with the right words, a dialogue seeks to understand *why* (under some but not all interpretations) the original opinion is indeed true—and thus might be transformed into real knowledge (*Meno* 97e6–98a8). Like a theme with variations, this tension seems to be played through in dialogue after dialogue. Thus on the one hand, there will be a logos formulated on the basis of opinion, which, although in one sense true, is nevertheless inadequately understood and so unanchored (like the statues of Daedalus: *Meno* 97d6–98a4; *Euth.* 11b9–d2, 15b7–10); on the other, there will be the same logos, which, now tethered by reasoning [19] and so properly understood, actually becomes the reflection and expression of knowledge (cf. *Rep.* 534b5–6; *Theae.* 202c3–5).

This is why Plato insists on those contrasting interpretations, why he highlights not only the false but *also* a true interpretation of the traditional phrase "minding one's own business" (compare *Charm.* 162b8–165b4, with *Rep.* 433a8–b4, 441d12–e2, 443c9–d4); why we are offered both false *and* true interpretations of Anaxagoras' doctrine that "nous is cause" (compare *Pho.* 97b8–99c6, with *Phil.* 26e2–27a2, 28c6–30d8); why Polemarchus' false interpretation is balanced by Socrates' true interpretation of Simonides' account of justice as "giving to each its due" (compare *Rep.* 332a7–8, 335e1–5, with 433e6–434a1, 443d1–4); why Lysias' false interpretation of love as a kind of madness is corrected by Socrates' true interpretation (*Phr.* 231d2–4, 244a5ff).

As already suggested, the problem with the interpretations offered by Lysias—or by Polemarchus or Theaetetus or whoever—turns out to be not that they are false but rather that they are inadequate and partial until properly (and differently) understood. When what is inadequate and partial is thus taken, or mis-taken, for the whole, it ends up as radically other—thus highlighting an original though hidden ambiguity. This explains why it is only Critias' superficial understanding of sophrosyne as self-knowledge that is at fault, not the Delphic injunction (*Charm.* 165b3–4, 166e5 et seq.); it is only Nicias' understanding of courage as the knowledge of that which is and is not dreadworthy, not the logos itself that is deficient (compare *La.* 199c3–e11, with *Prot.* 360d4–5); it is only Meno's understanding of the Platonic claim that virtue is knowledge that is rendered absurd, not the doctrine itself (*Meno* 87c11–12, 97b9–98a8). When at the end of the *Theaetetus* the final effort at definition echoes the Platonic claim that knowledge combines true opinion and logos, the problem is still the same since, as Socrates frankly admits, "the statement itself is probably all right" (*Theae.* 202d6); the persistent question remains, however, as to "What is meant by the doctrine that the most perfect knowledge arises from the addition of logos and true opinion?" (203c3–5); for, as Socrates goes on to warn him: "Let us not carelessly accuse him of talking nonsense who gave the definition of knowledge which we are now considering; for perhaps [your interpretation] is not what he meant" (*Theae.* 206e4–5). That under Theaetetus' interpretation the doctrine does not hold up need not alter the fact that his words can represent true opinion. As in the case of Meno's slave boy whose true opinions were stirred up in him "like a dream" (*hosper onar: Meno* 85c9), so likewise here in the *Theaetetus*, that last definition is represented as remembered from "a dream" (*onar:* 201d8, 202c5). One recalls that the goal, as reiterated in the *Statesman*, is not to destroy such dreaming opinion but rather to transform it into "waking" knowledge (278e10).[20]

This gradual process of coming to understand through pursuit of logical analysis—this kind of purificatory testing that pares away false or inadequate interpretations—constitutes, then, the discursive aspect of an education that helps us see beyond, or beneath, ambiguity. Since, however, merely discursive clarification still leaves us vulnerable to the original ambiguity that clings to language, Platonic inquiry includes not only a discursive but also a dramatic element, and so provides a second dimension through which we are led to deep-level meaning. In this next section I should therefore like to look at the action of the dialogues.

Ergon: the dramatic dimension of the dialogues

For some time now it has been conventional to read the dialogues as primarily works of philosophical argument and definition, the sometimes tedious logical development being interspersed with picturesque scenes and diverting characterization. Increasingly in recent times this view has been questioned, and the so-called literary aspect of the dialogues is now often taken seriously.[21] It is with this latter approach that I wish to join forces, for although the dialogues do indeed offer delights of characterization, action, imagery, wit, and whimsy, I argue that the purpose of Plato's dramatic presentation is *essentially philosophical*: in other words, the point of the literary dimension of the dialogues is not only (nor even primarily) to charm but rather to provide necessary parameters of interpretation that will allow us to cut through the ambiguity of the discursive level.

The need for actual instances or examples is a familiar Platonic theme. In resorting to example, however, Plato utilizes two types of *paradeigma*. First of all, there are those *external* examples—from cobblery (in the *Theaetetus*) to cookery (in the *Gorgias*), marketing (in the *Sophist*) to medicine (in the *Charmides*), shepherding (in the *Republic*) to ships and piloting (in the *Statesman*)—which run like bright threads through the pattern of the dialogues. But it is the *internal*, self-referential examples that are truly pivotal for this question of interpretation—that is to say, those examples Plato provides within the fabric of a concurrent discussion of the same topic. And at this level, there seem to be three main ways in which Plato structures his paradeigmata.

In the first, a paradigm or example is provided through reference to action outside the dialogue—as in the discussion of courage in the *Laches*, where specific reference is made to Socrates' courageous behavior at Delium, or in the case of Alcibiades' account of Socrates that climaxes the discussion of love in the *Symposium* by pointing to the actual love demonstrated by Socrates (in light of which the discussion itself must then be interpreted). A second mode of presentation works through the careful introduction and clever juxtaposition of characters—as, for example, in the case of the *Euthyphro*, where the inquiry into piety brings together two citizens both of whom make amazing claims to piety—one of whom we know will shortly be judged guilty of impiety, and the other perhaps ought to be. The actions and attitudes of each reflect, and are reflected in, their rather different ways of understanding the logoi that are here being discussed—and it is left to the reader to see (in light of their different behavior) in what sense their respective interpretations are to be rejected, in what sense maintained.[22] Again, in the dialogue devoted to a discussion of sophrosyne, Plato brings together Charmides and Critias, both of whom at the dramatic time of the conversation represent claims to that virtue— but both of whom at the time of actual writing (as the reader well knows) had demonstrated that their sophrosyne had in fact been only apparent, not real. And again, *for the reader*, that highlights the ambiguity in the traditional formulas to which they so readily appeal, forcing us to think about the difference between interpretations reflected in the behavior of Critias and Charmides, on the one hand (interpretations rejected as inadequate), and in that of Socrates, on the other (an interpretation Plato finds both true and worthy of enthusiastic emulation). It is, however, what I am distinguishing as a third mode of presentation that is perhaps the most subtle—and most illuminating as self-referential key whereby we look to erga (deeds) to interpret logoi (words)—for this focuses our attention on what is actually going on in the dialogue itself.

One of the most conspicuous instances, because explicitly adverted to at the time, occurs in the *Phaedrus'* discussion of logos, where deliberate reference to the examples provided in the deficient logos of Lysias and the masterly logos of Socrates enables us to see in what sense the stipulations about logos are and are not to be understood. But, of course, the *Phaedrus* is simultaneously an inquiry into love; and if not Phaedrus himself, then at least the reader must see that the discussion of love is likewise pursued with deliberate reference to the actual paradeigmata of love provided— and again, with specific reference to the contrast between the deficient love displayed by Lysias and the genuine love demonstrated by Socrates.

In the *Theaetetus*, their final search for a logos of logos must obviously be related to the *external* paradigm provided in the logos of surd, but even more subtly to the *internal* paradigm of the logos of knowledge that they are pursuing together and that constitutes the dialogue as such. So too, the *Meno*'s account of the method of hypothesis refers back not only to the obvious *external* example from geometry but more significantly to the *internal* example provided in the method he has himself been employing in the first part of the dialogue. Finally, in the *Sophist* we are given a double play. On the one hand, there is the obvious parallel between the definition by division of the angler and the definition by division of the sophist. On the other hand, the very activity of genuine "dividing by kinds," definitive of the true philosopher (*Soph.* 253c6–e2), is itself being self-consciously illustrated in that same process through which the Stranger has been leading us from the outset of the dialogue. The Stranger thereby helps us recognize what he calls a "slippery" distinction between the philosopher and the sophist (*Soph.* 231a6). In other words, we have been offered on a *practical* level an answer to the original question of the dialogue (*Soph.* 217a3–8).

To sum up then, what I am here arguing is that beyond the familiar external examples ("his talk of pack-asses, smiths, cobblers, and tanners"; *Symp.* 221e4–5), Plato makes a point of providing these self-referential internal examples in a deliberate effort to illumine the abstract and cru-cial—but ambiguous—concepts and doctrines of his philosophy; for, as the Athenian Stranger explains in the *Statesman*, "it is difficult to set forth any of the greater ideas except by the use of examples [*paradeigmasi*]" (*Pol.* 277d1–2). In short, our understanding of love or the art of logoi in the *Phaedrus*, of division in the *Sophist*, of limit and the unlimited in the *Philebus*, of hypothesis in the *Phaedo*, of episteme epistemes in the *Char-mides*, of discrimination and weaving in the *Cratylus*, of dialectic in the *Republic*, of logos in the *Theaetetus* will all to a large extent depend on our awareness of the practical demonstration or paradeigma that Plato has taken care to provide within the dramatic action that constitutes the context of the discussion. It is awareness of this constant need for interpretation that drives Plato to adopt a special kind of vehicle for his philosophy— that of dramatic dialogue that will not be forced to rely exclusively on its vulnerable discursive content.[23] Concrete and dynamic, these "perform-ances" ensure that discursive content is always aligned with, always illu-mined and qualified by, and always interpreted with reference to the dra-matic element provided by the action of the dialogue, for ultimately it is in what he calls "the rubbing together" of these two "like firesticks" (*Letter VII* 344b4–5) that genuine knowledge is kindled in the soul.

Tradition as Task

Standing back now to reflect on the activity of interpretation as this is found in the dialogues, one is struck by an interesting parallel between what Socrates as protagonist is doing within the dialogues and what Plato as author is doing in writing the dialogues. For each in his own way is seeking to interpret what has been received—Socrates, the insights and values embodied in the traditions of his culture; Plato, the conversations of his mentor and the Socratic tradition itself. In this sense the dialogues might even be seen as dialogues *with the tradition*.[24] Despite the disavowals of each, moreover, both Socrates as protagonist and Plato as author pursue this interrogation of their tradition in ardent commitment to educating any or all of us who will listen. When we stop to ask what exactly this education consists of, we find an answer both sophisticated and challenging.

Having first argued for the pervasiveness of the problem of ambiguity, and the need for interpretation, and having examined ways in which the dialogues seek to address that problem, I must now reflect more explicitly on how the dialogues envision—and thereby educate us too in the pursuit of—an appropriate response to a tradition. It is this reflection that finally highlights the subtlety of the dialogues' stance between two (by now) familiar approaches to tradition.[25]

Thus, at one extreme, there is the kind of uncritical subservience that seeks to preserve in some absolute sense what is taken to be the determinate and objective meaning of the original message, and at the other, a kind of critical independence that sees meaning as significantly indeterminate, with every interpretation of text or tradition as so historically conditioned by what the reader brings to the interpretation that even to talk of *the* meaning is to be deceived by a will-o'-the-wisp, since there will be as many meanings as there are individual, historically conditioned readers.

Thus to structure the problem is, I believe, fruitful for an understanding of the Platonic dialogues. For, according to my thesis, we are in the dialogues repeatedly presented with these alternatives—determinate versus indeterminate, fixed versus changing, absolute versus relative[26]—only to be led with the saving skill of an Odysseus between the Scylla and Charybdis they represent. Unlike the relativist, Socrates accepts with the utmost seriousness the tradition he inherits—not only in philosophy but also in myth, poetry, and the wise and "pithy" sayings of the ancients (*Prot.*, 343a6–b5). Unlike the absolutist, however, Socrates is impatient with hidebound and literal readings. The Socrates of the dialogues is, by contrast, always pressing to find an interpretation that will represent not simply some historically accurate thought from an earlier period but one rich enough and flexible enough to provide insight into problems current in his own time. The persistent challenge, to both participants and readers, is always to find beneath the literal text some deeper level meaning which, when translated into the contemporary language, will nourish their values and enrich their understanding.

In other words, in looking to the tradition for sustenance, the Platonic Socrates is trying, on the one hand, to avoid that literal and absolutist conservatism that leads to uncritical subservience to the text of the historical tradition and, on the other, to avoid a relativistic dilution that leads to the discarding of texts as they come now to be rendered irrelevant. He seems critically aware that either alternative will ultimately lead to the loss of the tradition. The first (the attitude of would-be objectivist absolutism) takes the written text too seriously, uncritically carving its literal expression into the shrine of cultural memory; the second (a wide-open relativism) takes it too lightly, ending up by emptying it of meaning. Either way, although for opposite reasons, the tradition—and with it, their educational patrimony—will be lost to the youth of the next generation. Self-understanding by contrast demands something different, something more, to which Socrates dedicates his life. It is his examination and cross-examination of the tradition that constitutes such a crucial aspect of the search for self-knowledge, the lifework of Socrates. He sought to defend that undertaking before the Athenian people, but it was rejected because he was seen not as interpreting but rather as abandoning the tradition, and hence as corrupting the youth. In giving us, therefore, the Socrates of the dialogues, with his persistent demand that the tradition make sense, that it be understood in such a way as to illumine and nourish, Plato has offered a subtle, yet powerfully eloquent defense of his master.

In making that defense, however, Plato himself now as author must struggle with an analogous challenge as he confronts his own tradition; for just as the Platonic Socrates seeks a way between these two extremes in interpreting the tradition, so Plato as author must try to steer between the same two extremes in interpreting the lifework of Socrates. At a first level this will dictate his attitude to Socrates himself; at a second level it will dictate his attitude to his own written work. It is easy enough to see that for Plato as author, the counterpart to taking the tradition too literally and absolutely would be some attempt at literal portrayal of the historical Socrates, whereas the counterpart to relativist dilution might be some kind of literary fiction with only vaguely remote ties to the original Socratic ideal. Plato's own resolution echoes the resolution he will attribute to Socrates: he presents us with an *interpretation* of Socrates and of the Socratic search for self-knowledge—"a Socrates become fair and young" as the *Second Letter* (usefully, even if inauthentically) puts it (314c4)—through which those of us who come after might continue, in our own times, to be challenged and edified.

But already the Platonic presentation of Socrates becomes in turn a tradition for all of us who follow. How then should Plato assess his own work, his account of Socrates that constitutes the text of the dialogues themselves? Here too, it would seem, he must face the same tension between, on the one hand, the danger of taking his own work too seriously as dogmatic and definitive and, on the other, the danger of so relativizing it that we discount what he wants to retain as the abiding message of Socrates' lifework. It is this tension that generates, of course, Plato's well-known paradox about writing. Instead of seeing this as a problem, however, it is my claim that the paradox arises precisely, and predictably, as a result of Plato's own response to the challenge of finding a dialectical way between those two extreme approaches to one's tradition. In other words, reading the dialogues in the way I am suggesting resolves both horns of our original dilemma. We now see the sense in which the dialogues are and are not to be taken seriously, and we understand the sense in which they do indeed offer a defense of Socrates.

Conclusion

Taking Plato's fundamental concern with interpretation as key to reading the dialogues, we realize that there is no important statement of doctrine or value—nor, because of the ongoing character of human life, could there be—whose meaning is absolutely static. This is why we must never take the merely literal text of the tradition too seriously. On the other hand, our coming to understand the texts of the tradition and their relevance to our own situation (so that, as he puts it in the *Phaedrus*, they will not be dead words on our lips but living illumination in our souls; 278a1–5) is educationally the most serious of all our undertakings, insofar as it leads to deeper understanding not only of the tradition but ultimately of ourselves. For at this point, yet one more interesting parallel becomes apparent.

As Socrates is shown to resolve the extremes of absolute objectivism and historicist relativism with respect to his own tradition, and as Plato in turn seeks to resolve the same extremes with respect to the Socratic tradition, so it becomes clear that one way of looking at what this chapter is trying to do is to see it in turn as seeking to resolve the same extremes with respect to the Platonic dialogues which have become so central to our own tradition.[27] In all three cases, what is right about the objectivist stance is that the tradition is indeed of paramount importance in making us be who we are; what is right about the historicist insight is the recognition that interpretation is never complete. Thus it is the quest for self-knowledge that, on the one hand, takes the tradition with utmost seriousness and, on the other, calls for relevant *interpretation* of that tradition and so goes on to search out those interpretations that, in the context of one's own time, will offer illumination and nourishment.

In our own time, this view of a perennial task in which each generation is called to confront its own tradition without falling into either dogmatic absolutism or critical relativism finds a familiar echo in Hans–Georg Gadamer's major work on hermeneutical understanding, *Truth and Method*.[28] In developing his hermeneutical approach, Gadamer is also seeking the kind of dialectical resolution I wish to attribute to Plato. For Gadamer too, "the hermeneutical experience is concerned with what has been transmitted in tradition. . . . For tradition is a genuine partner in communication" (*TM*, p. 231). Since moreover, as Gadamer puts it, "the proper realization of the historical task is to determine anew the meaning of what is examined," he too holds that "the text . . . if it is to be understood properly . . . must be understood at every moment, in every particular situation, in a new and different way" (*TM*, p. 275). Therefore, echoing the dialogues, he believes that "every age has to understand a transmitted text in its own way, for the text is part of the whole of the tradition . . . within which it seeks to understand itself" (*TM*, p. 263). For both Plato and Gadamer, self-understanding must seek to resolve that tension between acceptance and interrogation, respect and critique, reconstruction of the past and application in the present. To every generation, and to each of us in our own time, falls the task of integrating our historical past and historical present in what Gadamer so aptly calls "the fusion of horizons" (*TM*, p. 273).

8

On Socratic Dialogue

Jürgen Mittelstrass

> a dialogue we are.
> F. Hölderlin, *Friedensfeier*

The aim of conversation is to communicate who one is and what one means, as well as what is and should be the case. By way of contrast, the *philosophical dialogue*—a form of verbal communication distinct from this and other forms of discussion—aims at the acquisition of (philosophical) knowledge. Insofar as it is a *Socratic* dialogue, it also fulfills a function in addition to that of the acquisition of *knowledge*: developing a *philosophical orientation* and a *philosophical subject*. The philosophical dialogue, in other words, is a form of discussion designed to impart philosophical knowledge and to promote both a philosophical orientation and the development of an autonomous (philosophical) subject. In addition to elements such as question and answer or assertion and denial which are common to all forms of conversation, philosophical dialogue also contains the "theoretical" elements of proof and refutation. And in addition to "practical" elements like conflict and agreement, which are again common to all forms of con-

---

This chapter is a translation of "Versuch über den Sokratischen Dialog," in J. Mittelstrass, *Wissenschaft als Lebensform: Reden über philosophische Orientierungen in Wissenschaft und Universität*, suhrkamp taschenbuch wissenschaft, vol. 376 (Frankfurt: Suhrkamp, 1982), pp. 138–161; the original also appeared in K. Stierle and R. Warning, eds., *Das Gespräch*, Poetik und Hermeneutik, vol. 11 (Munich: Wilhelm Fink, 1984), pp. 11–27. The translation is by Steven Gillies (University of Constance). The author is grateful to Suhrkamp Verlag for permission to publish the translation.

versation, philosophical dialogue also contains an element of reciprocity in teaching and learning and aims at developing a dialogical (philosophical) subject of knowledge acquisition.

This conception of philosophical dialogue is Socratic since it is adopted from the Socratic practice of discussion. But it is also a Platonic conception since Plato presented it in a theoretical way in his literary dialogues. The crucial question, however, is whether this conception belongs merely to the historical perspective in philosophy—that is, philosophy's concern with itself and what it once was—or also to the idea of philosophy itself. In other words, does it still have something to do with how we arrive at philosophical knowledge? Does it contribute to the development of a philosophical orientation and of philosophical subjects? The aim of the following is to analyze both aspects—the Socratic-Platonic idea of the philosophical dialogue and the question concerning the practical value of such an idea for philosophical research—and to formulate the results in seven statements.

I

The aim of the philosophical dialogue is a philosophical orientation in which a philosophical understanding of situations or of oneself furthers the idea of man as a rational being. What is at stake in philosophical dialogue are not particular opinions or problems but the subjects who are to acquire philosophical knowledge. This is what constitutes the agonistic and Socratic character of this form of dialogue.

A *presumption of reason* (*Vernunftvermutung*) refers less to an action than to the ability to represent and judge past actions (also in institutional contexts) and to plan future actions according to alternatives that we are conscious of and hence anticipate. What makes us above all rational beings, both conceptually and anthropologically, is not action but nonaction, that is, the possibility of interrupting a sequence of actions in order to judge thoughtfully the effects of one's own or someone else's actions or the potential effects of future action. When we say that something—an action, a context of actions, a state brought about through action—reveals the presence of reason, we mean that whatever we are referring to—an action, a situation, a state—is the effect of a reasoned judgment. The demand for clearness, proof, and justification with respect to actions and their effects requires in this sense that we stop and think. The action is interrupted and made an object of reflection. (The distinction between "physical" action and "reflective" nonaction does not affect the pragmatic insight that both thinking and speaking are in a special sense also actions.)

Whoever interrupts an action in order to think is no longer sure of his ground. Aims and results of actions no longer coincide. The unity of the action, which is always a unity of designated and realized aims, disintegrates. It is "placed in question" and becomes a "problem." *Problems*, of course, are not the sole result of nonaction, that is, the result of reflection. On the whole they are just simply there, forcing themselves upon the actor. No longer being sure of one's ground is in this sense something that just "happens." It is a result of the world, both the world we can affect in view of what we have done (the socially constructed world) as well as the world we cannot affect given who we are (the nature that we are ourselves in part).

Problems that confront us as actors either are solved by conferring with each other or prove to be insoluble through deliberations accompanying actions that are futile or whose intentional unity has been thwarted. Philosophizing is a way of conferring. This is true even for the monologue: "Whoever philosophizes, simulates a dialogue and fails when the dialogue cannot be realized."[1] The philosophical dialogue, the idea of which also organizes the philosophical monologue, is, however, a way of conferring about problems that are not so much there in the sense we have used up to now. They are more *anticipated* by the way we confer. This does not mean anticipation in the way that problems are accessible to a consultation based on a model of technical problem-solving competence, that is, on the expertise model of technologically advanced cultures such as ours. Anticipation in this sense means asking questions that technical reason does not ask and seeking answers that transcend knowledge of technical application. In a certain sense, philosophical dialogue *simulates* problems: problems the world and the individuals involved do *not* have. *Realizing* their solution, however, should lead to the development of a "true" understanding of situations or oneself. Philosophical dialogue is thus the field where an understanding of situations or of oneself takes place in a way that is committed to the idea of orientation through reason.

Wherever there are problems there are also different *opinions*—opinions about how problems arise, are avoided or solved, and so on. The reverse is also true. Where there are no differences of opinion, there are no problems; everything seems clear, and the unity of action (and of life) seems undisrupted. The knowledge that philosophical dialogue imparts is that undisrupted agreement is based on an illusion. Philosophical dialogue (unlike technical understanding) is not meant to cause problems to disappear but to gain knowledge about the idea of man as a rational being as well as the idea of a rational life. In other words, philosophical dialogue is a way of conferring about problems that we—from the point of view of realizing the above-mentioned ideas—*should* have.

The idea of a rational being and a rational life cannot be connected with the solutions to problems provided by technical reason but only with the production of a *philosophical orientation* that serves these ideas and their realization. Philosophy, therefore, is always "in conflict," and philosophical dialogue is a means of conducting this conflict according to the idea of rational interaction. Philosophical reflection that interrupts action (in nature and society) also aims at changing the participating subjects and at constituting a dialogical subject (the subject of the development of philosophical knowledge). Such subjective achievements gained in philosophical dialogue are possible only in a give-and-take that involves not the opinions but the subjects themselves. The result of philosophical dialogue is a new subject with a new philosophical orientation, a subject that comes into existence with the decline of the old subject, inevitably through conflict or combat. *In philosophical dialogue it is the individuals and not their opinions that are at stake.* This is so not in the sense that they risk destruction but in the sense in which they can be made to live up to the idea of a rational being, that is, of their "becoming like god," as Plato puts it (at the same time compensating for that edifying perspective by pointing out the philosopher's ridiculousness) (*Theae.*, 176b). Where this goal is the content of the philosophical dialogue, the dialogue is *Socratic*. Its competitive character derives from the seriousness of the conflict in which not just some opinions or problems but the subjects themselves are at stake.

II

The practical and theoretical intentions of the philosophical dialogue are expressed in an orientation toward mutual understanding and justification. Both transcend the conditions for the subject's particularity determined in the agonality of the beginnings of reason (*Anfang der Vernunft*). Dialectic is characterized by these intentions and is the way in which the aim of philosophical research, namely a philosophical orientation, is realized.

Philosophical dialogue mirrors the competitive *beginnings of reason*. Heraclitus' statement that war is the father of all things[2] also applies, within the limits of a Socratic and Platonic understanding of the philosophical dialogue, to the genesis of a philosophical orientation. This means that as in all other aspects concerning the development of an autonomous subject, self-reliance is not *granted* but *achieved*: both against the world (the dominant objective orientation) and against itself (the dominant subjective orientation). The Socratic insight and the Socratic postulate for philosophical dialogues is that the agonality of the beginnings of reason is compatible with the development of a *dialogical subject* (the subject of philosophical acquisition of knowledge). Agonality helps to overcome divided subjectivity; it does not serve to isolate the subject. In the Socratic dialectic, derived as it is from the reciprocity inherent in dialogical relations, the agonality of the beginnings of reason transcends its own condition which lies in the particularity of the subjects.

Dialectic derives from διαλέγεσθαι: "to examine (something)," "to consider," "to confer with others (about something)." *Dialectic* was originally used to designate the function of dialogue as a means of conferring about something. According to Xenophon's remarks about the Socratic form of philosophizing, διαλέγεσθαι means "coming together and conferring with one another" (συνιόντας κοινῇ βουλεύεσθαι).[3] For Plato a dialectician is someone who "knows how to ask and answer questions" (*Crat.* 390c). Where conferring in dialogue has been institutionalized and made to conform to rules, *dialectic* serves to designate the use of such rules or an institutionalized form of conducting dialogues. This is the point where the dialectic splits up both historically and systematically into a sophistic and a Socratic approach. In the sophistic approach the "dialectical art" (διαλεκτικὴ τέχνη) involves an eristic method of argumentation. The method allows one to prove statements, including the negation of previously "proved" statements[4] (documenting in a sense the dialectical omnipotence), by making appropriate initial distinctions and choosing appropriate arguments: "Whoever knows the art of speaking will also be able to speak correctly about everything. For whoever wants to speak correctly speaks about what he knows. Thus, he knows everything. For he knows the art of all types of speech. All types of speech, however, refer to what exists."[5] Whoever can talk about everything knows everything. Reason appears here as a verbal, a dialectical capacity, but in such a way that the eristic artistic skill replaces a *searching* acquisition of knowledge. This makes agonality an aim in itself and *being* right a (supposed) proof of *doing* right.

The Socratic mode of dialectics also involves verbal conflict and the refutation of one's dialogue partner. In Socratic dialogue, however, *eristic* elements, which help one to assert one's own opinion and one's own will, are replaced by Socratic elenchus. It characterizes the part of the argument that reveals apparent knowledge for what it is. For this reason Socratic elenchus cannot be characterized as verbal deception, as is the eristic mode, but as following the postulate of truthfulness or explicitly renouncing deception.[6] Its goal is a justified agreement (homology) and not merely the assertion of one's own particular position. If we assume together with Socrates and Plato that being right at all costs is not the basic intention of dialogues, particularly philosophical dialogues, then the eristic, or what Plato—whether historically justified or not—called the sophistic, approach becomes the perversion of an original *dialectical intention* based on *mutual understanding* and *justification* in dialogues. According to Socrates and Plato, in dialectics the agonality of the beginnings of reason transcends the particularity of the individual through the presumption of reason (*Vernunftvermutung*). Dialectics is thus characterized both by a *practical intention*, which aims at mutual understanding and agreement, and a *theoretical intention*, which aims at justification. Mutual understanding, however, is based on a postulate of veracity, whereas justification is based on a postulate of conceptual clarity. In the Platonic λόγον διδόναι ("to give a logos"), both elements, the practical and the theoretical, are united. This makes dialectics in the sense of dialectical intention what it always had been: the essence of the philosophical dialogue. The eristic dialogue, on the other hand, is characterized by the absence of the practical intention and the reduction of the theoretical intention to an "art of contradiction" (ἀντιλογικὴ τέχνη), that is, the deduction of contradictions.

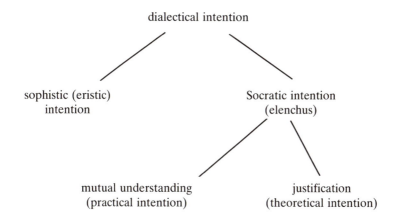

In Socratic dialogue (or in the Socratic form of a dialectical intention) the actual goal of any philosophical activity, a *philosophical orientation*, is already reached in the approach itself and not just by acquiring material knowledge. Doing something better and not knowing something better is what overcomes the sophistic intention. Dialectics in the Socratic-Platonic sense is not just a *form of argumentation* but also essentially a (philosophical) *form of life* (*Lebensform*).

Whereas Plato, in keeping with the Socratic orientation, attempts to present the *practical* beginnings of reason in its dialectical form, Aristotle presents its *theoretical* beginnings: the presumption of reason (*Vernunftvermutung*) is justified by explicating epistemologically the thesis that all men by nature seek knowledge (*Met.* A, 980a1). At the same time, by characterizing dialectics as "thinking in alternatives,"[7] Aristotle retains the dialectical origins of philosophical knowledge and the use of practical postulates to determine a philosophical orientation. Because men, as Heraclitus had already said, know neither what they do nor what they say, philosophical dialogue is the best place for realizing this anthropological embarrassment and overcoming it by developing a philosophical orientation. This constitutes once again, even in Aristotle, the agonality inherent in the beginnings of reason.

III

Plato's anamnesis theorem (knowledge as recollection) does not postulate a hidden world of the mind but instead preserves the constructive nature of theoretical knowledge and the imputation of autonomy (*Autonomie-unterstellung*). It uses the idea of "theoria" and independent learning in order to supplement the dialectical model of knowledge acquisition and the beginnings of reason.

Whoever reads about the problem of knowledge acquisition in the Platonic dialogues, particularly the so-called Socratic dialogues, will also find a completely different model accounting for the beginnings of reason. This model is based on the notion of "recollection" (*anamnesis*). In the anamnesis model reason begins "in the soul" and through contemplation and not, as in the dialectical model, "in speech" or "in conflict." Whoever has the best memory, not who "knows how to ask and answer questions," is on the right path. It seems as if the epistemological die is cast even before the philosophical subject begins to concern himself dialectically with a rational orientation and the acquisition of knowledge. Whoever reads Plato's doctrine of anamnesis that way, however, has the wording on his side, but possibly not the Platonic insight connected with the wording. This can be readily illustrated by examining the context in which this central aspect of Plato's epistemology is introduced.

In the *Meno* the central problem is whether or not virtue can be taught. But before the question can be answered, Socrates and his friends must first explain what virtue is. Plato approaches the problem of whether it is possible to seek what one does not know (in this case a clear understanding of virtue) by elaborating his anamnesis doctrine: the acquisition of knowledge through recollection. He uses a geometry problem—doubling a quadrangle—to show how it is possible to recollect knowledge (*Meno* 82b–85b). Socrates helps someone with no knowledge of geometry to solve this problem not by *teaching* him but *argumentatively*. For Plato the subject's problem-solving knowledge is explainable in terms of prenatal knowledge. The soul recollects this knowledge when encountering empirical objects (figures drawn in the sand) and empirical actions (constructive actions dealing with such illustrative figures). At first sight this actually seems like mythical anthropology put to epistemological ends, particularly since (in the *Phaedo*) the theory of anamnesis is presented in the context of an attempt to prove the existence of immortality. In the Book 10 of the *Republic* a mythical wanderer, the Pamphylian Er, who is given the chance to return to earth from the underworld in order to explain the astronomical system, recollects what he has seen.

But this is only a metaphorical representation. What is actually involved in the Platonic anamnesis theorem has nothing to do with retaining an archaic conception of rebirth in epistemological contexts but with three things, all of which were probably equally important to Plato: (1) the solution of an actual problem in geometry (this is relevant for the history of mathematics); (2) the representation of theoretical contexts and theoretical objects with respect to empirical contexts and empirical objects (this aspect is relevant for the development of the Platonic theory of ideas— ideas as the archetypes of empirical objects—as well as for supplementing epistemologically the concept of the theoretical proposition with the concept of the theoretical object);[8] and (3) the conception of the idea of independent learning (this is relevant for the development of the idea of a philosophical subject as the subject of knowledge acquisition). All three aspects, however, are not opposed to but correlate with the dialectical conception of the connection between the production and reproduction of knowledge. The anamnesis fiction, which allows the acquisition of knowledge to appear as the reassurance of what one already knows, guarantees the constructive character of theoretical knowledge and the *imputation of autonomy (Autonomieunterstellung)*. It is *our* constructions that constitute theoretical knowledge—that is, we derive our knowledge neither from the obtrusiveness of things nor from the "moods of the Gods," but only from ourselves. What we *do* we are "already capable of" and what we *perceive* we "already know." References to "another place" where the soul has already "seen" what constitutes knowledge in actual problem-solving situations[9] are nothing other than metaphorical expressions of a *theoretical* achievement with respect to the objectivity of (especially theoretical) knowledge and a *practical* achievement with respect to the subjectivity of knowledge acquisition and its autonomous structures. Theoria, in the Platonic and Aristotelian sense, serves as a representation for this achievement. Anamnesis, in other words, is not a theory about a hidden world of the mind but rather a metaphorical formulation of the beginnings of reason and the form of knowledge that is compatible with the dialectical model. The "Platonism" of Plato's anamnesis theorem is an invention of Platonism and its opponents.

What I have tried to show is that the Socratic maxim of learned ignorance (like that of Cusanus' *docta ignorantia*) is not opposed to the anamnesis theorem. Just as the question presupposes a certain horizon of knowledge, a framelike understanding of situations and oneself, so realizing one's own ignorance presupposes a prior knowledge of whatever is in question. And just as someone asks a question because he no longer knows or does not yet know something (although he knows what the question involves, what "is in question"), so someone like Socrates in the Socratic dialogues knows what to look for by recognizing his own ignorance. Recognizing one's own ignorance is not the "end" of an effort (as in the eristic dialogue) but a stage in the acquisition of knowledge. What we do not know is part of our knowledge, but a dialectical part. It is, in fact, the very same Socrates who advocates both the maxim of learned ignorance and the anamnesis theorem. Socrates, like Plato, is no "Platonist."

What is more important than the compatibility of maxim and theorem when examining the constitutive nature of philosophical dialogue is the fact that in Socratic dialogue the processes of knowledge acquisition are primarily conceived of as developmental processes, that is, as processes in which not only objectively valid knowledge but also subjective autonomy is produced. According to Socrates and Plato, knowledge cannot be divorced from the individual who knows something or acquires knowledge. This is true at least for philosophical knowledge. Behind this is the insight that knowledge has something to do with the life of an individual, with his (subjective) autonomy. In other words, the Socratic-Platonic concept of a *person* is defined in terms of achievements that are the practical and theoretical parts of knowledge acquisition processes. This is also the origin of the so-called intellectualism of Socratic ethics—the assertion that one cannot act against one's better knowledge or judgment, at least not without endangering the unity of person and action.

IV

In Socratic dialogue the beginnings of reason do not have their origins in reference to someone else's or to one's own authority. "To orient oneself in thought (in dialogue)" means finding together with others the place where reason resides. It does not mean putting oneself in someone else's place.

In the Platonic theory of philosophical dialogue the maieutic model of knowledge acquisition and of the beginnings of reason is connected both systematically and genetically to the anamnetic model. According to the principle of independent learning, the Platonic Socrates does not teach; he only assists, although in such a way that the dialogue, which helps one to acquire both knowledge and reason, is understandable as a learning process. Here the Socratic maxim of learned ignorance appears to be the central aspect of an *epistemological maieutic*. The function of this maieutic is to make methodical the transition from a state of mere opinion where people do not realize what they do or say, and from an eristically induced aporia where opinions as well as apparent knowledge are questionable, to a state of knowledge acquisition. The Socratic role is that of one who keeps the process of inquiry going and who assists it by disrupting one's apparent sense of security (Socrates as "electric ray"; *Meno* 80a–d) and by helping someone become more independent (Socrates as "midwife"; *Theae.* 148d–151d). That the Platonic Socrates knows more than he is willing to admit is insignificant from a systematic point of view. The aim of whoever adopts the role of the epistemic maieutic is actually to make himself superfluous.

It would be misleading to see in the reserved epistemic behavior of Plato's Socrates only the actions of a philosophical manipulator who keeps the dialogue going by keeping what he knows to himself. Quite the opposite is, in fact, the case. What is at stake with reference to the constitution of philosophical dialogue is the rejection of references not only to the authority of *others* (including commonly held opinions) but also to the authority of *oneself* as detrimental to matters of reason. The essence of rational independence (*vernünftige Selbständigkeit*) that philosophical dialogue should develop is a mode of thought that relies neither on the authority of others nor on the authority of oneself. One of the difficulties involved in philosophical dialogue, in other words, is that of *not putting oneself in someone else's place* when the aim is to "orient oneself in thought." This is so, provided, of course, that what is involved in the philosophical dialogue is not the transfer of accepted knowledge from one individual to another but the beginnings of reason and the entry into an independent acquisition of knowledge, or, in short, a philosophical orientation. Philosophical dialogue is that anthropological place where the attempt is made within the limits of a process of knowledge acquisition to cause both the singularity of others as well as *one's own singularity* to disappear. That the individuals themselves do not disappear, that is, that a properly understood subjectivity is not sacrificed, is an additional property of philosophical dialogue. This is in fact what distinguishes it, for example, from meditation, where the individual loses himself altogether by abandoning his own aims.

The subject in philosophical dialogue is the philosopher—although not as *magister artium* but as Socrates' partner in dialogue. The Platonic definition of the philosophical dialogue in dialectic, anamnetic, and maieutic terms also requires a certain amount of modesty. Approaching the idea of the rational being that philosophical dialogue should further is not possible without a significant restriction of worldly perspectives for both participants and nonparticipants, as the Platonic caricature in the *Theaetetus* reveals. Philosophers "have never known the way to marketplace" (*Theae.* 173d); "to take any interest in . . . merrymakings with flute-girls, never occurs to them even in dreams" (*Theae.* 173d); their soul "takes wings, as Pindar says, 'beyond the sky, beneath the earth,' " while only their body resides in the city (*Theae.* 173e). Ever since Plato gave philosophical expression to the story about Thales, who fell into a well and was soundly ridiculed by a Thracian maidservant because his star-gazing prevented him from seeing what lay before his feet, the anecdote has become a symbol of the philosopher whom "the whole rabble will join the maidservants in laughing at" and who "as from inexperience . . . walks blindly and stumbles into every pitfall" (*Theae.* 174c). But Thales is also a symbol for that which— unnoticed by Thracian maidservants and what one would call common (and practical) sense—does not become "dizzy from the heights" when the subject is justice and injustice or fortune and misery (*Theae.* 175c–d). Walking upright often leads into "pitfalls" and "all sorts of other embarrassments," but according to Plato, it also leads in "this region of our mortal nature" to our "becoming like God" (*Theae.* 176b). Once again, however, one should be wary of false hopes. Even the Greek gods, if one can believe those who tell the stories, could not avoid Thalean misfortunes in the "region of mortal nature." This in turn makes them like us, who are so unlike them. A philosophical orientation is apparently something that has to be left to men and gods—although with a slight advantage (from a Greek perspective) for mortals with respect to their willingness and ability to enter into a philosophical dialogue.

V

Philosophy cannot be spoken (in the form of textbook knowledge) but only practiced (in the form of philosophical dialogues or the realization of a philosophical orientation). Philosophy is an argumentative action conducted under the perspective of reason (*Vernunftperspektive*) and hence a form of life.

If philosophical dialogue is a medium for the (philosophical) acquisition of knowledge and the development of a philosophical orientation, then it exists as a concrete dialogue. The reason is itself dialogical: the written word does not answer. "Once a thing is put in writing, the composition, whatever it may be, drifts all over the place, getting into the hands not only of those who understand it, but equally of those who have no business with it."[10] This means first of all that what constitutes a dialogue is the possibility of questioning and answering. When nothing is questioned and nothing answered, a dialogue crosses over directly into inquiry or *research*. The results of research can be written down, but not in a strict sense the process of research. A *pragmatic* perspective is particularly important in this respect. What is involved are not meanings—that is, the semantic level—but the development of dialogues and, indirectly, of research. This leads, second, to Plato's thesis that philosophy "cannot be put into words" (*Letter* VII 341c). Where philosophy is put into words—written down—what is said loses its pragmatic connection with the situation (the dialogue) in which it is spoken. Even considering the potentially *exemplary* character of such a situation—clearly indicated in the written Platonic dialogues—the written word frees itself from its original context: it "drifts all over the place." It cannot adopt the role of philosophical dialogue—namely, that of providing a philosophical orientation. At best it does this only in the form of a report. It conveys meaning, not practice.[11]

In addition, what distinguishes philosophical knowledge from mere opinion in the context of an oral dialogue is lost in a written context. The communicability of philosophical knowledge through writing is purchased, according to Plato, at the expense of a transformation of knowledge into opinion. Where the pragmatic context is missing, the philosophical dialogue loses its characteristic function—to turn opinions into habitual knowledge, that is, into parts of a philosophical orientation. Only pragmatically do knowledge and opinions have a different structure; semantically they have the same. In this sense, philosophy is for Plato always *an argumentative action conducted under the perspective of reason* or, as it was termed under the heading of "dialectic," a *form of life*. The opposite of this form of philosophy is the monological meditation—in Plato's realm of experience this would be Heraclitus' "deep" thoughts—and the eristic controversy—represented in Plato's realm of experience by the sophists.

Accordingly, the Platonic critique of the written word no longer indicates the systematically incomplete character of Plato's dialogues, often maintained under the heading of "the unwritten doctrine."[12] Instead, it indicates the insight, represented ("made sensible" in the written word) through the chosen dialogue form, that philosophical knowledge—that is, a philosophical orientation realized through the concrete philosophical dialogue—cannot be transformed into textbook knowledge. For this reason, Plato also distinguishes between the knowledge (ἐπιστήμη) of the sciences and a dialectical knowledge (τοῦ διαλέγεσθαι ἐπιστήμη; *Rep.* 511b–c) without, however, making the current distinction between science and philosophy. This distinction stems from a semantic misunderstanding concerning different types of propositions: empirical and analytical propositions on the one side and metaphysical propositions on the other. What this actually means is that only the dialectical treatment of knowledge turns it into what it should be, according to Plato—namely, philosophical knowledge. Plato wants to show that orientation in the scientific acquisition of knowledge should be philosophical and that the conception of knowledge acquisition should be supplemented again by its dialectical beginnings. In this sense what at first sight seems so speculative—Plato's conception of the "idea of the Good" which guarantees both the "truth of things" as well as the "ability to know" (*Rep.* 508d–509b)—means nothing other than that the practical and theoretical aims of the dialectic should be realized in scientific knowledge. Plato's famous critique of mathematicians, which precedes the distinction between scientific and dialectical knowledge (*Rep.* 510c–e), clearly demonstrates that this supplementation does not mean a loss of scientific rationality but instead makes gaps (in this case, beginnings that are not really beginnings) visible.[13]

This also restrains the impression that philosophy is esoteric, suggested by the expression that philosophy "cannot be put into words." What is significant here are neither experiences that are remote from any form of control nor higher forms of knowledge accessible only to the initiated but the transmission of *attitudes* that should promote reason, as well as reason in the sciences. Thus, the λόγον διδόναι ("to give a logos"), that is, the emphasis on a *grounding obligation* (*Begründungsverpflichtung*) which includes both practical and theoretical elements, is not only a central aspect of Plato's philosophy but also part of his critique of mathematicians. As such this obligation is not at all *esoteric* since it can be applied to every form of knowledge acquisition. But it is also not purely *methodological* since adopting it depends on goodwill and so on the entry into the philosophical orientation that accompanies it. It is philosophical dialogue that leads to the adoption of such an obligation. The adoption cannot be demonstrated.

Today one refers at this point in ethics to "traces of decisionism," that is, to a "decision" in favor of reason.[14] From a Socratic-Platonic perspective this is seeing something correctly, but often it also gives a false impression. No demonstration and no *deduction* lead to a philosophical orientation. It is incorrect that the entry into a philosophical orientation is of the same order as an unpremeditated act (in the sense of "I do it because I want to"). Even the reference to an entry is, strictly speaking, misleading. In reality such a point of entry can never be isolated, not even in a philosophical dialogue. On the contrary, a philosophical dialogue must *show* through itself that a philosophical orientation exists and that the participants in a philosophical dialogue realize a philosophical orientation. More than this cannot be *said* about an individual's reason.

VI

Dialogical knowledge can only be presented in a dialogue. Whereas textbooks and philosophical treatises have to be systematically comprehensive, the literary (philosophical) dialogue "transports" experiences with thinking and with a philosophical orientation in a way that is both exemplary and makes the universal concrete.

By representing the philosophical acquisition of knowledge as a form of *dialogical knowledge*, Plato can acknowledge the view that philosophy cannot be put into words without having to dispense with that possibility of transmitting a philosophical orientation. In view of the Socratic practice of conducting dialogues, Plato represents in his dialogues his own *experience* with this practice. This is theoretically consistent and quite sensible from a literary point of view. The dialogue form, particularly when philosophical texts are involved, is capable of partially suspending its own textual character. The reader is drawn into the dialogue through identification and critical appraisal, even if what is involved has for the most part less to do with co-argumentation than with illusion. In other words, the dialogue is that form of writing best suited to mediate between the pursuit of a philosophical orientation and the process of reception. Any possibility of confusion with textbook knowledge is excluded. Aporetic structures underline the situation-variant character of a philosophy that seeks to transport not objective knowledge but philosophical attitudes.

The choice of the dialogue form that is based on the Platonic definition of philosophy as an argumentative action also provides from the perspective of reason certain advantages in presenting material that the otherwise common textbook or treatise forms do not possess. A Platonic dialogue allows the following. First, certain questions or problems can be excluded in the event that these cannot or cannot yet be dealt with in an acceptable way. Second, opinions, commonly accepted knowledge, and scientific knowledge can be presented without having to take an explicit stand. Third, one's own position can be kept in the background (this is the case in Plato's dialogues when there is a discrepancy between his position and that adopted by Socrates or when his own position has not yet been formulated in a discussable form). In all these cases what cannot or should not be discussed is simply not mentioned in the dialogue. There is no obligation to be systematically comprehensive, as is the case with textbooks and treatises. A dialogue, however, also allows, fourth, the revision of positions in the course of their formulation without having to rewrite the preceding sections that are no longer "correct" or can no longer be supported (again the contrast to the systematic character of textbooks or treatises, which do not allow one to say on page 188 that one made a mistake on page 73). And finally, fifth, a dialogue permits the use of literary techniques such as situational descriptions (essential for presenting philosophical knowledge as dialogic knowledge), irony, and mythical stories without breaking with the literary form. For example, the surprising number of myths in the Platonic dialogues help, on the one hand, to illustrate or explain in ways that cannot be accomplished dialogically. Myths are also used to present material that is not yet available in a systematically controllable form, such as the discussion about the soul and its immortality in the *Phaedo* and in the *Phaedrus*.

The advantages offered by the dialogue form by no means free the (written) philosophical dialogue only from the systematic constraints of textbooks and treatises. It also copes effectively with the dogmatic tendencies that are part of such systematic constraints. Theoretical (dogmatic) comprehensiveness is now replaced by exemplary presentation as an essential aspect of the philosophical acquisition of knowledge and its literary transmission. The dialogue transmits less theoretical than *exemplary* knowledge, a knowledge the acquisition of which the reader (as dialogical self) can identify with and which he can even continue (something other literary forms such as the novel and drama do not give rise to). Thus it coincides particularly well with the Aristotelian characterization of poetry as being "more philosophical" than the writing of history (*Art. Poet.* 9.145b5–6). Philosophical dialogue does this by representing the *universal*, here in the form of a philosophical orientation. The function of philosophical dialogue in exemplifying and making the universal *concrete* places it between the factual dialogue, in which philosophy is not spoken but performed, and the scientific text, which is incapable of transmitting a philosophical orientation by itself. According to Plato, the written philosophical dialogue renders in an exemplary way a philosophical *dialogical experience (Dialogerfahrung)*. By doing this it can also teach (indirectly) what "philosophy" is.

VII

Reason cannot be demonstrated; it reveals itself in philosophical dialogue. It is essentially dialogical reason just as transsubjectivity (as the content of the philosophical orientation) is a product of individuals, of subjectivity in the *Lebenswelt*.

References to Socratic dialogue imply that the development of a philosophical orientation and a philosophical subject is connected with the philosophical acquisition of knowledge. Only through a philosophical orientation and through subjects standing in such an orientation can knowledge be acquired philosophically. This constitutes the idea of philosophical dialogue in the Socratic and Platonic understanding of philosophy. It also indicates the extent to which processes of knowledge acquisition must be conceived of first and foremost as developmental processes. This conception, however, is not only suitable for transmitting a better understanding of philosophy and philosophical inquiry. It can also be applied to an analysis of the conditions constituting nonphilosophical knowledge. For example, it is part of the concept of the *reconstruction* of scientific knowledge that this knowledge is conceivable as a product both of *historical* as well as *argumentative* processes. All knowledge has a history and, in Platonic terms, a dialectical structure. With the distinction between internal and external history, such a conception was also adopted by the contemporary theory of the history of science. In Lakatos' writings it even determines the form of presentation. In the context of historical case studies in mathematics, for example, a dialogue between teacher and pupils constitutes the internal history (for example, of the Descartes-Eulerian theorem, which states that, for any simple polyhedron, $V - E + F = 2$, where V, E, and F are the number of vertices, edges, and faces, respectively), whereas historical and biographical information, which in this conception constitutes the external history, is placed in the footnotes.[15] The dialogue is not simply external to the presentation but reflects the inner structure of scientific developments ("the dialogue form should reflect the dialectic of the story").[16]

What holds for scientific developments is particularly true of philosophical developments. These are, in fact, scarcely understandable without the use of dialectical orientations—that is, without the implication that their acquisition of knowledge is based on the structure of dialogical relations. This is the case even when their (historical) appearances tend to indicate the opposite and philosophical developments almost appear as monuments of monological isolation.

The applicability of the dialogical model of knowledge constitution to scientific and philosophical developments is, however, not the decisive aspect. If it should prove to be absent, this does not mean that the Socratic conception of philosophical dialogue is itself obsolete. What is decisive is that according to this conception philosophical dialogue and only philosophical dialogue is capable of sustaining and realizing the presumption of reason (*Vernunftvermutung*). Reason is not something that can be demonstrated in just any way; it is something that *reveals* itself in a philosophical dialogue. It reveals itself in properly understood agonality: the subjects work off their subjectivity. *Transsubjectivity* as the content of the philosophical orientation is thus always an achievement of *concrete subjects*; otherwise it would not be distinguishable from objectivity as a characteristic of instrumental knowledge. In other words, transsubjectivity is something that only subjects, only the concrete subjectivity (in the Lebenswelt) are capable of. Philosophical dialogue is concerned neither with demonstrating subjective superiority (in the pursuit of the sophistic intention) nor with merely exchanging opinions, but rather with establishing a philosophical orientation and the transsubjectivity of philosophical subjects (the Socratic intention). Philosophical dialogue is thus the medium for what Plato calls "living in philosophy" (*Theae.*, 174a–b). Philosophy is here understood, once again, not as a model of knowledge acquisition designed to compete with the sciences but as a *form of life*.

Part of this life form is also philosophical inquiry (or philosophical research) in the form of theoretical elaborations (for example, in logic, ethics, and the philosophy of science), limited by restrictions that *dialogical reason*, that is, reason revealed only in the dialogue, itself determines. Its limits are the limits of transsubjectivity, not limits of things or of methods. This in no way contradicts the principle openness of the dialogue that lies in its form. Philosophical dialogue, therefore, also demonstrates the principle openness of philosophical inquiry. It is impossible to take a final stand on a philosophical orientation.

Against the background of his experience with Socratic dialogue, Plato made the idea of philosophical dialogue the essence of philosophy. But as he did so he gradually began to make philosophical inquiry independent of the form of life of which, in its Socratic form, it is a part. Besides passing on the Socratic dialogue experience, there is also the constitution of philosophical knowledge which to an increasing degree masks its place in a life form, although still retaining cooperative perspectives. The Socratic unity of the philosophical orientation now moves into the background. In the course of the history of philosophy the danger of shifting from dialogically or dialectically *systematic thinking* to monological *thinking in systems* begins to overshadow the original Platonic idea of the philosophical acquisition of knowledge. Platonism overtakes Plato.

According to Gilbert Ryle, it is the university that competes with Platonism: "The impersonality of Plato's late dialogues, like that of Aristotle's lectures, reflects the emergence of philosophy as an inquiry with an impetus, with techniques and even with an academic curriculum of its own. Plato is now creating professional philosophical prose. As disputing for the sake of victory gives way to discussion for the sake of discovery, so the literature of the elenctic duel gives way to the literature of cooperative philosophical investigation. The university has come into being."[17] This is a university in which a philosophical orientation also begins to disappear together with the philosophical dialogue. The university in our time still has philosophy (as one subject among others), but—Socrates and Plato help us, and Kant, Fichte and Hegel as well—it has no longer any philosophical orientation. For this reason, our attempt at explaining the Socratic dialogue is probably more a contribution to the past than to the present state of philosophy and the university.

9

Plato's Metaphilosophy: Why Plato Wrote Dialogues

Charles L. Griswold, Jr.

Why did Plato write *dialogues*? To oversimplify somewhat, at least three types of answers seem possible. The first focuses on the demands of pedagogy. Plato wrote dialogues, we are told, because he thought them effective in getting potential philosophers engaged in the search for truth. If he were writing for fellow philosophers already well on their way to the truth, the dialogue form would be optional, if it were not actually an obstacle to a precise articulation of the subject matter.

The second type of answer would have us focus on political considerations. Plato wrote in a way that allowed him both to present unorthodox points of view and to escape the fate of Socrates. Authorial anonymity, estericism, and irony would be heavily stressed in such an account.

The third type of answer focuses on various philosophical reasons for Plato's exceptional adherence to the dialogue form. In this chapter I shall argue for a version of this type of answer. My line of reasoning attributes philosophical significance to the oddly occasional and provisional character that Plato gave to his written dialogues; to Plato's anonymity vis-à-vis the dramatis personae in his compositions; to the role of irony; to his obsession with refuting sophists, poets, popular rhetoricians, and other critics of philosophy; and finally to his decision to make the origination of philosophy an omnipresent theme. I shall argue that Plato *must* write dialogues, and indeed dialogues possessing characteristics such as those just mentioned,

An earlier version of this chapter was published in *Platonic Investigations*, ed. D. O'Meara (Washington, D.C.: Catholic University of America Press, 1985), pp. 1–33. My thanks to the publisher for permission to reprint.

if he is to avoid begging the question when maintaining that the philosophically unexamined life is not worth living for a human being. In a moment I shall explain the connection between that argument and the issue of "metaphilosophy."

The whole issue of the role of "dialogue" or "dialectic" (for now I will not distinguish between them) in philosophy has recently come to the fore once again thanks to the criticisms of nondialectical, systematic rationality put forward by (if I may vastly oversimplify the genealogy) descendants of both Nietzsche (such as Heidegger, Gadamer, Derrida, Foucault, and Rorty) and Hegel (such as Rescher and Habermas), as well as by philosophers of science such as Kuhn and Feyerabend. These critics themselves fall into at least two major camps, the one (to which Rorty and Derrida belong) hostile to philosophy as such, the other critical of nondialectical philosophy but partisan to dialectical philosophy (Hegel, Rescher). Thus, in spite of their common opposition to nondialectical philosophizing, these two camps have a debate of their own. This second debate is more radical than the debate between dialectical and nondialectical philosophers because it concerns the viability of philosophy *simpliciter*. I believe that an understanding of these two levels of debate can be of considerable assistance in clarifying why Plato wrote dialogues. Since the philosophical issue at stake concerns the nature of philosophy itself, the debates are metaphilosophical in character.

I will begin by establishing a working definition of "metaphilosophy." Having then discussed the two metalevel debates, I shall try to show how sound metaphilosophical considerations make Plato's choice of the dialogue form and the associated phenomena intelligible. This demonstration will require a fairly detailed discussion of several other figures in the history of philosophy. After arguing that dialogue carries with it important ontological commitments, in the final section of this chapter I discuss the Platonic response to Richard Rorty's notion of "conversation." The general form of my argument looks like an example of "rational reconstruction." I do believe, however, that there is sufficient evidence in Plato's dialogues to indicate that the argument I will be presenting was, in general outline, understood and endorsed by Plato.

I

The term *metaphilosophy* is a recent invention. It seems to have been coined by, not surprisingly, a follower of the later Wittgenstein, in order to refer to the "investigation of the nature of philosophy, with the central aim of arriving at a satisfactory explanation of the absence of uncontested philosophical claims and arguments."[1] The prefix *meta* had, of course, long since been put to work by philosophers intent on carving out a discipline that is one step above, or prior to, its object. The term *metacritique*, for example, was used by Herder in this sense.[2] Even the term *metaphysics* is used by Kant in the distinctly non-Aristotelian and by now familiar sense of "the study of the conditions for the possibility of" a given science. Indeed, Kant repeatedly remarks that the *Kritik der reinen Vernunft* (*KRV*) is itself an example of the new "metaphysics" (for example, B22–24, A841 = B869 ff.; see also Axix–xxi). Kant also characterizes the *Critique* as a "treatise on the method" (Bxxii) whose purpose is to determine the limits of reason in advance of particular attempts to reason. Since reason itself undertakes this task, Kant holds that in the *Critique* reason is "occupied only with itself" (A680). Since reason alone can judge of itself, all claims to knowledge are brought before it as before a "tribunal" (Axi, A751 = B779). Knowledge of "transcendental" rules or concepts will thus perform a veridical function (B26).

The second level, or transcendental, focus of "criticism" requires a concentration on *form*. The *KRV* studies our (formal) knowledge of objects, not objects themselves, a knowledge that is not itself an "object" in the same sense (A402). This metalevel project thus consists, as Kant repeatedly says with respect to reason's "critique" of itself, in *self-knowledge* (Axi, A735 = B763, A849 = B877). The project thus seems fully in keeping with the *goal* of philosophy as traditionally understood.

In the simplest terms, metaphilosophy is the effort to philosophize about *how* we reason about things and so to understand, "before" we reason about them, what we can and cannot know. Thus metaphilosophy in the primary sense of the term is naturally understood within the Kantian framework just adumbrated. This framework, anticipated by Descartes (and still more clearly by Locke), is definitive of a great deal of modern philosophy, according to modern philosophers themselves. The rise of the notion of subjectivity, the emphasis on certainty as a criterion of knowing, the description of knowledge in terms of formal rules and concepts, the thesis that knowledge is an instrument or *techne*, as well as the concern for method, system, scientific procedure—all characterize the tradition derived from the Cartesian-Kantian "turn" to a metaphilosophical interpretation of the Delphic "know thyself." Although Kant in particular denies that this amounts to a metaphysics of the self in the classical sense (the *Paralogisms* is an attack on the possibility of such a project), he admits that the "transcendental conditions" of knowledge are, in some difficult to define sense, "in us."

The metalevel study of the conditions of our knowledge of objects cannot, as I have already suggested, list these same objects *as* conditions, unless it is to move in a circle. Hence the turn to metaphilosophy results in something like the substitution of "epistemology" for "ontology," or at least the view that the former is logically prior to the latter (*KRV*,A247-B303). This is why metaphilosophy has an endlessly "preparatory" or "anticipatory" nature (*KRV*,B26). Of course, even *this* tradition of modern philosophy is full of revolutions and counterrevolutions. But there is a family resemblance between them; the quarrel is an intramural one. Each new claim to legitimate rule rests on an intensification of the "critical" turn; new, more rigorously drawn limits (whether "transcendental," "logical," "categorial," or "linguistic") of reason are constantly touted, and the work of one's predecessors rejected as sloppy, speculative, unscientific, guilty of transgressing the bounds of what is knowable, and so forth.[3] Even the history of German idealism, I think, should be read in this way.[4]

In my opinion, the logic behind this turn to "critical" philosophizing— that is, to metaphilosophy—is very persuasive. There really is a problem concerning *beginnings* in philosophy, and metaphilosophy concentrates on this problem directly. Moreover, there would simply seem to be a difference between knowledge claims that are *made* and those that are *used* in the claims themselves, between claims made on the "object level" and evidence used to support the claims, or between what Hegel calls the "truth" and "knowledge" of claims. Still further, there would seem to be a difference between, on the one hand, the metalevel rules that allow one to define the problem or area one wishes to investigate, the rules for investigation, as well as the rules that determine when the investigation is complete, and, on the other hand, the investigation itself. Just as (to use one of Kant's own analogies) a language possesses a grammar containing its rules, so knowledge claims possess a metaphilosophy (a "transcendental grammar") containing the rules for making knowledge claims. This argument looks like a distant epigone of the Platonic demand for an "ascent" to the forms.[5]

In sum, before we make a claim to know an object, we must know our knowledge of this object (*KRV*, A11 = B25). Arguments *ad rem*, that is, prove little in philosophy; they do not answer the *quid iuris* question. Philosophers must first locate the *arche*, and this arche (starting point) seems necessarily to be a "concept" of knowledge, not of being. For, to repeat, every statement about "what is" is an implicit knowledge claim, which therefore reflects assumptions we are making in formulating the claim. Moreover, it does seem to be a distinguishing mark of philosophy to be self-reflexive; while other branches of knowledge cannot serve as the instruments for self-reflection (there is no biology of biology, only a philosophy of biology), philosophy alone possesses this capacity. So persuasive is this formulation of the self-knowledge issue that most modern interpreters of ancient philosophy assume without further ado that Plato too *must* have had an "epistemology," in however primitive a form. It is thus typical to find modern philosophers construing the history of philosophy as a continuous development toward the goal they believe themselves to have reached: namely, that of specifying the "architectonic" (for example, *KRV*, A856 = B884 and context), the "logic," "syntax," or the "grammar" of reason. Critical metaphilosophy, in short, seems to be an intensification (and inevitably also a correction) of philosophy as traditionally understood.[6]

Our metaphilosophically oriented philosophers also claim that there is no way of ending the proverbial disputes of the philosophers,[7] of distinguishing between defensible and indefensible philosophies,[8] or of answering skepticism convincingly,[9] unless some new, more self-conscious "method" is brought to light (*KRV*, A751 = B779 ff.). The reasoning here is, again, persuasive.

II

I would like to bring this discussion to bear on Plato. We should admit from the start, I think, that judged by the standards of metaphilosophy, Plato seems hopelessly naive and clumsy. His dialogues contain no systematic doctrine of logic or of the a priori principles of knowledge. Plato does not even furnish us, as Aristotle does in Book VIII of the *Topics*, with a systematic analysis of dialectical reasoning. Most of Plato's discussions about the nature of philosophy are framed against a moral or political canvas, and so avoid the purely theoretical discussions we would expect from a self-conscious thinker. The Platonic discussions of the matter tend also to be stated in a literary or poetic form (philosophy is "midwifery," and so forth), and so fail to measure up, as Hegel and countless others have said, to the demands of "scientific" thinking.[10] That is, there is a close connection between Plato's dialogue form of writing and his seeming inarticulateness in metaphilosophical matters. The one dialogue that would have dealt directly with metaphilosophical problems, namely the *Philosopher*, was never written, although it is promised in the *Sophist* and *Statesman*. And on the occasion when Plato brings the mature Socrates together with the one person competent to enter into a good metaphilosophical discussion with him, namely the Eleatic Stranger, Plato has Socrates sit in virtual silence. Yet this is the only time in the Platonic dialogues in which two mature philosophers are brought together.[11]

To be sure, there are indications in the dialogues that Plato understood, in principle, what a Kantian "critique" would be like. The discussion in the *Charmides* about an "episteme of episteme," and the various descriptions in the later dialogues about the "method of division and collection," constitute some evidence of that. But the *Charmides* ends in aporia, self-reflexive episteme is dismissed as an impossibility, and the method of division and collection never replaces for long the haphazard movement

of dialogue. In the *Theaetetus* Plato seems to be groping for an epistemology, but of course that dialogue also ends in aporia. There are some
statements in the dialogues that look like fragments of an epistemology,
such as the occasional talk about "ἀνάμνησις" (recollection), about the
difference between knowledge and belief (δόξα), and so on. But such talk
is often cast in the form of a myth (as in the *Phaedrus*) and is never
presented systematically and in a manner that is unencumbered by digressions, rhetorical pronouncements, in short by the whole "dramatic" dimension. The incomplete epistemological doctrines even seem to change
throughout Plato's career. None of this constitutes a reason for dismissing
the epistemological (or metaphysical) passages in the dialogues as unimportant. But these passages are radically unsatisfactory from a metaphilosophical point of view.

Still more important, we repeatedly find that in his discussions about
knowledge Plato just *assumes* or *asserts* that the Ideas exist, and *then*
explains what "knowledge" is (for example, *Rep.* 476a ff., 507a–b ff., 596a
and context; *Pho.* 100b ff.). We do not seem to get an account of how we
know these ontological assumptions to be true. Indeed, one is justified in
wondering whether Plato has a "theory" of Ideas at all.[12] Thus in the
Phaedrus, for example, Episteme is listed as one of the Ideas, the knowledge of which is the province of godly souls especially (247c–e and context).
But in the *Phaedrus* little thought seems given to working out how we
could claim to "know" even an Idea of Knowledge, or rather, to how we
could know we know it. Similarly, the sun/Good analogy in the *Republic*,
and the image of the Divided Line, do explain something about our knowledge, but without explaining how we know this very analogy to be true.
In any case, the "ontological" principles of the *Phaedrus* and *Republic*
seem to be beyond the grasp of merely mortal intellects. Correspondingly,
the Platonic dialogues never supply us with a thorough discussion of the
nature of "dialectic" (cf. *Rep.* 532e–533a; *Phr.* 266b8–9 and context). To
these points we must add that Plato's dialogues evidence a studious and
frustrating avoidance of "technical" terminology. There is no Platonic an-
alogue to book Delta of Aristotle's *Metaphysics*.

In sum, Plato's dialogues seem both fantastically naive—because of
the absence of systematic reflection on the conditions for the possibility of
knowing, as well as the ubiquity of unproven assumptions about the existence and nature of essences—and utterly inconclusive—because the
assumptions always seem vitiated by the paucity, and poor logical structure,
of arguments in favor of them as well as by the fact that they are presented
in a rhetorical and dramatic context. The result would seem to be, de-
pending which of these aspects one stresses, either dogmatism (supported,
perhaps, by theories about Plato's "secret teaching") or skepticism (knowledge of ignorance, and nothing more). This is precisely the dilemma from

which Kant seeks to extricate both himself and philosophy. The dilemma seems to arise from the fact that Plato has no "critical" metaphilosophy, even though he understood, in broad outlines, the notion itself. When everything is said and done, we seem drawn to the conclusion that Plato philosophizes unselfconsciously.

Having sketched out (in properly dialectical fashion) a negative construal of the failure in Plato's dialogues to pursue systematic and metaphilosophically oriented self-knowledge, I would like now to argue for a positive, and I believe far more persuasive, analysis of the same phenomena. Plato's decision to write dialogues can and should be explained as part of a deliberate and plausible philosophical position. In order to present this interpretation, I would like to return to the two debates referred to at the start of this chapter.

III

In the history of philosophy a movement critical of the very idea that philosophers should, or can, possess a metaphilosophy seems to dog every attempt to formulate one. The "constructive" efforts of the history of philosophy seem always shadowed by ever-present criticisms of "positive" or "systematic" philosophy. In recent years the criticisms have been developed, in a variety of ways and with a variety of intentions, by writers such as Nietzsche, Heidegger, Goodman, Gadamer, Derrida, and Rorty. One perfectly obvious, but very powerful criticism of metaphilosophy may be roughly stated as follows. Metaphilosophy either leads to an infinite regress or begs the question. If a metaphilosophy can itself be reasoned about, then we will require a meta-metaphilosophy, and so on ad infinitum, there being no Archimedean point in philosophy. If we hold at the outset that the principles *about* which we wish to reason are the only principles *for* reasoning, or if we simply stipulate or believe in our metaphilosophical principles, then we are assuming what we want to prove, namely, that our claims to knowledge on the object level are reasonable. Metaphilosophy, after all, is a form of philosophy. That is, we are simply assuming, in advance of metaphilosophical analysis, the very principles that the analysis is supposed to uncover.

That the objection can be made with a variety of intentions is evident from the fact that Hegel—and not just some of the simply antiphilosophical thinkers mentioned above—also made this criticism of Kant. Since I regard Hegel's formulation of the criticism as unanswerable by the nondialectical advocates of metaphilosophy (such as Kant) who wish to avoid the criticism, and since the criticism will shed light on Plato's preference for dialectic, I would like to quote Hegel's own words:

A main line of argument in the Critical Philosophy bids us pause before proceeding to inquire into God or into the true being of things, and tells us first of all to examine the faculty of cognition and see whether it is equal to such an effort. We ought, says Kant, to become acquainted with the instrument, before we undertake the work for which it is to be employed; for if the instrument be insufficient, all our trouble will be spent in vain. The plausibility of this suggestion has won for it general assent and admiration; the result of which has been to withdraw cognition from an interest in its objects and absorption in the study of them, and to direct it back upon itself; and so turn it to a question of form. Unless we wish to be deceived by words, it is easy to see what this amounts to. In the case of other instruments, we can try to criticize them in other ways than by setting about the special work for which they are destined. But the examination of knowledge can only be carried out by an act of knowledge. To examine this so-called instrument is the same thing as to know it. But to seek to know before we know is as absurd as the wise resolution of Scholasticus, not to venture into the water until he had learned to swim.[13]

Hegel does not deny the need for metaphilosophy; on the contrary. But he insists that the project can be completed only dialectically, and correspondingly that the effort to set limits compels us to make increasingly comprehensive claims. Dialectic and the search for wholeness seem closely connected, at least for both Hegel and Plato (see below). Kant's effort to assign dialectical reason a noncognitive status is thus self-defeating. As is clear from Kant's own words, reason's (*Vernunft*) knowledge of the a priori conditions for the understanding (*Verstand*) cannot be obtained within those conditions. *Verstand* is modeled on techne (art, skill); but the knowledge of techne cannot be an example of it. Techne made reflexive negates itself. Hegel's criticism of Kant, and of nondialectical philosophy in general, has this ad hominem structure.

The Hegelian point is, in my opinion, shared by Plato. The least controversial evidence for this claim is the *Charmides'* criticism of an "episteme of episteme" (episteme is said to be analogous here to the techne of mathematics). Socrates seems here to initially equate "episteme of itself, of all other epistemai, and of the lack of episteme" (166e) with self-knowledge and "knowing what you know and do not know," that is, with his regular knowledge of ignorance (for example, 167a–b). However, the two are not the same. Ironically, the very refutation of the "episteme of episteme" formulation *contributes* to the "knowledge of ignorance," and so to the self-knowledge, of those present.[14] As in Hegel's *Phenomenology*, a claim is allowed to "negate" itself and find its "truth" in a larger "whole." The negation is dialectical, and a moment in the larger dialogue. Our efforts to philosophize presuppose an ideal of "wisdom." Further evidence for the thesis that for Plato techne, episteme, or method cannot "ground" itself without integrating itself into a broader conception of knowledge may be found in the *Phaedrus*,[15] as well as in the distinction in the *Republic* between "ascending" dialectic and "descending" techne (511b–c and context). In sum: the criticism of nondialectical philosophy, which has been undertaken with such devastating effects by figures such as Hegel, seems conclusive. This brings us, then, to a more fundamental issue, namely that of the ability of dialectical philosophy to establish *its* own "metaphilosophy" without opening itself to the objections just directed toward the Kantian sort of metaphilosophy.

Hegel agrees that we must appeal to *some* standard in order to be able to say that we know even the conditions of knowledge; he holds, like Kant, that this standard is reason itself. Hegel argues that the efforts of Kant, Fichte, and others to "know" the limits of reason nondialectically, must terminate in a faith (or in some undefinable "intuition") which just stipulates that it "thinks" (perhaps with the putative guarantee of a benevolent God) the conditions of knowledge truly. Stated broadly, Hegel argues that Kant and Fichte share the Enlightenment's characteristic *faith in reason*. This result, Hegel thinks, can be avoided if we understand that the relationship between object- and metalevels of reasoning is itself dialectical. Dialectic is thus the solution to the seemingly impossible effort of philosophers to, as Rescher puts it, "pull ourselves up by our own bootstraps."[16]

As the discussion thus far suggests, the really fundamental dispute is not between Hegel and Kant, between proponents of dialectic and those of nondialectical epistemology, but between the dialecticians and the critics of philosophizing or "reason giving" as such. This latter debate is the second, and deeper, of the two debates I mentioned at the start. As a rule, these critics do not share in the philosopher's faith in reason. Nietzsche and his descendants, for example, fully agree with Hegel's criticisms of Kant and, more broadly, of nondialectical rationality. But they deny that the putative "circularity" or "completeness" of Hegel's system escapes a *petitio principii*. In a by now familiar move, they focus on the supposed *Aufhebung*, in the *Phenomenology of Spirit* and *Encyclopaedia*, of art and religion into "absolute knowledge." They assert that Hegel is simply showing that art and religion contain the "conceptual truth" that he has already read into them. In fact, so the objection runs, art and religion are not really assertions about "conceptual truth" at all. They are simply not continuous with philosophy. It is not the case, they claim, that (to take one example) poems secretly harbor philosophical questions. The questions exist only in the minds of philosophers, and all the grandiose claims made by philosophers on behalf of the supremacy of their questions are self-serving myths.

From this radical standpoint, Hegel's error is the same as that of all philosophers, indeed, of philosophy per se. The error derives from the philosophical effort to impose (and then to pretend to discover) a structure on all spiritual activity, a structure in terms of which philosophy inevitably emerges as dominant. A presupposition of the demand that one give a logos for one's opinions is that there is Truth, and correspondingly that there is a "whole" in terms of which opinions somehow reflect what really *is*. The effort to make the philosopher ruler of the life of the soul begins, so the objection continues, with Plato. Plato's harsh polemics against the poets, the sophists, and those who just do not care about giving reasons for their views—in short, his effort to legitimize the philosopher's *quid iuris* question—simply sets the agenda for all philosophers.[17] The thesis that all significant forms of spiritual activity are incipient forms of philosophy is, we might say, Plato's legacy. Indeed, Nietzsche and Rorty *do* say just this. Socrates too, so Nietzsche argues, has an indefensible, indeed absurd, faith in reason.[18] From the standpoint of the critics of reason, philosophical questions are pseudoquestions not worth asking, questions that carry no weight. Nietzsche argues that we should substitute the "aesthetic" justification of life for the philosophical effort to "justify" by appeals to "grounds" and "conditions."[19] The resolve to live well need not be supported by moralizing or metaphysical and theological considerations. At the very least, then, we seem left with an irreducible pluralism; philosophy is just one form of spiritual activity among others—one form of creativity, perhaps.

That is—to restate the main point of the previous paragraph—the really fundamental debate is the "ancient quarrel between philosophy and poetry," as Socrates puts it in the *Republic* (607b).[20] This remark in the *Republic* (along with its context), as well as many other passages, indicate that Plato understands that his *fundamental* argument is not with other philosophers, let alone with epistemologists, but with the hordes of antiphilosophers. This argument cannot be settled nondialectically (and for reasons I will examine in a moment, it is also very difficult to settle dialectically). I have tried to suggest thus far that the decision to consider the "quarrel" between poets and philosophers as the fundamental dispute makes sense in the light of the general problem of metaphilosophy. From this vantage point, two features of the Platonic dialogues are quite natural.

The first feature is simply the ubiquity of the effort to refute the poets, sophists, and popular rhetoricians in such a way as to justify the activity of philosophy. Both sophists and rhetoricians resemble the philosopher in their love of discourse and in their willingness to talk and dispute about all things (consider *Phil.* 58a–59a, *Rep.* 596c–e, *Grg.* 452e–453a, *Soph.* 232c–233c). Characteristically, however, they care not about the truth but about persuasion. Hence, they are concerned not with giving reasons for insights with the aim of restoring to the soul forgotten knowledge and lost wholeness, but in controversy and refutation for the sake of "goods," such as reputation, wealth, power, and the like. The self-conscious critics of philosophy, to be sure, recognize that no one can escape making assumptions. They offer a variety of reflections on their own assumptions which seem to philosophers to lead to relativism, historicism, or nihilism. As Nelson Goodman puts it, philosophy is just one "way of world-making." Philosophy, we might say, has its own language game and its own history. The "ground" of a philosopher's assumptions then seems to consist in little more than the fact that he has faith in them, or believes in them, wills them, or finds them interesting and useful.

Thus, given that a basic and unavoidable "quarrel" concerns the viability of the philosophical enterprise, the constant (some have said wearisome) demonstration in Plato's dialogues that there are philosophical questions makes perfect sense. Plato's dialogues are full of characters who are, in one way or another, either hostile or indifferent to philosophy.[21] *The origination of philosophy itself out of the medium of opinion is the most comprehensive theme in Plato's dialogues.* This point is so preliminary that most philosophers have thought it absurd to make much of it. Most philosophers follow Hegel's lead here; his polemics against the critics of reason tend to be confined to the prefaces and introductions to his works—outside of his main argument, as it were. Yet it is precisely these polemics that are rejected by many proponents of popular rhetoric, sophistry, poetry, religion, and common sense.[22] I suggest that Plato understood this and was eager to *show* us the philosopher's response to his critics. The prefaces of other philosophers constitute the bulk of Plato's text. Perhaps this is an indication that Plato would agree with Hegel's critics that Hegelian dialectic begs the really fundamental question. However that may be, it is a fact that dialogue after dialogue raises, at one point or another, the question "why philosophize?" Does not this question go right to the root of the dispute between philosophers and nonphilosophers? Would not an answer to this question require a comprehensive justification of the whole project of "giving reasons," and so an account of a universe in which it makes sense to want to give reasons? With the madness attributed in the *Phaedrus* to philosophy itself, Plato's dialogues seem obsessed with the fundamental questions concerning the justification of philosophy.

Moreover, the experience of controversy, which is tirelessly depicted by Plato, shows (as does our own experience in the matter) that fundamental disagreements can be extremely difficult to resolve. Refutations of philosophical positions are rarely, if ever, conclusive. A clever interlocutor can always find an answer somewhere in the vast sea of discourse. Every proposition and argument seems to depend on and lead to myriad others. A discussion limits itself to this or that topic and leaves the rest undefined.

But a clever arguer can always build a bridge to a related topic or to related aspects of the present topic under discussion.

And if it is the case, as I have been suggesting, that the defense of philosophy is a prime theme of Plato's dialogues, and that this defense is best accomplished in the medium of a dialogue with the critics of philosophy, then we have the basis for an explanation of another very odd feature of the Platonic texts—namely, that they do not contain a discussion between two mature philosophers. As I said above, the occasion for such a dialogue exists in the *Sophist* and *Statesman*; Socrates' silence there is dramatic. But a dialogue between him and the Eleatic Stranger would be a departure from Plato's overriding concern with the problem of the genesis of philosophy—a genesis that is no longer a live issue in a conversation between mature philosophers.[23]

However, understanding what kind of debate Plato wants to carry on does not fully explain why he wrote *dialogues*. I would like to turn next to this issue.

IV

I begin by noting that, as the debate between dialecticians and their critics suggests, it is not possible to successfully attack *or* defend philosophy *directly*, a fact that sheds light on the form of Plato's texts. I would like to discuss this point by reverting to the just mentioned debate.

The cleverest of those who reject the rationality of the love of wisdom understand that to argue *against* philosophy is to engage in it and so, it seems, to fall prey to the same dialectic of reason they turned on those who argued *for* philosophy. The notion of a "limit" to reason, as Hegel insists, is a dialectical one. Consider the self-refutation of those who *argue* that, say, reason is (unlike faith) powerless to grasp "objective truth"; in arguing this they are claiming that something is objectively true It is as though someone were to write a weighty book in which it is claimed that writing books is something a serious philosopher should never do. The inconsistency here is of the "pragmatic" sort, as it is called today; it turns on conflict between logos (word) and ergon (deed) (on the *Phaedrus* and *Seventh Letter*, see below).

The self-refutation seems to point to Hegel's famous view that "the truth is the whole." However, our clever critics of dialectical philosophy have a way of arguing that there is no "whole" in the sense required. They practice a form of elenchus and criticism called "deconstruction" (a term derived from Heidegger). The critique proceeds on purely ad hominem grounds; one shows one's opponent that within his own framework the argument is either question-begging or incomplete, or leads to an infinite regress. The success of the critique depends on the critic not making any claims to knowledge not also made by his opponent (except, perhaps, a sly claim to "knowledge of ignorance"). Thus Rorty characterizes his approach as "reactive" and "parasitic."[24] Only the critic's *intention* should distinguish him from his opponent. The strategy of these critics necessarily involves an element of ruse, dissemblance, and irony.[25] This strategy is familiar to us, of course, from Plato's Socrates, as well as from the "classical skeptics."[26] Thus there is a significant resemblance between the procedure of the critics of reason and that of its Socratic defenders.

The critic will try to show, then, that the defense of dialectical reason is necessarily question-begging, and therefore that it too cannot be argued directly. He will then try to suggest that the defense of reason is also interminable (Kant's "tribunal" of reason to one side). Since the *hope* of the closure of philosophical discourse animates philosophers, the critic of reason may thus succeed in *persuading* the philosopher that philosophy is a hopeless, Sisyphean task. This persuasion is not, in the final analysis, an argument. It is a rhetorical effort to shake the philosopher's faith in reason by raising ever more difficult metaphilosophical questions that the philosopher cannot yet answer and soon despairs of ever answering. Elenchic deconstruction is dialectic unaccompanied by the insight that there is a Whole—hence the great emphasis placed by the critics of reason on fragmentation, partiality, dissolution, difference, otherness, nonbeing. It is Socraticism without the Good.

In this way a philosopher is prepared to receive that insight that comes in the dead of night as the soul silently looks into itself, the insight that extinguishes the desire for reason giving and kindles the poet's desire for "creativity," the intellectual's interest in cultured "conversation," the believer's resolve to trumpet his faith regardless of what is said or done, the skeptic's desire to free himself from the illusions of the love of wisdom, the orator's desire for power through the art of persuasion. In one way or another, the philosopher is prepared to imitate the self-negation of Wittgenstein's *Tractatus* and to leap into a more profitable, or at least satisfying, way of life. Neither the self-negation nor its result are supposed to constitute "a philosophy." In the final analysis, none of the skeptics or critics of reason has a "position." To even announce that he has a position, let alone that there are arguments in favor of it, is already to concede the game to the philosophers. As Rorty puts it, "edifying philosophers [such as Rorty] have to decry the very notion of having a view, while avoiding having a view about having views. This is an awkward, but not impossible, position."[27] It may be replied that Rorty is advancing a "view" at least while he is engaging in debate with his opponents; but there is no reason for Rorty to deny it. Derrida too freely confesses that the terminology used in his own deconstructionist program must itself be deconstructed, put "sous rature."[28] An unending series of polemics that undermine themselves even as they undermine others is the deconstructionist's way of avoiding being either reduced to silence or being forced to appeal in propria persona to a priori standards.

In sum, if reason cannot be either defended or attacked directly, then both the defense of and attack on reason must be dialectical. Not only are there (if one accepts the just mentioned proposition) no irrefragable systems or doctrines, and no unquestionable metaphilosophies, the defense of philosophy cannot be successfully generated in the absence of fundamental objections to philosophy. Like Hegel, Socrates reduces nonreflexive objections to absurdity by asking for *their* grounds (as in his critique of Protagoras in the *Theaetetus*). However, the debate between critics and defenders of reason more closely resembles Platonic dialogue than Hegelian dialectic, and it is here that a preliminary distinction between dialogue and dialectic should be drawn. The debate cannot fairly be seen as the dialectical self-explication of Reason. That is, it does seem that Hegel's decision to confine this dispute to prefaces and introductions, and to reconstitute it in terms of abstractly formulated "positions," is open to the criticism that he is begging the question. If one wishes to avoid this criticism, the dispute would have to be seen as taking place not between positions, but between the persons who hold them. In a dispute as radical as the one I have been discussing, the philosopher is compelled to question not just this or that doctrine but also why anyone should be persuaded by the metaphilosophical view that philosophy as such is possible. In this sort of dispute, there are no "commensurating" principles (to borrow Rorty's terminology); hence a regression to the level of individual agreement is inevitable. As Socrates claims at the end of the *Phaedrus*, this dispute is best undertaken in the responsive medium of the "living" word. And, of course, this is precisely what all of Plato's "published" (if one may use the word) works depict.

Thus Platonic dialectic is crucially dependent on someone's asserting or denying something, agreeing to defend what he says, agreeing to say what he means, and acknowledging consequences of his position when they are pointed out to him (all of which is regularly insisted upon by Socrates).[29] The Platonic dialogue with the critics of philosophy is inescapably "empirical," unscientific, a posteriori, occasional, and rhetorical. Another reason that the debate between defenders and critics of philosophy must take the form of a dialogue (Plato) and not of a dialectic of positions (Hegel) is that, as noted above, the critics of philosophy deny that they have a "position" in the first place.

If the present line of reasoning is accepted, then we can see that, and why, Socrates cannot "justify" or "demonstrate" his own activity except by coming across or finding someone who is *not* already persuaded by its possibility and worth. Socrates cannot ever allow himself to claim that the critics of reason have been permanently refuted. He can claim to have refuted an antiphilosophical position only to the extent that he has refuted the person who holds it. And this limits him to a finite number of demonstrations, whose occurrence is contingent on a number of factors. Thus he must, as he explains in the *Phaedrus*, spend his time inside the walls of the city, rarely wandering out to peaceful nature; for the "open country and the trees do not wish to teach me anything, whereas men in the town do" (*Phr.* 230d4–5). Unless Socrates can *persuade* his interlocutors to agree that there are philosophical questions, he cannot allow himself to persuade himself of it.

Correspondingly, philosophical rhetoric is unavoidably pedagogic. As Socrates puts it in the *Phaedrus*, rhetoric is "psychagogia," the leading of the soul. Socrates accomplishes this "leading" by getting his interlocutors to *desire* philosophy—hence the unendingly protreptic character of the Platonic dialogues. This is one reason Socrates claims that the only thing he understands is erotic matters ("τὰ ἐρωτικά"; *Symp.* 177d7–8), and that he possesses an "ἐρωτικὴ τέχνη" (erotic art; *Phr.* 257a7–8). It is as though eros is the basis of Socrates' defense against skepticism. The philosopher is characterized by the fact that he cannot be satisfied with himself unless he knows why he is satisfied; that is, he remains unsatisfied until he can know himself discursively.[30] Obviously, Socrates' erotic art is meant to destroy the self-satisfaction of his interlocutors, a turn of events that is essential to Socrates' demonstration of the view that philosophy is not optional. The "post metaphysical conversation" advocated by Derrida and Rorty would amount, from Socrates' perspective, to talk unanimated by the desire for truth. It would amount to unerotic rhetoric, in short. Socrates cannot refute his adversaries directly, or simply announce some metaphilosophical program of his own. He can refute them indirectly if he can change their intentions—hence the crucial role of rhetoric for Socrates, and specifically of dialogical rhetoric. Socrates' erotic art is the art of questioning and answering, and so of carrying on a conversation; it is the work of *phronesis* (thoughtfulness, prudence). These strange claims make sense if we understand Socrates to be concerned above all with the defense of philosophy in the sense that I have outlined.

To sum up: if reflection on the "beginnings" of philosophy is unavoidable, if the fundamental question of metaphilosophy concerns the "quarrel" between the proponents of philosophy and its various critics, if philosophy cannot be attacked or defended directly, and finally if the defense of philosophy requires a conversation with the critics of philosophy (and not just with abstract formulations of their "positions"), then it makes sense for a philosopher who agrees to all this to write *dialogues*.[31]

Nevertheless, one might object, my comments about Socrates' rhetoric and erotic art seem to reduce philosophy to the art of persuasion. The indirectness of the Socratic defense of philosophy seems to sabotage it. How will the dialogical defense of philosophy establish anything of a "positive" nature? I would like now to make some comments about this question.

V

In the *Meno*, Meno offers his famous "paradox," the conclusion of which is that learning is impossible. If we do not at all know what we are looking for, we cannot seek it. There are many things we do not know, and we would be unable to select one of them as that which is to be investigated. Even if we hit upon what we do not know, we would not know that it is the thing we were seeking (*Meno* 80d). Socrates immediately restates the puzzle in the form of a dilemma and omits the last of these points.

It is striking that in the *Meno* Socrates twice inveighs against the laziness and intellectual cowardice to which Meno's paradox would lead (81d, 86b). "Trusting" (*pisteuon*; 81e1) in the view that it is necessary to inquire, we are braver and less idle. Socrates here uses the language of war, thus trumpeting his courage; on behalf of the worth of inquiry "I am determined to do battle, so far as I am able, both in word and deed" (86c1–2; Lamb trans.). Similarly, at a difficult juncture in the *Laches* Socrates urges his interlocutors on with the remark that they must endure further conversation, lest courage laugh at them for their cowardice in the search for courage (194a1–5; cf. *Euthyd.* 306d1, 307c3). Although Socrates is never, in the Platonic dialogues, explicitly referred to as courageous (with the ambiguous exception of *Symp.* 219d5), courage is the one virtue he attributes in his *Symposium* speech to eros (203d5). The erotic Socrates certainly exhibits the sort of courage in question. He also says in the *Symposium* that eros is a "philosopher through all of life, a clever sorcerer and enchanter and sophist" (203d7–8). Socrates concludes his encomium of eros by saying that now as before he worships "eros' power and courage" (212b7–8). The fainthearted misologist is, it seems, unerotic.

But the skeptic might argue that the emphasis on courage is a sign that Socrates' "knowledge of ignorance" is "justified" *only* by an individual's desire for it, and so only for that individual. The exhortations to have courage may be necessary precisely because there is no rational justification for the philosophical enterprise. Courage seems to be a substitute for the possession of wisdom. It is striking, in fact, that philosophers such as Nietzsche and Heidegger, who reject the Platonic ideal of wisdom, emphasize heavily the importance of courage, resoluteness (Heidegger's *Entschlossenheit*), and the will. In still another tradition of thought, Socratic courage would be replaced with faith. I am far from suggesting that Socratic courage and Heideggerean "Entschlossenheit" are the same. But on many occasions Socrates seems to argue that we ought to philosophize even though we cannot really prove that it makes sense to do so. A function of many of the myths in Plato's dialogues seems to be to reassure us that there are grounds for the hope that philosophy is a worthwhile enterprise; but myths are not proofs.

Without commenting on Meno's (nontrivial) puzzle in detail, I would like to point out Socrates' answer to the sort of objection just adumbrated. The refutation has two parts. The first is a short myth about the soul, and its affinity with the natural whole. The second is a demonstration (*epideixis*) of somebody "learning," or rather, "recollecting," something. That is, Socrates does not provide a direct rebuttal of Meno's radically skeptical position. Instead he tries to *show* Meno a *deed* from which Meno is himself compelled to draw the conclusion that his own puzzle can be answered. This demonstration of an absolutely fundamental point (namely, that there is, loosely speaking, "learning") illustrates a crucial feature of Socrates' indirect refutation of the critics of philosophy, namely the reliance on the *deed* of learning which is itself generated through questions and answers. Meno is supposed to learn not the solution of the geometrical problem but the solution to a "meta" problem about learning. The slave boy is said to "recollect" the solution to the former; but in spite of Socrates' remark at 82a, it cannot be said that Meno "recollects" that the boy *is* recollecting. There is no meta-recollection. Nevertheless, Socrates' indirect demonstration to Meno confirms his view that philosophical knowledge cannot be taught in the way that other kinds of knowledge can be.

Socrates concedes that he is not confident of every point in his demonstration in the *Meno*—indeed, how could he be certain of the myth that preceded it, or the thesis that learning is recollection of previously known truths?—but he affirms in the strongest possible terms that we should inquire into what we do not know. As I have already noted, he is willing to do battle, both in word and deed, for the proposition that we should seek the truth. As Socrates says, Meno's paradox reduces dialogue to eristics—to disputation devoid of the *desire* for the truth. This is the bottom line of the battle with the critics of reason. It is not, as I have argued, a line that Socrates can draw nondialectically. Socrates' ad hominem argument against those who reject the possibility or worth of philosophical inquiry uses not just their words but also the evidence of deeds to persuade them otherwise. That is, a crucial refutation of the skeptics is simply the deed that *there is learning* (in a sense other than memorization). The refutation works only when the skeptic has either learned or acknowledges that someone has just done so—hence, once again, the necessarily occasional, empirical, and contingent character of Socratic dialogue about these fundamental issues. As Gadamer remarks, "There is no such thing as a method of learning to ask questions, of learning to see what needs to be questioned."[32] Philosophy certifies itself in the perfect tense. Differently put, Socrates' "erotic art" submits his interlocutor to the power of the question and the corresponding insight that the way one is leading one's life is not satisfactory. Our lives are not linguistic constructions, and Socrates' ability to arouse us to understand our lives better than we think we already do *shows* us that the questions are real and worth pondering.

Until Socrates can yoke his critic into the activity of philosophizing, then, he lacks his most potent weapon against him, namely, the deed of philosophizing itself. The inference from this experience is the proposition that there are philosophical questions, an understanding of which brings one closer to what is. This inference from the deed, however, cannot itself be presented separately as a doctrine or teaching, at least not successfully. This is why the *Meno*'s "slave boy passage" contains *two* conversations: one between Socrates and the boy and another between Socrates and Meno about the conversation between Socrates and the boy.

VI

If *showing* (rather than merely *saying* or *asserting*) the viability of philosophizing is a necessary component in the dialogical refutation of the critics of philosophy, then Plato's decision to write *dialogues* (indeed, "dramatic" dialogues) once again makes sense. In a way that is strikingly similar to Hegel's view that the demonstration of a philosophical standpoint is just the history of the experience of "consciousness" coming to know itself, Plato's dialogues contain no assertions by Plato, only depictions of people becoming and failing to become philosophers. Just as Hegel offers, not a treatise in which he "criticizes" various positions, but rather a "phenomenology" in which various nonreflexive positions show their defects and rewrite themselves in a more satisfactory way, so Plato presents us with dramatic *imitations* of the practice of philosophizing. Indeed, by withholding his own answers from his texts Plato seduces the reader into finding an answer for himself (just as Socrates did with respect to his interlocutors). The point of this maneuver is not simply a subjective or pedagogic one. On the contrary, given that the fundamental debate concerns the defense of philosophy, and given that this defense is necessarily dialectical, it is of the utmost importance that Plato draw the reader into philosophizing and only *then* allow him to reflect on the extraordinarily difficult problem of "justifying" this activity. Thus poetry and mimesis are indispensable to Plato's presentation of the nature of philosophy.[33]

We now have, moreover, a further explanation of Plato's distance

from his own texts. Simply put, the fact that Plato nowhere contributes to
the discussions he portrays allows him to convey something about the
nature of philosophy without asserting it in his own name to be so. If he
did assert it, he would be open to the kind of criticism Hegel leveled against
Kant, and which the critics of philosophy have frequently leveled against
philosophers. An extradialogical postscript or preface by Plato would amount
to a short treatise by him about philosophy; it is easy to see, from what I
have said above, that this move would immediately fall prey to the difficulties already mentioned. Plato cannot stand outside his thought and set
limits to it from some supradialectical standpoint. But, we now want to
ask, is there any way for Plato to supply us *indirectly* with a commentary
on what he is trying to accomplish without falling into self-contradiction?[34]

In order to see that the answer to this question is affirmative, it is
necessary to compare something that is said in one of the dialogues with
the deed of the dialogue itself. I am thinking of Socrates' criticisms of
writing presented at the end of the *Phaedrus*. Plato wrote the criticisms,
a fact that shows—to make a long interpretation short—that he both
rejects the criticisms (since, unlike Socrates, he wrote) and that he accepts
them (since he wrote dialogues). Plato accepts Socrates' arguments in favor
of dialectical discourse, but he thinks that he has found a form of writing
that blunts Socrates' criticisms of writing. On the essential points about
the nature of philosophy, that is, Plato and the Platonic Socrates are in
agreement. By recording all this, Plato allows us to understand his philosophical reasons for writing *dialogues*.[35] He also allows us to see the
limitations of writing and the need for our engaging in spoken philosophical
dialogue. This is Plato's silent postscript to his texts. Just as Socrates "answers" Meno's skeptical paradox with an exhibition of somebody learning,
so Plato "answers" the critics of philosophy with a similar depiction. In
each case, the onlooker is and must be left to draw his own conclusions.
Plato's deed of writing dialogues supplies a basis for an indirect self-com-
mentary.

The relationship between Plato and Socrates in this matter of writing
looks rather like one of Hegel's "determinate negations." Or, to put it in
more Platonic terms, Plato's qualified acceptance of Socrates' conception
of philosophy is indicated *ironically* by Plato. Irony is the medium in which
Plato can express his "philosophy of philosophy" without compromising
his own view on the matter. Hence there is a good philosophical rationale
for Platonic irony.[36]

I note that to the extent to which the articulation of Plato's self-
commentary depends on his "negation" of Socrates in the manner just
referred to, Plato's defense of philosophy *must* be conveyed through the
artifice of the written word. The written word is at one remove from the
"ensouled" activity of dialectic (*Phr.* 276a8 and context) which itself is at

one remove from the Ideas. The written word affords Plato an indirect commentary about the nature of philosophy, but the dialogue form of writing releases him from the ensuing consequences that plague metaphilosophical self-reflection. Contrary to Socrates' remarks at the end of the *Phaedrus* about the inability of the written word (unlike the spoken) to defend itself, the present argument suggests that it is by virtue of being written that Platonic philosophizing can defend itself.

A final aspect of Plato's dialogues that makes some philosophical sense if we keep in mind the roots of dialectic as I have specified them is the lack of closure in the Platonic corpus as a whole. It seems that if Plato had written one more or one less dialogue, the unity of the corpus would suffer little, precisely because its unity derives from a common goal, not the systematization of the means. Moreover, it is difficult to see how any one dialogue could explicitly claim to "close" or "complete" Platonic philosophy without falling prey, once again, to the usual objections against "metaphilosophy" (in the primary sense of the term). Perhaps that is why the *Philosopher*—a dialogue that might have been the "definitive" statement of Platonic philosophy—was never written.

If one goes along with my general argument concerning Plato's use of the dialogue form, his choice of the positions he wants to argue with, his distance from his own texts, his irony, and the lack of closure in the corpus, then it would seem that Plato does not so much have "a philosophy" as a philosophy about the making of philosophical claims. But this cannot be said to amount to a "metaphilosophy" in the primary sense of the term. However, to restate an objection already discussed above, all this still doesn't seem to allay the old suspicion that Socratic and Platonic philosophizing is essentially "negative," elenchic, parasitic on the claims of others, and without any "positive" content of its own—as barren as the "midwife" Socrates claims to be. Are there, however, "ontological" consequences of Socratic and Platonic philosophizing (as I have adumbrated it) that mitigate the just mentioned criticism?

VII

The answer to this question is, I think, affirmative. In keeping with what I have said above, I suggest that we understand these consequences not so much as "theories" posited to round out an epistemology but as reflections on the implications of the fact that there is philosophical learning and inquiry (in a sense other than memorization). As Gadamer puts this point: "The assumption that there are ideas remains for Plato an inescapable conclusion to be drawn from the nature of discussion and the process of reaching an understanding of something." And "the purpose of the

Socratic art of conversing was to avoid being talked out of the fact that there is such a thing as the Just, the Beautiful, and the Good."[37] That is, inquiry, or philosophical questioning, or simply understanding something, have implications concerning the presence of intelligibility. In the *Republic*, Socrates explains this in terms of the sun-like Good. In the *Philebus*, he asserts that the Good shows itself as measure, symmetry, appropriateness, truth, and beauty (64e–65a, 66a–b). In the *Phaedrus*, Beauty is cited as the principle underlying the presence of intelligibility. In the myth of the *Meno* Socrates speaks of "all nature being akin" (81d). In the *Gorgias* he says that "heaven and earth, gods and men, are held together by the principles of sharing, by friendship and order, by self-control and justice; that, my friend, is the reason they call this Whole 'cosmos,' and not disorder or licentiousness."[38] There is a Whole ordered according to the principles of geometrical equality (*Grg.* 508a). This is an implication of the "aporetic" as much as the "nonaporetic" dialogues.

Plato would want to argue for all this indirectly and in an ad hominem way. He might say (and does say in the criticism of Protagoras in the *Theaetetus*) that that to which we implicitly appeal in defending or attacking reason is the truth of our own thoughts and assertions—even if these be directed against the very notion of truth.[39] Even the antiphilosopher's inner dialogue with himself assumes, Plato wants to argue, the *presence* of the very intelligibility and wholeness that he thinks is the fabrication of the philosophers.

Deconstructionists who truly understand deconstruction do indeed truly understand something; they *see* their own point, as well as their opponent's point, and they do so in the light of intelligibility. The true "forms" and "looks" (εἴδη, ἰδέαι) of things cannot be entirely inaccessible; for even the efforts to deny their accessibility or existence assume them. Or at least, this is the sort of deeply reflexive strategy Plato uses at this level of the argument. He then wants, of course, to introduce other notions to draw out his point. That of ἀνάμνησις (recollection), for example, expresses (among other things) the thought that the soul by nature knows something of what *is* (*Phr.* 249e4–250a1). Plato's language in these matters necessarily becomes imprecise, metaphorical, or analogical; poetry is not dispensable for the Platonist. But there is also a good deal to be said about the "logic" of these forms and about their instantiation in language, as well as about the nature of the soul. I am not arguing that the sorts of metaphilosophical issues considered here somehow exhaust Platonic philosophy or the actual discussions Plato presents in his dialogues. In fact, my explanation of Plato's choice of the dialogue form of writing requires the philosopher to philosophize about the many issues that are discussed in Plato's dialogues, as well as in the history of philosophy. For progress in these object-level discussions is the evidence for the metalevel inferences concerning the εἴδη (forms).

Now, there are responses to this Platonic ad hominem attack on the critic of philosophy that need to be considered. The critic can simply ignore it, reject it, or simultaneously both deny and affirm it. In each case dialogue seems to grind to a halt; and insofar as the success of the attack depends on the opponent's admission that he is wrong, the attack fails. The impossibility of dialogue with the Homericists-Heracliteans (and implicitly the Protagoreans as well) is vividly described by Theodorus (*Theae.*,179e–180b). As a matter of fact, the anti-philosophers reject the very idea of a "dialogue" in the philosophical sense (along with the idea, discussed above with reference to the *Meno*, that there is "learning" in any philosophically suggestive sense), as Socrates explicitly notes in his attack on Protagoras.[40] Thus Socrates' dialogues with such persons are, one might argue, proto-dialogues, for they are not animated by a *mutual* search for the truth (hence they border on the eristic). But in the face of a sufficiently tough or clever opponent, it would seem that even this protodialogue must falter and, as in the *Gorgias*, that the philosopher must end up conversing with himself. The antiphilosopher in question professes no care for the truth and therefore does not mind being labeled "irrational" in the philosopher's sense; all that is just an expression, for him, of the very framework that he has rejected. That is, having argued that, for Plato, dialogue with the critics of philosophy is necessary, we now begin to wonder whether it is possible even in the "indirect" senses I have discussed. Do we have, in effect, a paradoxical necessity for an impossibility?[41] In the last section of this chapter I would like to take a brief look at this issue.

VIII

The idea that a very intelligent person (such as Protagoras or Derrida) could profess no interest in the love of wisdom is, we must admit, profoundly disturbing. One might wish to dismiss their failure to give in to Plato's "deeply reflexive strategy" mentioned above as a sign of an obstinate streak, a character defect, or some such. That is, it would be easy to dismiss their disagreement as a sign of their deficiency, not as a sign that there is something wrong with the sort of ad hominem argument sketched above. Thus Aristotle terms a "vegetable" the man who resolutely rejects the principle of noncontradiction (*Met.* IV, 4, 1006a15, 1008b13).[42] Plato also sees, as Aristotle does, that the debate is *so* deep that *everything* is at stake, and that nothing of "philosophy" will survive if the other side wins (we cannot proceed with our metaphysics until we have settled this debate in our favor); and Plato certainly thinks that philosophy is the superior of the two. But Plato rightly seems unwilling to let the insult be the last word, and this because he seems especially aware of just how difficult it is to "win" the quarrel between philosophy and its critics without begging the question. I have argued that the dialogue form, and everything associated with the genre as it is molded by Plato, can be understood as consequences of these observations.

Thus, to repeat, a true mediation between philosophy and its critics may well seem impossible. However, the rhetorical, dramatic, or mimetic dimension of Plato's dialogues may serve as a partial response to this point. This pervasive and sustaining dimension represents what might be called the world of ordinary experience, the "life-world," or to use a more Platonic expression, the "political." Even the debates with the anti- or non-philosophers emerge, in Plato, from this context, and they never lose touch with it. These debates could have been structured by Plato "academically," without this elaborately crafted context, but they are not. That is, it seems that when faced with the ultimate challenge or "quarrel," Plato thinks he can draw on prephilosophical experience. At least two reasons for this suggest themselves.

First, the prephilosophical is not already a construction of the philosopher, and so provides a common starting point for philosophy as well as its critics, thus eliminating one basis for accusing the philosopher of begging the question. The framework that contains distinctions such as those between truth and judgments about the truth is not, on this account, a philosophical construction but a fact of life. In Plato's dialogues even the fundamental philosophical problems are depicted as arising out of the rich tapestry of ordinary experience and not (as is so often the case today) from an "academic" tradition. Moreover, if agreement is the "starting point" of philosophizing, then the starting point is unsystematic. This starting point is opinion, the multihued, receptaclelike medium in which the "Whole" is reflected. That opinion is the context of philosophizing in Plato has frequently been thought, particularly by metaphilosophically oriented philosophers, to constitute its weakness. But given the problems I have discussed concerning the beginnings of metaphilosophy itself, Plato's doxic starting point is a virtue, not a vice. Opinion is not an axiom or theoretical construction; it gives us an *already intelligible*, but nonmethodological, "beginning" for our philosophizing. Thus, for Plato, opinion is not a starting point that can ever be left behind. These points help explain Plato's decision to write dialogues.

Moreover, the "political" does already contain and exhibit the threads of the great issues: those of life and death, self-interest and justice, freedom and slavery, war and peace, desire, power, and so on. It also exhibits, unavoidably, moral judgments and moral sense, along with their naive realism (see below). It seems to me that, in the final analysis, it is only by returning to this level—the level that defines what our concerns should be and defines the issues as real, the level in which our basic moral intuitions (such as "the courageous man is better than the coward") are grounded— that Socrates can draw his opponent into a context from which the origination of philosophy can command assent. Moral judgments in this sphere are not viewed by people in a relativistic or historicist way. Allegiances to family and country are deeply felt. The force of moral opinion is enormous. And the stakes in both war and peace are of universal import. In his debates with nonphilosophers Socrates appeals regularly to all this; for example, he frequently tries to shame his interlocutors into changing their outlook.[43] Correspondingly, Plato's phenomenology of human life is not value neutral, in the way that Heidegger's phenomenology of *Dasein* is. For Plato, philosophical rhetoric is always tied to the political (in the broadest sense of the term); this cannot be said of the comparatively apolitical thought of Wittgenstein, Heidegger, Rorty, and Derrida. Plato's wager is, I think, that the "political" dimension of human experience is more or less stable throughout history. Hence his portrayals of it can function as mirrors in which we can recognize, and be reminded of, our own moral intuitions— above all, the intuition that the great issues of life are great because they are somehow tied to the truth and the good in nonrelativistic senses of the terms.

Socrates is known for his criticisms of δόξα (opinion); but these do not amount to anything like a complete negation of it. His ability to drive home the power of the question brings him into conflict with the polis. But in his view that these "moral" issues are to be understood as "real" (and not just as social or linguistic conventions) he is at one with the polis, even though he wants to show that ordinary moral intuitions, when thought through, "really" depend on things like "recollection" and "Ideas." Rorty's postmetaphysical culture, by contrast, is considerably more alien to common sense than Socrates' analyses of true virtue. His deconstruction of philosophy seems to me also to entail a deconstruction of the political.[44] Rorty does, to be sure, talk about moral commitment; indeed, he does so in the last sentence of *Philosophy and the Mirror of Nature*. One wonders what he could possibly mean by such talk. Indeed, one wonders what it would mean to say, on Rortean grounds (if that is the right word), that one should have a moral commitment to keep a "conversation" going.[45]

But what if, to borrow the terminology of a recent reviewer of Rorty's *Philosophy*, our antiphilosopher is a "cheerful nihilist"?[46] What if he "deconstructs" political life? At this point (given that all our other strategies have been exhausted) the limits of dialogue really are reached, and such a person is dialogically irrefutable. Plato certainly does not mask this fact. But his depiction of it actually leaves the reader with more than this breakdown would suggest. Understanding the limits self-consciously and dialectically, with full awareness of all the pitfalls, and with the deeds and words of both philosopher and his opponent in front of us, we are justified in drawing the conclusion that the unexamined life is not worth living.

Part II

Dialogues

10

Liberalizing the *Crito:* Richard Kraut on Socrates and the State

Clifford Orwin

Although Professor Richard Kraut's *Socrates and the State* ranges widely, it is primarily a challenging reading of the *Crito,* and that is how I will treat it here.[1] Kraut aims to vindicate both the consistency of the early Plato and the power of the argument of the laws in the *Crito,* taken as an argument of Socrates. His intransigence on these points, and the tenacity with which he defends them, are highly impressive. His claim is not that the other dialogues in fact preach blind submission to the laws but that the *Crito* in fact does not, and that the submissiveness the personified laws require of the citizen is, in the end, not submissiveness at all.

Before addressing the particulars of Kraut's argument, I should say something about his approach to interpreting the dialogues. The only interpretive principle that he states is that wherever possible we should interpret the dialogues as consistent with one another (p. 12). I certainly agree. But consistent in what sense? Although or because Kraut does not appear to have entertained this question, his answer to it is never in doubt. We must read each of Socrates' sayings so as to make it compatible, taken as a philosophical argument, with all his other sayings, taken as philosophical arguments. If Socrates says X in the *Apology,* we must not if we can at all help it read him to say not-X in the *Crito.* If the arguments in the former establish (as they do; pp. 13–24) limits to the authority of law, we must try to avoid reading the argument of the laws in the *Crito* (taken as an argument of Socrates) as demanding submission beyond those limits. We vindicate the consistency of the dialogues when we show, by cutting and pasting the remarks of Socrates, that no such remark clashes with any other.

My reservations about this approach are simply stated. The first thing that must be interpreted about the dialogues—the most glaring thing about them—is that they are dialogues. Like many other scholars, however, Kraut tends to interpret this fact by minimizing, even ignoring it. For him one learns what Plato thinks by listening to what Socrates says.

That the speeches of Socrates occur only within the contexts of particular conversations conducted with particular people under particular circumstances is therefore not of great importance to Kraut. Neither in the *Crito* nor elsewhere is the dramatic situation to be held to qualify the definitiveness of Socrates' statements; we are not to take the statements as (at most) definitive relative to their situations. That of the *Crito* provides a plausible occasion for Socrates' definitive statement on the duty of law-abidingness, and Kriton is a plausible addressee (p. 3, n. 1). Of course Kraut would not deny that Socrates has a practical ad hominem intention in speaking as he does—namely, to persuade Kriton of something. What he would deny is that the requirements of persuasion, here or elsewhere in Plato, deviate from those of truth.

In order to be dissatisfied with this approach to what Socrates says, in the *Crito* or elsewhere, one must begin by being dissatisfied with what Socrates says. If the speeches of Socrates are adequate as treatises, that pretty much clinches the case for viewing the dialogues as treatises doused in drama sauce. If, however, his speeches are, taken as treatises, defective—if, among other things, they contradict each other—new problems and possibilities arise. We would have to seek for consistency on a deeper level, and questions of context would come to the fore. What would be contradictions in a treatise—or between them—need not be such in drama or in life. For there is no inconsistency in addressing different situations differently. Indeed there would be some in failing to do so. We would look, then, to Socrates as a kind of Prospero of the dialogues. Precisely because he has achieved that consistent understanding of the human situation that eludes the rest of us, he attends to the diversity of human types and dilemmas and of the speeches appropriate to them.

In Kraut's view, again, the speeches of Socrates *are* adequate as treatises, and they do not contradict one another. Socrates' argument in the *Crito* is one for which no apology is needed. That includes the speech of the laws, which comprises indeed the "philosophic heart" of Socrates' argument. The heart of Kraut's treatment of that speech is his discussion of "persuade or obey."

Just what is it, Kraut asks, that the Laws in the *Crito* require of the citizens in general and of Socrates in particular? That they "persuade or obey" the city (51b, 51c) or the Laws themselves (51e–52a). Previous critics have read this as meaning that where we have failed to persuade the city or the Laws as to what justice is (whether in the assembly or in the law court or wherever else), we must obey them. This seems the most obvious reading, and in fact the Laws never clarify their meaning or hint that clarification is required. Instead they devote their efforts to explaining *why* we are obliged to persuade or obey. And although Kraut denies that the Laws are necessarily defending the situation prevailing at Athens, it is the Laws of Athens that are speaking, and their purpose is clearly to justify whatever it is that, as Laws of Athens, they require.

We might summarize Kraut's interpretation of "persuade or obey" somewhat as follows: "Obey us where you deem our commands just; where you will not obey you owe it to us to try to persuade us; if unpersuaded we reserve the right to punish you; in no case, however, need you obey us where you deem that unjust." The Laws leave it to the citizen to judge the justice of the law and allow him to refuse to do an injustice although not to refuse to suffer one.

Kraut insists on this interpretation not because anything in the speech of the Laws demands it but because consistency does. A little earlier in the *Crito,* Socrates has suggested that one must do the things that one has agreed upon—when they are just (49e). This in itself is neither here nor there: according to the Laws, what we have justly agreed upon is to "persuade or obey," whatever that may mean. But Kraut is mindful that the Socrates of the *Apology* would reject an agreement to obey all laws, because laws must be disobeyed when they bid us do anything unjust. We cannot, then, defer to the laws or the city as the ultimate arbiter of justice. "Persuade or obey," as commonly interpreted, implies such deference; the common interpretation must be wrong.

Yet Kraut's interpretation is highly improbable. What the Laws tell Socrates is that "you must persuade [the fatherland] *or do whatever it bids"* (51b); that "you must *do whatever the city and fatherland bid,* or else persuade it what the just is by nature" (51c); that "we do not order [anyone] crudely *to do whatever we bid,* but permit either of two things—either to persuade us *or to do it"* (52a) (emphasis supplied).[2] Now this is a curious way to put what Kraut says the Laws mean, given that it is so much more plausibly read to mean the opposite. If the Laws want to shame Socrates by stressing their deference to Socratic scruples, and to point out that they have never required him to do injustice, but at most to suffer it, why don't they come out and say so? In fact the Laws would deny having imposed either of these evils on Socrates. It is not, however, that they honor his claim as the rightful arbiter of their justice. It is rather that they say what all laws necessarily say, that *they* are the rightful arbiters of justice.

The Laws do not argue that as laws they are necessarily just. They do argue, however, that where we have failed to persuade them of their injustice, it is just that we obey them. The just remains the legal; we may seek to change the law, but we are not free to defy it. To advert to a distinction of Thomas Hobbes, our own opinions concerning justice we are free to advance as "counsel," but counsel is authoritative only if it becomes law. Kraut's interpretation of "persuade or obey" reconciles the teaching of the Laws with the utterances of Socrates in the *Apology*. Mine, apart from finding more support in the text, respects the facts of life and of law. That the justice (and therefore the authority) of the laws is for the individual to admit or reject is something that no laws could accept: if they did, they would cease to be laws. So it is that when we appeal the command of legal authority, though we invoke a "higher law," it is to legal authority that we must appeal it. In the end it is the polity that decides whether we must abide by the decision of the polity—which is to say that we must abide by the decision of the polity.

In a chapter entitled "Citizens and Offspring," Kraut adduces in favor of his interpretation of "persuade or obey" that the obligation in question rests on an analogy between one's duties to one's father and to one's fatherland. For in Athens as in most other places, parental injunctions, however much respect might have been due them, were not binding on grown children. This, argues Kraut, supports his thesis that the Laws do not present their own injunctions as binding, either.

If, however, this is how the Laws interpret duties to parents, then the analogy simply falls through. Our obligation to the law could not be as weak as that to parents so conceived. That would reduce law to mere advice, to counsel rather than command. "Obey if you wish," the Law would demand, "and if you don't, at least try to show a little respect."

The Laws, moreover, clearly grant parents the right to demand that children submit to punishment at their hands (50e–51a; cf. 51b–c). Indeed in this regard parents stand to offspring as masters to slaves. To be sure, we can distinguish in theory between a duty of obedience and one of submission to punishment (pp. 105–8). No one in his right mind, however, would concede what amounts to a right to punish to any authority to which he would deny a right to command. "I claim no right to tell you what to do, but if you won't do what I tell you, then you must submit to being punished for it." Less plausible words have rarely been uttered.

In the end Kraut fails to persuade that the Laws assert anything short of a right to command, comparable to that of masters over slaves and of parents over small children. Insofar as they require submission to punishment, they already go far beyond what parents may demand of *grown* children. Kraut is therefore compelled to argue that it is only respect that the Laws demand on the analogy of parents, deriving our duty to submit to their chastisement from consent rather than gratitude (pp. 111–14). In fact, it is clear from 50e–51a and 51b–c that the Laws of the *Crito* do require children to bow to the beatings of their parents. It is equally clear that the teachings of the Platonic Socrates do not, except where the parents are wiser than the children.

There is much else in Kraut's book, novel and stimulating and a challenge to anyone who thinks that he knows the *Crito*. I will here raise just one point more which particularly addresses our different notions of Socratic consistency.

Kraut considers the argument of the Laws that in addition to being obliged to them by benefits received, Socrates is obliged because he has consented to them, not in word but in deed (51e, 52d), by the manner in which he has passed his life. Kraut is at pains to show that this argument, closely considered, is much better than most have thought it. All to no avail, however, for even on his reading the argument suffers from a "devastating defect: it adopt[s] the false assumption that if citizens are satisfied with their country they must be satisfied with its laws." Kraut's interpretive principles compel him to ascribe the error to Socrates himself, "who generalizes from his own case." "He sees no reason to like a city apart from its laws, for he thinks that the legal system shapes the moral outlook of the citizen . . ., and nothing is more important to him" (p. 191).

Kraut is driven to this interpretation because he takes Socrates' sayings at face value and treats the sayings of the Laws as sayings of Socrates. Here, however, his concern for preserving the consistency of Socrates should have deterred him. There is ample evidence that Socrates does not regard the laws of Athens as good, and least of all as good at inculcating virtue. At *Apology*, 24d, he asks Meletos who in Athens improves the young; Meletos replies "the laws." Without challenging this reply directly—for that would not serve his present purpose—Socrates does so obliquely by impugning the competence of the many to improve the young: the laws at Athens proceed from the many. So too in the *Crito,* where Socrates and Kriton agree that the opinion of the many is to be disregarded, especially where virtue is concerned (47a–48b). When the Laws make their shining appearance, they are silent as to their dependence on the opinion of the many. Their godlike authority rests entirely on suppressing the question of the regime. (The Laws are also silent as to their success at fostering virtue.) As for Socrates' position, the Laws themselves put it quite precisely: Socrates has passed his whole life in Athens while praising *other cities* for having good laws (52e). Had he ever so praised Athens, we may be sure the Laws would leap to remind him.

There is then no reason to foist on Socrates this bit of special pleading by the Laws. So far is he from equating the cities with good laws with the ones congenial to him that he has shunned the former all his life for a city whose laws he has never praised. We need not seek far for the reason. Suppose that a criminal has persisted in infesting a certain city because the pickings are good and the laws (in comparison with those of other cities) flabby. Would anyone maintain that, having continued in this city for the odds that it offered of avoiding punishment, he has obliged himself to remain there to face it? The criminal is Socrates, and the crime philosophy, with its implicit impiety and corruption (as these are viewed by the city). Proscribed in the best-governed places, philosophy flourishes in democratic Athens, as one of that riot of activities that thrives precisely in laxly governed cities (cf. *La.* 179a 4–8; *Rep.* 557d–559d, 561d).

If, then, Socrates was somewhat satisfied with the laws of Athens, it was not because they were good ones, and not in a way that can be understood as obliging him to obey them. Kraut rightly goes on to suggest that what Socrates valued in Athens was its very great freedom (p. 228), a freedom so great that it enabled him, for a long time anyway, to get away even with philosophy. Kraut wrongly adduces this, however, as an aspect of *eunomia*. Nowhere does Socrates suggest that such freedom is desirable for a city as city; what is best for philosophy is not best for the city as city. Kraut blurs this distinction because, like most philosophy professors who are comfortable in a liberal democracy, he underestimates the tension between philosophy and the city. He thereby underestimates as well the distance between what Socrates thinks and what Kriton can understand, or that between what the philosopher is and how he must present himself to the many (as faithfully law-abiding, for example).

Kraut refers to the teaching of the Laws in the *Crito* as the "philosophy that led [Socrates] to his death" (p. 4). In fact it is superfluous to that end, as the laws themselves remind us (52c). When Socrates might have proposed at his trial to leave Athens with the Laws' blessing, he declined to do so. He had sufficient reasons for meeting his fate that had nothing to do with law-abidingness. The *appearance* of law-abidingness, however, before both Kriton and the many, had something to do with his decision. Kraut's Socrates is in no way concerned with appearances (p. 121). He wears his mind on his sleeve. Although he knows that most people are immune to persuasion (pp. 201–3), he badgers one and all with as much truth about virtue as he knows. There is surely no danger that he is hiding his wisdom (pp. 245–49). According to Kraut, it is confirmation of Plato's disdain for a certain view of Socrates that it not only contradicts Socrates' presentation of himself but that we find it in the mouth of Thrasymachos (p. 246 n. 6; cf. *Rep.* 337a ff.). The view in question is that Socrates is a master of irony. Kraut's approach to the dialogues is such that he could entertain this possibility only if Socrates were to avow it, that is, only if Socrates were not a master of irony.[3]

Reply to Clifford Orwin

Richard Kraut

Professor Clifford Orwin says that I misread the *Crito* because I bring to this work a naive methodology that ignores the fact that Plato wrote *dialogues*. I will therefore begin with some remarks about how I think these dialogues should be read. Then I will turn to some specific questions about the *Crito*.

It cannot be assumed a priori that when a philosophical work is presented to us in the form of a dialogue, it is not at the same time a straightforward treatise. For example, if we wanted to, we could rewrite Berkeley's *Three Dialogues between Hylas and Philonous,* eliminating its two characters, and the result would be a less dramatic presentation of the same ideas and arguments. The content of the work could easily be preserved through this stylistic transformation, and its presentation in the form of a conversation is therefore peripheral.

Could we do the same for any of Plato's writings? That wide-ranging question cannot be answered simply by taking note of the fact that these works are dialogues. What we must do is go through each of them, one by one, examine their content, and ask ourselves, in each case, what would happen if we tried to transform that particular work into a straightforward treatise. And we cannot assume a priori that this experiment would yield the same result in every instance. There may be some dialogues that could not possibly survive such dedramatization, and others that could.

For example, if we tried to transform the *Lysis* into an essay on friendship, it would be difficult to decide what the resulting essay ought to look like, and in any case much that is valuable in this work would be lost. We might come to the conclusion that the experiment would be not only pointless and undesirable but impossible to carry out, since the result would be a completely different work, and the *Lysis* would have been destroyed. At the other extreme, we have such works as the *Menexenus* and the *Timaeus*: in each, there is an introductory conversation among a cast of characters, and then the body of the work consists in a discourse that is largely or entirely uninterrupted. In these cases, the dialogue form seems unimportant, and its elimination would not radically transform the work.

Are there examples that fall between these extremes? That is a difficult and controversial question. For some readers of the *Republic,* the personalities of Glaucon and Adeimantus are crucial, and any interpretation of the entire work must center around its dramatic form. For others, the fact that Books 2–10 retain the form of a conversation can be safely ignored. The point I am making is not that the former approach cannot be right, but that the question of what the right methodology is must be decided by looking at the text and seeking, on a case-by-case basis, the most illuminating and best supported interpretation. There can be many different reasons for using conversations in a philosophical work, and it should not be assumed without argument that Plato always had the same reasons for composing these discussions, or that the dialogue form is always equally important to him. So the mere fact that his works are dialogues by itself counts for nothing. And this is compatible with saying that in some cases—perhaps many—the dramatic structure and interplay of characters is crucial.

In fact, at certain points, my own interpretation relies heavily on the drama and irony of the early dialogues—although Orwin does not mention this. For example, in the *Protagoras,* Socrates argues that virtue cannot be taught, since Pericles, one of the wisest and best of the Athenians, was unable to teach it to his children (319e–320b). If we take this argument at face value, it conflicts with the low estimation Socrates gives of Pericles at *Gorgias* 514c–519c. And so I suggest (pp. 292–93) that we explain the compliment Socrates pays to Pericles in the *Protagoras* as a piece of irony required by the dramatic occasion: Socrates takes himself to be the wisest Athenian, but substitutes the name of Pericles because it is Protagoras he is talking to.

Orwin is therefore guilty of oversimplification when he describes me as someone who "takes Socrates' sayings at face value." It would be more accurate to say that *as a general rule* I do take Socrates at his word. I adopt this approach because I insist upon textual evidence before I come to the conclusion that Socrates should not be taken to mean what he explicitly says. In the example just mentioned, it is the *Gorgias* that provides solid evidence for not taking portions of the *Protagoras* at face value. We must take Socrates at his word at least some of the time if we are to have any basis for finding irony at other points. And, as I have been saying, the question of how much of what Socrates says has to be reinterpreted as irony can be decided only by careful and intelligent examination of texts.

In his final paragraph, Orwin (citing p. 246 n. 6) reports that in my opinion Plato has "disdain" for the view that "Socrates is a master of irony." But what I say Plato has disdain for is the view that when Socrates disclaims knowledge, he is merely being ironic. I take those disavowals of knowledge at face value, but I do not arrive at this conclusion because I naively assume that Socrates must always mean what he says. Rather, I argue (pp. 245–67) that the balance of textual evidence favors the straightforward acceptance of these disclaimers. That Socrates is a master of irony I would never deny, but I do not think he is *always* being ironic. It is unsound to assume that *whenever* Socrates says something to somebody, it is not because he believes it but only because that is what his interlocutor needs to hear. (For further examples, genuine and spurious, of irony in the early dialogues, see *irony* in the index to my book.)

Turning now to the *Crito,* we should first of all acknowledge the obvious point that only part of this work involves considerable conversational interchange. The speech of the Laws is almost entirely unpunctuated by dialogue, and although it does contain a few brief expressions of assent, I assume Orwin does not want to make heavy weather of them. And so, even if we accepted the point that no dialogue should be interpreted as though it were a treatise (and I see no a priori reason to assume this), that methodological principle would no more apply to the speech of the Laws than it does to the bulk of the *Timaeus.*

It is, of course, true that the speech of the Laws is preceded by dialogue. But what is the significance of this fact for our understanding of that speech? There is no evidence in that part of the work that Socrates is being less than straightforward in his conversation with Crito. Certainly the latter is a less than brilliant conformist whose devotion to Socrates conflicts with his acceptance of traditional Greek values. But he is nonetheless one of the few who has been persuaded by the Socratic principle that one must never do injustice to others, and nothing suggests that Socrates regards him as a dope who cannot really understand the higher mysteries of philosophy. So there is no good evidence, prior to the speech of the Laws, that in this work Socrates is hiding his real opinions and aiming at mere persuasiveness. (I am assuming here that Socrates does have some convictions, and that it is possible to come to know what they are by studying Plato. This assumption is entirely compatible with the recognition that drama and irony sometimes play an important role in the dialogues.)

Therefore, those who wish to argue that the speech of the Laws does not present Socrates' real opinions must rely on two claims: (1) that speech is not given by Socrates himself—and this suggests that he wished to distance himself from its doctrines; and (2) that speech is so authoritarian that the Socrates of the *Apology* could not have accepted it. Of these two arguments, the second is surely the more important. For if we could, without strain, interpret the speech of the Laws in a way that makes it consistent with the *Apology,* then the first argument by itself will carry little weight. After all, the *Crito* would not be the only dialogue in which the ideas being endorsed come from a speaker other than Socrates. And those who emphasize the importance of drama in Plato's works ought to recognize the dramatic reasons for putting the argument against escape into the mouth of the personified Laws of Athens. (For further discussion, see pp. 40–41 of my book.)

Orwin wisely puts his emphasis on the second argument. He thinks that if we try to read the *Crito* as a straightforward treatise, ignoring its dramatic quality, it will turn out to be a defective treatise, since it will conflict with the *Apology.* He argues, on the basis of the text, that my "liberalizing" reading of the speech of the Laws is implausible, and then proposes that the resulting contradiction with the *Apology* be explained in dramatic terms: Socrates merely wants to create the impression, in the many and in Crito, that he is a law-abiding man. For philosophy as Socrates practices it is inherently at odds with the requirements of civic order. The city must take the position that it alone is the rightful arbiter of justice, and this is a claim to authority that the philosopher cannot concede. That is why the Laws expound an authoritarian doctrine: Plato correctly saw that this is the position civil authority must always take. Socrates only pretends to accept the speech of the Laws because Crito cannot understand the true Socratic doctrine.

I think this reading faces an insuperable objection: in the *Apology,* Socrates openly says, in front of the entire city, that he is prepared to disobey the many, should they command him to give up philosophy (29c–d). Since he makes no attempt to deceive the general public about his attitude toward authority, why should he put on a mask when he discusses this question at greater length with one of his closest friends? Furthermore, if the speech of the Laws is unacceptable to Socrates, then we have in the *Crito* something that is without parallel in the other early dialogues: Socrates leaving unanswered a reasoned argument that he rejects. The ideas of Thrasymachus and Callicles are ruthlessly picked apart, and those of Protagoras are subtly and ironically undermined. Is it plausible, then, that Socrates would leave untouched the elaborate argument of the Laws if he rejected it? Can he be an earnest seeker of truth and physician of the soul if, like the sophists, he persuades people (including his closest associates!) to embrace doctrines that he takes to be false?

Orwin claims that his reading of the *Crito* finds "more support in the text" than mine, but at several points he misreports what the text actually says. For example, he attributes to Socrates the belief that philosophy is "proscribed in the best-governed places," and although he does not specify which places he has in mind, he is presumably thinking of Socrates' belief that Sparta and Crete are "well governed" (*Crito* 52e). But there is a crucial difference between Sparta being *well* governed, and its being *best* governed: the latter opinion is never attributed to Socrates, whereas the former is. And the fact that Socrates takes Sparta to be well governed is perfectly compatible with my thesis that he had an even higher opinion of the Athenian legal system.

A more serious error occurs when Orwin tries to specify the content of Socrates' agreement. Without citing any text, he says, "according to the Laws, what we have justly agreed upon is to 'persuade or obey'. " But that differs, subtly but crucially, from what the Laws actually say: citizens like Socrates have agreed "to do whatever we command" (51e4–5). The citizen does not agree to adopt one of two alternatives—to persuade or obey—but, quite simply, to obey the city; persuasion is not part of the content of the agreement. Now, this raises a fundamental question: since the citizen has agreed, simply, to do whatever the city commands, ought he to honor every one of those agreements, regardless of its content?

We are given a strong indication of how Socrates answers this question, for he insists at 49e that one must abide by one's agreements—if they are just. These last words can plausibly be taken to imply that unjust agreements are *not* to be honored. So, even when a citizen has agreed to do whatever the city commands, Socrates can call upon him to break that agreement and disobey if the law requires the citizen to act unjustly. And this enables us to understand the relationship between persuasion and obedience: persuasion is the course to be adopted when one refuses to obey on the grounds that the city's order is unjust. Since persuasion is not part of one's agreement, the Laws must mean that when one fails to honor that agreement, one still owes it to the city to defend onself in court. In this way, the speech of the Laws makes the citizen accountable to the city (he must persuade when he disobeys) without assuming that the city's judgment is constitutive of justice.

Orwin thinks he can cast strong doubt on my understanding of the "persuade or obey" doctrine simply by quoting from the speech of the Laws and emphasizing selected portions. "You must persuade [the fatherland] *or do whatever it bids* (51b)." I don't see how calling attention to one of the two alternatives undermines the fact that the other is left open. The Laws are clearly recognizing the possibility that something other than obedience might be justified. Isn't it plausible to suppose that this something else might be *dis*obedience?

One final point. Orwin's review creates the impression that I find a high degree of permissiveness both in the social atmosphere of late fifth-century Athens and in the speech of the Laws. I am said to believe that "in Athens . . . parental injunctions . . . were not binding on grown children." Orwin even takes me to be saying that parents "claim no right" to tell their children what to do; analogously, the city on my interpretation is supposedly telling the citizen "in no case . . . need you obey us where you deem that unjust." In view of this misunderstanding, there is little wonder that Orwin rejects my interpretation out of hand. But my real position is this: The Laws make use of the widespread assumption that "parents were entitled to give adult male children orders on any subject whatever" (p. 110, n. 16). In this sense, parental and civic injunctions *were* binding on grown children and resident citizens. But (and here is the point Orwin misses) the *Crito* can (1) insist that parents and cities are entitled to give orders, (2) even while admitting that circumstances might sometimes require adult children and citizens to set those valid commands aside. On my interpretation, the Laws hold that grown children owe their parents obedience, and by parity of reasoning citizens owe obedience to their parent-cities. These debts are not made void by the mere allegation that a command is unjust. Nonetheless, when this allegation is correct, it will be wrong to pay one's parent or city the obedience one owes (see especially pp. 99–100).

These, then, are some of the differences that separate Orwin from me. But I do not reject his central point—that dramatic situation, personality, and irony are often important features of Plato's dialogues. These elements deserve more careful study than they have been given, and I look forward to learning more about them from Orwin. They received little attention in my interpretation of the *Crito* because my aim was to show that a straightforward reading of the dialogue could succeed. I may not have achieved this aim, but surely it cannot be wrong, in principle, to try taking Socrates at his word and seeing how far this gets you.

11

Terence Irwin's Reading of Plato

David L. Roochnik

Terence Irwin's recent work on Plato, particularly his *Plato's Moral Theory (PMT)*, has received wide notice and acclaim. We are told by Malcolm Schofield that Irwin has produced "what is in some ways the most important and instructive book about Plato for a generation."[1] C. C. W. Taylor claims that *PMT* "will be an essential point of reference for anyone interested in Plato, in ancient ethics, or more widely, in ancient society and civilization."[2] And Gregory Vlastos states, "I have never had more valuable help from a critic."[3]

Perhaps equally remarkable as the positive reception accorded to Irwin by his distinguished colleagues in academe is the fact that his is one of the few works on Plato to have been brought to the attention of the wider reading public. *PMT* has been reviewed in the *New York Review of Books* (by M. F. Burnyeat) and in the *TLS* (by Gregory Vlastos).[4] This is noteworthy because it reveals a perception held by the intellectual community to the effect that Terence Irwin is now taken to be emblematic of twentieth-century Platonism. Even if Burnyeat and Vlastos (among others) have found much that is wrong in detail with *PMT*, they have done so only in the context of high praise for its scholarship, intentions, and interpretive method, and this makes *PMT* an important work indeed.[5]

In this chapter I join several of Irwin's critics and examine some of his more controversial claims. I will do so, however, by situating these

---

My thanks to Charles Griswold for his assistance with this essay. If my discussion has any merit, it is due in large measure to his numerous criticisms of earlier drafts. Of course, I bear responsibility for whatever shortcomings may remain.

particular issues within a larger context—namely, a critique of Irwin's general interpretive strategy and method of reading Plato. I will argue that Irwin misreads a number of critical passages and does so because he accepts a faulty set of hermeneutical principles. Schofield described Irwin's project by saying that *PMT* "applies the precise analytic techniques of contemporary Anglo-American philosophy to the Platonic corpus on a much more extensive scale than we have seen done before." It is just this application that will here be called into question.[6] Contrary to the impression given by Irwin, as well as by reviewers such as Vlastos and Burnyeat, there are other ways of reading Plato that produce plausible results. These not only disagree with *PMT* in detail, but take an entirely different orientation to the text. Irwin has other (potential) critics, such as Strauss, Rosen, Gadamer, and Klein (none of whom, nor their many students, is mentioned in his otherwise massive bibliography), who would challenge him on the most basic question of how to read the dialogues. This chapter will argue that *PMT*'s account of Plato is inadequate because it does not address, and in fact cannot refute, critics such as these.

I

The following principles, roughly stated, are implicit in Irwin's interpretive strategy:

1. Plato's thought underwent significant transformations as he matured. His work can be divided into an early, "Socratic" period, and a middle, "Platonic" one. (*PMT* does not address the later dialogues.)

2. The interpreter should articulate the pivotal transitions of this development and outline the chronological development of the philosophical content of the dialogues.

3. In both periods philosophical content is equivalent to theoretical doctrine, which is divisible into various disciplines (ethical theory, epistemology, and so on). The core of Plato's thinking can be formulated into a series of positions (assertions), buttressed by logical argumentation.

4. The interpreter should isolate and analyze the individual arguments that constitute each discipline.

5. The context that surrounds such arguments, be it dramatic, rhetorical, mythic, or humorous, should be dismissed in the search for correct analysis of isolated arguments.

6. If inconsistencies or anomalies are found among positions extracted from different dialogues, these are to be resolved by appealing to Plato's "development." As a result, the relevant whole or object of the interpretation is the corpus itself (or a large segment of it), and

not individual dialogues. Even further, it is the entirety of Plato's putative development that is the concern of the interpreter.

7. An essential criterion of a successful developmental account is its coherence.

Principle 1 is so widely accepted that Irwin sees no reason to comment on it. Perhaps he is simply relying on the defense of it provided by others. Since the dialogues contain many apparently contradictory claims, and since they can be grouped on stylometric grounds as well as by argumentative and dramatic structure, principle 1 has been taken for granted among commentators for much of this century.[7] Irwin's unique contribution within this tradition is his claim that even in the earliest phase a positive moral theory can be attributed to Socrates. Most developmental accounts consider the initial stages of Plato's thought to have been "negative" in character— that is, the early dialogues have been thought to be elenchic, refutative, or aporetic. In contrast, Irwin argues that the foundations of a positive moral doctrine can be discovered in Socrates' use of the elenchus and that Socrates had an actual moral theory, "a coherent set of mutually supporting principles for understanding the virtues and moral choice" (p. 94).[8]

It should be stated at the outset that Irwin is unclear to whom he refers when he uses the name "Socrates." As Klosko puts it, "Irwin's Socrates is a curious figure. His relationship to the historical Socrates is never discussed and the reader takes him to be the Socrates of the early dialogues. Yet Irwin cites Aristotle without compunction, without explanation (e.g., pp. 40, 42, 87). The relationship of Plato to his Socrates is never discussed. Are we to take Plato as ascribing to every sentence Socrates utters?"[9] I share Klosko's discomfort on this critical hermeneutical point. It will be seen below that it is altogether unclear whose moral theory is under consideration in *PMT*.

Irwin is thorough in his adherence to principles 3, 4, and 5. He is committed to articulating the logical structure of Plato's moral theory; he isolates individual arguments to such an extent that he is able to number his paragraphs decimally; his account is so context-free that it has virtually nothing to say about the dramatic structure or the characters of the dialogues, and is composed almost exclusively of the analysis of arguments.[10] His use of principle 6, particularly in treating the *Protagoras,* is ingenious, but problematic, and will be discussed below.

Irwin comments on his general approach in his Introduction:

> The following chapters are meant to be an exposition of Plato's views. I cite textual evidence as fully as I can, to show that I am discussing some views he really holds. But I do not claim that the arguments for or against a particular view, or the consequences I draw from it, are always to be found in Plato, or even that he would accept them if he were asked. This way of "reading into" the text is hard to avoid in discussing any philosopher, if we want to raise the most interesting questions about him, and

> to discuss him critically, instead of merely reporting what he says. With Plato it is essential. (p. 3)

There are immediate problems with this. First, how does Irwin know what views Plato really held? Plato never wrote treatises in which he explicitly set forth his ideas, nor did he appear as a speaker in any of his dialogues. Socrates is the main character in the works with which *PMT* is concerned, but as Klosko noted, we cannot assume that all his utterances are identical to Plato's views. Exactly how one gains access to Plato's thought is a difficult question, but one that is completely ignored by Irwin. Principles 1 to 7 above all assume that the interpreter can discover who Plato is and how his thinking evolved, but this is an assumption made intrinsically problematic by the dialogue form itself. Irwin does not address the troublesome hermeneutical question of how the reader disentangles the complex dramas that are the dialogues in order to discover their author's true intentions. This is because his primary concern, as stated in his introduction, is not with a thorough exposition of the text but with extracting an interesting moral theory from the text. This he has surely succeeded in doing, but is the result genuinely Platonic? Irwin is ambiguous. When is he reading into the dialogues, and when is he not? The reader of *PMT* is not told. A related question is, what does Irwin mean by "interesting"? It is neither obvious nor necessary that philosophers (including Plato) be exclusively interested in the kind of logical analysis Irwin practices. Unless one can show otherwise, the varieties of philosophical discourse are many and are not restricted to the analysis of formal arguments or, in this case, the construction of moral theories. Irwin continues:

> What I say about Plato will sometimes sound excessively "charitable," in so far as I sometimes discount flaws or obscurities in his arguments, or in his defences of his claim; and in general I try to discuss those parts of his doctrine which I think are more plausible in more detail than the parts I think less plausible. (p. 3)

In order to construct his account Irwin analyzes in detail only those portions of the text he finds "plausible." But what is the standard by which he measures plausibility? When is a doctrine likely to be acceptable to Irwin? Apparently, it is when it can be formulated and then analyzed by the "precise techniques of contemporary Anglo-American philosophy." In other words, if a passage contains, or can be reformulated to contain, the kind of formal argumentation that contributes to moral theory as Irwin understands it, it will be included in *PMT*. If it does not, it is ignored. This is a procedure that will prove successful only if Plato envisioned moral theory of the same type as does Irwin. But to ask again what I take to be the central question: how can we determine what views Plato really held? In a preliminary fashion, I would answer as follows: we must read the text as comprehensively as possible and do so with a minimum number of preconceptions about what it might contain. In contrast, Irwin discounts from the outset large portions of the text because they do not measure up to his standard of philosophical plausibility. But did Plato hold to the same standard? *PMT* is not equipped to answer this question. Despite an appearance of comprehensiveness it is but a partial treatment of the dialogues, since it concentrates only on what its author believes to be philosophically significant.

As mentioned before, Irwin is thorough in his adherence to principle 5. In the search for Platonic theory, "we must sometimes try to free moral doctrines from their distorting context" (p. 3). But when does a context distort? Is it when Plato mistakenly takes an issue in ontology to be one in ethics? Or is it when an ironical or humorous moment infects the purity of logical argumentation? The success of *PMT* depends on its being able to separate fairly and accurately relevant from irrelevant textual material. Presumably Irwin would employ the same standard for this separation as the one he would use to measure plausibility—susceptibility to philosophical analysis. But the same problem arises, for how does Irwin know that such a standard is actually appropriate for a reading of the dialogues? He assumes without argument that much of the text Plato wrote distorts or obscures what is philosophically relevant. What justifies such an assumption? Irwin cannot rely on principle 3, which comprises (the outline of) a conception of philosophy, to support principle 5, for if he dismisses context because he believes his task to be that of discovering theoretical content he begs the question: the context may well call into doubt the very identification of philosophy with such content. Similarly, he cannot use 5 to justify 3, for that would be a method of reconstructing the text after a preconceived notion of philosophy.

These objections become particularly sharp if *PMT* is read in the light of the commentators alluded to above. For example, according to Strauss, "one cannot take seriously enough the law of logographic necessity. Nothing is accidental in a Platonic dialogue; everything is necessary at the place where it occurs."[11] In other words, there is no such thing as a distorting context in the Platonic dialogues. Every bit of detail that describes the characters, every example a speaker uses to illustrate his point, all the jokes, need to be taken into consideration when the reader attempts to understand the philosophical import of the dialogues. This is not to say that Plato was a god who unerringly fitted each word into its appropriate slot. Nor does it suggest that the analysis of, for example, the dramatic context will of itself result in a complete philosophical interpretation. Indeed, following Strauss's dictum may never yield a systematic or clearly defined Platonic doctrine. But why should the reader assume that such a doctrine was what Plato intended to be elicited from his writings (as Irwin does in principle 3)? To quote Tigerstedt, "how can we ever be quite sure that the difficulties which oppose any systematization of Plato are not intentional?"[12]

Strauss's hermeneutical principle may itself be accused of being an assumption about how to read the dialogues. This is no doubt true, but it is one that insists we take Plato seriously as a thinker who knew what he was doing and wrote self-consciously. As a result, following Strauss's advice leads to what may be termed "hermeneutical prudence." It forces us to minimize our preconceptions and furnishes us with a method to avoid imposing our views upon the text. As such, it provides us with the best hope for understanding the author as he wanted to be understood, a step that is certainly prior to any criticism of that author.[13]

Perhaps Irwin would answer these objections by arguing that his interpretive strategy is justified by the coherent account it elicits from the text (principle 7). If, in other words, he can construct a consistent description of Plato's theoretical development, then the principles used to reach that description have been vindicated. Burnyeat rightly called *PMT,* "a developmental story of extraordinary coherence."[14] But is the story true, or is it a myth? Strauss too generates a coherent account, yet his results are quite different from Irwin's. Irwin might strenuously object to Strauss's interpretation of the *Republic,* Rosen's reading of the *Sophist,* Klein's *Meno,* or Hyland's *Charmides.*[15] He might accuse these commentaries of being overly literary since they scrutinize all the small details of the dialogues' dramatic context. Nevertheless, they are internally coherent. Each of these works concentrates on a single dialogue and makes no appeal to Plato's chronological development.[16] Each insists upon a contextual reading of all argumentation. As Strauss again puts it, one must "read the speeches of all Platonic characters in light of the deeds. The deeds are in the first place the setting and the actions of the individual dialogue: on what kind of men does Socrates act with his speeches? What is the age, the character, the abilities, the position in society, and the appearance of each?"[17] All of these are questions in which Irwin takes no interest. He has not, however, demonstrated that they deserve to be ignored.

None of this is intended to deny the value of logical analysis. Rather, it is to insist that the dialogues are complex wholes that include not only serious argumentation, but dramatic confrontation, rhetorical interplay, and irony. It is impossible to predict in advance when a given speech will be more or less characterized by one of these factors. There is, for example, no algorithm to determine under what circumstances Plato intended Socrates to be speaking ironically. As a result, the commentator, in order to avoid ascribing his own views to Plato, must read the dialogues as individual works, as the fictions they are, and as texts whose every dimension may modify the meaning of the arguments they contain.

If commentaries such as Strauss's are in fact coherent, how does one adjudicate a dispute between their results and Irwin's? Clearly a standard other than coherence must be invoked, and this I suggest may be called "the principle of quantity." The nod must be given to that interpretation that incorporates more of the text as it is written into its account. The interpretation that recognizes the law of logographic necessity and is not predisposed to dismiss large segments of the text because they appear philosophically implausible will read the dialogues more openly and comprehensively than the one that does not. It will include detailed examinations of characters, settings, digressions, and myths. As a result, it will be more tentative in tone than *PMT*, whose author regularly speaks with confidence of Socrates' doctrines and theories. Finally, such an interpretation may well terminate in questions rather than in doctrines (in contrast to principle 3 above), and so will not contain the kind of theoretical results that Irwin finds most interesting. This is not, however, to say that it is any less philosophical than *PMT*. From Irwin's point of view it may be less plausible, but in fact it may also be more Platonic.

II

In what follows I shall illustrate my general criticism with one particular issue, namely, *PMT*'s treatment of the "craft analogy" (CA). The CA is pivotal to Irwin's developmental story. He claims that Socrates "argues that virtue is simply craft-knowledge" (p. 7). (I have already mentioned the troubling ambiguity of Irwin's use of the name "Socrates." Presumably it here refers to the younger Plato.) Irwin believes that when Socrates uses the CA in his discussions, as he does regularly, Plato intends it to be read as a conceptual outline of a theoretical project. For example, in the *Apology* Socrates describes his conversation with Callias. If Callias' two sons were colts or calves, he would hire a horse trainer or a farmer as an "overseer" (*epistates*; 20a8) to make them excellent in their appropriate virtue. Callias' sons, however, are men. Who, then, is knowledgeable about the human and political virtue (20b4–5) appropriate to them? Callias says that Evenus of Paros, a sophist, has this techne (20c1). Socrates' irony makes it certain that he thinks Evenus has no such knowledge. In addition, he claims he himself does not possess it. Thus, the analogy is left as follows: as the horse trainer is to the virtue of colts, so X is to the virtue appropriate to human beings. If *hippike,* the techne of horse training, is substituted for the horse trainer, X will refer to a kind of knowledge.[18]

Variations of this analogy are used throughout the dialogues. Irwin's essential point is that the younger Plato believed that the X, moral knowledge, could be supplied and was strictly analogous to a craft. This becomes the basis of the moral theory he ascribes to Socrates. Such a thesis, which I would call the "theoretical reading of the CA," brings with it problematic consequences. For example, according to Irwin the kind of knowledge illustrated by the first term in the analogy is productive in nature.[19] A craft, such as carpentry, issues in a product distinct from itself, namely, houses. The quality of a carpenter's skill and the value of the knowledge he possesses are measured only by the houses he makes. Since Irwin believes the analogy is strict, the knowledge that is virtue must be productive as well. Therefore, its value is instrumental since its worth derives only from the good (happiness) that it is able to produce. Such a reading stands at odds with the more traditional belief that for Plato virtue is a good valued in and of itself. Vlastos has strongly disagreed with Irwin on this point and their debate over it is recorded in a fascinating exchange of letters in *TLS*.[20]

Irwin's entire argument hinges on the role he gives to the CA. This is made quite clear by his reading of the *Protagoras*. He claims that although the earliest dialogues contain the position that "happiness is a determinate end to which virtue prescribes instrumental means" (p. 84), they did not make clear what this end is. Such a lack is remedied by the hedonism introduced by Socrates after 351b: "Hedonism is Socrates' own view, intended like the rest of the *Protagoras* to support the positions assumed without defence in the Socratic dialogues. Hedonism explains the rather indefinite talk of the final good, provides a clear subject matter for the craft of virtue" (p. 103).

I alluded to this above when mentioning the sixth of the hermeneutical principles operative in *PMT*. The hedonism of the *Protagoras* has long troubled commentators, for it is "not in keeping with the general temper or method of Socratic ethics,"[21] and it contradicts Socrates' denial of the same position in other dialogues. Irwin argues that in order to make sense as a working ethical theory, the CA requires a determinate end, a final good, to function as the object of virtue as craft. "And pleasure is a plausible candidate for the final good" (p. 108). The word *plausible* is striking here. Irwin believes that since he can extract from the *Protagoras* a thesis that logically coheres with the other theses he has outlined, he has demonstrated Plato's true intention. The *metretike* techne (356d4) described by Socrates is, for Irwin, a serious theoretical proposal: "virtue is the craft of measuring pleasures and pain" (p. 109).

Irwin's proposal for synthesizing the *Protagoras* with the earlier dialogues is elegant, economical, and, simply as a moral theory, interesting. But is it Platonic? As Vlastos has noted, a majority of commentators have read this passage not as one that espouses Socrates' own view but as an ad hominem and a reductio. The "homo" to whom the argument is being addressed has been variously described as the "average man" (Taylor), the "many" (Sullivan), or Protagoras himself (Grube).[22] My own suggestion is that the primary audience of Socrates' remarks is young Hippocrates, the character for whose benefit the entire debate with Protagoras is taking place and whom I would label a "protohedonist."[23] None of these proposals can be pursued here; the point is that they all (especially Grube's and my own) seek to find internal or dramatic grounds from which to explain the introduction of hedonism, which, when coming from Socrates, is surely anomalous. All consider this passage to be in some measure rhetorical or ironic. Irwin, on the other hand, does not discuss any of the dramatic components of the dialogue. He is concerned solely with the analysis of arguments and the charting of Plato's theoretical development. His position altogether depends on Plato's having perceived a deficiency in his earlier work in need of correction: "The *Protagoras*, and especially the hedonism . . . offers solutions to central problems in Socratic ethics; and this is one reason to find the hedonism theory attractive" (p. 108).

In other words, Irwin argues that because the passage introducing hedonism can be formulated so as to form a coherent account of a developing ethical theory, hedonism can be attributed to Plato as a doctrine sincerely held at a stage of his career. There is no way of apodictically proving this false. It is, however, an argument that appeals to a psychological transformation that took place twenty-five hundred years ago. Furthermore, Plato's changes of mind were, according to *PMT*, somewhat erratic. (Irwin states that "the earlier dialogues . . . neither endorsed nor rejected hedonism"[p. 103], whereas "the *Gorgias* rejects it" [p. 116].) Most important is the fact Plato left behind no *Nachlass* in which he described his own development and that the dialogues themselves offer no commentary on their author's evolution. As a result, Irwin's argument is entirely speculative. His analysis is painstaking, and his results coherent, but there is little evidence to show that they are genuinely Platonic. The kinds of interpretations mentioned above, which rely on internal (or textual) grounds alone for their account, must surely be preferred. They are, one might say, more empirical than that provided in *PMT*, for they account for more of the "data"—the text—that can be observed.

It is clear that *PMT*'s reading of the *Protagoras* depends on its account of the CA in earlier dialogues. How does Irwin marshal evidence in support of his interpretation, his theoretical reading, of the CA in these dialogues? Space permits discussion of only one example: *Charmides* 165c4–e2.[24] Irwin believes that this passage is evidence for the following statement: "In the *Charmides* he [Socrates] argues that temperance is not modesty; he does not ask if it is wise modesty, but considers what kind of craft it must be. . . . he must assume it is no more than a craft" (p. 70). This is a peculiar interpretation of the passage, for the definition here under consideration is no longer modesty, but Critias' "knowing oneself" (165b2). To this Socrates asks, "for if temperance is a knowing something [*gignoskein ti*] obviously it must be some episteme and of something. Or is this not so?" (165c3–5). The "is this not so" (*ē ou*) may well be important, as Hyland believes,[25] for it leaves open the possibility that Socrates himself does not believe that the knowledge that is temperance is explicable via the model of epistemai such as medicine and house building. Critias rejects this potentially fruitful option and proceeds on the basis of the CA. This is what causes his downfall, since an object analogous to health or houses cannot be located for "self-knowledge." Indeed, much of the remainder of the dialogue explores the aporiai that ensue if one explicates temperance through the CA. As Klosko puts it, "Exactly what the *Charmides* established is not clear, but it seems to damage the CA more than support it."[26]

If the *Charmides* does damage the CA, why and how is it being used? Critias is a man who needs to be refuted. As historical figures, both he and Charmides were infamous as intemperate villains. From the outset, then, this dialogue is permeated by a profound irony. Much like Meno, Critias' arrogance and thoughtlessness parallel his political viciousness.[27] Thus, there is a need to defeat him in public argument in order to inform the audience (and the readers of the dialogue) where, in Plato's estimation, this man went wrong. The CA provides a useful tool for doing this. It forces Critias to formulate his knowledge claim in the most unambiguous terms available—those belonging to the typical technai. Once so formulated, Socrates can demand that Critias' definition be explicated as clearly as medicine. By here employing techne as a model of knowledge, Socrates brings about the downfall of the definition.

It is clear that in some sense Socrates adopts techne as the operative model of knowledge in this passage. But in what sense does it operate? As I have mentioned, the *Charmides* is a profoundly ironic work, and I am suggesting that the CA as it occurs in this dialogue is part of its irony. Critias is neither a reflective nor a moral man. Consequently, it is unlikely that he has spent much time wondering about the nature of moral knowledge. The conception of knowledge he adopts is that belonging to the ordinary, prephilosophical world, namely, techne. The refutation proceeds on the basis of *Critias'* conception of knowledge. In other words, Socrates adopts the standpoint of his interlocutor in order to demonstrate its weakness. He does so, not to articulate a moral theory, but to refute Critias and instruct his listeners. The refutation leaves open the question of the nature of moral knowledge, a question that Plato invites the more philosophically inclined among his audience to explore. Such, at least, would be the outline of an interpretation that takes into account the text as it is written.[28]

Irwin is convinced that the only interesting and philosophically plausible results of the early dialogues are axioms or theorems of an ethical doctrine based upon a theoretical reading of the CA. He has ignored important facets of the dialogues and so greatly narrowed his scope. As a result, this portion of *PMT,* although coherent, is not a genuine or comprehensive commentary on Plato, but a sometimes fascinating muthos generated by tenaciously weaving together and then expanding a series of propositions suggested by various speeches in the dialogues. But this is not exposition of the text, and so *PMT* has the wrong title. Irwin's book articulates not Plato's moral theory but Irwin's theory about what Plato's moral theory should have been. I certainly agree that ancient texts, like modern ones, often merit criticism. But if the dialogues are not read faithfully *as dialogues,* they cannot be accurately understood, and any criticism aimed at them will be premature and lack force.

Reply to David L. Roochnik

Terence Irwin

David L. Roochnik's remarks include specific criticisms of my book and more general criticisms of the approach to Plato that he takes to be implicit in it. I would like to reply briefly to some of the specific criticisms, and to say a bit more about the wider issues he raises.

1. Roochnik states seven principles that he takes to be "implicit" in my interpretive strategy. I agree roughly with the first two, but I reject the other five and do not see why he thinks they are implicit in my book.

2. On his principle 5: If I ignored dramatic structure altogether, I could not draw the conclusions I draw from the *Laches* and the *Hippias Minor* (see *PMT*, pp. 299 n. 48, 302 n. 62). Nor do I think the character of the interlocutors unimportant; see *PMT*, p. 290 n. 28 (on Charmides and Critias), p. 303 n. 65 (on Nicias). Roochnik and I do not disagree in principle here.

3. Roochnik is wrong to suggest that my "unique contribution within this tradition" (I am not sure of the exact referent of "this") is my claim that even in the earliest phase a positive moral theory can be attributed to Socrates. I believe such a claim is at least as old as Aristotle, and is shared by Zeller, Guthrie, and Vlastos (to pick just three distinguished and very different scholars). The view I actually ascribe to Socrates is quite similar on some important points to that suggested by Zeller (see reference, *PMT*, p. 304 n. 71).

4. I mention these precedents not for the sake of self-protection but to counter a suggestion about the philosophical basis of my views. Roochnik sometimes seems to think my interpretation is somehow characteristic of, or at least dependent on (see his n. 6), what he calls (quoting Schofield) "precise analytic techniques of contemporary Anglo-American philosophy." I disagree on two counts: (a) acquaintance with the works of Zeller,

Pohlenz, Raeder, and Moreau will show that the main theses I offer are not essentially novel; and (b) the "precise analytic techniques" consist largely in setting out some arguments contained in the dialogues in numbered steps for convenience of reference and analysis. I wouldn't have thought that identifying the steps of an argument was a peculiar concern of contemporary Anglo-American philosophy. Perhaps it is the practice of numbering the steps, or filling in those left implicit in the initial statement of the argument, that is peculiarly contemporary and Anglo-American? By this criterion Kant proves himself to be contemporary and Anglo-American in his exposition of the Antinomies.

I rather deprecate the use of the term *Anglo-American* to refer to a philosophical school or outlook. And I doubt if there are any techniques characteristic of contemporary Anglo-American (as opposed to medieval Latin or eighteenth-century German) philosophy; and Roochnik hasn't said what they are. Modern philosophy (including Butler, Hume, Kant, Mill, Sidgwick, Bradley, Quine, Putnam, and Rawls) has certainly influenced my view (and many other people's views) of Plato; but it seems to me misguided to associate this influence with some set of techniques.

5. Roochnik complains that "Irwin is unclear to whom he refers when he uses the name 'Socrates.' " Unfortunately he does not refer to the place where I try to say (too briefly) to whom I refer; at page 291 I say that I accept Aristotle's testimony that Socrates held three doctrines found in the "first group" of Platonic dialogues. On the other hand, I evidently don't always take the character "Socrates" to state the views that Plato holds at the time of writing a dialogue (see the discussion of *Rep.* 1, pp. 183 ff.).

In any case I am not sure why Roochnik thinks this question important for evaluating my argument. If I'm wrong to think Aristotle is a good source for the historical Socrates, then the development I trace (unless it is open to some other objection) is a development wholly within Plato's own thinking. The question of historicity affects the question of whether it is a development between the historical Socrates and Plato, but it does not affect the question of whether there is a development or not.

6. It is surprising that Roochnik thinks I am "convinced that the only interesting and philosophically plausible results of the early dialogues are anxioms or theorems of an ethical doctrine based upon a theoretical reading of the craft analogy." I sharply distinguish the principles associated with the craft analogy from those associated with the elenchos (*PMT*, p. 94); and I argue that Plato (of the middle dialogues) differs from Socrates insofar as he accepts the latter principles and rejects the former. I think it should be fairly plain that I think the Socratic and Platonic principles associated with the elenchos are interesting and philosophically plausible.

7. Roochnik claims about me that "his primary concern, as stated in his introduction, is not with a thorough exposition of the text but with

extracting an interesting moral theory from the text." This claim is unsupported by any passage that he quotes from me. I agree that the exposition is not thorough, if a thorough exposition would require equal attention to every part of every dialogue that I discuss. But I don't believe I ever claimed or implied that my main concern was to extract a theory rather than to expound Plato.

8. I turn now to some of the more general issues that Roochnik raises. He believes that before we consider the results we reach by any particular line of interpretation, we can establish at least a presumptive case for one interpretive strategy and against others; in his view the choice of interpretive strategy does not depend on assumptions about Plato's likely philosophical aims or on our views about the merits of one Platonic doctrine or another. We need only assume that Plato is "a thinker who knew what he was doing and wrote self-consciously." Roochnik refers with approval to a method of interpretation (attributed to Leo Strauss) that "(a) concentrates on a single dialogue and (b) makes no appeal to Plato's chronological development" (reference letters added). Certainly (b) is defensible; some argument is needed to show that the dialogues reflect any particular line of chronological development. But I wonder why there should be a presumption in favor of (a). It is not a peculiarity of developmental accounts of Plato to find striking convergences and apparent conflicts between the arguments of different dialogues. Shorey and, more recently, O'Brien have argued powerfully for a "unitarian" interpretation of these features of the dialogues; and I regard such an interpretation as a plausible and serious rival to my own. But the issues that arise here are not to be settled by refusal to compare the apparent results of one dialogue with those of another.

9. Fortunately, Roochnik does not actually follow the self-denying ordinance he appears to endorse here. For in the *Protagoras* he seeks "internal or dramatic grounds from which to explain the introduction of hedonism which, when coming from Socrates, is surely anomalous," and he quotes with approval Vlastos's claim that hedonism is "not in keeping with the general temper or method of Socratic ethics." I do not see how such an argument is consistent with Roochnik's point (a), which insists on concentrating on each dialogue by itself. Vlastos's claim is certainly not based on the *Protagoras* alone; and if we look at this dialogue alone, we find nothing anomalous in attributing hedonism to Socrates. The argument for seeking "internal or dramatic grounds" rests on (i) an appeal to other dialogues, and (ii) the claim that hedonism is incongruous with these other dialogues. But (i) is inconsistent with Roochnik's interpretive principles, and (ii) rests on very controversial exegetical and philosophical assumptions that he does not defend. (I attacked them briefly in *PMT*, and they have been attacked more fully by Gosling and Taylor.)

10. This strikes me as a fairly significant example. Roochnik favors some methods of interpretation because they involve fewer philosophical or interpretive presuppositions. We can fairly ask (a) if such methods really involve fewer such presuppositions, and (b) if it would be a good thing if they did. The example of the *Protagoras* suggests that we should answer no to both questions. As soon as he tries out the sort of interpretation he favors, he turns out to be relying on just the sort of presupposition that he professes to eschew. If he didn't, his method would get nowhere at all.

Like many others who profess to be approaching a text with no, or few, presuppositions, Roochnik is in fact approaching it with many controversial, concealed, and undefended presuppositions. I believe it is futile to try to avoid presuppositions, and I see no reason for trying to get by with as few as possible. We should want to approach the text with the right presuppositions—those suitable for discovering the truth about it. I don't deny that these are hard to find, but we should not be diverted from the task of finding them by Roochnik's counsels of "hermeneutical prudence" that "forces us to minimize our preconceptions." Roochnik's approach to the *Protagoras* well illustrates the failure of this method. He doesn't actually rely on it, and he would discover nothing if he did.

11. A related point may be illustrated from Roochnik's remarks on the *Charmides*. He appeals freely to the bad reputation of Critias and Charmides as "intemperate villains" and uses this fact about them to explain the point of the dialogue. Now nothing is said in the dialogue about their reputation; why should we not say that Plato actually approves of them, or that he represents Socrates as not disapproving of them, in order to put Socrates in a bad light? Each of these views is as consistent with the text as Roochnik's view is.

We might well reject these views by claiming to have good reason for thinking Plato disapproves of these people and that he does not intend to put Socrates in a bad light. But such claims must rest on evidence outside the *Charmides* itself, and in particular on a philosophical assessment of other dialogues; we must, for instance, rule out the assumption that Plato intends to make fun of Socrates by attributing plainly ridiculous philosophical views to him. I have no objection to these appeals outside a particular dialogue; I insist only that the picture of an interpretive strategy that "concentrates on a single dialogue" and "forces us to minimize our preconceptions" is a distracting illusion.

12. It would be unwise of me to try to pronounce definitely on the interpretive principles that Roochnik advocates. But I would like to comment on the "principle of quantity." Taken one way, this principle is uncontroversial; it says that the best interpretation of a given dialogue is the one that explains the whole dialogue. Such an interpretation can readily include the claim that parts of the dialogue embody mistaken views or bad arguments. Roochnik perhaps introduces some unclarity here when he

suggests that I am "predisposed to dismiss large segments of the text because they appear philosophically implausible." If "dismiss" simply means (i) "reject as probably false," then I am certainly ready to dismiss segments of Platonic text. But if it means (ii) "leave out of account in the interpretation of the text," then I quite agree with Roochnik that large segments of the text should not be dismissed simply because they appear implausible. Roochnik and I disagree, then, only if he can show I accept (ii); but he offers evidence only of my acceptance of (i), and he gives no argument to show that (ii) follows from (i). I don't believe that philosophically implausible parts of the *Phaedo* or *Republic,* for example, should be dismissed in the interpretation of these dialogues.

13. Roochnik's principle, however, becomes controversial if it says that everything in a given dialogue is of equal importance for its interpretation (so that, for example, dramatic setting, characterization of the interlocutors, or interjections are as important as the explicit or implicit arguments in fixing the interpretation of the dialogue). it becomes even more controversial when he adds the assumption that "nothing is accidental in a Platonic dialogue; everything is necessary at the place where it occurs" (quoted from Strauss). I see no reason to accept the principle of quantity so understood. There is room for reasonable discussion about which features of a given dialogue matter more for its interpretation; but I don't see why an interpreter should refuse to say that some features matter more than others. In fact, I doubt if Roochnik or anyone else can consistently refuse to say this (even if we could make a list of all the features to be taken into account); in claiming to regard each feature as equally important, we simply conceal from ourselves our grounds for discriminating in favor of some. Similarly, the assumption that Plato is a competent and self-conscious writer doesn't justify the inference that everything in a dialogue is necessary at the place where it occurs. Some competent and self-conscious writers write some things casually, could have written something else instead of what they wrote at a particular place, and attach more importance to some things they write than to others. Why should Plato not be one of these self-conscious and competent writers, instead of the rather strange sort that Roochnik takes him to be? We might find ourselves agreeing with Roochnik when we compare his claim and its results with the results of other interpretations of the dialogues. But I can't see (to put it mildly) any initial presumption in favor of his principle of quantity.

Perhaps, however, I have misunderstood Roochnik's principle of quantity, and it is neither (understood one way) unhelpful and uncontroversial nor (understood the other way) false. But if it isn't to be understood in either of these ways, I'm not sure how to understand it.

14. I would like to touch on one very controversial matter alluded to by Roochnik, when he mentions my use of Aristotle (see also my point 5 above). When we are thinking about how to read Plato's dialogues, and

especially his treatment of Socrates, I believe we are rather unwise if we reject Aristotle's testimony. Indeed, I think we are unwise if we ignore the indirect testimony about Socrates that is incorporated in the views of the main schools of Hellenistic ethics, beginning with the Cynics and Cyrenaics. The view that Socrates disavowed knowledge, held that incontinence is impossible, and believed that all the virtues are instances of knowledge is not simply the view of overingenious modern interpreters; it is also Aristotle's view of Socrates, as opposed to Plato. Aristotle was in a much better position than we are to know about Plato's intentions; and he has a strong prima facie claim to be heard. The claim may be overridden if the contrary arguments are strong enough, but they need to be rather strong. I may be wrong in my estimate of Aristotle or in my claims about how he understands Plato and Socrates; but we cannot sensibly decide how to read the dialogues by our views of what they suggest or hint without considering Aristotle's views of them.

15. In the ten years since I wrote *PMT* it has been sharply and deservedly challenged by many helpful critics. If I were revising it, I would probably be well advised to say more on the general questions that Roochnik raises on methods and strategies of interpretation. But, without denying the importance of these questions, I don't think students of Plato should concentrate on them too exclusively. We are likely to take a method of interpretation more seriously if it produces philosophically interesting and significant results, and so it is important to display the results. It is an illusion to think we can find the right interpretive methods and strategies in advance of considering the philosophical merits of the conclusions they yield. I don't think there is necessarily anything to worry about here, or that if we admit this we abandon our chances of finding true and historically accurate accounts of Plato. We rightly evaluate methods of scientific investigation partly by their capacity to reach interesting and plausible results; and I see no difference in principle in the proper way to evaluate methods of studying Plato.

In saying this I have made several assumptions about what we might be trying to do in studying Plato, and about the reliability of our own philosophical judgments about what is interesting and plausible. These assumptions deserve philosophical debate; and this is part of the reason that study of the history of philosophy should be a task for philosophers (although not only for them). But it would be a mistake for philosophers to give up philosophy in favor of metaphilosophy; it is philosophical progress that leads us to rethink metaphilosophical issues. For similar reasons it would be a mistake for students of Plato to spend all their time worrying about how to read Plato; they may learn more about this by looking for what is philosophically interesting and provocative in him.

12
Reading Plato: Paul Woodruff and the *Hippias Major*

Ronald Polansky

Professor Paul Woodruff's recent book on the *Hippias Major* gives rise to important queries regarding interpretation of Plato's dialogues.[1] In his preface, Woodruff makes some statements about his interpretive approach well worth critical attention. First, he says, "The most interesting questions about the *Hippias Major* concern Socrates' method and Hippias' character" (p. ix). One is immediately provoked to ponder how one determines just which questions in connection with a Platonic text are truly the most interesting. Are these questions those that are taken up explicitly *in* the dialogue or those we ask *about* it? Second, when Woodruff states that "the Essay does not consider wider questions about Plato and Socrates except insofar as the *Hippias Major* helps answer them. I try to be neutral on the interpretation of the rest of Plato's work" (p. ix), one wonders to what extent Woodruff succeeds in being "neutral," and indeed whether any interpreter could or should be so. How does the background of interpretation of the other dialogues govern the reading of any particular dialogue?

Third, Woodruff advises us, "Chapters Two through Four of the Essay are introductory. They discuss literary features of the *Hippias Major* in terms I believe are accessible to laymen. The remaining chapters treat subjects of interest mainly to Plato scholars" (p. x). From comments he makes below these lines and at the very start of the preface, it appears that Woodruff began his work with scholars in mind (chapters 5–8 were previously published or presented), and the part laymen might find useful was added subsequently to round out the book. Here, then, is a division between the literary approach to Plato, possibly accessible to laymen, and the recondite treatment appropriate to scholars. The implication is that serious scholarship begins only with the sorts of philosophical topics taken up in chapter 5, whereas literary and dramatic aspects of the dialogue have less scholarly interest and doubtful import for the philosophical points. Hence, there is likely to be little that is recondite or esoteric in the analysis of literary aspects of the dialogue.

Thus, I find three key issues raised by Woodruff's opening methodological comments: What are the interesting questions pertaining to a dialogue? What impact should interpretation of the rest of the Platonic corpus have on the treatment of a particular dialogue? Are literary aspects of a dialogue easy and separable from its philosophical content, so that the dialogue form is not essential to the content? My discussion of Woodruff's work on the *Hippias Major* will focus on these three questions. I begin with the first.

In lines quoted above, Woodruff states that Hippias' character and Socrates' method are the most interesting questions about the dialogue. Elsewhere Woodruff observes:

> Like most early Platonic dialogues, the *Hippias Major* carries no explicit message. . . . There is not even a single subject or theme to unify the piece. We could say equally well it is about Hippias, or about definition, or about the fine, or about Socrates himself. The elusiveness of Plato's purpose in writing such works frustrates scholars, but it is part of Plato's fascination for us. And despite its complexities, the *Hippias Major* is a unified work; the themes are related mutually, . . . and the arguments take an orderly sequence. (p. 181)

Both passages are surprising. The first seems to separate Socrates' method of interrogation from the character of the person with whom he speaks. The second appears to overlook the obvious way in which the question "What is *to kalon*?" dominates the dialogue.

Woodruff's two announced interests, the character of Hippias and the method of Socrates, divide his work into literary and scholarly parts. In his literary explorations of Hippias' character, Woodruff finds that Hippias is the supremely disturbing sophist because of his extraordinary versatility (p. 115). Moreover, Hippias is distressingly shallow. Yet, most important for this dialogue, Hippias is far from stupid. His answers to Socrates' questions are not so obtuse as they appear. Woodruff defends him with the novel proposal that Hippias really understands Socratic questioning and its hopelessness (pp. 127–30), and that instead of seriously trying to answer Socrates, he dodges. Furthermore, his toleration of Socrates' abuse is explicable in terms of his ambassadorial tendency to agreeableness (p. 125). These are key points of Woodruff's literary analysis. In his treatment of Socrates' method, Woodruff concentrates upon what is presupposed as essential for a successful definition and whether what is presupposed entails a full-fledged ontology. He shows that Socrates assumes that what is to be defined, such as the fine, is that which is the explanation for all its further instances, that which is strictly and purely what it is, and that which is the same in all the instances. Or, in Woodruff's technical vocabulary, a definition must satisfy the explanation, self-predication, and unity requirements.[2] In this dialogue, according to Woodruff, the *definiendum* satisfying these requirements is not yet the transcendental form of the middle dialogues. I shall return to these points after taking up the second passage I have quoted.[3]

In spite of the fact that the *Hippias Major* "carries no explicit message," it does have an explicit, single, unifying theme, *to kalon* or the fine, which organizes the dialogue and may direct our interest in it. That the topic of the fine does unify the dialogue and properly direct its interpretation requires justification. Woodruff has allowed that "the themes [of the dialogue] are related mutually." But this does not go far enough. In the context of this dialogue, inquiry into who Hippias and Socrates are ought to center upon their link with the fine. Woodruff offers some excellent insights along this line, but does not fully utilize them. For example, on page 130 he observes in regard to Hippias:

> In his amazing flexibility he is personally a model for the logical behavior of the word *kalos*. Neither one stands for anything by itself; both depend on their contexts for what they are. As Hippias is a mathematician in Athens, but an antiquarian in Sparta, so fineness could be *gold* for jewelry but *figwood* for cooking spoons. Thus the long opening of the dialogue has the effect of calling our attention to ways in which Hippias is a living metaphor for its philosophical subject.

Woodruff adds on the same page that "Socrates calls our attention to another way in which Hippias is personally connected with his subject. Hippias is *kalos*; he is dressed *kalōs*; and, most important of all, he speaks *kalōs*." Unfortunately, these insights are not followed up in Woodruff's work. Rather little is made of Hippias as "a living metaphor" for the fine.[4] By the same token, Woodruff does not consider the way in which Socrates too may be a living exemplar of it. Woodruff notes that "Plato uses Socrates as the example to set against the nonphilosophical sophists" (p. 118), yet he does not elaborate the possibility that Socrates himself provides some sort of an answer to the question of the dialogue. Woodruff aptly states that the topic of the fine is closely joined to virtue, since in every Socratic attempt to define a virtue it is early established that the virtue is fine (p. 111, n. 2).[5] Hence, Woodruff urges, "The *Hippias Major* has virtue as its underlying theme" (p. 112). But who better exemplifies for Plato the possibility of human virtue than Socrates? Is it not necessary to discern in Socrates himself, in the life of questioning, an answer to the questions at issue in the early dialogues of search? Socrates in *Apology* 23a–b indicates that he is a "paradigm" of true human knowledge, and might he not as well serve as an account of what the other human virtues are? Thus, the questions that Woodruff saw as separate—"Who are Hippias and Socrates?" and "What is the fine?" and even perhaps "What is Socrates' technique of inquiry and definition"—connect intimately with the topic of the fine.

The value of taking the two interlocutors as representatives of the fine may be best appreciated by observing the tension in the dialogue between the apparent fine and the truly fine and the association of each of the interlocutors with one of these. That Hippias concerns himself merely with what appears fine to the many emerges in his three attempts at definition of the fine and becomes explicit in the section that considers the fine as *to prepon* or the appropriate (293c–294e). This section serves, in fact, to divide the three attempts of Hippias to determine what appears beautiful and the Socratic definitions of the truly beautiful. Nonetheless, even after Socrates takes over, Hippias remains committed to appearances, for he offers as proof that power is fine the evidence that the finest thing is political power, whereas Socrates responds that the finest thing is wisdom (296a). These are but a few indications that there is much material in the dialogue useful for contrasting the manners in which the interlocutors are fine.[6]

Some of the passages I have cited from Woodruff's book suggest that he is often prepared to recognize that the dialogue has a single theme, which is virtue or the fine.[7] The reason he seems less occupied with this at other times is that he wishes to explore how the *Hippias Major* fits into the story of Plato's development as a philosopher, and especially in connection with the dispute over the authenticity of this dialogue. The attempt to trace an account of Plato's development has been the center of much scholarship over at least the last hundred years. Woodruff's attention to this theme, particularly as involved with authenticity, diminishes his attention to the fine and the unity of the dialogue because the study of development cannot remain within this dialogue. In spite of Woodruff's claim that he is "neutral on the rest of Plato's work," this is hardly so. His whole analysis is colored by acceptance of the view that the *Socratic* quest for definitions of the early dialogues need only make modest suppositions which *Plato* subsequently elaborates into a full metaphysical doctrine. Woodruff is remarkably reluctant to avoid flat assertion of the various parts of this story of development, but it governs his topics and his use of evidence.

My remarks on which questions pertaining to the dialogues ought to hold our attention tend to champion the question explicitly raised in the dialogue, rather than questions provoked by systematic interests, such as, "What is the ontological standpoint attained in this dialogue?" or "Is this dialogue genuine?" Such orientation may appear of doubtful value. Every interpretation does take up the explicit question of the dialogue, no matter how it allows others to overshadow it. Moreover, it seems inescapable that we turn to any particular dialogue with broader questions resulting from our reading of the others. Yet it must be recognized that all approaches to the dialogues other than the one I propose are always threatened with becoming curiosities of scholarship since they begin from what is unobvious and presuppose an unestablished global view of the corpus. Nothing can be more obvious in regard to many of the dialogues than that they present a discussion about a particular moral notion. Other questions about these dialogues presuppose a much less obvious global interpretation. But to start from a global view that is unobvious and undemonstrated, and indeed demonstrable only by interpretation of particular dialogues, risks forcing the evidence to fit the hypothesis. For those who accept such a global view, of course, the questions seem so evident and the possible answers so clear that both the questions and their procedure are impervious to challenge. However, as this global view of the dialogues fades from conviction, or for nonbelievers, the questions and the assumptions behind them are of doubtful value. Furthermore, I suggest that the most philosophical approach to a dialogue is to take it as provocation for reflection upon its announced topic. In the case of the *Hippias*, whether it is by Plato or not and however it fits into a story of intellectual development, interpretation concentrated upon the bearing of the dialogue on its topic, the fine, promises us philosophical reward. For in asking "What is the fine?" under the challenge of this historical text, we aim to find the truth about a matter of concern to us, rather than just to confirm our general presumptions about Plato or the early history of philosophy.

Fortunately, as noted above, Woodruff is remarkably free from bald assertion of any story of Socrates' or Plato's development. He even allows that "we do not know for certain whether Plato ever changed his mind on philosophical matters, and we never shall. . . . His written works can at least be stretched to allow either interpretation: the unitarian view that Plato's theory of Forms is presupposed in dialogues that do not mention it, or the developmental view that Plato's theory emerged in a middle period" (p. 175). Yet Woodruff argues that the *Hippias Major* contains no full-fledged ontological theory, and for him much rides on this, specifically, the authenticity of the dialogue. Rather than employing criteria, such as matters of style, to determine the authenticity of the dialogue, Woodruff suggests that if it can be objectively determined that the *Hippias* fits into a good story of Plato's development then there is much evidence for its being genuine. Let us trace the argument and thereby extend our reflection upon the second issue I set out at the beginning—namely, how interpretation of the rest of the dialogues should have an impact upon interpretation of a particular dialogue.

Woodruff's strategy is to list what are generally agreed to be the prominent features of the "mature" theory of forms and then to determine the extent of their presence in the *Hippias Major* and the other early dialogues. He finds three of eight features in the *Hippias*, but urges that these three (requirements for explanation, self-predication, and unity) are actually just requirements for a satisfactory definition rather than a full theory of forms. He argues that the dialogue is innocent of the five remaining features and even that it evidences naïveté in regard to them. This latter is an important point, for there may be many reasons for an author's silence about some of his ideas. But if it could be shown that the characters are naive in such a way that it is likely the author is too, then there is good evidence for claiming intellectual development in the author.

The only real arguments for Plato's naïveté, however, occur on page 166. Here Woodruff claims that the *Hippias* is naive in its utilization of language that points to the immanence of the forms in perceptible things. Yet Woodruff also states that "the various expressions Plato uses to connect a form and its namesakes do not at any stage in his career clearly betoken an ontological choice." Hence the absence from the *Hippias* of explicit talk of the transcendence of the forms amounts to an argument from silence. On the same page he notes that the dichotomy of being and becoming characteristic of the mature theory of forms is "incompatible with the linking of the two at 293c2, but is nowhere directly considered." Once again this hardly amounts to a compelling argument for doctrinal disparities explicable only as being due to evolution of thought. So it seems all we have are arguments from silence. Just how far can we go with the claim that since the *Hippias* does not utilize features of the theory of forms— such as their transcendence of particular sensibles and the contrast of their *being* to everything else's *becoming*—that it marks immaturity in the author's intellectual progress?

If we assume that an author has fully worked out his thoughts on certain issues, or merely that he holds some views on them, need we expect the author to introduce them into every work or even to allude to them? Since Plato's writings take the form of dramatic dialogues rather than treatises, we ought to be wary of this expectation. Nonetheless, many interpreters of Plato more or less explicitly believe his dialogues to be principally vehicles of his doctrines. An extreme version of the position may be found in these comments from Dorothy Tarrant: "It is inconceivable that a thinker like Plato should at any point go back upon his own development and revert to a more primitive stage of metaphysical theory," and "Plato will vary his emphasis from one dialogue to another; he may set metaphysic aside to concentrate on ethical or logical problems. . . .

What metaphysic Plato does introduce will, however, always represent the actual stage of thought at which he has arrived."[8] As extraordinary and oracular as these statements are, most efforts to elaborate the Platonic system of thought end up working from a similar position.

In less extreme form it is assumed in Woodruff's book when he argues that the *Hippias* is authentic because it has a doctrinal niche in Plato's intellectual development. In particular, on page 178, Woodruff contends that the *Hippias* should come between the *Euthyphro* and the *Republic*. The claim about its following the *Euthyphro* is made thus: "Had the fine-girl argument of the *Hippias* been in the air [that is, the argument that no perceptible thing is solely fine and not also ugly in comparison with something finer], Socrates could not simply have assumed the overly strict requirement in the *Euthyphro* [that there might be an action that is solely pious]." And in regard to the *Republic*, Woodruff asserts that there is a gap in the passage at 479a that is supplied by the *Hippias*. He says, "We may, therefore, understand the *Republic* as generalizing from the three first arguments of the *Hippias* to the conclusion that *any* of the many fine things will be seen to be foul. Without the *Hippias Major*, we could not explain why Plato leaves the gap; with it, we can reasonably suppose Plato thought the point too well-known to require argument." Do such arguments carry much conviction, and do they reflect Woodruff's pledge to neutrality in the interpretation of the rest of the dialogues? I think answers to both questions must be negative.

Woodruff seems to hold that the dialogues are written to supply the latest pieces of an evolving Platonic philosophy and that their author presupposes familiarity with his earlier dialogues on the part of his readers. That this general view is hardly "neutral" about the dialogues becomes obvious when an alternative possibility is considered. Suppose the direction of the argumentation of each dialogue is governed by the sorts of interlocutors engaged in them.[9] We would then need to ask whether it would be appropriate or pertinent for Socrates to introduce into the *Hippias* or any other of the early dialogues the five features of the mature theory of forms that Woodruff misses. Hippias is not an enthusiastic fellow investigator with Socrates. So long as moral virtues are being sought in conversation with rather antagonistic interlocutors, as is the case in many of the early dialogues, there appears to be little reason to introduce the full theory of forms. We do not expect the theory of forms in the *Apology* and *Crito* because of their settings. Why might not the same be the case for the other early dialogues?

In those dialogues in which the theory is found (the middle and later dialogues), Socrates speaks principally with friendly, inquisitive, and sophisticated interlocutors. Of course, we may ask why Plato chose to use such interlocutors and even whether this choice reflects evolving philosophical interests. Yet, this does not just push back the question of possible development one step. To take seriously the influence on the course of the dialogue of its particular interlocutors is to allow that Plato's concerns go well beyond systematic metaphysics. He is fundamentally concerned with the relationship of universal wisdom and particular human souls. Plato may find it rewarding to deal with certain topics through certain interlocutors without delving into the complete theory of forms. In short, there are possible explanations for the absence of explicit treatment of doctrines besides evolution in Plato's metaphysics. Unless it can be made compelling that the early dialogues really demand the introduction of the full theory of forms—and how could this ever be compelling except on the view that Plato would always introduce his most difficult thoughts into every dialogue—we would do better to seek for reasons it is not introduced other than that the author was unaware of it.

I have presented reason to doubt Woodruff's strategy of interpreting the *Hippias Major* by fitting it into a pattern of Plato's emerging thought. His strategy, I fear, employs the unknown—Plato's own supposed doctrinal positions gleaned from the rest of the corpus—to elucidate what is obscure, the argument of a single dialogue. My counterproposal is that we account for the doctrines that appear in various dialogues by the interlocutors involved and the dramatic situations depicted—that is, what is present in each dialogue itself—rather than by any presumed understanding of their author's views.[10] Persistence in my approach promises an interpretation of each dialogue that understands it as a fully coherent work, since all that occurs in the dialogue will be read as motivated by its participants. The value for this approach of familiarity with other dialogues is not only enhanced sensitivity to matters likely to be significant in a Platonic dialogue but also stimulation to employ the approach vigorously. I believe that just where statements and arguments from different dialogues appear inconsistent is where one needs especially to locate purposes in each of the several dialogues that lead to the conflicting positions. Ultimately, then, the development of fully coherent interpretations of the individual dialogues by invoking their dramatic situations as motivating their philosophical directions will contribute to the elaboration of a coherent interpretation of the entire Platonic corpus. In following up the topic of the role of interlocutors in providing dialogues a direction, I shall be dealing with the third issue I proposed to examine, the relationship of the literary and philosophical components of the dialogue.

Woodruff does have occasion to concentrate upon the role of the interlocutor in directing the dialogue. There is in his book some attempt at the approach I have suggested. Woodruff pursues this line, however, exclusively to defend Hippias against the appearance of terrible stupidity. He offers, as previously noted, the novel view that Hippias deliberately fumbles Socrates' request for a definition. Woodruff states, "Hippias probably knows, as having some experience of Socrates (301b), that no one wins by seriously trying to answer Socratic questions. He therefore shifts ground. Instead of trying to say what the fine is, he tries to get away with mentioning something that is fine. He tries this three times. Had he an audience, as he is accustomed, he might have succeeded in turning aside Socrates' question with laughter" (p. 169). Woodruff also remarks that "alone among Socrates' interlocutors in dialogues of search, Hippias cares nothing for the subject or the method of Socratic inquiry. No wonder he and Socrates are talking at cross purposes" (pp. 124–25). The trouble with such interpretation of the course of the dialogue is that it does not accord with the evidence of the text. Admittedly Hippias is not especially enthusiastic (see, for example, 291b7–8), but there is little reason to think that he is saying anything other than what he believes to be the best answer and nearly none that he is doing this because he understands the futility of trying to answer Socrates.

Woodruff's case ultimately depends upon the plausibility of this claim: "It is impossible to read the dialogue and believe that Hippias did not recognize the Questioner. . . . He must have recognized the Questioner: we know from their greetings and the interchange at 301b, ff., that Hippias was familiar with Socrates and his methods" (p. 108). Yet what Woodruff thinks impossible I think quite possible. Hippias does not really show much understanding of Socrates. The opening exchange reveals that Socrates has a good grasp of Hippias' activities and motivations, but not vice versa. Only well into the dialogue, at 301b, does Woodruff find the evidence that Hippias knows the Socratic style of questioning; Hippias' outburst, however, need only reflect his response to his present interchange with Socrates. Generally, all those passages in which Hippias suggests that he will have an easy time answering Socrates (for example, 286e5–287b3, 288a3–5, 289d6–290a2, 291d6–7, and 295a3–6) indicate how unfamiliar he is with Socratic cross-examinations. Moreover, Socrates explicitly insists in 290d10–e2 that Hippias does not know the questioner. Also, Hippias seems more willing to engage in the conversation than he should be were Woodruff correct that he aims to evade Socrates (see esp. 293e9–10 and 295a1–6). Finally, I urge that Socrates can test his interlocutors only if they are saying what they believe. In the *Protagoras* and *Republic* 1, Socrates protests against an interlocutor saying anything else, and so it is unlikely that he would not object were Hippias to respond with other than his own beliefs. If it is doubtful that Hippias really understands Socrates, then it is unlikely that he aims to duck his questions.

We see that Woodruff does utilize dramatic aspects of the dialogue in his interpretation. In fact, he even uses the main insight from his literary interpretation in the scholarly section of his book, since the point we have been considering—namely, to what extent Hippias is serious in answering Socrates' questions—enters crucially into chapter 7 on the ontology of the dialogue. This is as it should be. For Plato so embeds consideration of questions in a dialogue setting—since he always seems most concerned with the relationship of the particular soul with wisdom—that the philosophy of the dialogue can never be disentangled from its participants. Woodruff properly turns toward the dramatic side of the dialogue and begins breaking down the distinction between literary and philosophical interpretation. My main objection to his manner of doing so is in his use of evidence. For points that he considers purely philosophical, Woodruff pursues the text diligently and marshals as much support as he can. When, however, he turns to assessing the interaction of the characters in the dialogue, he tends toward less minute inquiry. But the dialogue must be mined as strenuously for the evidence of an interpretation of the character of its participants as for the presuppositions of its arguments. Ultimately, these are not very far removed from each other. Neither the presuppositions of arguments nor the motivations of the interlocutors are openly stated, and the motivations are very much linked with the presuppositions shaping the arguments. I suggest, then, that Woodruff's division between literary features "accessible to laymen" and "subjects of interest mainly to Plato scholars" (p. x) interferes with an accurate account of the dialogue.[11]

In regard to the three issues concerning the interpretation of Plato provoked by Woodruff's book, I have proposed the following. The key question for us in interpreting a dialogue should be that question explicitly raised in the dialogue itself. In pursuing that question through the text, we must be attentive to Socrates' interlocutors' roles in shaping the course of the dialogue. And we must be ever cognizant that all the argumentation concerning the matter at issue is inextricably woven into the dramatic situation of the dialogue.

Reply to Ronald Polansky

Paul Woodruff

I agree with so many of Ronald Polansky's principles that in reading his review I am surprised to see the extent of our disagreement on particulars. We share a conception of the goals one should have in interpreting Plato, but we disagree as to how close I have come to meeting them on specific points. Rather than tire the reader with a rehearsal of the arguments I made in the book, I shall concentrate on the larger issues Polansky raises.

Subject of the Dialogue. Ought one to ask what is *the* subject of a dialogue like the *Hippias Major*? That would be a good question to ask of Berkeley's dialogues, but a very bad one to ask of, say *Oedipus Tyrannus*. On its face the *Hippias Major* is about the fine, τὸ καλόν; but it is equally about Hippias and Socrates, and the differences between them and their generic methods. It is, besides, an illustration of a method of inquiry that serves more to show the limits of human understanding than it does to illuminate the truth of things. At this deep level, it shares themes with Sophocles' play—the limits fixed on human wisdom and the hubris of human claims to knowledge. But to say that the play and the dialogue are about the same things would not be of much use to an interpretation of either; we merely begin to understand such works by noticing that they share a theme that runs through much of Attic literature. "What is this play or dialogue *about*?" is a beginner's question and should not occupy a serious reader very long, unless it is shorthand for requesting a thorough interpretation of a work understood to be complex.

The various themes of the *Hippias Major* are related, of course; and Polansky is right that they cluster around the mysterious nature of the fine. To say this, however, is informative only insofar as we know what the fine is; but that knowledge is no more granted to us than to Socrates. I am drawn to Polansky's suggestion that Socrates himself is an illustration of an implicit account of the fine. The point must be taken weakly: Socrates would not allow that an adequate account could be derived simply from an example;[1] and in any case Socrates is plainly dissatisfied with himself and with his grasp of the fine in the *Hippias Major* (304c ff). Nor is Plato himself an unqualified admirer of Socrates. The comedy Plato writes is not such as to present us with a character that is simply ideal.

The wisest course is to admit that we do not know exactly what the fine is, and that we are therefore unable to say how much of its nature we can learn from the example of Socrates. Showing Socrates at work, and investigating the nature of the fine, belong in the same structured whole; but they are not the same thing.

The Relevance of Global Interpretation. Should a global view of Plato's work affect the interpretation of a single dialogue? Yes and no. Three points for the affirmative follow. First, broad questions that arise from attempts to view Plato's work as a whole must be answered with reference to particular works. Some of the questions a reader brings to the *Hippias Major* (or any other dialogue) should be motivated by global concerns. Second, in considering the grave challenge to the authenticity of the *Hippias Major*, we must ask whether the dialogue is consistent in style and doctrine with Plato's other work, and to do that one must be informed by general views about Plato's style and doctrine. Authenticating a particular work must depend on a view of the whole oeuvre. There is no escaping that. Third, uniformity within a set of Plato's works is relevant to the interpretation of each member of the set; and this uniformity is observed by an overview of Plato's work. It is an important feature of the *Hippias Major*, for example, that the rules Socrates introduces for definition are essentially the same as those he uses elsewhere on other subjects with other partners. It is astonishing how uniformly Socrates proceeds in the dialogues of search, almost heedless of the protests of his various antagonists.[2] This uniformity must be part of an adequate account of each particular dialogue: it shows how little in each case Socrates is actually responding to his partner, and how considerable is Socrates' own stake in the presuppositions of the inquiry on which he insists.

On the other hand, it would be a poor method to force an interpretation to yield results predicted by a global view. I do not think I have done this. I was in doubt during more than a year's work as to the authenticity of the *Hippias Major* and found myself assenting to it only after completing the greater part of my interpretation. My larger views about Plato determined the questions I asked but not (unless I deceive myself) the answers I found. Polansky gives the impression that my reading of the *Hippias Major* was guided by my desire to fit the work into a certain developmental scheme. Quite the contrary. I do not entirely subscribe to the scheme in question; but finding that the dialogue fit into it nevertheless, I thought it useful to point this out. At no point did I appeal to a global view of Plato's development in my interpretation of the dialogue itself.

In this context, Polansky wonders why I paid attention to ontological issues on which the author of the *Hippias Major* is silent.[3] I do not think I should need to defend a way of reading Plato that asks questions about his ontology; this interest is shared by virtually all readers of Plato. I found that the *Hippias Major* did not commit its author to the ontology associated with Plato's middle period works, and this finding allowed me to argue that the dialogue is similar in respect of doctrine to the *Euthyphro*, with which it has other affinities. I do not myself have a view about the unity of Plato's doctrine or of his alleged development. But I thought it useful to mention in the book my discovery that the dialogue fits neatly into the widely held theory that Plato proceeded from ontological neutrality toward a transcendent ontology. This answers dialectically one objection to the dialogue's authenticity: some readers have thought the dialogue too mature philosophically for the relatively early place to which its style would assign it. I have answered this objection in my book, although I admit that the objection presupposes a scheme about which I retain considerable skepticism.[4]

I agree with most of Polansky's general comments on developmental interpretations of Plato. They tend, however, to use shaky assumptions that I disclaim in my book and that I do not hold:

1. Silence on a point is no proof that the author has not considered it, but silence on an ontological distinction is evidence that a given text does not commit its author to that distinction. If the *Hippias Major* is silent on the being/becoming distinction, for example, that fact may be used (with other evidence) to support the conclusion that its author did not think he had to make that distinction in order to do adequately what he attempts in that dialogue. Moreover, it is quite proper to point out that the *Euthyphro* and the *Hippias Major* are silent on similar issues. That conclusion supports the case for authenticity without presupposing a developmental model.

2. Discrepancies among dialogues need not imply a change of mind on Plato's part; Polansky is surely right that some of these are due to differences in the dramatis personae. Still, Plato is responsible for his characters and for how they affect the arguments. Also, as I have said, Socrates has an amazing ability *not* to be affected by the par-

ticular features of a situation (and this is consistent with his being the exemplar for the famous description of the philosopher at *Theaetetus* 173d ff). Some discrepancies, then, are evidence for a change of mind.[5]

Because of the challenge to its authenticity, the *Hippias Major* demands special attention to the question of discrepancies with other dialogues. Discrepancy does not disprove authenticity; nor does its absence refute the athetizers. But a case for the *Hippias Major* would be badly marred if it were unable to place the dialogue in a family of Platonic works with which it has close affinities. We do not need to accept a developmental model for Plato's works to notice that they do fall naturally into several groups united by similarities of style and substance (*Plato: Hippias Major*, p. 175).

Literature or Philosophy? How should an interpretation deal with the relationship between what Polansky calls literary and philosophical components of the dialogue?[6] Here I think we are in almost total agreement on strategy, although we disagree perhaps about the order in which the material in a dialogue should be covered.

I did not write the book in the order Polansky supposes. I mention this only because it illustrates the dangers of inferring authorial intention from a text. Apparently I give the impression of having set out to write a book for scholars primarily about philosophical topics and added the literary chapters "to round out the book." Actually, I offered the manuscript to the publisher without the scholarly chapters, these being of less interest to me; I added them later at the publisher's request, meaning them to deal with questions that scholars had been asking about the dialogue, but that were not directly related to my reading of the work. That was why I warned the general reader away from them in my preface. I do not want any part of a debate as to whether literary or philosophical components deserve more serious attention in Plato's work.

Polansky is quite right: there are a number of defects in my literary chapters; I hope the charitable reader will not ascribe these to contempt for the subject. As a practicing playwright, I take Plato's technique very seriously indeed. My arguments in the book depended rather too much on abstract considerations of dramaturgy.[7] I think now that an adequate literary reading of Plato should make more use of the literature of Plato's period. I would have done better to appeal especially to parallels from Greek comedic literature.

I agree with Polansky that literary and philosophical interpretation of a Platonic dialogue should proceed side by side; but I do not think that we should apply the same methodology to literary and philosophical questions alike. Polansky faults me for using different styles of argument in the two areas, but I think he would have to do the same. That is partly because of the divergence in tradition between literary and philosophical scholars (who must be satisfied in different ways) but also because of the different sorts of evidence required and the different sorts of presuppositions for charitable inference. Philosophical charity calls us to read every argument in such a way that it is valid, but literary charity might lead us to expect the same arguments to be glaring fallacies. A consistent character may say inconsistent things.

For such reasons as this, tension rises between literary and philosophical attempts to interpret a dialogue. This too is inescapable. Reading Plato is hard work and inevitably frustrating: total satisfaction in interpretation eludes us. Nevertheless, χαλεπὰ τὰ καλά; the experience is good for us. In the Socratic spirit, I should be grateful to Polansky for reminding me not to be too comfortable with my views about Socrates and his quest.

13

Kenneth Dorter's Interpretation of the *Phaedo*

Joachim Dalfen

In his book on the *Phaedo*, Kenneth Dorter attempts to come to a general understanding of the philosophy of Plato.[1] He considers the best way to achieve this to be the careful reading of a particular dialogue. He tries to combine two methods that are regarded as inimical to each other—the analytic approach (the analysis of individual isolated arguments and the evaluation of their logical correctness or uncorrectness) and the dramatic approach (whereby the dialogue is viewed as a dramatic unity rather than as the sum of its arguments and proofs). As I myself have been trying for more than ten years to show that only an interpretation that also takes into account the literary-artistic organization of the dialogues can hope to capture adequately Plato's messages and intentions, I readily agree with Dorter when he says that the individual arguments and proofs deserve serious consideration only as additional events within the drama, and that it constitutes a distortion of Plato's intentions and achievement to look for objective validity in them (p. ix).

In my opinion, Dorter is also right when he says (p. 134) that the insight into the boundaries of our wisdom is a persistent theme in the dialogues of Plato, and that Plato was convinced that some questions can be answered only tentatively, while at the same time, however, Plato's aporetic (and not skeptical) attitude is closer to the truth than the claims of other philosophers to have found absolute resolutions (p. 140). Dorter likewise tells us what consequences the insight into the limitations of human wisdom had for Plato's manner of writing, among others the consequence

My thanks to R. Philippi for translating this review into English.

that Plato never stated doctrines in his own name but only through the persons of his dialogues, ad hoc and ad hominem in the particular dramatic situation. Since I agree with him on this point, I also consider right and essential Dorter's statements about Plato's undogmatic and unsystematic approach to philosophy (p. 179) and about the theory of forms (pp. 120ff.): the different versions of the theory of forms in different dialogues do not indicate changes in Plato's point of view; rather they depend on the particular dialogue, on the particular questions, on the participants in the dialogue, and so on.

How then does Dorter proceed to interpret the *Phaedo*, intending thereby to synthesize two methods? He goes through the dialogue bit by bit, from the introduction to the first scene by way of the individual stages of the discussion to the myth and the final scene. He divides this continuous treatment of the dialogue into eleven chapters: "Introduction" (*Pho.* 57a1–61b7), "Life, Death, and Suicide" (61b7–69e5), "The First Argument: Reciprocity in Nature" (69e6–72e2), "The Second Argument: Recollection" (72e3–77a5), and so on. The headings of the chapters already indicate that in Dorter's treatment of the text one of the two methods dominates: the analysis of the statements, arguments, and proofs.

Dorter proceeds in each case in the following way: he analyzes the arguments presented in each piece of the text, he divides them into single steps, and he examines the relation of the individual statements to each other, and their progression and logical correctness; often he reports as well the opinions of other interpreters and discusses them. The discussion of the *locus vexatus* at 61b7–69e5 is, for example, very good: Dorter compares four interpretations that tried to explain the paradox posed here that death is indeed better than life, but that suicide is forbidden. Finally he suggests that the whole of the rest of the dialogue is an attempt to solve this paradox. The solution he himself proposes for the paradox of suicide is, incidentally, not an especially new one (pp. 31ff.).

But Dorter does not stop at analyzing what the characters in Plato's *Phaedo* state. The chapter about the soul as attunement (pp. 98ff.) is an example of how Dorter puts problems into the statements of Socrates and then tries to solve these self-created problems. His analysis and interpretation seems to me to be much harder to understand than Plato's text. He questions not just whether Socrates' answer to Simmias' objection that the soul is perhaps merely the attunement of the body is adequate but also whether it serves as a reply to epiphenomenalism (a theory of modern physiology that considers the soul an epiphenomenon of the nervous system). I do not think that the inclusion of epiphenomenalism contributes to making Socrates' words clearer.

The preliminaries to this book say that it is an attempt to radically rethink and reinterpret the *Phaedo* and, by means of the *Phaedo*, Plato's philosophy as a whole. Where are the radical new insights? Obviously they lie in a thesis that Dorter poses and attempts to assert again and again throughout the whole interpretation of the *Phaedo*. The reader finds this thesis for the first time at the beginning of the third chapter (p. 33) in the form of a question: Did Plato want to present the arguments for the immortality of the soul as serious demonstrations of the eternal perpetuation of our individual consciousness? Somewhat later (pp. 40ff.) he declares that Plato does not make it unmistakably clear that the proofs are not meant to be applied to personal immortality and the particular soul, but to soul in general; he says that one could postulate an argument like that of the soul as principle of motion, such an argument being in fact implied here (72a11–e2). To convince the reader, Dorter distinguishes three levels of the argument: the religious level, at which it is meant to appeal to Socrates' troubled audience; the second level, at which the notion of soul is already conceived more broadly (soul as vital principle); and finally the third, at which the conception of the soul is broader still, being seen as world-soul or principle of energy from which even the characteristic of life can be abstracted. Dorter, on the one hand, is conscious that Plato developed this conception of the soul only in the *Phaedrus* and the *Laws*, but he suggests that Plato could already have had the conception of the soul as principle of motion when he wrote the *Phaedo*. That may be true, but Plato wrote for readers who did not yet know the *Phaedrus* and the *Laws*. Dorter proceeds in the same way as some philologists, who interpret the *Oedipus Tyrannus* in the light of the *Oedipus Colonus*, as if Sophocles had walked out before his audience and said: "Today I'm showing you the *Oedipus Tyrannus*. In about twenty years I will show you the *Oedipus Colonus*, and then you will know how to understand the *Tyrannus*."

Dorter observes rightly, on the one hand, that the conversation in the *Phaedo* is constantly about the personal immortality of the individual soul. On the other hand, he maintains (pp. 62ff.) that Plato did not believe our immortality to be of a personal nature, but that he considered the dramatic setting in the *Phaedo* dialogue an inadequate place to make this explicit. Plato wanted therefore to obscure deliberately the boundary between personal and impersonal immortality (p. 68; the assertion that Plato obscured what he actually wanted to say is repeated several times: pp. 154ff., 159, 161, and so on). The thesis that Plato does not speak about personal immortality is given another aspect in addition to the first one (that Plato thinks of the soul's immortality as a world-soul and a principle of motion)— namely, Dorter thinks (p. 77) *Phaedo*'s arguments furnish us with a conception of immortality closer to the discovery of eternity within ourselves than to unending individual perpetuity in time. Apart from the question of whether it is appropriate to look for statements of Plato about "unending individual perpetuity in time" in view of what he says about reincarnation and anamnesis, Dorter himself shows why he does not want to believe in Plato's believing in a life after death for the individual soul. To prove this thesis, he refers to Croesus' injunction to "count no one happy until he is dead" (p. 82). He interprets it as follows: as long as we are alive, our nature is subject to constant modification; as soon as we are dead, it is enduringly fixed. Our life after death can be conceived as an image of the perpetuity of our individual nature in the memory of, and in its effects on, future generations. Here the reader gets the strong impression that Dorter is not interpreting Plato, but rather that he wants to find in Plato what he himself believes in.

By means of his thesis Dorter also answers the question of why Plato lets Cebes agree to a conclusion (about the immortality and imperishability of the soul) that as such is not cogent (pp. 154ff.). First he asks some other questions: whether Plato perhaps was not aware of the weakness of the argument or lets Cebes agree because of the readers (Dorter several times thinks of the possibility of a noble lie) or whether Plato identifies himself with Cebes. Once again he answers by means of a recourse to, or better, an anticipation of, the *Phaedrus* and the *Laws*: the agreement of Cebes is legitimate if the soul is taken as the world-soul. Since, however, Socrates wants to lead his audience in the *Phaedo* to a particular belief because he realizes that this belief is the basis for moral behavior, Plato has to obscure the distinction between personal and impersonal immortality, and this is what he does throughout the whole dialogue. Dorter attributes falsely to Cebes what he himself believes. He seeks a confirmation of this from 107a9–b8, where Socrates says that the arguments need further analysis (where does he not say this?). Dorter gives the following interpretation (p. 161): Socrates hoped that his listeners, when they had more critical judgment, would analyze the argument and uncover its true implications.

Dorter correctly perceives that the author Plato shows in the *Phaedo* dialogue a situation where the deciding factor is that Socrates convinces his audience and gives them confidence that death is not the end of our existence. Dorter rightly stresses the importance of words like πίστις (belief) and πείθειν (to persuade), as well as παραμυθία (exhortation) as leitmotifs in the *Phaedo* (pp 8, 84ff., 94). He correctly recognizes that Socrates takes a role in the *Phaedo* different from his roles in the other dialogues. Dorter speaks of the role of the advocate (p. 8), and of the fear we all, like children, suffer from and must overcome. He does not draw the right consequences, however. In spite of saying that Plato was aware of the boundaries of human insight, he misses the signal Plato gives by means of the word διαμυθολογεῖν (70b). This word tells much about the degree of validity that Plato wants to be attributed to the "proofs" for the immortality of the soul. Dorter says (p. 214 n. 6) that the word ranges in meaning from "mythologize about" to simply "talk about," the best approximation being "speculate." This is what Dorter does himself; Plato, however, wanted to say something else with it. Dorter wants to interpret the *Phaedo* dramatically, and in a certain way he does just this. But what is one supposed to think of the author Plato (whom many regard not only as a great philosopher but also as a great writer) who, according to Dorter's interpretation, creates a dialogue with particular scenery, figures, and dramatic setting, but does so in such a way that the figures do not say what he actually wants them to say, but constantly obscure it? Socrates must hope that some time an able thinker will turn up who will reveal the true interpretations.

Dorter sees, too, that the myth at the end of the *Phaedo* relates to the particular soul and its life after death. Nevertheless, he keeps to his thesis that Plato did not take seriously the doctrine of the personal immortality of the soul (cf. also pp. 179ff.). To rescue his thesis he demands that we distinguish between a literal and a metaphorical reading of the myth (pp. 162ff.): one part should be understood literally and another part metaphorically (the difficulties and a possible criterion for the distinction are discussed on pp. 166ff.). Dorter sees in this myth a symbolic description of what we do to ourselves during life (summarizing, he says on p. 175 that the fate of the soul after death turns out to be an image of what it makes of itself during life); Plato's pretending to speak about the fate of the soul after death is a noble lie, like much else in the *Phaedo*. Dorter puts it in the following way, and I think he thereby admits the dilemma of his radical reinterpretation: "I have argued in preceding chapters that Plato does not put forth a serious doctrine of personal immortality in the *Phaedo*, in the sense of indefinite perpetuity. In the present chapter I would like to show that the myth is perfectly compatible with this view, without, however, denying that it is compatible with the traditional view as well" (p. 167). Already earlier (pp. 78ff.) Dorter has maintained that in the *Phaedo* one has to distinguish between metaphorical and literal statements: in a popular dialogue like the *Phaedo* Plato uses conceptions of popular religion as metaphors and speaks on a level intelligible to all, but the religious metaphors are meant to express abstract relationships.

One such metaphor for Dorter is the concept of Hades as Plato employs it in the *Phaedo*. Hades is, according to the words of Socrates, that place where the other, the good gods are, to whom the soul comes after having been separated from the body. Hades is the invisible i.e., the intelligible: the traditional religious conceptions are exchanged for a philosophical revision of these conceptions. Hades is taken as a symbol for a source of truth, understood in the philosophical sense. Dorter is certainly right in stating that Plato is giving a new philosophical meaning and dimension to the mythical-religious concept of Hades within the *Phaedo*. But I wonder whether the concepts of "metaphor" and "symbol"—both are critical for Dorter's method of interpretation—are appropriate. Plato is playing here with etymology, like other ancient philosophers, and the result of this playing is easy for every reader to recognize. Dorter, however, infers from Plato's using the concept of Hades "metaphorically" (in Dorter's sense) the right also to understand other statements of Plato in a way different from how they are put—for example, to maintain that Plato does not speak about the afterlife (the connection between the symbolic interpretation of Hades and Dorter's own thesis shows up clearly at pp. 37ff.).

Most of what Dorter calls "dramatic interpretation" is "symbolic." Here he offers some very accurate and appropriate remarks. He sees a relationship that Plato establishes between Theseus' voyage to Crete mentioned at the beginning of the dialogue and the dialogue as a whole. Theseus sailed to Crete with twice seven young Athenians and saved them and himself; in the *Phaedo* exactly fourteen present friends of Socrates are mentioned by name, and the motif of rescue plays a big role as well as that of the sea voyage (pp. 4ff., 84ff.). He is also certainly right in what he says about the relation between Socrates' interlocutors, Orphic-Pythagorean thinking, and the content of the *Phaedo* (p. 9). Moreover, he proposes an excellent answer to the question of why Plato chose Phaedo for the narrator and his name for the title of the dialogue: through his fate Phaedo could become a symbol for the theme of liberation, which runs throughout the dialogue—liberation in both the literal and the figurative senses (conversion to philosophy, p. 10).

Dorter also interprets the final scene symbolically (pp. 176ff.); that is, he interprets it on the basis of Orphic-Pythagorean conceptions of the themes of purification and liberation. The bathing of Socrates before his death is, for Dorter, a reference to Orphic rites of purification (in the Platonic dialogue Socrates says at 115a that he wants to save the women the toil of bathing his corpse); he sees in Orphic rites the reason for the exclusion of the women. He also sees an Orphic element in the mention of Socrates' legs and feet. Socrates dies lying on a bed, so that his feet do not touch the earth. Feet touching the earth symbolize the connection with the corporeal; having Socrates die without touching the earth with his feet is supposed to symbolize that his connection with the mortal world is broken forever. Here Dorter has probably seen far too much; above all he has failed to notice that his symbolic interpretation does not match his thesis. For Orphic-Pythagorean symbolism must be related to the conception of the afterlife of the personal, particular soul, albeit in the form of reincarnation. Yet it is just this conception that Plato is said not to believe in.

The dramatic interpretation—the task of which would be to show that the author is hinting at something relevant for the content and the progress of the philosophical discussion by means of the organization of the treatment of the dialogue, the behavior of the figures of the text, and the like—

is only occasionally applied by Dorter. It has already been mentioned that he correctly describes the role that Plato gives to Socrates in the *Phaedo* and that is different from that in the other dialogues, and that he draws the right conclusion concerning Plato's intention in the *Phaedo*. He also states correctly that at 76a–b the behavior of one person in the text—Simmias' hesitation in deciding between the two possible alternatives—is a sign that there is a problem in the content of the discussion (pp. 62ff.). Yet immediately he draws the wrong conclusion, because he brings in his own thesis, namely, that Plato did not believe in personal immortality, but rather wanted to leave this obscure. Dorter also discusses well the function of the interlude at 84c1ff.: Plato lets skepticism and worries arise among the audience, and these worries demand a new argument and indeed a justification of the possibility of an argument against the skepticism that the audience begins to feel (p. 83). Since Dorter, however, builds up his interpretation of the *Phaedo* on the theses that Plato meant something other than what he had the figures of his text utter, and that the apparent casualness of the "dramatic naturalism" and the ostensible appeal to popular religious conceptions mask the rigor of the organic structure of the arguments (p. 46), Dorter ultimately is not able to make much out of a "dramatic" interpretation.

What I consider good, nevertheless, are his observations that the linguistic formulation of one argument (78c1ff.) is imprecise, that some premises are weakened by qualifications, and that this procedure is meant to call our attention to the fact that the argument is not a rigorous deduction (pp. 75ff.); good too are his remarks about the function of Socrates' autobiographical account (p. 130; i.e., about the background for the understanding from which the theory of forms was developed).

Although Dorter gives many fundamentally relevant insights into Plato's manner of philosophizing, and contributes many valuable remarks and good analyses and interpretations of individual arguments, he generally does not understand the *Phaedo* correctly. First of all, notwithstanding the text he wants to prove his thesis that Plato means something other than what he makes his characters say. As far as method is concerned, this procedure leads him again and again to bring ideas from later dialogues into the *Phaedo* (apart from what has already been mentioned, see also pp. 22, 30, 108ff., where ideas from the *Republic, Philebus, Phaedrus*, and *Timaeus* may be found). Moreover, he skips over parts of the text that contradict his thesis. For example, at the very beginning of the *Phaedo*, the question of the afterlife of the human soul and the continued existence of individual consciousness is posed explicitly, and this question is maintained and constantly called to the attention of the reader (95bc, 106e). At 70a–b it likewise is said that the question of the soul's afterlife demands much ἐλπίς (hope), παραμυθία (exhortation), and πίστις (belief), and the interlocutors want to διαμυθολογεῖν (converse) with each other, whether this be εἰκός (probable) or not. Dorter rightly observes that Socrates' task in this dialogue consists in overcoming the fear of his interlocutors by arguments that affect their feelings (by ἐπᾴδειν). He pursues the leitmotif of πίστις (belief) throughout the text and rightly states that the correctness of arguments is not discussed by people who are not touched emotionally by the problem under discussion; he is also right in maintaining that Plato is aware of the boundaries of human wisdom. Yet he misses the signals Plato gives by the words διαμυθολογεῖν (to discuss) and εἰκός (probable), or rather he understands them in the wrong way. Plato shows through them that in a question like that of immortality there cannot exist cogent rational proofs (see also 85c). It is significant that Dorter does not examine the end of the rational argumentation and discussion at all (107a–d): Cebes declares that he cannot ἀπιστεῖν (disbelieve) the λόγοι (arguments). Simmias is likewise incapable of this; because of the magnitude of the problem and his human weakness, some ἀπιστία (lack of belief) still remains in him. Socrates agrees and adds that the first ὑποθέσεις (hypotheses), although they seem to be πισταί (believable), must be examined further, and that his interlocutors, if they proceed carefully, will follow the logos. Then Socrates talks about the consequences that the belief in the immortality of the soul has for human life.

Dorter skips this part of text (likewise, for example, the interlude at 102a) and fails to appreciate the weight of this statement because (like almost all interpreters of Plato) he neglects one circumstance that is essential for Plato's philosophizing and for his conception of philosophy. For this reason, too, he does not know what to do about the final scene (115a3ff.)—apart from the symbolic interpretation. Socrates' instructions to his friends to look after themselves and to live according to what has just been said, the jailor's statements about Socrates and Socrates' behavior toward death—all these point to what I call existential philosophizing and the commitment of philosophizing. The demeanor of Socrates, which Plato describes as early as the introductory scene and in some interludes, is the strongest argument for the hope of an afterlife. The reminder to the friends to keep to what has been said in their future life expresses Plato's attitude that philosophy does not consist of theoretical discussion about particular propositions, but rather that the conclusions to which the interlocutors together come are binding for their behavior as long as they cannot replace the logos they have found with a better one. Socrates expresses this in the *Phaedo* (100a) and indeed with words that strongly recall the *Crito* (46b–c). The structure of the *Phaedo's* discussion is also the same as the discussion with *Crito*. This structure is marked by the words ὁμολογεῖν, ὁμολογία (agreement): the interlocutors examine a logos and determine whether they agree, and the agreement then becomes the basis for further examination. The agreement remains valid and binding for the interlocutors as long as it cannot be replaced by a better logos.[2]

Dorter may indeed conclude (p. 35) that Socrates formulates the outcome of the first argument with reservation (71e–72a), but he expresses his astonishment that Socrates afterwards treats it as established without reservation. The reason for this is that the interlocutors have agreed on this point and from then on continue the discussion on the basis of this "agreement." The motif of "agreement" is completely disregarded by Dorter. He does not mention it, even though Plato indicates it clearly enough by the frequency with which his characters utter the words ὁμολογία, ὁμολογεῖν and the like (72a4, 9, 11, d7, 73c1, 74d9, 75a5, 76d2, 77c8, 93d1, 2, 94c3, 8, 95a3, 102b1, 8, 103a6, c7, 10, 105d11, 106b8, c4, 9, d7). At the end Socrates explicitly points out the existential importance of "agreement": if the friends are not willing to live according to what has been said now and in earlier times, then they will not do better in the future, even if they agree now (115b). "Agreement" is meaningful only if one abides by the opinion to which one agrees.

Since Dorter completely misses the importance of ὁμολογεῖν and ὁμολογία (agreement), he also misinterprets the "method of hypothesis." Socrates applies it in the *Phaedo* after that passage (100a) that so strongly reminds us of the *Crito*. He states that he always takes as a basis (ὑποθέμενος) that logos which seems to him the strongest one, and in each case takes for true that which seems to be in harmony (συμφωνεῖν) with that logos. Transferred to the dialogue, συμφωνεῖν (to be in harmony) corresponds to the ὁμολογεῖν (to agree) of the interlocutors. Dorter understands (pp. 115ff.) the Greek word *hypothesis* in the contemporary sense. This is not entirely wrong, nor is it entirely right. Thus Dorter is led to the inappropriate question of whether Socrates' "hypothesis" is a premise, a proposition, or a definition (pp. 120ff.). And since he obviously misinterprets ἄνωθεν ("from above"; 101d), he looks at length and in vain for a "higher hypothesis" and discusses many questions the text gives no reason to consider.

Several things have already been said about Dorter's treatment of the myth, but let me add a few more. Above all he interprets the myth metaphorically, and he relates what is said about the fates of the soul after death to worldly life. Thus punishment and rewards in Hades are supposed to be symbols of what we do to ourselves during our lifetime; the daimon is interpreted in the sense of behaviorism. Neither the question of why Plato in the *Phaedo* (as in the *Gorgias*) has a myth follow the rational discussion, the logos, nor the question of the myth's function is put by Dorter. The change in the manner of speaking and arguing at the end of such a dialogue must have some significance; it is surely connected with Plato's insight into the boundaries of our knowledge and wisdom, which

Dorter has correctly recognized. Plato has Socrates in the discussion with his friends look as successfully as he can for rational arguments and proofs for possible answers to the existential question of the immortality of the soul. Yet again and again Plato draws attention to the fact that definite knowledge cannot here be attained. In the end one must venture forth on a conviction; one must sail out into the ocean on a flimsy raft. Plato presents conviction and its basis in the form of religious speech, in the form of myth. The function of the myth and its relation to the preceding rational discussion (the logos) is misunderstood if the myth is interpreted symbolically and metaphorically (this does not, of course, mean that Plato imagined the other world literally as he described it in the myth).

In conclusion I would like to summarize the main points of my criticism of Dorter's book, the merits of which I have also tried to show.

1. Dorter argues the incorrect thesis that in the *Phaedo* Plato is not speaking seriously of the personal immortality of the particular soul, but rather is thinking of the world-soul and the soul as principle of motion. (Dorter dedicates a special chapter to the Platonic conception of the soul, pp. 179ff., at the beginning of which he says that it is of speculative character and that the preceding discussion is independent of any particular theory about what Plato thought was the ultimate nature of the soul.) This thesis has consequences for Dorter's method of interpretation—namely, his attempt to distinguish between literal and metaphorical statements, and his inclusion of ideas from later dialogues.

2. In spite of a correct basic approach, Dorter misinterprets an essential part of Platonic philosophizing and the Platonic conception of philosophy. He therefore skips some parts of the text whose importance for the message of the *Phaedo* he does not recognize, and he fails to understand others in the sense that Plato presumably intended.

3. Although Dorter tries to combine two methods—the analysis of arguments and the interpretation of the dramatic action—he mostly uses the first method (as is usual in the traditional interpretation of Plato), which takes as a starting point the premise that philosophy is an abstract system of theoretical propositions. But Plato tries to show, precisely by means of the literary-artistic form of the dialogue, that philosophy is always the convergence of the subject matter with concrete people in particular situations, and that the questions and possible answers are related to these people and their existence.

Reply to Joachim Dalfen

Kenneth Dorter

The first of the two sections of my discussion addresses the general problem of how to read a Platonic dialogue, and indirectly addresses some of the questions raised by Joachim Dalfen's critique of my book on the *Phaedo*. The second section deals with the review explicitly, in order to correct Dalfen's misrepresentations of what I have written.

I

Any philosopher of worth gives rise to difficulties of interpretation since he presents us with unaccustomed ways of thinking, but Plato occasions special difficulty because of his mixture of two such disparate modes of expression as conceptual argument and literary drama. How are they meant to react upon each other? Are they meant to be reconciled in interpretation, or is one to be subordinated to the other, or, indeed, is their conflict meant to *prevent* any interpretation from giving a fully satisfactory account of the dialogue as a whole? Within the confines of this short presentation I should like to sketch briefly one plausible approach to the problem, while recognizing that none is likely to be definitive.

The *Republic* presents us with a convenient starting point, since one finds in it statements about the value of both conceptual and artistic pursuits. In Book 7, when Socrates raises the question of how to turn the soul around from its preoccupation with the corporeal to an apprehension of the intelligible dimension, he argues that this is best begun by acquaintance with mathematical relations (521c ff), since relations are not reducible to corporeal properties per se (the bigness of a thing exists only in relation to something *else* that is smaller). Socrates advocates a sequence of five disciplines, the mastery of which will prepare us for proficiency in philosophical dialectic: arithmetic, plane geometry, solid geometry, astronomy, and harmony. Each of them is analytical in nature, belonging on the dianoetic level of the Divided Line, rather than the noetic (531d), for they operate essentially in deductive terms proceeding from basic ("hypothetical") principles; indeed mathematical studies are explicit examples of the workings of *dianoia* (understanding; 511a–b). Now, since Socrates is not content simply to use the irreducibility of relations as a way of making one aware of the intelligible *in general*, but insists in addition that one devote oneself between the ages of twenty and thirty (537b–d) to these rigorously analytic disciplines, followed by a further five years' study of dialectic (539e), it seems reasonable to conclude that Plato regarded analytical and conceptual rigor as very important indeed. Consequently it is only by arbitrarily disregarding the theoretical discussions in the dialogues that one can insist upon reading him without careful regard for and analysis of the arguments he presents. The *Parmenides, Theaetetus,* and *Sophist* in particular testify to an intellect fascinated with the nature of argument at the minutest level.

What, then, of the artistic dimension? Here one can point to the *Republic*'s emphasis on the arts in early education and the importance of the study of harmony later on. But this emphasis is in both cases qualified, and to an extent that leaves art with little reason to be pleased. In the first case it turns out that art is useful in early education only because the age of reason has not yet been achieved (401c–402a); in the second case the study of harmony is to remain an abstract theoretical study of the *principles* of harmony rather than an exposure to its *influence* (531b–c). Nor are any other dialogues more encouraging. Why then do we not simply conclude— as is often enough done—that the conceptual component of Platonic dialogues is important and the literary component is not?

The answer is that although Plato considered analytic conceptual rigor to be a necessary condition for philosophical attainment, he did not consider it by itself to be sufficient. If it were, philosophy at its highest level could be taught as other disciplines are (the previous examples of mathematics, astronomy, and harmony, for instance); but this, Plato believes, is impossible. Other disciplines can be taught extraneously, with the teacher exhibiting what is to be learned, and the student absorbing it. Philosophy, however, cannot be put into words like other subjects, as we are told in the *Seventh Letter*: it can effectively be "taught" only by kindling within the soul of the "learner" a spark that becomes self-sustaining (341c–d). (Recall also Socrates' remark about the impossibility of pouring wisdom from one soul into another like cups of wine [*Symp.* 175d].) A similar metaphor occurs in the *Phaedrus* (whose authenticity at least is not in question), where it is said that the only effective way to transmit philosophy is indirectly, by planting in a properly cultivated soul words whose seed will become self-sustaining (275e–277a). This ideal is illustrated in a noteworthy passage of the *Sophist* (265d–e):

> Theaetetus: Perhaps because I am young I often vacillate between both opinions, but now, looking at you and believing that you consider these things to have a divine origin, I too accept this.
>
> Stranger: That is fine, Theaetetus. And if we considered it possible that you might change your opinion in the future, we would now try by force of persuasion to make you agree with this account. But since I understand your nature, and that even without our arguments you yourself will come to the conclusion that you now say attracts you, I will let it go.

This is the same attitude that is conveyed in the *Theaetetus* by Socrates' comparison of his role as a teacher to that of a midwife who assists in delivering and passing judgment on the "conceptions" of his students (149a–151d). Passages like these, which emphasize the importance of cultivating enlightenment *within* the learner, rather than attempting to introduce it *into* him from without, are all the more significant in light of Socrates' decision not to write. And in view of Plato's sensitivity to this problem we may assume that his decision to write and publish philosophy was accompanied by an attempt to overcome the problem, by writing in such a way as to prevent his writings from being taken at face value, as if they were treatises. Certainly his choice of the dialogue form suggest that this was the case.

Here one can see the positive import of the literary dimension of the dialogues, for it prevents the reader in at least two ways from reading them as if they were treatises. First, since Plato himself never speaks in the dialogues, none of the views that the interlocutors express in them can be attributed to him with confidence. Second, the authority of the views expressed by Plato's presumptive spokesmen is continually compromised by reservations expressed either by the speaker himself or members of his audience, and occasionally by more subtle devices, such as a surreptitious inclusion of counterexamples, indirect references to other matters that reflect on the present discussion, or allusions to other dialogues or theories that suggest other directions in which the present discussion might be carried. The reader is thus forced to pursue the inquiry within himself rather than believing that he can accept it ready-made from the dialogue.

There is also a second, negative function of the literary dimension. Where Plato gives voice to his belief that philosophy cannot ultimately be put into words like other subjects, he also remarks that even if it could be, it would be dangerous to do so because very few people can be exposed to its tradition-dissolving power without ill effect. Thus even to the extent that philosophy can be put into words, this should be done in such a way that it will not speak to the wrong people (*Phr.* 275e), lest it excite contempt or arrogance in them (*Letter* VII, 341e), and destroy the simple faith of ordinary people (*Theae.* 180d). The dialogue form seems designed not only to provoke us into pursuing the inquiry within ourselves by subtly undermining any illusion that the words themselves are definitive; it also seems to aim at reinforcing the traditional values of those who do not respond to that subtle provocation, that is, those less likely to have the philosophical temper to support the iconoclastic implications of some of the inquiries.

These two claims, however, seem to contradict each other. How can the dialogue form be said on one hand to pull us deeper into the potentially tradition-dissolving philosophical inquiry, and on the other to hold us back from it by reaffirming traditional beliefs? What makes this double, nearly contradictory, thrust possible is the fact that Plato always says less than he might. Although philosophy ultimately cannot be put into words like other matters, Plato does not seem to want to put even as much of it into words as he could, and he thereby accomplishes both goals. First, by not making any of the iconoclastic implications of philosophy explicit, he reduces the chances that his dialogues will "speak to the wrong people": taken at face value the Platonic dialogues never completely deny, and usually seem to affirm, traditional values and faith. Second, by such dramatic means as were adumbrated above, he creates in more critical readers a dissatisfaction with those easy affirmations and inconclusive questionings, which seems intended to lead us beyond what he did say—not only to what he chose not to say but eventually to what cannot be said.

II

Professor Dalfen claims that his basic disagreement with my approach to Plato is that I emphasize the arguments while he believes that the emphasis should be on the dramatic aspect. This, however, is not the case at all. The real difference between us is that I believe that *both* the arguments and the drama are meant to be read with meticulous care, while Dalfen does not seem to believe that *either* of them is. In support of his claim that I have a predilection for the argumentative over the literary component of the dialogue, he points to the fact that I have, for the most part, organized the chapters of the book around the individual arguments, but this shows no such thing: since the dramatic "plot" of the dialogue consists of Socrates' arguments for immortality, the plot is the natural organizational principle whether on conceptual *or* literary grounds. The balance between my comments on the dramatic and conceptual aspects of the dialogue was dictated by their balance within the dialogue itself, and if I do not devote many sections of my commentary to purely dramatic episodes, it is because there are not many such episodes in the *Phaedo*. The literary aspect of the dialogue functions conjointly with the arguments, and my analyses of the arguments accordingly make continuous reference to the dramatic and literary nuances that accompany them.

Dalfen's real objection seems indeed not to be to my approach as such so much as to the conclusions to which it leads. He is particularly opposed to the conclusion that the arguments operate on at least two levels—the level of popular religious imagery and a deeper level on which the concept of *personal* immortality is replaced by an impersonal conception—and he accuses me of overinterpreting the text and reading into the dialogue things that Plato did not intend. In support of this contention, as well as for other purposes, Dalfen misrepresents my text to the reader in a number of places, as may be seen from the following examples.

First, he writes: "I readily agree with Dorter when he says that the individual arguments and proofs deserve serious consideration only as additional events within the drama, and that it constitutes a distortion of Plato's intentions and achievement to look for objective validity in them." He then proceeds, as we have seen, to chastise me for betraying this principle. *In fact* what I said was that my commentary "seeks to synthesize two methods that generally regard themselves as inimical to each other. One is the analytic approach, which isolates individual arguments and evaluates their logical success or failure (usually the latter); the other may be called the dramatic approach, which prefers to view the dialogue as a dramatic unity rather than an aggregate of arguments" (*Plato's Phaedo*, p. ix). Although I make it very clear that I regard each of these, taken by itself, to be one-sided, it is my detailed description of the "one-sided" dramatic method that Dalfen puts forward as representing *my own* view, despite the words quoted above (which precede the lines Dalfen cites) and those that follow four lines later: "In the present study an approximately equal emphasis is given to both, and I hope to show that neither one can be properly understood without the other and that Plato cannot be properly understood without both."

Second, Dalfen refers to the flyleaf (what he calls "the preliminaries"), where it is said that my book "attempts a radical rethinking and reinterpretation of the *Phaedo*." By this is meant simply that I attempt to read the dialogue as far as possible without any preconceptions about what Plato is supposed to have meant and to read it in an unusual way (by attempting to combine the two methods mentioned above). Dalfen, however, presents this as a boast that I have discovered a radically new interpretation of (a new thesis about) the *Phaedo*, even though nowhere do I make or imply any such claim. The closest I come is in the preface, where I call *the attempt to combine the two methods* "somewhat novel." He even tells the reader that this "radically new" thesis is my view that the immortality treated in the *Phaedo* is ultimately impersonal in nature. But this interpretation of the *Phaedo* goes back to antiquity.

Third, when I suggest that the "argument from motion" (which Plato first explicates only later, in the *Phaedrus* and *Laws*) is already implicit in the first argument of the *Phaedo*, Dalfen says: "Dorter proceeds in the same way as some philologists, who interpret the *Oedipus Tyrannus* in the light of the *Oedipus Colonus*, as if Sophocles had walked out before his audience and said: 'Today I'm showing you the *Oedipus Tyrannus*. In about twenty years I will show you the *Oedipus Colonus*, and then you will know how to understand the *Tyrannus*.' " Thus Dalfen leads the reader to believe that I have not addressed myself to nor indeed even recognized this problem. He does not tell the reader that in the very section that he is reporting I explicitly pointed out that "although the *Phaedo* was presumably written before these dialogues, one should not infer that Plato had not yet thought of this, for it is in principle a fairly venerable conception" (p. 42); nor that I went on to present evidence that the general principles of the argument were well known even before Plato, so that hints at it would be readily intelligible to his audience even though he himself had not yet given it an explicit formulation. I even mentioned that the view that this line of argument precedes Plato is supported by such scholars as A. E. Taylor and W. K. C. Guthrie, and cited a passage from Guthrie in which he calls it an old Ionian conception (p. 42).

Fourth, after discussing the "affinity" argument (*Pho.* 77a–84b), and concluding that it leads to a conception of immortality that is impersonal rather than personal, I wrote:

> There is *in addition* a genuine sense in which our individuality survives death, and although Plato makes no mention of it here the temporal dimension of the image of "afterlife" *may be intended partially to reflect it.* Croesus' injunction to "Count no one happy until he is dead" . . . implies not only that while we are alive our nature is always subject to modification, but also the converse, that once we die our nature has become enduringly fixed. Our "survival" can be taken as an image of the perpetuity of our individual nature in the memory of and in its effects on future generations. (p. 82, emphasis added)

Dalfen quotes all the rest of this paragraph but leaves out the first sentence, and thereby suppresses my claim that the succeeding remarks were intended only as *additional* reflections whose relevance to the preceding conclusions was in no way insisted upon. This allows him to tell the reader that I have claimed just the opposite: I have introduced those remarks, he says, "to prove this thesis about Plato." Having thus diametrically reversed my expression of uncertainty as to whether these considerations are actually present in the dialogue, he observes: "Here the reader gets the strong impression that Dorter is not interpreting Plato but rather that he wants to find in Plato what he himself believes in." I hope it is clear from the above which of us it is who finds in the text what he himself puts there. Other examples of how Dalfen distorts my position could be given but these four should suffice to deter the reader from giving too much credence to Dalfen's account.

I would prefer to turn to a more basic question: by what criterion does Dalfen arrive at these assessments of my interpretation—that is, how does *he* read Plato? Since he endorses the view "that the individual arguments and proofs deserve serious consideration *only* as additional events within the drama" (emphasis added), it is clear that he does not regard the *arguments* as having any intrinsic importance. But neither does he pay serious attention (regardless of whether he agrees with them) to my *dramatic and literary* analyses. Where I conclude, on the basis of such analyses, that Plato intends a second level of meaning that differs from the surface meaning, I make clear what my evidence is and how strongly or tenuously I think it supports that conclusion. I do not expect everyone to be convinced by all my arguments, but they are in any case serious arguments, not the nonsequiturs that Dalfen misrepresents them to be. As far as I can tell, however, Dalfen has made no attempt to actually consider the evidence I offer for any of these conclusions. If the true import of the dialogue lies in its dramatic dimension, as Dalfen believes, why does he completely ignore—not merely dispute—all the dramatic evidence I adduce for my views? The answer is that for Dalfen the drama is important only in a general way. The dramatic meaning of the *Phaedo* is *obvious* and therefore needs no careful interpretation:

> The demeanor of Socrates, which Plato describes as early as the introductory scene and in some interludes, is the strongest argument for the hope of an afterlife. The reminder to the friends to keep to what has been said in their future life expresses Plato's attitude that philosophy does not consist of theoretical discussion about particular propositions, but rather that the conclusions to which the interlocutors together come are binding for their behavior as long as they cannot replace the logos they have found with a better one.

Now one may wonder how an accepted logos can be replaced with a better one without undertaking "theoretical discussion about particular propositions," or for that matter how the original logos can command our respect if it was embraced so uncritically to begin with. On Dalfen's view it doesn't matter whether the arguments actually prove anything or not, which is presumably why Socrates' demeanor outweighs them. One can see from this quotation that for Dalfen the dramatic *surface* of the dialogue—the overt plot—*is* the basic meaning of the dialogue. That is why, where I argue that the nuances of the dialogue (whether dramatic or conceptual) point to a level of meaning beneath the surface that differs significantly from the surface meaning, Dalfen feels that he can reject my arguments simply on the basis of the conclusions to which they lead, without any regard for my evidence. If my conclusions differ from the surface they are wrong a priori, since the meaning of the dialogue *is* its surface. Thus the difference between my reading of Plato and Dalfen's turns on a disagreement not about the importance of the dramatic aspect of the dialogue but about what it means to read a Platonic dialogue carefully.

14

Recollection, Dialectic, and Ontology: Kenneth M. Sayre on the Solution to a Platonic Riddle

Jon Moline

Why did Plato write dialogues? Other genres were available to him, and they have proved far more appealing to almost all subsequent philosophers. Yet Plato not only wrote dialogues but persisted in doing so throughout his career. Both his making the choice and his persisting in it require explanation.

The most appealing explanations are based on accounts of Plato's conception of philosophy. Kenneth M. Sayre's recent book, *Plato's Late Ontology*, presents such an account.[1] Professor Sayre claims that Plato accepted and retained the Socratic conception of the love of wisdom as nurtured in conversation, and a view of philosophical achievement as lying more in discernment than in argument and counterargument (p. ix). Sayre's book thus suggests an interesting explanation for Plato's choosing dialogue as his genre.

In Sayre's interpretation of Plato's views, there is a special fittingness to Plato's initially choosing to write dialogues. The choice was founded on Plato's having adopted the doctrine of recollection. As Sayre interprets it, this doctrine rested on three assumptions:

1. There is a certain fundamental knowledge that rests on no prior knowledge.
2. This fundamental knowledge exists in the human mind prior to sense experience. Moreover,

    "No form of experience provides an access to knowledge" (p. 189).
    "Bodily experience actually is hostile to knowledge, and is the cause of the mind's forgetting upon incarnation" (p. 189).
    "The influence of sense-perception begins at birth" (p. 190).

3. "Recollection can be accomplished by nullifying the effects of those influences that caused forgetting in the first place. The influences are those of bodily experience; and their effects—in the cognitive realm at least—are deception and false opinion" (p. 190).

Sayre notes that Socratic elenchus (refutation) is tailored expressly to overcome deception and false opinion (p. 190). Moreover, if the theory of recollection is a good one and the practice of elenchus is successful, then, Sayre suggests, elenchus should be not just necessary but sufficient to return the answerer to "an explicit state of knowledge" (p. 190).

Interestingly, this "explicit state of knowledge" seems not to be an articulate one, in Sayre's interpretation. This figures in his diagnosis of the inconclusive character of several Socratic dialogues. In his interpretation, "If the process of elenchus has been successfully applied (in the *Euthyphro*, for instance, or the *Laches*, or the *Charmides*), then no explicit statement of the result (the nature of Piety, Courage, Moderation, or whatever) is called for—since the result will be present already in the mind of the subject" (p. 190).

This extraordinary claim seems to rest on two related points in Sayre's argument: the first is his claim that Plato's conception of philosophical achievement involved more of discernment than of argument and counterargument (p. ix). The second is his view that the early and middle Forms were "absolute" in the sense of being simple, single-characteristic entities, and hence presumably not knowable by description or account (pp. 34–37, 46, 89).

Sayre concludes that Plato saw that the theory of recollection is not an adequate one, however, and that he abandoned it before the end of the *Phaedo* and certainly before *Republic*, replacing it with a new method of hypothesis (p. 188). Sayre claims that elenchus was demoted from a necessary and sufficient condition for attaining episteme (knowledge) to a merely necessary one, remarking that "refutation itself, however artfully practiced, does not bring knowledge in its wake" (p. 191).

Sayre's interpretation has the merit of recognizing a feature of the early dialogues that has been insufficiently remarked upon—namely, Socrates' epistemic optimism about his dialectical methods.[2] But despite its initial plausibility, Sayre's account of recollection—and hence his interpretation of early Platonic dialectic and of the dialogue form—does not explain or cohere with a number of important texts.

It is important to distinguish between Socratic elenchus and recollection. Elenchus is a method of testing and refuting *false* opinions. Recollection is a process by which answerers are held to be able to supply *true* opinions on matters on which they have not been instructed. Recollection explains how the Socratic method or any other method is able to bring people into a condition of episteme. It is not itself a method, but rather a very tentative notion of the ontological and psychological basis on which philosophical methods can work.[3]

That Sayre sometimes confuses recollection with elenchus is apparent from one of the reasons he supplies for Plato's rejecting the theory of recollection—namely, that "removal of false opinion is not sufficient for bringing the mind to a state of knowledge" (p. 191).[4] Recollection was not wedded to the epistemic sufficiency of elenchus. Indeed, elenchus by itself had never been seen as sufficient for episteme by Plato.

A close examination of the arguments in the *Meno* will confirm that elenchus is finished at 84a, before recollection begins. Elenchus removes the false opinion that one already has episteme and thus has no need to inquire (to embark on the process of recollection that Plato identifies with inquiry). Elenchus culminates in aporia (perplexity) and in the realization that one does not understand what one thought one did. Inquiry with the slave boy begins at 84d. At 84c, Socrates points out to Meno that as a result of the perplexity the boy now feels, he "will discover something by inquiring with me." Only at 85c does the boy "recover true opinion out of himself," that is, recollect. Clearly elenchus by itself was no more sufficient for attaining episteme in Plato's view in the *Meno* than it was later in the *Sophist*. Any deficiencies Plato later finds in the Socratic testing of answers or in the structure and presuppositions of those answers do not touch the recollection story.

Viewed in this light, at least some references to recollection in later dialogues may be interpreted differently than Sayre does. He attempts to explain them away, believing that because Plato had concluded that Socratic elenchus was not sufficient for attaining episteme, Plato had given up the notion of recollection. But as we have seen the *Meno* does not support such a close association between elenchus and anamnesis (recollection). And the *Phaedo* makes explicit one requirement for episteme that was implicit even in the Socratic practice of elenchus—namely, that one who has episteme can give an account of its objects (*Phaedo* 76b). Thus recollection should result in the ability to articulate a logos. Certainly Plato often spoke as if episteme involved discernment, but he consistently held that episteme brought with it the ability to give and defend a logos of what one had discerned. All elenchus achieves is the realization that one cannot at present give a defensible account. By itself it does not enable one to articulate any further account. If Plato had thought it did, the early dialogues would have ended with accounts he thought defensible.

It is simply not true that in Plato's early view of dialectic, no explicit statement of the nature of the object under inquiry is called for once elenchus has been achieved. Socrates is still attempting to get Euthyphro to state the nature of holiness at the end of the *Euthyphro* despite abundant refutations. At the end of the *Laches*, all parties are eager to inquire further even though all have been refuted (200e–201c). They inquire because they are conscious that they are ignorant (199e–200b), that is, that elenchus alone has *not* been sufficient to give them episteme. The most important inquiries have yet to begin. At the end of the *Charmides*, at 175a–b, Socrates confesses that they have all been shown ignorant, and Charmides confesses at 176b that he needs the *epode* (charm) Socrates spoke of in the beginning (157a–b), that is, treatment of his psyche by means of words that will engender sophrosyne (moderation). By an exercise in *Modus Tollens*, Charmides' inability to say what sophrosyne consists in is represented here not simply as his lacking episteme of what sophrosyne is but as his lacking sophrosyne itself. It was assumed at 159a that if one has sophrosyne, one will have some opinion of what it is, but Charmides in the end appears to have had all his opinions about it removed (176a–b). Hence elenchus is very far from having brought Charmides or any of the other participants into an explicit state of episteme or of the *arete* (virtue) which Socrates equated with it. The utter conceptual independence of elenchus and recollection should be apparent.

Plato's notion of recollection was a tentative and perhaps mythical account of the basis on which any method of inquiry can work. It was independent of early Platonic methods of inquiry, which consisted of repeatedly asking the same questions in a variety of forms (*Meno* 85c). Thus if Plato indeed changed his method of inquiry when he adopted the method of hypothesis at the end of the *Phaedo*, it does not follow that this new method replaced recollection, for recollection was never a method at all. It is compatible with hypothesis and also with the method of collection and division with which it is associated at *Phaedrus* 249c and 250a.

Plato's notion of recollection would *not* be compatible with any method of inquiry tied to a conception of the objects of episteme which did not allow them to preexist one's incarnate life along with the psyche which is said to "behold" them prior to that life. Hence, even though the recollection story was offered, perhaps as a salutary myth, there are certain ontological presuppositions without which the myth would not be intelligible. If at some point Plato adopted an ontology that did not meet these requirements, one would expect him to abandon talk of recollection. Did his ontology change so radically that he no longer conceived of both Forms and psyche as preexisting any particular round in a series of incarnations? Any answer to this will turn on what one takes Plato's prerecollection ontology to have been. And the key issue in the interpretation of this ontology is his talk of *chorismos*, usually rendered "separation."

Sayre appears to take Plato's "separation" metaphors quite literally, and believes that Plato abandoned the doctrine that he takes them to express. He argues that Plato's theory of Forms was radically modified in the *Philebus*, where recollection is mentioned at 34b. On his interpretation,

Forms in the *Philebus* are "ontologically derivative" (pp. 14–15), "not separate" (pp. 155, 184), "not ontologically basic" (p. 184), and not distinct from sensibles in their mode of being (p. 184). Would such modifications rule out the preexistence of the Forms and thus contradict one of the major ontological assumptions of the recollection story?

Sayre's argument for these modifications is elaborate, ingenious, illuminating, and, except for his treatment of the separation metaphor, largely convincing.[5] It sheds more light on Plato's late ontology than any work known to me and establishes important connections between Plato's later ontology and ancient mathematics. It also validates most of Aristotle's long-perplexing claims about Plato's ontology in *Metaphysics* A.

Sayre's account does not, however, make sense of Aristotle's claim that Plato regarded the Forms as "separate" from sensibles (*Met.* 991b, 991a). This is a feature of the theory that Sayre (pp. 14, 36) claims Plato had given up in late views. Sayre relies so heavily on Aristotle's testimony in interpreting Plato's late ontology that it is rather awkward for his view when Aristotle does not distinguish different periods in Platonic ontology and talks as if Plato continued to believe in chorismos. I find no hint in Aristotle that Plato's "mathematicized" Forms were any less separate than their predecessors.

In any case Sayre's account does not establish that Plato's earlier recollection story and his late ontology are incompatible, for that recollection story requires neither that forms be sempiternal nor that they be atemporal. It simply requires that they preexist the incarnation of human psyches. They can so preexist and still be ontologically dependent upon unity and the great and the small.[6] Plato's late forms turn out to be "the numbers and measures by which the Great and (the) Small is made definite and determinate," in Sayre's interpretation (p. 164). I find no reason to think that Plato believed these numbers and measures did not predate one's birth, and thus no reason here to see any incompatibility between this conception of forms and the recollection story. Moreover, if Forms "do not exist independently," but exist owing to "the interaction of Limit and Unlimited" (p. 163), then only a dating of that interaction subsequent to one's birth would be incompatible with the requirements of the recollection story. I find no argument for such a dating in Sayre's book.

Thus there is reason to believe that whatever its inadequacies when treated as a literal logos or account, Plato continued to mention his notion of recollection as figuring in a story that explained in mythical fashion how inquiry could succeed. There is no reason Plato could not have continued to mention recollection even in the *Philebus* and *Laws* in the belief that it played the same role as in the *Meno*, namely, grounding after a fashion the possibility of inquiry. Changes in his mode of inquiry and in the structure of the accounts he wished to find do not count against adherence to the recollection myth. This myth is compatible with many different interpretations of the structure of inquiry and of the structure of the objects of inquiry. It demands only that these objects (whether separate in some sense or not) exist along with the psyche before the psyche's current embodiment and that they be accessible to it before that embodiment.

This brings us again to the question of why Plato wrote and persisted in writing dialogues. The diagnosis of why Plato initially wrote dialogues which I find implicit in Sayre's book is in my judgment inadequate for the reasons cited. The book presents no clear suggestion as to why Plato would have persisted in writing dialogues if he had given up the theory of recollection as Sayre interprets it. Space does not permit me to develop fully an alternative answer, but I have already sketched most of the elements of this in *Plato's Theory of Understanding*, and will simply draw them together and supplement them here.

Dialogues can have enormous heuristic power. There are several reasons for this. Among them are that (1) well-written dialogue does not permit one to forget that philosophical conversation involves complex human beings who interact not simply at a rational level but at other levels as well, and that (2) dialogue permits one to teach philosophical method much more perspicuously than one could in other genres, for it permits one to portray vividly the complex process of trial and error, conjecture and refutation, by which inquiry proceeds. It permits one to depict quite elaborate failures and, by diagnosing these as they occur, teach the standards for philosophical inquiry that one believes appropriate. As Gilbert Ryle remarked, "To have learned a method is to have learned to take care against specified kinds of risk, muddle, blind alley, waste, etc."[7]

Plato doubtless taught standards of philosophical inquiry with more grace and literary polish in earlier dialogues than in later ones, but he continued to depict and diagnose philosophical failures even in such late dialogues as the *Statesman*, where we learn how not to confuse statesmen with swineherds (226c). One learns there how *not* to carry out collection and division; one learns how the process can go awry. One could not learn this so easily from a straightforward presentation of the method, far less from a straightforward and putatively successful *application* of the method to a major problem.

Dialogue depicting flesh-and-blood human beings can also teach that the obstacles to understanding are often not cognitive. Recall the Spartan's incredulity at the Athenian's proposal for wine parties as tests for prospective officials (*Laws* Bk. I), or Philebus' confidence that he will always think precisely what he now thinks about the relative merits of pleasure and wisdom (*Phil.* 12a). Plato's conception of philosophy remained a conception of the loving pursuit of *sophia* (wisdom) or episteme. This episteme demanded harmony between the parts of the psyche of its possessor.[8] Plato held that not all these parts are accessible to the best sort of logos. Some are inferior to others.[9] Hence his conception of philosophy demanded that his philosophical writing employ a genre rich enough to speak to us in all of our complexity, a form that allowed for muthos as well as logos. This demand is satisfied better perhaps by the dialogue form than by any other.

Reply to Jon Moline

Kenneth M. Sayre

Professor Jon Moline finds my book largely convincing in its main endeavor, which was to shed light on the ontology of the *Philebus* and to establish connections between that dialogue and Aristotle's account of Plato's philosophy in *Metaphysics* A. I am grateful for this appraisal and thank him for his careful reading of my sometimes convoluted argument.

Moline's reservations concern (1) my (very brief) treatment of the theory of recollection and (2) the rationale he finds implicit in this treatment for Plato's having written in dialogue form. Regarding the first, he suggests that I confuse recollection with elenchus, and that in arguing that recollection does not appear in the later dialogues both my conclusion and the reasons for it are at odds with the text. Regarding the second, the complaint seems to be that the rationale in question is no longer available if Plato did in fact relinquish the theory of recollection in his later years, and that my treatment is remiss in not having provided an alternative rationale for the dialogue form. Both topics are inherently interesting, and since I did not find occasion to say much about them in the book I welcome this opportunity to look at them a bit more closely.

Recollection and Elenchus. Moline is justified in finding fault with my reconstruction of the theory of recollection. I plead guilty to oversimplification, but I want to offer a defense against the more serious charges of confusion and infidelity to texts.

A point to begin with is that *some* reconstruction is necessary for a responsible discussion of the theory, since it takes on different forms in each of the three dialogues that mention it explicitly. In the *Meno*, the theory is introduced in response to the so-called paradox of the learner. Divested of its rhetorical trappings, the paradox poses the authentic problem of how it is possible to know anything at all, inasmuch as all inquiry seems to rely upon something previously known. In more recent writings the problem is met by postulating some level of cognition (clear and distinct ideas, sense-datum statements, self-authenticating beliefs) where prior knowledge is not required. Plato's response in the *Meno* was to postulate an unmediated apprehension of the Forms, which (being unmediated) does not depend upon any previous knowledge. The knowledge gained in this direct encounter is overshadowed at birth by the deception of sense experience and can be recovered only when the false opinions generated by that deception have been cleared away—the professed learning by recollection that Socrates demonstrates with Meno's slave boy. In the *Republic* Plato's response was quite different, relying upon the notion of a nonhypothetical first principle (apparently to be identified with the Good itself) with no explicit mention of prenatal knowledge. Yet other approaches seem to be working in the *Sophist* and the *Philebus*, where he expounds methodologies that bear little resemblance to the procedures of the *Meno*.

In the *Meno*, at any rate, the theory of recollection serves as background for an account of learning in which four stages are clearly distinguished: (1) knowledge of Forms by direct encounter prior to birth, (2) obscuration of this prior knowledge by sensory deception, (3) elenchus for the removal of false opinion, and (4) an orderly recall (82e13) in response to variously repeated (85c11)—and artfully posed—leading questions. In the *Phaedo*, Socrates offers an alternative version of the theory (in case Simmias doesn't find the former version convincing; 73b3) in which recall is stimulated by association of thoughts and images instead of by a teacher's questioning. And in the *Phaedrus*, which is the only other dialogue in which the theory is explicitly mentioned, recollection is described only as a passage from a plurality of perceptions to a unity of reason—a clear allusion to the procedure of collection later developed in the *Sophist* and the *Statesman*. So Moline is right in pointing out that Plato never represents elenchus as sufficient by itself for the recovery of prenatal knowledge. Putting the three contexts together, in fact, there is no consistent story of what is supposed to be sufficient; and this is the reason reconstruction is necessary if we are to speak responsibly of *the* theory of recollection. The reconstruction in my book was based on the *Meno*, which provides the most complete account of recollection to be found in the dialogues. But, as far as the *Meno* goes, there is no apparent reason elenchus itself should not be sufficient for this purpose. Given that the loss of prenatal knowledge is due to deception generated by sense experience, wiping away this deception (by elenchus or any other means) should be enough to reawaken that prior knowledge. To be sure, in Socrates' purported demonstration of recollection with the slave boy the process of elenchus is followed by a series of questions cleverly formulated to elicit the appropriate answer. But there is no indication in the *Meno* itself why this additional stage should be necessary, and one might wonder whether Socrates' astute questioning was anything more than a practical necessity for contriving a more or less convincing demonstration of the theory. Considerations of this sort stand behind my treating elenchus as the primary technique for the recovery of knowledge in the reconstruction of the theory of recollection offered in my book. But Moline is right in pointing out that this version of the theory represents a considerable simplification.

He is justified also in questioning the reasons suggested in my appendix for why Plato gave up the theory in the later dialogues. The most conclusive reason, I suggested, is that elenchus does not prove sufficient for a return to knowledge in any of the dialogues in which it might have been intended to bring about that result. Now although this does seem ample reason to give up the theory of recollection in the version specified by my reconstruction, the reason, like the reconstruction, is an oversimplification. To avoid simplifying matters unduly, what I should have suggested is that elenchus followed by suggestive questioning, or by association of images, or what have you, never proves sufficient for a return to knowledge. But none of these attempted explanations involves a confusion between recollection and elenchus as Moline suggests. Even in my simplified version there is a clear distinction between the process of recollection sustained in the soul of the learner and the technique of elenchus by which the teacher is supposed to help stimulate that process. Recollection itself is not a technique; rather, it is the result of applying a technique (namely, elenchus), according to the account proposed in the *Meno*.

The Absence of Recollection in the Later Dialogues. My conjectures regarding Plato's reasons for giving up the theory of recollection in the later dialogues were not offered as reasons for believing that the theory does not appear in those dialogues. That it does not appear after the *Phaedrus* seems to me to be evident, amounting to a fact to be explained rather than an opinion to be justified. It is of course true that the term ἀνάμνησις (recollection) and its cognates occur several times in the *Philebus* and the *Laws*, and also less frequently in the *Theaetetus* and the *Sophist*. But an item-by-item examination of the texts involved shows not even a remote connection with the earlier theory of prenatal knowledge. At any rate, it is not correct to cite these passages as contexts in the later dialogues where the theory of recollection is *mentioned*. To use the term ἀνάμνησις is not ipso facto to mention a theory that went by that name in earlier contexts.

Nonetheless, I agree with Moline that there is nothing about the ontology of the later dialogues that would have precluded Plato's having maintained the theory to the end if he had so elected. Whatever it might amount to in detail, the theory of recollection does not seem to require the ontological separation of the objects of prenatal knowledge from sensible things. All it requires, as Moline points out, is that these objects be accessible to the soul before its current embodiment. Although I believe the separation thesis has been relinquished by the time of the *Philebus*, I do not see anything in the ontology of this dialogue that would prevent access of the type required.

In response to Moline's interesting point that Aristotle says nothing about Plato's having given up the separation thesis in later years, it should be noted that I do not rely upon Aristotle's testimony in establishing Plato's later views. That is, I do not argue to the conclusion that Plato held such-and-such views from the premise that Aristotle said he did. For reasons Moline himself surveys in the introduction of his *PTU*, Aristotle's testimony must be treated with considerable caution by any commentator bent upon discovering the doctrinal content of Plato's writings. My concern with that testimony was not so much to use it as evidence that Plato held certain views in the *Philebus* as to show that Plato's having held certain views in that dialogue enables us to make sense of that otherwise baffling testimony.

Granting all this, however, one still might feel the need for a more persuasive answer to the question of why Plato abandoned the theory of recollection as he moved into his later period. Moline points in the direction of what might be a more complete answer with his observation that elenchus is never represented as sufficient for the recovery of prenatal knowledge. But if not elenchus, then what? Not just carefully contrived questioning, which shares the stage with elenchus in the *Meno*, or association of thoughts and images as cited in the *Phaedo*, because neither of these constitutes anything resembling a method of inquiry. But suppose Plato at some point were to have hit upon a method showing promise of being effective in moving the mind from a state of professed ignorance to explicit knowledge—a method of retroductive reasoning like that adumbrated in Book 6 of the *Republic*, for example, or a method of collection and division like that featured in several late dialogues. The more effective such a method might prove to be, the more informative it would become about the type of response appropriate to the question posed in the paradox of the learner— the question of how knowledge is possible—and the more informative indeed about how that question should be formulated. The more successful the method in moving the mind from professed ignorance to knowledge, at the same time the less important would become any accompanying story about how the mind arrived at the state of ignorance in the first place. The upshot is that considerations of the mind's status before inquiry begins become less relevant as Plato's methodological investigations become more successful. And Plato's methodological investigations certainly become more successful in the later dialogues.

This line of reasoning not only indicates a plausible explanation of why Plato in fact gave up the theory of recollection in later years but also undercuts the only prima facie plausible argument I know to the effect that the theory is mentioned in the later dialogues. At *Phaedrus* 249b8–c3 Socrates remarks that passing from a plurality of perceptions to a reasoned unity is a recollection of those things seen by the soul before entering human form. This could be construed as a strict identification of recollection with the procedure of collection clearly present in the *Sophist*, the *Statesman*, and the *Philebus*, from which identification it could be argued that recollection figures in those dialogues as well. (Gulley seems to argue in approximately this fashion in the passage cited favorably by Moline in *PTU*, p. 260 n. 25.) But apart from the dubious reading of ἔστιν at 249c2 as the "is" of identity, this way of arguing involves interpreting the method of collection and division as a response to the paradox of the learner as it appears in the *Meno*. This interpretation seems misguided for several reasons, not least of which is that the method of collection and division is a response to the quite different problem of specifying the logos characteristic of philosophic knowledge. This latter problem, in fact, is focused with the help of a new version of the paradox at *Theaetetus* 198c7–8, which concerns the need for a criterion to distinguish knowledge from ignorance (my *Plato's Analytic Method*, pp. 114–17, discusses the relationship between the model of the aviary, which generates this version of the paradox, and later methodological developments in the *Sophist*). In the *Meno*, the central epistemological problem is how it is possible to arrive at knowledge, and the theory of recollection responds to this problem. By the time of the *Theaetetus* and the *Sophist*, however, the predominant epistemological problem has become one of distinguishing knowledge from its various pretenders, and this is the problem to which the new method responds. The association of recollection with the method of collection at *Phaedrus* 249c thus does not constitute the continuation of an old response to a question posed in a much earlier dialogue, but rather marks an entirely new approach to the problem of how knowledge is possible.

Why Plato Wrote Dialogues. If knowledge begins with a direct apprehension of the Forms and is reawakened by a process (elenchus) that eradicates the false opinion that obscures it at birth, then the result should be the return of the soul to a state of knowledge (recollection). In the purported demonstration of this reawakening process with the slave boy in the *Meno*, elenchus takes the form of a cross-examination by Socrates himself. That is to say, conversation with Socrates provides both the occasion and the stimulation for the removal of the boy's false opinions on the geometrical matters at issue. For someone unable to converse with Socrates directly, however, the next best alternative would be sustained exposure to recorded Socratic conversations with persons beset with approximately the same misapprehensions—to be subjected to elenchus, as it were, at secondhand. If all goes well, then the mind of the reader should be returned to a state of knowledge in much the same manner as that of the respondent in the dialogue. Like the slave boy, the reader should have recollected what he or she had previously known. Unlike the case with the slave boy, however, the occasion would be not an actual conversation with Socrates but rather an attentive reading of a Socratic conversation as reported by Plato. To provide an occasion of this sort is one intelligible explanation of why Plato wrote dialogues, and I gather is the explanation Moline finds implicit in my simplified reconstruction of the theory of recollection.

Although obviously sympathetic with this explanation, Moline finds it problematic on two counts. For one, *Phaedo* 76b (along with several other passages, including *Meno* 81b where the theory of recollection is first introduced) makes it explicit that the possession of knowledge enables one to give an account of what one knows, and the explanation sketched above makes no mention of such an ability. But someone wishing to defend that explanation could readily respond along the following lines. Any person whose soul has been returned to a state of knowledge on a given topic would thereby be rendered capable of articulating an account of that knowledge in whatever manner (written or oral, long or short) appropriate to a given occasion. But being in a state of knowledge does not require that an account ever be actually articulated. The actual giving of logos is not essential to knowledge, which (as Moline expresses it in my behalf) results from discernment and not from argument.

Moline's second complaint about this implicit explanation is that it is no longer available to someone who maintains as I do that the theory of recollection had been relinquished by the time of the late dialogues. As far as the account in my book is concerned, the objection presumably is not that the explanation in question is not implicit in it after all (how could that be an objection?) but rather that after banishing the theory from the later dialogues I give no indication of how else Plato's adherence to the dialogue form might be explained. Since this is certainly correct as far as the book is concerned, it is fortunate that I have found an opportunity to address this question explicitly in my other essay in this volume. For present purposes it is enough to point out that explanations of the sort Moline finds appealing—those based on accounts of Plato's conception of philosophy—do not depend upon Plato's having maintained the theory of recollection to the end of his productive career. They do not depend upon his ever having held the theory of recollection at all (for all we know, the theory may have been strictly a Socratic doctrine). The only thing required is that (for whatever reason) Plato thought that philosophic knowledge is a state of the mind that could be fostered by conversations presented in dialogue form. One possible reason Plato might have thought this, which has nothing essentially to do with recollection, is the conviction that philosophic knowledge arises in the properly prepared mind in something like the manner of spontaneous combustion, and that conversation with master dialecticians like Socrates (either direct or recorded) are particularly effective means of preparation. This is the drift of the explanation I offer in chapter 6 above.

At the end of his provocative comment, Moline offers in summary form several suggestions of his own that might figure in an explanation of why Plato wrote dialogues. All these suggestions seem entirely plausible from my point of view. The remarkable thing about them is that none of these suggestions makes any mention of the theory of recollection. As we know from *PTU*, Moline does in fact believe that Plato maintained this theory throughout his later period. But it is interesting how much Moline himself is able to say about the philosophical effectiveness of the dialogue form in Plato's hands without alluding to this problematic theory.

15

Observations and Questions about Hans-Georg Gadamer's Interpretation of Plato

Nicholas P. White

Professor Hans-Georg Gadamer's distinguished reputation as an interpreter of Plato rests in part on the view that his hermeneutical approach will offer insights not otherwise available. The most conspicuous feature of his approach is his attempt to explain Plato's use of the dialogue by insisting that it was more than merely clothing for his philosophy—it had an organic connection with it. He holds that we should take what is said in a dialogue in the context of the situation in which it is presented, especially the interlocutors' state of mind, and should regard each dialogue itself as framed by a context in which Plato is trying to teach something to us, the readers.

As I understand Gadamer,[1] he thinks Plato regarded the dialogue as appropriate for philosophy because he believed that the means by which the truth about reality might be explained and demonstrated are inevitably incomplete. Whatever you might think you know, you can never be sure that some refutation, perhaps sophistic, will convince you to the contrary. The best you can do is to hold that a claim is established only relative to the resources of a given discussion and its participants. We lack certainty because nothing can be known or understood in isolation and without complete knowledge of all of its relations with all other things, and because such complete knowledge is impossible. The gaps in our judgments leave openings for refutations of them. The dialogue, by showing our dependence on actual other people for criticisms of what we believe, is supposed to make this state of affairs clear.[2]

To begin, let me grant that in an important way Gadamer seems to me correct: Plato does embrace a kind of fallibilism, and his use of dialogue is meant to convey it. But once this is conceded, many important questions still remain. I shall develop only three, and those only cursorily, in this chapter. First, how far does the uncertainy indicated by Plato's use of dialogue extend? Does it include even the most general propositions about method, such as the idea that if one is shown to be committed to two conflicting propositions, one ought to try to alter that state of affairs? And does it include even things that Socrates says he is quite sure of, such as the idea that it is worthwhile to inquire into what one does not know? Next, there is a question whose very formulation is problematical: in suggesting that our judgments are not immune from possible refutation, is Plato also suggesting that the states of affairs about which we judge are themselves indeterminate, or does he think that the reality is fixed regardless of whether we are able to know it with certainty? If we accept the latter alternative, one can ask, third, whether Plato really thinks that *all* types of knowledge of these facts are impossible, or whether there is a type of possible knowledge or cognition different from the type whose limitations the dialogue indicates. I have in mind one contrast between types of cognition that has been thought pertinent to Plato's views—namely, a contrast between cognition that the cognizer formulates in language or some other system of "symbols," and cognition that is sometimes labeled "intuition" or "direct apprehension," not involving any formulation in linguistic or other such form.

I choose these questions partly because they seem to me interesting and important, and partly because I do not find Gadamer's views on them altogether easy to determine. But before I discuss them, let me very briefly indicate my own responses to them, so as to make clear my motivations in raising them.[3]

The first question seems to me extremely difficult, but I am inclined to think Plato's fallibilism is quite unrestricted. On the second question, it seems to me that Plato believes that very many facts about Forms (and possibly also "mathematicals," if indeed he believes in such things) are completely determinate, even if we might be unable in some strong sense to know what they are. Here I think that Plato is entitled to be called a "Platonist" in the sense commonly meant in the philosophy of mathematics, although I think he extends his Platonism far beyond mathematics. On the third question, I think that Plato does believe there is a kind of intuition or direct apprehension of Forms (although one needs to describe it very carefully to avoid confusion). Moreover, I think that he probably holds it possible, *in principle*, for a soul to have complete intuition of all Forms, individually or collectively. But if by "knowledge" we mean something essentially formulated in words or the like, then I would agree with Gadamer that Plato does not think that (at least much) such putative knowledge is irrefutable.

As I have said, I am not completely sure what Gadamer's account of Plato's views on these questions are. In answer to the first, he seems to picture Plato as holding that the uncertainty and incompleteness of our putative knowledge extends to all subject matters. On the second question, although Gadamer certainly does not portray Plato as a relativist about truth, at least not in the style of Protagoras,[4] he does seem to suggest that not all facts about reality are determinate, not merely that we are unable to know what they are. On the third question, although he does seem to believe that Plato makes room for some sort of "intuition" of Forms, Gadamer evidently thinks that it is subject to the same incompleteness that affects judgments essentially cast in language. But it is unclear to me whether he thinks that this limitation on the intuitability of the Forms arises from something in the nature of the Forms themselves or rather from limitations on human souls that might not apply to all possible souls or minds.

Let me now discuss each of these questions more fully. I can be brief with the first. It is difficult to see in Plato, either explicitly or implicitly marked, any boundary between judgments susceptible to possible future refutation and those held immune to it. For one thing, although Socrates is occasionally made to suggest that he holds fast to something, neverthless even when he does this, as at *Meno* 86c1–2, *Parmenides* 135b5–c4, or *Timaeus* 51d3–7, he does not claim that it is incontrovertible. In particular, *Parmenides* 135b–c is not a "transcendental" argument for the certainty of the existence of forms. It is an argument that there are forms if *dialegesthai* (dialectic) is possible, but the antecedent of the conditional is pointedly—I think–not asserted, and given that in Plato's view dialegesthai is far more than the observable mouthing of words to each other, I do not think that Plato can take its occurrence to be beyond all possible question, even though it may seem so to common sense, or to a philosophical outlook that takes common sense as firm ground.

In the second place, I do not think that Plato regards general methodological judgments as less open to uncertainty than what one might call substantive judgments about particular forms. Some philosophers think that methodological judgments concern linguistic usage or things easily accessible through it (such as concepts) and go on to suppose that such judgments are therefore less subject to doubt than those concerning some putative reality. In addition, since they see methodological issues dominating in many of Plato's later works, and also see that those works have less of an air of genuine dialectical debate, they may well think that Plato later became less hesitant about the chances of reaching utterly firm philosophical conclusions. I do not myself think that Plato tends at all, even in the later dialogues, to become more assertive as he becomes more methodological. Moreover, I do not think that he ever expounds any philosophical rationale that would justify him in doing so. The picture of philosophy as the study of concepts, language, or syntax, and as immune from the uncertainties of the studies of "metaphysical reality," although it has something to be said for it as philosophy, seems to me to have nothing to be said for it as an interpretation of Plato. *If*, then, Plato adopted a fallibilistic attitude, I doubt that he restricted it to any particular area of subject matter.

On the second question, it seems to me possible to be fairly definite, with one qualification. If one considers Plato's dialogues themselves, and also the *Seventh Letter*, I think one finds no indication that Plato was anything but Platonist (or alternatively realist) in the sense alluded to above. That is, he seems to me steadfastly to assume that however problematical the attempt to gain genuine knowledge may be, nevertheless what knowledge must have as its subject matter is fully determinate in every way. So to speak, the facts about the Forms are what they are, completely independently of what we may happen to judge or be able to discover or demonstrate.

The dialogues seem to me to support this interpretation, and I do not think that it can be argued that their being dialogues undercuts the support they give the interpretation. As we have seen, Plato is willing to leave open some question (however small) of whether there are Forms by asserting that they exist *if*, for example, dialegesthai is possible and *if* there is knowledge as distinct from opinion (*Tim.* 51d; cf. *Rep.* 477b5–6, e4–478al). This may leave it open that there may not be forms. It does not, however, make it less determinate whether there are forms or not. More important, if there are forms, then the dialogues seem to me to make it clear that all facts involving them are fully determinate. The dialogues contain nothing, so far as I can see, of the conceptualist doctrine that we *construct* facts involving forms by holding beliefs about them or by giving what we ourselves accept as proofs about them, and that if we have not yet demonstrated S nor not-S, then there is as yet no fact of the matter about whether S or not-S. As I shall indicate in a moment, moreover, I think that the *Seventh Letter* upholds the same interpretation.

The one qualification that must be entered is the inevitable one arising from the reports about Plato's "unwritten doctrines," especially those concerning the notion of the "indeterminate dyad" (as I would translate *aoristos dyas*). Gadamer is rightly cautious about ascribing views to Plato simply on the basis of these reports (pp. 126ff.). But he also thinks, perhaps rightly, that they reflect something in Plato's thought. The problem is to tell what that something is. This I cannot do, but I can indicate the one idea from the reports that would, *if* it could be attributed to Plato—as seems to me very far from certain—make necessary a substantial modification of what I have just maintained. It is the idea that the indeterminate dyad, or (so to speak) the indeterminacy that attaches to it, is somehow a constituent of the Forms, *in the particular sense that* because of it there are facts involving Forms that neither determinately hold nor do not hold. This would mean, of course, some of the facts involving Forms would have a status rather like that of the famous sea battle in chapter 9 of Aristotle's *De Interpretatione*. And I suppose something like this to be in Gadamer's mind when he writes, "Perhaps in the final analysis in indeterminacy of the Two is meant precisely to imply that for us there exists no clear, unambiguous structure of Being" (p. 110). I do not think that this possibility can be ruled out completely, although I think it has to be doubted. Whatever exactly they were, the ideas about the indeterminate dyad were developed partly in connection with the philosophy of mathematics, and in particular the notion of various sorts of the mathematical infinite. It is well known that considerations about the infinite can lead, as it has especially among intuitionists in mathematics like Heyting, to the notion that some facts about numbers are indeterminate. And perhaps we should see some such considerations at work in the *Parmenides* and the *Philebus* or even *Timaeus*. But specific connections between "unwritten doctrines" and these dialogues seem to me even more speculative than general hypotheses ascribing parts of those doctrines to unwritten parts of Plato's thinking, so I would be wary of saying anything confidently about these matters. The facts about the "unwritten doctrines" being so uncertain, however, I take it as a working hypothesis that the evidence of the dialogues is as I have maintained, and that Plato did in fact think that the facts involving the forms are fully determinate.

On the basis of that hypothesis, let me turn now to the third question. I want to argue that even if Plato does think that any knowledge formulated in language must be inevitably incomplete, and perhaps for that reason subject to possible refutation, he nevertheless allows for the possibility of a complete direct apprehension of the Forms, whether of particular Forms or structures of forms, or of all of them together. But an important part of what I shall say involves an explanation of what I mean by "direct apprehension," because that notion as it figures in Plato is often misunderstood.

But I cannot possibly treat this issue fully here, and so I shall confine myself to only some of the pertinent considerations, notably some arising from the *Seventh Letter*. I think that it is clear that the dialogues, particularly Books 6–7 of the *Republic* and parts of the *Phaedrus* (247c–249d, esp. 247c–e) and the *Symposium* (210a–212a), allow for the possibility of a human soul's apprehending either a single Form fully, as in the *Symposium*, or of a divine soul's apprehending the whole structure of Forms, as in the *Phaedrus*. Even if these passages are mythical or allegorical, what they portray is obviously meant to be in some sense conceivable. But the *Seventh Letter* is especially interesting because it might seeem to rule out the possibility of any knowledge, strictly so called, of the Forms, on grounds of the defectiveness of the medium in which such knowledge would have to be formulated. The *Seventh Letter* is not a dialogue, to be sure, and so the canons of interpreting it are arguably different from those applicable to Plato's other works. Since Gadamer (like myself), however, accepts its authenticity and uses it to argue, seemingly, for the impossibility of complete cognition of reality, and since he even grants that it comes the closest of Plato's works to being explicitly addressed to us, the readers (pp. 96–98), I take its evidence to be of eminent interest.[5]

Plato offers his philosophical excursus as a treatment of five types of things—names, definitions, *eidola* (by which I think he means any sort of nonlinguistic representation or symbol, whether in one's mind or not), knowledge (episteme), and finally the Forms themselves, that is, the class of what is *gnoston* (knowable) and truly *on* (real; 342b1). For reasons we shall see, he disparages the first three as aids to our cognition of the fifth. Gadamer appears to think that Plato disparages the fourth in the same terms and to the same degree (pp. 105, 112), but here I disagree. Plato does call attention to inadequacies in something he calls episteme, at 342c–5 where he lumps it together with *alethes doxa* (true opinion), at 342c7, where he emphasizes the distinctness of it from the forms, at 343b6–7, where he says that there are many reasons things of the first four types are "unclear" (*asaphes*), and then in c1–5, where he indicts them all for tending to make what we "say and show" easily refuted by encouraging the confusion of *ti* and *poion* (see also d9).[6]

On the other hand it seems equally clear that he allows for a kind of cognition of Forms, which he sometimes calls episteme, and which he regards as exempt to a degree from the indictment of the other four types. I do not, for example, see any other way to interpret 344b3–c1. Here he says that if we carefully and in the right spirit bring to bear on each other (literally, "rub them together") *all* of the first *four* types of things, there shines forth (*eklampein*) what he here calls *phronesis* (understanding) and *nous* (intelligence) concerning each thing (cf. *Tim.* 51d3–4 for this use of *nous*). *Phronesis* and *nous* here plainly designate something different from the defective *episteme* ("knowledge") mentioned before. Moreover, Plato uses the word *episteme* for the nondefective sort of cognition, both at 342e1, where he says that the first four types are all indispensable for gaining episteme of the fifth, and at 343e2, where he says that the use of all of the first four engender, with difficulty, episteme. These passages would be nonsense if he did not mean to distinguish two types of episteme, one of which he does not disparage (much as at *Phr.* 247d6–e2). When he wishes to refer to cognition in a general way, without regard to degree of adequacy, he uses a noncommittal phrase like "the fourth" (342c4), which he acknowledges to be a grab bag (342b5; *hos de hen touto au pan theteon*), whose distinguishing feature is simply that its instances occur in souls rather than sounds or bodies. He also uses *aisthesis* in a general sense to stand for it (344b5). So the fourth type, sometimes called episteme in a loose sense, includes various types of cognition, most of which are defective, but at least one of which is not, namely, phronesis or nous or episteme in the narrow sense.

What then is this nondefective knowledge? We can tell best by seeing what makes defective cognition defective. Limitations of space prevent discussion of the evidence of the dialogues, but the answer in the *Seventh Letter* is important and explicit (343c5–e1). It is embodied in his criticism of language, "names" and "definitions" (*onoma* and *logos*, the "first" and "second" types of things), a criticism he says applies also to "images" (*eidola*, the "third" type) and also, as we shall see, to the "fourth" (343b7ff., esp. c2). The criticism is focused on the idea that language fails to maintain securely the distinction between *ti* and *poion*, "what a thing is" and (roughly) "what is it like." The trouble with both names and definitions is that, in general, words are not bound indissolubly to things—they are not "firm," or *bebaion*—but can be transferred from one thing to another and could have been used for different things from what they in fact are used for. From 343c5–e1, it emerges that Plato thinks that this produces problems, because there can be a discrepancy between the words a person says and, roughly, the reality about which he is trying to convey knowledge, so that what he says can be refuted even though his thought was correct (d7–e1). Plato emphasizes the way in which this can involve the distinction between *ti* and *poion* (342e2–343a1, 343b7–c5). To judge by 343b7–e1, he appears to think that a person may be misled by the linguistic designation that someone gives into supposing that a feature that is really accidental is essential (343c2–3), so that when he tries to state in a definition what is essential to a thing, what it is, he is open to refutation. I think Plato's thought must be roughly that because of the lack of an indissoluble bond between a word and a thing, in particular a Form, it becomes possible to be mistaken about which Form is being associated in a given context with the use of a particular word, so that one becomes confused about whether a word signifies a certain Form or instead some other Form whose extension only partially or contingently overlaps with its.[7] Eidola—by which I think he means any nonlinguistic representation of a Form that might be used by way of example—are misleading in an exactly parallel way.

But since the same difficulty is said to apply also to defective instances of the "fourth" type (343c2), it is easy to see what Plato thinks distinguishes defective from adequate cognition. Defective cognition is cognition essentially formulated either in language or through eidola.[8] Plato's criticism of language makes no exception for language used *in foro interno* as a vehicle of thought. The knowledge that is nondefective, therefore, must be knowledge that is not cast in language or any medium similarly defective—that is, defective in the sense of involving symbols or representations only contingently bound to objects. But since Plato shows no sign of thinking that any symbolic or representational medium lacks this defect, nondefective knowledge must dispense with anything of that kind and be in that sense direct cognition.

Because it is easy to confuse different notions of intuition and direct apprehension, some clarification is in order. In the view that I am suggesting, there is one particular sense in which the cognition that the *Seventh Letter* presents as adequate must be direct: that it not involve a formulation in symbols, or any representation in the mind of the cognizer because that would impose the risk of a mistaken inference (particularly one that could confuse *ti* and *poion*, as noted) from features of what was in the cognizer's mind to features of the things cognized. This is one reason other philosophers, such as Russell, have held that some cognition must be in this sense direct and without any formulation or representation in symbols or ideas or concepts of the like.[9]

Once this is said, it must be emphasized that it is a *further*, *additional* question whether (a) the entities that can thus be cognized are necessarily simple or may be complex, and (b) whether, if they may be complex, they may have "propositional structure," in the sense of being properly described (by us, not the person directly cognizing them) by expressions of propositional form. Thus, it is a further question whether a person could cognize directly, in the relevant sense, such a thing as *the fact that* two plus two equals four, or whether that fact's apparently having a propositional structure disqualifies it from being directly cognized. Strange as it may initially seem, it is *also* an additional question (c) whether a person who, by hypothesis, has direct cognition of such a thing as the *fact that* two plus two equals four can or cannot be said, by someone else, to *know that* two plus two equals four. It is currently the subject of debate in Anglo-American philosophy (I must confess ignorance of other current discussions of this issue) whether it is possible for S to know that P without having some sort of mental representation of the proposition P.[10] It seems clear, however, that if this is not possible, the reason is *not* that "S knows that P" *logically entails* "S has a mental representation of P," but is rather a matter of whether an adequately explanatory psychological theory could support the former without the latter. Beyond these questions, there is also the further question (d) whether a person engaged in direct apprehension of a thing could be said to be therein engaged in any sort of *recognition*. It seems that to recognize an object is to recognize it *as* having a certain feature or as being identical with some specified object, and that this is to recognize *that* the object has a certain feature or is such-and-such (pp. 102,

127). If so, then direct apprehension could be recognition only if a direct apprehender could be said—in answer to (c)—to know *that* something was the case.

I distinguish these questions mainly to point out that merely by holding that there is direct apprehension in the sense described, Plato does not thereby commit himself to answering these further questions in a particular way. I see nothing in the *Seventh Letter* to suggest that in answer to (a) he would hold that intuition must only be of simple objects (as Aristotle seems to hold, for example, in *Met.* IX.10), and I doubt that he would say this. There are grave difficulties in determining what he would say in response to (b) and (c), and although there is some relevant evidence in the *Sophist* especially, it is too involved to be discussed here, and I tend to doubt that it is conclusive. It is equally hard to be sure how he would respond to (d). Gadamer says that in Plato's view, "philosophical knowing is identification of something as what it is and has the structure of recognition" (p. 127).[11] This seems to me importantly true for a good deal of what Plato thinks of as knowledge, but it would have to be shown that it also holds for the direct cognition of the *Seventh Letter*, in view of the issues raised above.

Finally there is (e) the issue of whether direct apprehension of the Forms can be said to be in any sense *infallible*. Usually, infallibility is thought of as the impossibility of a mistaken belief with regard to a *proposition*. In part, then, the answer to (e) depends on the answers to (a) through (d), and I must therefore defer it. But since directly cognizing in our present sense means having in one's own mind no representation, and therefore no propositional representation, involved in one's cognition, it is clear that direct cognition cannot in and of itself contain anything that could be called infallible. Rather, it could only at best be in some sense the basis of some other, infallible knowledge, formulated in one's mind in propositional form. But we have already seen that any such formulation would be subject to the inadequacies of which Plato complains in the *Seventh Letter*. So if infallibility requires having a propositional representation in mind, direct cognition cannot be in that sense infallible.

What value would intuition of Forms have? It is clear from *Rep.* 519–521, 540–541, that Plato thought it intrinsically enjoyable, and the same view seems to appear in the *Seventh Letter*. But the rulers of Plato's ideal city in the *Republic* also seem to make use of their contemplation of the Forms in their governing of the city (520c, 540a–b). Here there is need to explain exactly how a direct apprehension of Forms, without any representation, could lead to better judgments about what sensible things are eidola of what forms (520c4–5), but that is beyond the scope of this essay.

Does Plato think that a human soul can ever adequately intuit Forms?

I think that the *Seventh Letter* indicates an affirmative answer. Some dialogues, such as the *Meno* and the *Phaedrus* (249bff.), might be taken to mean that in embodied life we can have only recollection through images and languages, but can never have intuition, of the Forms. But it seems to me that the *Republic* and the *Symposium* indicate otherwise. Could the apprehension be complete? This is hard to be sure about. *Phaedrus* 247–249 indicates that only the gods can have a view of all the Forms, and that humans, even disembodied philosophical humans, can have only a partial view. If this is Plato's meaning, however, his view is that what prevents a complete apprehension of the Forms is nothing intrinsic to them but rather a limitation on our souls that need not attach to all minds.

And, of course, there is the inevitable question: how does one know that one is in fact directly apprehending the Forms, as opposed to knowing that one is directly apprehending a particular Form, which I have already discussed under (d), rather than, say, simply hallucinating? Or rather, if we can only approximate that state distantly, how does one know when one really is closer to it? Here Gadamer refers to a difficulty in ordinary knowledge—that "an opinion or insight is always my opinion or insight and always has such and such a particular character" (p. 112). I suspect that he is here alluding to what seems to me Plato's answer to the question. I think that Plato regards as *the* fundamental cause of our mistakes and our disagreements that we apprehend the world, spatio-temporal as both it and our positions in it are, from different *perspectives*. I experience things from my position, and you do so from yours; I make evaluations from my position and experience as you do from yours. For Plato held (overoptimistically, I believe) that to the extent that one freed oneself from spatial and temporal perspective, one's judgments would be free from sources of error and would be susceptible of objective determinations of truth and falsity that would be accepted by all who were themselves freed from perspective-bound judgments.[12] He may have thought that this freedom could never be complete (although certainly *Rep.* 7 seems optimistic). But I think that in the notion that some judgments, in their very content, are more dependent on a perspective than others are, Plato thought that he had a way of telling when one was approaching a more adequate apprehension of the Forms.

Let me return to the three questions I raised at the beginning. As I have said, I am not completely sure how Gadamer does or would answer them. To my way of thinking, however, *if* Plato thinks that the facts about Forms are determinate, even if we cannot have knowledge of them formulated in language or eidola, and especially if he thinks that divine souls could apprehend them directly, even if we perhaps cannot, then by far the most important thing about Plato's outlook is not his fallibilism about our own judgments, but rather this: that he thinks that a full apprehension of reality is a notion that human beings can, if only sketchily and metaphorically, make intelligible to themselves.

Reply to Nicholas P. White

Hans-Georg Gadamer

When I gave the title *Dialogue and Dialectic* to an English edition of my Plato studies, I wanted to emphasize the dimension of the public give-and-take of dialogue that is absolutely necessary for a correct understanding of Plato. This was the dimension in which Plato himself had experienced the sophistic misuse of the new art of argumentation. He knew about the ἀγήρατον πάθος τῶν λογῶν ("ageless condition of words") and knew also that the logoi (discourses) are the only way to a more knowledgeable knowing. That was the direction Greek life took with Socrates, and it also characterized Plato's own historical situation as that in which he attempted to give the Socratic question a new validity, and out of which he developed his own new knowledgeable ignorance, the human wisdom of dialectic. All questions that can be meaningfully directed toward Plato can be answered only if they are asked from this perspective. In this point we are far removed from the requirement of certainty that statements or judgments must meet if they are to satisfy the scientific consciousness of the modern world. That which corresponds to certainty in this life-worldly dimension of the logoi can be described only by the other, the partner in the discourse, best stated perhaps by the German expressions *Unbeirrbarkeit* and *Unverwirrbarkeit* (imperturbability and disentanglement). *Aptōtōs* is the Greek word designating the sense of "knowing" which is put to the test in dialogic-dialectic discourse. The epistemological concept of fallibilism that White uses does not completely do justice to it. In general, the

---

This essay was translated by Roger C. Norton and Dennis J. Schmidt of the State University of New York at Binghamton.

epistemological approach makes it difficult to address the questions put to me in his critique. I feel as if I were being asked to leave the elderly Natorp, who was my teacher, and return to the younger Natorp, who likewise sought in Plato nothing but "epistemology." My resistance to this approach comes not so much from the lack of historical sense that I feel in its application of this epistemological standard as it does from a substantial problem that I believe I recognize in Plato and yet that becomes unrecognizable in epistemological alienation.

In my opinion, sophistry has, by means of its glittering illusions, weakened the sense for truth, and not only for a particular historical situation. All philosophical discourse has been and will continue to be threatened and hounded by this challenge to our thinking as human beings. We can perhaps call it "empty sagacity." It is found especially within the dimension of the problem of good, opened up by Socrates, as that which poses questions over and beyond all knowledge of reality. Aristotle constructed a picture of the world upon this "transcendent" idea, one that was for two thousand years our knowledge of the world and was called philosophy. It is now past. But since philosophy is, also in the narrow modern sense, the science of reason, it remains exposed to dialectical bewilderment. Not in vain did Kant, in the second division of the *Critique of Pure Reason* (the transcendental dialectic), reveal the unavoidable antinomy of pure reason. In doing this he had an eye on modern science, which extended the methodology of certain empirical knowledge and at the same time disputed the legitimacy of the final causes of such knowledge. It, too, created that other scientific concept that is characterized by methodologically ensured objectivity. What has since then been carried on as philosophy or metaphysics lacks legitimacy and inevitably has difficulty in escaping the accusation of sophistry, just as Plato had difficulty in making himself understood by the citizens of his city and in fulfilling his desire to reexamine the faulty judgment of the Attic court that had murdered Socrates. It is in this respect that we can recognize ourselves in Plato. That is the reason Plato's dialogues appeal to us as a basic text of philosophy.

It is no accident that Plato documented only in fictional conversations his disavowal of the idle talk of the sophists and his self-distancing from their actions. However much his criticism of writing in the *Phaedrus* is motivated by particular occasions insofar as it is directed at written speeches and similarly in the *Seventh Letter* insofar as this exposes the plagiaristic impertinence of Dionysius II, it is still in agreement with his own behavior. He calls his own wisdom the art of discourse, dialectic, so that, in his view, real thinking is always like conducting a conversation. Even the doctrine of ideas introduced by his Socrates (for which in English the unfortunate Aristotelian translation "forms" is customary—as if Plato knew of "matter") is, in the *Parmenides* dialogue, wrung out of Socrates by his great and superior inquisitor Parmenides and torn apart in a true frenzy of wild argumentations. We must take seriously the fact that sophia, "complete knowledge of all of its—the thing's—relations with all other things" is only for gods. And yet, despite this, not all our discourse is empty talk.

There are three questions that White poses. For the reasons I have presented in these introductory remarks, the first does not seem to be directed at Plato at all, and, if we keep the Good in mind, also not at us. The epistemological question, which speaks of universal fallibilism, is posed here in a vacuum. Refutability, which Plato certainly attributes to all language—here White is completely right—simply does not claim to be so unconditionally a refutation of the soul. That is said in the *Seventh Letter* (see 343d).

The second question cannot be asked of Plato at all if one takes seriously what he himself says. After all the *apeiron* (the "boundless" or "infinite") is, according to Plato, an essential element of Being, whether it is introduced in his dialogues as the principle of duality or as the *chora* or otherwise in mythic language. So here too White's epistemological approach is difficult to reconcile with the text. Plato most certainly does not intend his "ideas" to mean "facts about reality." What he seeks knowledge of must be something that human beings can have reasons to know so that they may be answerable for it. These are, to be sure, "forms" of reality, if we accept in consequence the English translation of *idea* with "form." Then one may, in White's strangely modernistic language, call them "facts about the forms." I certainly agree, if it is true that White means to say thereby only that in Plato there is no trace to be found of what the author calls conceptualism. If one had to make a choice, as Plato himself suggests in the *Parmenides* (132b ff.), ideas might be better understood as constant models (*paradeigmata hestota*) than as mere *noemata*. To be sure, the *Parmenides* intends to show that that is no real alternative. Whoever takes seriously the flight into the logoi and the dialegesthai will not be able to do anything here with the notion either of conceptualism or of realism. Ideas are for Plato the real granite of Being. One must certainly not let the "idea" degenerate into a mere hypothesis. But neither should one set apart the world of forms, of ideas, for the gods, and seek to reserve for man the world of phenomena in separation from it, as would perhaps correspond to the nominalism of the modern theory of science. The *Parmenides* teaches irrefutably that the two-world theory is not Plato. We may, indeed, presuppose that phenomena play a part in the "forms," but how they do it is not a problem for Plato. Rather, it is a distinctive feature of the discussion of ideas that phenomena play a part in them. Plato was not a Platonist who taught two worlds. May I refer in this regard to my book *Die Idee des Guten*, which has recently been published in English.[1]

The third question—whether there is a perception of such forms or ideas without the logoi and separate from them–is worked out by White in more detail in connection with the excursus of the *Seventh Letter* and thus requires examination on the same textual basis. This text does indeed give us a firm ground under our feet in its few precious pages. I have attempted to clarify the direction and purpose of this piece in my essay "Dialectic and Sophism in Plato's *Seventh Letter.*"[2] But that is not so important here; once again the problem has more to do with content. I must firmly contradict my esteemed colleague, who labels as "direct, unmediated knowledge" that which here, from the first to the last word, is introduced by Plato as necessary mediation and inevitable weakness of all mediating factors! After all, the entire text intends to show how much mediation the knowledge of the *Fifth Letter* needs and how easily confusion can be caused by the fact that it needs this mediation. *Mogis*, "scarcely," "with difficulty," "just barely," "finally," "perhaps," may be illuminated by means of such mediation of real knowledge of the object. It is the way of knowledge itself to hold fast to the object through all these mediations as that which it is, and not to be prematurely taken over by that which it seems to be. Here (343c) Plato is speaking of the difference between *ti* (what a thing is) and *poion* (what it is like). That could be very nicely illustrated with the aid of our knowledge of Greek mathematics, and that I have done in my essay. Such an example is found in the proof for the squaring of the circle, accomplished by visual evidence. Another is found in a person blinded by such deeply rooted prejudices that he lacks the good will requisite for insight. Such is the case with the Protagorean polemic against mathematics, when he speaks of the angle of the tangent. It becomes clear to us immediately that this image is falsely called an "angle" and that in this way a sophism is being created. In all of this, one must also keep in mind that the example of a circle is only an example and, indeed, of something that is far more difficult to hold fast to, namely, the *arete* (virtue) and *kakia* (moral badness) and the *aletheia* (truth) and the *pseudos* (falsehood) of all of existence. The *Letter* expressly states this.

Therefore it seems unfortunate or, better said, superfluous to differentiate a good episteme (knowledge) from a bad episteme. If one considers a mathematical figure, intended only to be an illustration, as the object itself, there is no episteme involved. Likewise there is no good or bad definition. The correct definition of the circle, which Plato cites, is in itself good. But it leads to knowledge only when one does not let his view of the object, the circle itself, be diverted. It is and remains "weak," like all speech. There is, of course, for us human beings no special power to perceive the thing itself without words and observation and inquiring discourse. Plato reminds us of that again and again, in the *Cratylus* as in the

Symposium, where Diotima emphasizes the weakness of the episteme and the necessity of ever renewed practice and repetition. This is very true for the *Parmenides* on the whole, which depicts in almost word-for-word similarity the incessant practicing of the "back and forth" through which alone insight is achieved. No, the pure nous, inasmuch as it is "in the soul," must also be corruptible. Plato well knows that there is no nous in us without soul. Nous within the psyche appears also in the line of argumentation found in the *Seventh Letter*. Elsewhere it is the same. The gods, who from their heavenly chariots serenely contemplate the firmament of eternal forms, may be different. But we human beings need benevolent argumentations, the *eumeneis elenchoi*, carried on in the long communal life of dialogue (*suzēn*), along with all the other factors of language and intuition. Fallibility and confusion of all four factors enumerated in the *Seventh Letter* are the unavoidable conditions imposed by our mortality. That does not mean that corruption must always succeed. The force of empty talk is opposed by the dialectical energy that lies in the act of speaking. It is able, "ergō," not "logō" (in deed, not word), finally to banish corruption.

Aristotle also knew that. The nous that goes to the *archai* (origins, first principles), is not like a pious opening of the eyes. This "eye of the soul" is present only in the logos and can "see" only with the logos. The Sixth Book of the *Nicomachean Ethics* shows that clearly. Here real knowledge is designated as sophia (wisdom) in which there is nous. This perfection of knowledge, which is called sophia, exists, however, only with episteme or techne (art)! Likewise, even in the perfection of *phronesis* (understanding), nous is present only with the logos that leads to concrete realization of the ethical *arete* (*eubolia*). Thus in the Sixth Book of the *Nicomachean Ethics* the kinds of knowledge that mankind may have are strictly differentiated. But the nous has its special character. It is not encountered by itself, but only in sophia and phronesis. In my opinion, *Metaphysics*, Theta 10, would be misunderstood if one should seek to separate the contact ascribed there to the nous from the logos in which it has its place (*Met.* Theta 10, 1051b 24). The *Seventh Letter* makes the same point. When it says there that the nous always comes closest to the object, the reason this is said is that it has no determination of its own other than that obtained through the object. We have known that since Anaxagoras and especially clearly in Aristotle, and we see it again in Aristotle where the nous is called *apathēs* (without feeling). This by no means excludes the idea that it too is threatened by darkness, for example, from emotional storms, so that the eye is not held fast to the archai (*N. Eth.*, VI.6 and context, *euthus ou phainetai he arche*).

We can learn from this. Logos and logoi are not only that which is expressed, in both its content and in its conclusiveness. It must not only be spoken. It must also be understood. The excursus of the *Seventh Letter* deals precisely with how episteme takes place (Exc. VII, 342a; *paragignetai*). We have the same experience. Writing and speaking after the fact are not enough where philosophy is concerned. Our scientific world of today, dedicated to security and certainty, may not like to hear that, but it is true. That which language is able to express lags necessarily behind what it intends. *Kat'onoma dioikein* was considered already by Plato as the great seduction lurking in the logos. The empirical sciences, which we call science (what might Plato have called them?—certainly not episteme!), have their own different forms of verification or, as the case may be, of falsification. Pure thought is, however, also not simply a vague fantasizing. It too needs verification. It constructs itself, under considerable jeopardy, in the mutual give-and-take of dialogue and, finally, in the continuity of a never-ending dialogue. To know means to become a part of this discourse. That is why Plato calls thinking dialectic. So I entirely agree with White that Plato's criticism of the weakness of the logoi does not lead to skepticism, but rather to the purge of all dogmatism. In that point I completely share his opinion. I also am far from denying that the direction the West has taken in philosophy includes the overcoming of rhetorical-sophistic deception and that, instead, mathematics and its advancement through Platonic dialectic represents a decisive step. Nevertheless, Plato stands, as it were, before the separation of "science" from the one who "has" it. Mathematics represents for him, to be sure, a wonderful model of clear rationality. The articulation of the world in its entirety, given lasting expression in language, can find no better model than this ideal of rationality that is mathematics. And yet it too remains a way of the soul. It teaches one to think and to stand up for one's opinions. So the weakness of the logoi is and remains what Plato always has in mind and does not recognize only in his old age, in the *Seventh Letter*. His entire ideal of dialectic is accompanied by the knowledge of the weakness of the logoi.

Those who perhaps believe that the logical genius of Aristotle put an end to that are, in my opinion, confusing "mathematics" with the way in which it too is transmitted by language alone and thus is connected with rhetoric and dialectic. But even more are they mistaking the theoretical insight into the logical function of thinking and speaking—which Aristotle analyzed both in the scientific argumentation of mathematics as well as by means of rhetoric—for the thinking of things themselves. This thinking remains exposed to enthrallment by the lasting fascination that emanates from rhetoric. *Rhētōr* means master of the power of persuasion (Gorgias). Until the beginnings of the modern era, dialectic (in the diminished sense of the Aristotelian use of the word) and rhetoric played the decisive role in the scholasticism of the *artes liberales*. The system of derivation established by Euclid remained, to be sure, unaffected but was limited to itself. It included no knowledge of reality.

When I now read White's own Plato work and search for a way to better understand his doubtlessly meritorious critique of my Plato studies, I find myself in a difficult position. It is regrettable enough that more than half a year passed before I, in Germany, had any opportunity to look at his book, *Plato on Knowledge and Reality*.[3] There is still a great distance between our little continent and the English-speaking world. I also did not find it easy to accept the information contained in his book. His leitmotif is "epistemological realism." As the modifier shows, "realism" can be understood here only in the modern, post-Kantian sense. Its application to Plato is then incomprehensible to me, as is likewise the application of this concept to the other great thinkers of tradition. Who is not a realist in the sense of believing that the reality of the world does not depend on us, our thinking, or our opinions? Only in the Kantian sense can the transcendental idealism stemming from Kant be designated as empirical realism.

I have the feeling when I read White's book that the Plato who is characterized by White as an epistemologist is being put in the difficult position of being expected to answer questions that he himself does not pose. My own efforts to understand Plato encounter a similar difficulty in regard to White's critique. From my understanding of Plato, the matter can be construed as follows: White considers the flight into the logoi, which Socrates speaks of in his autobiography in the *Phaedo* (97c ff.), as a mere phase in the series of Platonic attempts to come to terms with the doctrine of ideas. He does not recognize it as an element of the epochal change that Plato's entire thought signaled and that led to the development of physics, the metaphysics of Aristotle based on the theological principle, and to a two-thousand-year-old tradition. So he considers the *Seventh Letter* also as merely a phase that reflects Plato's doubts as to whether the approach to the world by means of language is really dependable. White seems in all seriousness to think that the *Cratylus* might even have intended to say such a thing. I can only imagine that this deserving Plato scholar is seeking, in an extralinguistic, direct approach to "ideas," a way to solve difficulties.

I do not wish to make a judgment as to whether such an ideal-typical (*idealtypische*) construction, which regards the dialogues under discussion as a logical series of problem-solving attempts, is heuristically rewarding. I really do not feel very much at home with the Anglo-Saxon manner of thinking. But I am surprised that such an intelligent, solid, and learned scholar as White would, under the hermeneutic pressure of his epistemological biases, twist the *Seventh Letter* in such a way as to suggest that

Plato here bypasses the dialectics and assumes a "direct" cognition of reality. For Plato it is the reality of the forms alone, the ideas, that is involved in cognition, and I should like to stress that these forms, according to their own definition, can never "be the case." They do not become "the case" for us as does the actuality of our experience of reality. But they are also not a world for themselves or for the gods. Plato did not wish to claim for mankind the knowledge of the gods. Mankind has recourse to the way of constant mediation that Plato called dialectic. Thus it will remain.

I do not wish, of course, to make the false assumption that the interest of modern epistemology in Plato has misled it into reading such positions into Plato in the same way, for example, that epistemological sensualism and relativism were read into the figure of Protagoras. Indeed, Protagoras has stood before us as the ancestor of ancient skepticism ever since Plato characterized him thus in the *Theaetetus*. I believe, however, that in the meantime I have learned more about Plato,[4] especially through the work of Hermann Langerbeck.[5] White, like Natorp, takes modern science as his starting point, although he does not seek, as Natorp always did, to recognize Kant in Plato and natural law in the "idea." But that "science" means mathematical natural science—that is for White as self-evident as it was for Natorp.

I am well aware that the development of mathematics as a science was the great accomplishment of the Greeks, and I fully understand that ancient skepticism was predominantly directed precisely against the mathematicians. In any case, it was not directed against the empirical sciences, whatever it might have called them—perhaps *historiē*. That is undeniable. If we wish to understand Plato's real contribution to philosophy, we must keep in mind what function the model of mathematics had for him. This function is based on the fact that mathematics is a rational, not an empirical, science. Therefore it represents the first step toward real science, namely, toward the dialectic of the pure science of reason superior to all experience and independent of all experience. Certainly such a science means "reality," but it is the true reality, that is, this communal world as it is encountered in words and discourse that mediate ideas. I must point out again that what we call reality is thought of in Plato as a mixture of peras (limit, end) and apeiron, thus coming from the ideas which meet by virtue of their inherence in things. This is, in the sense of modern science, no real explanation and yields no knowledge of reality. What we call reality is mediated only in mythic metaphors, for example, in the activity of the demiurge in the *Timaeus* or in the mixing of the drink of life in the *Philebus*. That is the extent of it. The existence of ideas within phenomena, this so-called participation, is for Plato a condition for the reception of ideas that is never questioned because it is self-evident. When the word *forms* is used in English to express the German *Ideen*, one cannot emphasize strongly enough: this is Aristotle, not Plato. Only then does one understand the Aristotelian critique of the doctrine of ideas.

I should like to conclude the account of my reaction to White's critique with a general statement. When one submits a text to a line of questioning to which the text contains no answer, illusory problems arise. As a student of Natorp I have endeavored with great effort, my whole life long, to free myself from this approach. Unfortunately, I cannot judge whether the research that I have seen illustrated in White's work has a merit equal to that which Natorp's once undeniably had. It is bad enough that I have to admit that. But a quarter century of isolation such as we have lived through has left its mark on my generation. I must continue to insist that in Plato the discussion is about dialectic, whether in the *Phaedo*, *Republic*, *Phaedrus*, *Sophist*, *Parmenides*, or the *Seventh Letter*. It always has to do with resisting the sophistic tricks of obfuscation in the use of arguments, and to hold fast to the idea of what is really meant by dialogue. That seems to me to be Platonic and to be our philosophical heritage. It lies beyond the inquiry of the modern epistemological contrast between idealism or conceptualism and realism. I think that philosophy would do well not only to strive to be a philosophy of the sciences but also to learn to move within this beyond, which is at the same time the here and now of our "life world."

Notes

Introduction

1. Both quotations are from Whitehead's *Process and Reality: An Essay in Cosmology*, corrected ed., ed. D. R. Griffin and D. W. Sherburne (New York: Free Press, 1978), p. 39.

2. *Poetics*, bk. I, chap. 1, 1447a28–1447b11, trans. I. Bywater in *The Rhetoric and the Poetics of Aristotle* (New York: Modern Library, 1984), pp. 223–24. See also Aristotle's remark in the *Rhetoric*, bk. III, chap. 16, 1417a19–21, that the Socratic dialogues, unlike mathematical discourses, "depict character, being concerned with moral questions" (trans. W. R. Roberts in *The Rhetoric and the Poetics of Aristotle*, p. 209).

3. See *Anonymous Prolegomena to Platonic Philosophy*, ed. and trans. L. G. Westerink (Amsterdam: North-Holland Publishing Co., 1962). The topics discussed in that text include the dramatic chronology and setting, the style, and the characters, and Plato's reasons for choosing them in each case; the reasons for his choice of various titles; the question as to how to divide up individual dialogues as well as the corpus (and in particular the question as to the ways in which the dialogues can be ordered); the distinction between narrated and performed dialogues; and Plato's reasons for writing *dialogues*.

4. Diogenes Laertius, *Lives of Eminent Philosophers*, III, 48–62.

5. See M. W. Haslam's "Plato, Sophron, and the Dramatic Dialogue," *Bulletin of the Institute for Classical Studies* (London) 19 (1972): 17–38.

6. I do not mean to imply that no work has been done on the problem of interpreting Plato. For example, see the works by T. A. Szlezák cited in the Bibliography to this book, as well as *Philologie und Hermeneutik im 19. Jahrhundert*, ed. H. Flashar, K. Gründer, A. Horstmann (Göttingen: Vandenhoeck & Ruprecht, 1979), particularly the papers by R. Wiehl ("Schleiermachers Hermeneutik—Ihre Bedeutung für die Philologie in Theorie und Praxis") and G. Scholtz ("Zur Darstellung der griechischen Philosophie bei den Schülern Hegels und Schleiermachers"). Not just Schleiermacher's *Introductions* (1804) but also Hegel's lectures on Plato (as well as Hegel's review of Solger's posthumous works) would also be apposite to subsequent discussions of the issue (for the complete references see the Bibliography). *Das Platonbild: Zehn Beiträge zum Platonverständnis*, ed. K. Gaiser (Hildesheim: Olms, 1969), contains some overlapping material of an older date (including essays by Natorp,

Stenzel, Jaeger, and so on) that complements this volume. Other relevant works (including E. N. Tigerstedt's *Interpreting Plato*, discussed by Bowen in chapter 3) are cited in the Bibliography.

7. The differences between fundamental interpretive assumptions, combined with a certain lack of self-conscious analysis of the given assumptions, helps account for the bitterness of the polemics that have accompanied recent exchanges about the problem of interpretation (exchanges that are, furthermore, rare enough in the first place). My own approach to the problem of reading Plato may be found in the Introduction to my *Self-Knowledge in Plato's Phaedrus* (New Haven: Yale University Press, 1986).

8. For the work on economic literature, see D. N. McCloskey's *The Rhetoric of Economics* (Madison: University of Wisconsin Press, 1985). Among recent debates concerning the interpretation of the law are works by proponents and opponents of the Critical Legal Studies school. The difficulties of interpreting documents such as the American Constitution have a long history. For a remarkable statement of the problem of interpretation in the context of law, consider James Madison's remark in *Federalist* no. 37 about the inherent equivocality of words: "But no language is so copious as to supply words and phrases for every complex idea, or so correct as not to include many equivocally denoting different ideas. Hence it must happen that however accurately objects may be discriminated in themselves, and however accurately the discrimination may be considered, the definition of them may be rendered inaccurate by the inaccuracy of the terms in which it is delivered. And this unavoidable inaccuracy must be greater or less, according to the complexity and novelty of the objects defined. When the Almighty himself condescends to address mankind in their own language, his meaning, luminous as it must be, is rendered dim and doubtful by the cloudy medium through which it is communicated" (*The Federalist Papers*, ed. C. Rossiter [New York: New American Library, 1961], p. 229).

9. All the exchanges, and almost all the essays, were written especially for this volume. With two exceptions, none of the contributions to this collection has been published elsewhere. The exceptions are my "Plato's Metaphilosophy: Why Plato Wrote Dialogues," first published in marginally different form in *Platonic Investigations*, ed. D. O'Meara (Washington: Catholic University of America Press, 1985), and Mittelstrass's essay, which originally formed chapter 7 of *Wissenschaft als Lebensform* (Frankfurt: Suhrkamp, 1982). The translation was prepared especially for this volume and has not appeared elsewhere.

10. See F. E. Manuel and F. P. Manuel, *Utopian Thought in the Western World* (Cambridge: Harvard University Press, Belknap Press, 1979), pp. 104–12. The authors note that in an important fifteenth-century defense by Bessarion of Plato's political ideas, Bessarion insisted that "it was an error to accept the opinions of various participants in the dialogues as Plato's own. Socrates alone was his true mouthpiece" (p. 107).

11. See, for example, Jefferson's letter to John Adams of July 5, 1814, as well as Adams's letters to Jefferson of February 3, 1812, June 28, 1812, and July 16, 1814 (all available in volume 2 of *The Adams-Jefferson Letters*, ed. L. J. Cappon, 2 vols. [Chapel Hill: University of North Carolina Press, 1959]). Also revealing is Jefferson's letter to W. Short of August 4, 1820 (in *Thomas Jefferson: Writings*, ed. M. Peterson [New York: Library of America, 1984], pp. 1436–37).

12. For an example, see the exchanges between M. F. Burnyeat and students of L. Strauss cited in the Bibliography to this book.

13. J. Findlay, *Plato: The Written and Unwritten Doctrines* (London: Routledge & Kegan Paul, 1974). On p. ix, Findlay says that publication of the work was encouraged in part by the appearance of works by Krämer and Gaiser. Findlay goes on to state that "my

first and most fundamental conviction is that the Platonic Dialogues are not, taken by themselves, the sort of works in which anyone's views on any matter could be clearly set forth: they point beyond themselves, and without going beyond them they are not to be understood." On p. xiii, he remarks that "there are many requirements for a good interpreter of Plato: the ability to follow intricate arguments and fill in their gaps, the ability to feel the drift of speculative passages and see where they tend without going off into speculative excursions of one's own, the deep feeling for an ultimate mysticism which is not incompatible with clearness and commonsense."

14. For relevant works by Derrida, Gaiser, and Krämer, see the Bibliography. The work by Lacoue-Labarthe cited there is also helpful in assessing the Derridean and Heideggerean approach to Plato. The Epilogue to my *Self-Knowledge in Plato's Phaedrus* offers further discussion of Derrida's interpretation of Plato.

15. For some discussion of the question, see *Esoterik und Exoterik der Philosophie*, ed. H. Holzhey and W. C. Zimmerli (Basel and Stuttgart: Schwabe Verlag, 1977), particularly the essays by R. Marten on Plato and by H. Kimmerle on Hegel.

1. Reading the *Republic*

1. "Et comme une même ville regardée de differens côtés paroît toute autre, et est comme multipliée perspectivement . . .," *Monadologie* para. 57, in G. W. Leibniz, *Vernunftprinzipien der Natur und der Gnade, Monodologie*, ed. H. Herring (Hamburg: F. Meiner, 1956).

2. I anticipate a theme I treat in what follows and document in n. 25 below.

3. The very title of More's *Utopia* reflects an appreciation of the reaction of most readers to Hythlodaeus' description of the society of Utopia which is Platonic. Such a society can exist "nowhere," just as the proposals of the *Republic* can be described as "nothing" (οὐδὲν; *Rep.* 7.527E). Another feature of More's *Utopia* that reflects his reading of the *Republic* is his decision to adopt Plato's indirect approach to the questions of social reform: "What you cannot turn to good you must make as little bad as you can" (*Utopia*, ed. Edward Surtz [New Haven: Yale University Press, 1964], p. 50). The dialogue form of the *Utopia* is another sign of More's appreciation of Plato's "indirect approach."

4. All this and more can be gotten from the indictment of Karl Popper's *The Open Society and Its Enemies*, vol. 1, *The Spell of Plato*, 5th ed. (Princeton: Princeton University Press, 1966), by a simple reference to his generous index under the headings totalitarianism, lordly lie, lying, infanticide, and individuals and society. It is not my purpose here to enter into the controversies the book has generated. For the purposes of this essay, the most noteworthy thing about Popper's attack on Plato's political philosophy is the lack of preliminary reflection on the nature of Platonic writing. One of the difficulties in Popper's characterization of Plato's thought is that it is global and embraces the *Republic* and the *Laws* without distinction. His contrast is rather between the "Socratic" *Apology* and *Crito* and the "Platonic" *Republic* and *Laws*: "the differences between the *Republic* and the *Statesman* as well as the *Laws* are very slight indeed" (p. 306). The same lack of awareness of the fundamental problems of Platonic interpretation is one of the many failures of the apology for Plato of R. B. Levinson, in his *In Defense of Plato* (Cambridge, Mass.: Harvard University Press, 1953). The closest Levinson comes to the issues raised in this essay is in a paragraph of his treatment of Plato, "The Literary Artist," where he observes that "Simmias and Cebes, in the *Phaedo*, might reasonably be called the reader disguised as participant" (p. 29).

5. The artisans, it appears, are free to leave the state for travel; cf. *Rep.* 2.370E and. 4.420B. Yet they are bound to contribute their labor to society; cf. *Rep.* 4.420E–421C. As for the emergent and ill-defined ruling class, its members are compelled to serve society; cf. *Rep.* 6.499C–D; 7.516D–517A; 519D; 520C; 539E; and 1.346E.

6. The full theory of the polity of Kallipolis cannot, of course, appear before Socrates has introduced the philosopher king in Book 5 (473C–D) and addressed the problem of the development of the ruling class in Books 6 and 7, although the class representing the ruling element of the soul is introduced in the psychology of *Rep.* 4.440E–441A. Yet, in his analysis of Plato's political theory, Aristotle centers almost exclusively on the guardian class, *Politics* 2.1260b27–1262b35, and only touches on the artisans in 1264a11 and the rulers in 1264b6.

7. Cf. most notably the proposals of *Rep.* 5.458D and 459B; cf. 3.413D. But only the solemn controversialist can take offense at the representation of the character of the guardian class as canine; cf. *Rep.* 2.375A; 376A–B; and 4.404A.

8. *Rep.* 5.459E–460A (marriage hymns); 468D–E (hymns to the brave); 469A–B (hero worship). The new and anonymous poetry of Kallipolis would be the counterpart to the poetry of Tyrtaeus in Sparta (cf. *Laws* 1.629C). There is, of course, the new mythology of the state, which gives its powerful sanction to the fixity of the lines dividing the classes (*Rep.* 3.414B–415D).

9. For the "eugenic" policies of the new state, cf. *Rep.* 5.458D–461E; for infanticide, 460C.

10. There is no cloak to palliate this version of what was known as *paidomasoma* during the Civil War in Greece. Popper is quite justified in holding his grounds against Levinson's objections to his interpretation of this passage (*Open Society*, pp. 326–28).

11. As he did with absolute consistency in his discussion of the *Republic* in *Politics* 2.1260b27–1264b25. (He only names Plato in introducing his theme, 2.1261a6.) In this careful distinction he is followed by Proclus, who treats Aristotle's criticisms of Plato's *Republic* in an appendix to his commentary on the *Republic, Proclus Diadochus in Platonis Rem Publicam,* ed. W. Kroll (Leipzig: Teubner, 1901), 2:361–68.

12. In this century, Paul Friedländer has been the most powerful spokesman for the view that Book 1 of the *Republic* was originally a dialogue of Plato's early period (*Plato: The Dialogues*, trans. Hans Meyerhoff [Princeton: Princeton University Press, 1969]), 3:63–67; cf. 2:50–66).

13. I discuss this antagonism in greater detail in connection with the historical allusions of Book 6 in what follows, but it can be noted here that this antagonism surfaces in the dialogue as Socrates embarks on his three waves of paradox in Book 5. He is quite aware of the laughter and derision his proposals will provoke in the world outside the house of Cephalus; cf. *Rep.* 5.451A, 452A–B, and 457B. This incredulous laughter prepares for the reaction Socrates' old associate, Adeimantus, predicts for his proposal of the philosopher king in Book 6 (487B). It is in Book 6 especially that the theme of philosophy brings to mind "the present condition of societies" (cf. 493A; and 497A and E).

14. "We might compare the *Republic* to a city built in stages according to a magnificent and uniform plan—a city that has incorporated, as a suburb, a settlement dating back to earlier times" (Friedländer, *Plato*, p. 63). His remarks on the effect of the themes taken up only in Books 7 and 8 (p. 94) and the meaning of Socrates' enigmatic statement that the argument of their conversation has slipped by without attracting attention (*Rep.* 6.503E) are juster than his image of a suburban Book 1, for they suggest that Plato's design in the *Republic* becomes known only as it seems to have been disrupted. As Karl Reinhardt said in another context (the *Symposium*), "one plays with a plan only when he has one" (*Platons Mythen,*

in *Vermächtnis der Antike*, ed. C. Becker, 2nd ed. [Göttingen: Vandenhoeck & Ruprecht, 1960], p. 245).

15. The theme of the two lives begins in *Rep.* 1.344A, continues through the dialogue (as in 2.364E, 347E; 6.506C), and culminates in the contrast between the life of the tyrant and that of the philosopher in 9.576–579C. It last appears in the choice of lives set out in the myth of Er (*Rep.* 10.617D–620C).

16. The fundamental problem with this analogy is that the individual who is made out to be a composite of appetite, a sense of honor, and intellect is fragmented as he is stretched on the frame of society, and the classes of the polity of Kallipolis reflect only a single level of the human soul. As a consequence the individuals who belong to these classes are not what we would now regard as "whole persons." N. R. Murphy, *The Interpretation of Plato's Republic* (Oxford: Oxford University Press, 1951), p. 20, addresses this problem, as does R. M. Hall in his *Plato and the Individual* (The Hague: Nijhoff, 1963), pp. 163–86. Both are right in pointing out that the society in which the individual lives can determine his capacity for development (as in *Rep.* 6.497A) and that the inner harmony (that is the "justice") of the individual is necessary for him to function in society (cf. *Rep.* 4.443E). Hall's conclusion— "it is, of course, personal justice which is the end of the just *polis*" (p. 185)—could be modified. For "the just *polis*" read "Plato's *Republic*." The dialogue ends with Socrates' exhortation to his companions, all of whom are involved directly or indirectly with the polis of Athens, εὖ πράττωμεν ("let us fare well").

17. The theme of medicine is as important to this dialogue as it is to the *Charmides* or *Gorgias*. But it goes beyond these dialogues (and the elaborate scheme of equivalences of *Gorgias* 463E–466A and 477E–479A) to advance the view that the philosopher is the physician, not to the individual soul, but to the "body politic" (cf. *Rep.* 3.389B; 470C; and 6.496C). Yet, in the end, it is the spiritual health of the individual that concerns Socrates (*Rep.* 9.591C).

18. *Ego men, ephe, ouk ennoō, o Sokrates, ei me pom en amton tomton chreia tini te pros allelous.* At this stage of the evolution of society, needs are innocent enough, but Adeimantus seems to be thinking of a more developed society in which χρεία amounts not to need but to dealings (cf. *Rep.* 5.465C–D). My interpretation of the word is that of LS-J, *sv.* IV.

19. This passage in Book 2 adumbrates one of Socrates' complaints against Homer— that he, unlike the societies founded by Pythagoras, failed to transmit a "Homeric way of life" (*Rep.* 10.600B; cf. 599B). The other contrasting way of life is, of course, the Socratic and Platonic (cf. *Letter* 7.328A).

20. Victor Ehrenberg has contributed a fundamental study of that virtue of Athenian political life which Plato saw as the typification of injustice, in "Polyprogmosyne: A Study in Greek Politics," *Journal of Hellenic Studies* 67 (1947): 46–67. This new Platonic conception of injustice as the doing of many things is essential to Socrates' criticism of poetry in Book 10 of the *Republic*, where the poets are represented as being "all-wise" and jacks-of-all-trades (598C). And, as I shall argue, the meddlesomeness of Athens makes the life of the philosopher who lives in the city but refuses to engage in its civic life (that is the ἀπράγμων) a life of justice (cf. *Rep.* 6.496D, discussed in the conclusion to this essay; 496D, 10.620C, and *Apol.* 31E–32A).

21. Cf. *Rep.* 1.351D, 9.590D, 591A, 592A, and 10.621C.

22. Cf. *Rep.* 6.489B, where the doctor and the statesman are drawn into the analogy, and n. 17 above.

23. This is Paul Shorey's comment in his note to the passage in his Loeb edition of the *Republic* (reprint, Cambridge, Mass.: Harvard University Press, 1978), 1:502.

24. *Laws* 3.702B–D; 4.704A; 8.848D; and 9.860E. Glenn Morrow offers an essential characterization of the Socratic fiction that he, Glaukon, and Adeimantus are the founders of a new city in *Plato's Cretan City: A Historical Interpretation* (Princeton: Princeton University Press, 1960), p. 580 (and for the passages, n. 12). There is a very revealing summary of the practice that lies behind this hypothesis in both the *Republic* and *Laws* in A. J. Graham, *Colony and Mother City in Ancient Greece* (New York: Barnes and Noble, 1964), pp. 29–39. It is, perhaps, significant for an evaluation of this theme in the *Republic* that in the early period of Greek colonization "the oikists seem to have been all-responsible, even monarchical" (p. 39).

25. Especially significant for Socrates' changing conception is the language of *Rep.* 5.450D, where the proposals of Book 5 are recognized as striking others as a daydream (cf. 456C). The metaphor from artistry also comes into prominence in these three books. It is announced programmatically in Book 4 (420C–D) and develops in 5.472D–E; 6.484C; 500C–E and 588B.

26. As Popper claimed with his best pulpit oratory (*Open Society*, p. 104).

27. Ehrenberg, "Polypragmosyne," pp. 60–671.

2. Shame and Truth in Plato's *Gorgias*

1. E. R. Dodds, *Plato: Gorgias* (Oxford: Oxford University Press, 1959) (hereafter "Dodds"), remains the greatest of all commentaries on a Platonic dialogue, invaluable for both the philosophical and literary study of the work. T. Irwin's commentary, *Plato's Gorgias* (Oxford: Clarendon Press, 1980) (hereafter "Irwin, *PG*"), for all its intellectual acuity, is an extreme example of how obsessive logical analysis can smother our appreciation of the dialogue as dramas. After Dodds, by far the most insightful work on the *Gorgias* as a drama is C. Kahn, "Drama and Dialectic in Plato's *Gorgias*," *Oxford Studies in Ancient Philosophy* 1 (1983): 75–121 (hereafter "Kahn"), although my own reading is fundamentally at odds with his on a number of counts.

2. I prefer "answerer" to the standard "interlocutor" both because the latter is even clumsier and much harder to say and because the former emphasizes the questioner-answerer role-playing so central to the rules of Socratic, as of Aristotelian, dialectic (although the "answerer" in both has a limited latitude to ask questions, lodge objections, and so on). A proper defense of my term lies beyond this essay's scope but will appear in the near future.

3. See T. Irwin, *Plato's Moral Theory* (Oxford: Clarendon Press, 1977) (hereafter "Irwin, *PMT*"), pp. 39f.

4. I argue for this interpretation of Socratic ignorance in "Socratic Self-Knowledge and 'Knowledge of Knowledge' in the *Charmides*," *Transactions of the American Philological Association* 115 (1985): 59–77.

5. Every reader of the early dialogues is struck by S.'s extraordinary confidence in the *Grg.* that the elenchus, even with so unprepossessing an answerer as Polus, will prove the truth (for example, 467a, 472bc, 473b, 473e–474b, 475e–476a). Again, it is important to realize that this confidence pertains to the Axiom in particular, not to true beliefs in general.

6. Contrast the insightful but analytic view of G. Vlastos, "The Socratic Elenchus," *Oxford Studies in Ancient Philosophy* 1 (1983): 49: "Anyone who ever has a false moral belief will always have at the same time true beliefs entailing the negation of that false belief"

(cf. Irwin, *PG*, p. 151). As Vlastos's language shows, he assumes that S. is always trying for logical proofs and that the answerers always believe everything they say or think they believe.

7.   All translations are my own except where noted.

8.   The following summary covers Callicles' opening harangue (esp. 482e–484e) and his tirade against temperance at 491e–492c.

9.   Cf. Irwin, *PMT*, pp. 19–24.

10.   Dodds, p. 263; Irwin, *PG*, pp. 170–72; Kahn, p. 94; R. Schaerer, *La question platonicienne*, 2nd ed. (Paris: Vrin, 1969), p. 52.

11.   Even Kahn, pp. 83–84 and 94–95, for all his dramatic sensitivity, fails to see that Callicles' view of shame is presented as anti-Socratic and false, and thus he follows the traditional Calliclean-Doddsian line that Gorgias and Polus do not really believe what they say out of shame. The only modern reference to shame in Plato that I have found to approximate to mine is briefly expressed (with reference to S.'s use of shame against Thrasymachus in *Rep.* 1) by Schaerer, *Question*, p. 102. Oddly enough, Dodds himself comes close in a by-the-way remark in his Introduction (p. 30, n. 2). W. H. Race, "Shame in Plato's *Gorgias*," *Classical Journal* 74 (1979): 197–202, is not particularly helpful on any account.

12.   Dodds, p. 263.

13.   For this lukewarm translation of *epieikōs philōs*, see Dodds, p. 276.

14.   See esp. 484c–486d, 489b, 490cd, 490e, 491e. Dodds, pp. 282f, completely misses the irony of S.'s pretense to be flattered.

15.   Schaerer, *Question*, p. 103, is the only commentator I have found to state that these complements are ironical, although even he thinks them only half so and makes nothing of the irony he senses.

16.   Cf. esp. 457d–495b and 470c; also, for example, *Charm.* 165c, 166cd; *La.* 190b, 196c, 198b, 199a, 200e; *Prot.* 331be.

17.   S. admonishes Callicles not to "succumb to shame like the others" at one earlier point (489a), but there he refers to what we might call C.'s competitive shame as a debater, for C. is hesitating to grant an inference that clearly follows from premises he has granted but that although not morally shameful, would result in his "losing" a round (cf. Dodds, *ad* 489a2). The irony here is that "the others" do *not* succumb to competitive shame, whereas C. does, just as they *do* "succumb" to moral shame as C. boasts he will not.

18.   Why does Plato not have Callicles advocate a more discriminating hedonism such as S. develops in the *Prot.*? Is he not making C.'s position too easy for S. to refute? The answer is that Plato is not concerned here with whether there is a defensible form of hedonism, but with dramatizing what an absurd conception of the good life results if we deny that temperance is beneficial. Thus he drives home the point not just that the Axiom must be true of temperance but also that our recognition of the absurdity shows that we already believe this. For different, complementary answers, see Kahn, pp. 104–5.

19.   *Pace* Dodds, p. 309, who takes this to mean that Callicles has spotted a fallacy.

20.   Cf. Dodds, p. 314.

21.   It is a measure of how badly S.'s shaming method has been traditionally misunderstood that W. K. C. Guthrie should refer to Callicles' capitulation here as a "shameless *volte face*" (*A History of Greek Philosophy* [Cambridge: Cambridge University Press, 1975], 4:291). What was "shameless" was his refusal for so long to *make* the volte face by admitting to his shame.

22.   Irwin, *PG*, p. 167, complains that hedonism does not follow from Callicles' doctrine

of natural justice, so that the latter remains unrefuted. But this ignores the fact that the elimination of temperance from the good life is the essence of C.'s natural justice—justice is for the superior man to be allowed as much pleasure as he desires. Thus to incorporate temperance into the good life does destroy that doctrine.

23.   For Polus' appeal to the mob, see 470c4–5, 471c6,d1, 473b12–d2, 473e2–5. For Socrates' response, 471e–472c, 474ab, 475e–476a.

24.   Irwin, *PG*, p. 159, like Callicles, thinks Polus should have denied ST in order to be consistent with his thesis. Like Callicles, too, he fails to see that Polus really believes ST and that to deny it would therefore be a debating tactic contrary to the rules of elenchus.

25.   See esp. Kahn, pp. 93 and 113, n. 62.

26.   G. Vlastos, "Was Polus Refuted?" *American Journal of Philology* 88 (1967): 454–60.

27.   Cf. Irwin, *PG*, pp. 157f: Dodds, p. 249; Kahn, pp. 92f; and, ineffectively contra Vlastos, Guthrie, *Greek Philosophy*, pp. 311f.

28.   Cf. Kahn, pp. 89f.

29.   Irwin, *PMT*, p. 310, n. 8, rightly rejects the logical-error and conscious-trick theories of S.'s move here (for the accusation of "trickery," see Kahn, pp. 91f), realizing that it rests on "assumptions." But he still wants Polus to object that S. must prove his assumptions regardless of the dramatic fact that Polus already accepts them. Cf. n. 24 above.

30.   Vlastos, "Was Polus Refuted?" pp. 458f.

31.   This is a large and controversial claim and space forbids proper substantiation. But see, for example, *Charm.* 165e–166c with McKim, "Socratic Self-Knowledge," pp. 60f; *Prot.* 350c–351b; and R. Sprague, *Plato's Use of Fallacy* (New York: Barnes & Noble, 1962) on the *Euthyd., Theae.,* and other dialogues. For a heavily qualified appraisal of "Plato's Consciousness of Fallacy," see R. Robinson in *Mind* 51 (1942): 97–114, esp. pp. 105–9 on types of ambiguity (reprinted in *Essays in Greek Philosophy* [Oxford: Oxford University Press, 1969], pp. 16–38).

32.   Robinson (ibid., p. 109) argues that the "irony" required of Plato on this sort of hypothesis is "superhuman," but one is tempted to respond that the logical naïveté required of him by denying it is, if not *sub*human, at least beyond excusing as pre-Aristotelian. Robinson claims that few modern readers catch the unremarked fallacies, but, of course, those trained to spot them do, and the dialogues were no doubt written in part as study pieces for students in the Academy in order to train them to do just that.

33.   A study of Polus' responses down to Callicles' interruption points up the instructive parallel between the dramatic structures of *Grg.* and *Rep.* 1. In both dialogues, a corrupt but affable old man (Gorgias, Cephalus) gives way to a rash but morally salvageable youth (Polus, Polemarchus), whose progress is disrupted by the intervention of an implacable anti-Socratic (Callicles, Thrasymachus).

34.   Cf. Dodds, p. 249, and Irwin, *PG*, pp. 157f.

35.   Irwin, *PG, ad* 477a, characteristically complains that S. "has not yet shown how justice is as obviously desirable as health." Plato's dramatic point is that Polus already believes it to be *more desirable*.

36.   This is the simple answer to Irwin's criticism (*PG*, pp. 125f) that S.'s moral theory gives us "no good reason" why it is beneficial to us to behave justly toward others. There is no reason "good" enough to make us believe it more strongly than we already do.

3. On Interpreting Plato

1. See H. F. Cherniss, "Plato: 1950–1957," *Lustrum* 4–5 (1959–60): 5–648; T. G. Rosenmeyer, "Platonic Scholarship: 1945–1955," *Classical World* 50 (1957): 173–82, 185–96, 199–201, 209–11; R. D. McKirahan, *Plato and Socrates: A Comprehensive Bibliography, 1958–1973* (New York: Garland Press, 1978); E. M. Manasse, "Bücher über Plato, I–III." *Philosophische Rundschau* 1–2, 7 (1957–76); L. Brisson, "Platon: 1958–1975," *Lustrum* 20 (1977): 5–304.

2. Stockholm Studies in the History of Literature no. 17 (Stockholm: Almqvist & Wicksell, 1976). I shall refer in the text to this work by means of page numbers only.

3. See also E. N. Tigerstedt, *The Decline and Fall of the Neoplatonic Interpretation of Plato*, Commentationes Humanarum Litterarum no. 52 (Helsinki: Societas Scientiarum Fennica, 1974).

4. Cf. H. Thesleff, *Studies in Platonic Chronology*, Commentationes Humanarum Litterarum no. 70 (Helsinki: Societas Scietiarum Fennica, 1982), pp. 2–7, for a much less discriminating outline of interpretive strategies.

5. See T. A. Szlezák, "Probleme der Platoninterpretation," *Göttingische Gelehrte Anzeigen* 230 (1978): 1–73.

6. And when they do admit this, they sometimes see such communication of ideas as a vice of their rivals; see, for example, M. F. Burnyeat, rev. of Leo Strauss' *Studies in Platonic Political Thought* (Chicago and London: University of Chicago Press, 1976), in *New York Review of Books* 32, no. 9 (1985): 30–36. But see M. Frede, *Essays in Ancient Philosophy* (Minneapolis: University of Minnesota, 1987), p. xvii.

7. Thesleff, *Studies*, pp. 19–20.

8. See R. E. Allen, *The Dialogues of Plato, Translated with Analysis* (New Haven and London: Yale University Press, 1984), 1:16.

9. There are, Tigerstedt says, many ways in which dialogues are effectively excised. The usual procedure among those who refrain from arguing authenticity is to concentrate exclusively on those dialogues that suit their picture of Plato's philosophy. See n. 11 below.

10. There are two main problems for all geneticists and both concern the specification of the terminus ad quem of Plato's development: the difficulty of connecting the *Laws*, a work in progress at Plato's death, with the rest of the corpus, and the relevance of Aristotelian testimony. Solutions among geneticists vary greatly. Susemihl, for example, saw the *Laws* as the end point of Plato's intellectual progress and considered this progress to be a disintegration or devolution. Ribbing simply denies the authenticity of the *Laws*; others, like Hermann, never lay out the Platonic system (Tigerstedt, *Interpreting Plato*, pp. 26–30, 92).

11. As Thesleff (*Studies*, pp. 4–5) observes, stylometry is even today still closely connected with geneticism. But this connection is only circumstantial: it is neither logically nor psychologically necessary that changes in linguistic style signify changes in thought. So this connection cannot license Thesleff's claim that nongeneticist interpretations of the dialogues "call for a total reconsideration" of the question of authenticity and chronology (pp. iii, 6–7). If one distinguishes the stylometric analysis of language used and the interpretation of what this language means philosophically, and allows the likelihood that Plato occasionally worked on dialogues that were in different stages of completion during the same period, it appears that the first contribution of stylometry is to ascertain authenticity (see Allen, *Dialogues*, p. 10 n. 15) and that the second is to argue some plausible order for groups of dialogues. To expect more of stylometric analysis—in particular, to attempt a precise ordering and dating of dialogues within their groups—is to misconceive what is possible (we lack

sufficient biographical data to attempt this with any certainty) and to abuse this technique (cf. Tigerstedt, *Interpreting Plato*, p. 92). Thus, the fact that scholars have in the past sought such false precision and have disagreed in their results is likewise no reason for Thesleff's project of settling debate by showing through historical and philosophical speculation that some dialogues are only semi-authentic and that others are partially revised (cf. *Studies*, pp. 236–38). The criticism I offer below of the tenet that the dialogues are evidence of Plato's philosophy is further grounds for rejecting what Thesleff proposes; and the distinction suggested of the philological and the philosophical responses to the dialogues entails that only the question of authenticity is interesting to the philosopher and philologist, that matters of chronology are limited to historical studies.

12.   Wilamowitz did not claim that Plato is primarily a political theorist, but he did emphasize Plato's interest in politics (Tigerstedt, *Interpreting Plato*, p. 47). Tigerstedt's remarks on Stefan George and his school are sketchy: for a more detailed assessment, see H. F. Cherniss, "The Biographical Fashion in Literary Criticism," *University of California Publications in Classical Philology* 12 (1943): 287–89. On the biographical school and its English proponents, see F. M. Cornford, "Plato's *Euthyphro* or How to Read a Socratic Dialogue" (a lecture read to the Peterhouse Classical Society, 1941), in A. C. Bowen, ed., *F. M. Cornford: Selected Papers* (New York: Garland Press, 1987), pp. 221–38.

13.   Although Tigerstedt quotes Leo Strauss for his own purposes (*Interpreting Plato*, p. 107 and n. 96), it is curious that Tigerstedt says so little about Strauss and his method of interpreting Plato, beyond citing Strauss as one who would turn Platonic thought into mere "philosophizing" (*Interpreting Plato*, pp. 102–3; cf. n. 14 below). In fact, those who follow Strauss seem to assume that Plato deliberately conceals his thought in the dialogues, and that only those who know how to read them can discern his secret meaning. This is perhaps enough to group them as a new species of esotericist to be distinguished from those who depreciate the dialogues and rely on the oral tradition. So viewed, Strauss's followers would on Tigerstedt's account be kin to Numenius (*Interpreting Plato*, p. 65)—at least in the way they read the dialogues. On Rosen, one who is influenced by Strauss, see *Interpreting Plato*, pp. 79, 144 n. 150.

14.   Tigerstedt criticizes R. E. Allen for treating Platonic thought as empty of content and, thus, as receptive of all manner of interpretation (*Interpreting Plato*, p. 103). But see Allen, *Dialogues*, pp. 23–24, in which the claim that the aim of Plato's teaching is education and not instruction is coupled with the assertion that to interpret the dialogues is to interpret a text and not Plato's thought. This qualification, as I shall argue, averts the original criticism.

15.   For a precise account of the sort of conversation Platonic dialogue is, see H. F. Cherniss, "Ancient Forms of Philosophic Discourse" (the first annual George Boas Lecture, May 1, 1970), in L. Tarán, ed., *Harold Cherniss: Selected Papers* (Leiden: Brill, 1977), pp. 24–33; cf. Cornford, "Plato's *Euthyphro*."

16.   See H. F. Cherniss, "The History of Ideas and Ancient Greek Philosophy," in *Studies in Intellectual History* (Baltimore: Johns Hopkins University Press, 1953); Cornford, "Plato's *Euthyphro*"; Frede, *Essays*, pp. xxiii–xxiv.

17.   Tigerstedt (*Interpreting Plato*, pp. 65–66) seems to suggest that the modern assumptions about interpreting Plato are in fact perennial, that the ancients like the moderns are concerned with reading the corpus as a (or the) basis for constructing and testing interpretations of Plato's philosophy: note "Thus, the interpretation of Plato *ceases* to be a problem" and "the problem of interpreting Plato *again became* urgent" (my italics). For an interesting account of how the Neoplatonists (especially Proclus) approached the problem of interpreting the dialogues, see J. A. Coulter, *The Literary Microcosm: Theories of Interpre-*

lation of the Later Neoplatonists, Columbia Studies in the Classical Tradition no. 2 (Leiden: Brill, 1976).

18.   In light of Tigerstedt's remarks on the nature of the dialogue, one would expect him to deny that certain interlocutors speak for Plato (thus C. Griswold, rev. of E. N. Tigerstedt, *Interpreting Plato*, in *Review of Metaphysics* 37 [1983]: 151). So it is strange to read that the Athenian Stranger is Plato's mouthpiece (*Interpreting Plato*, p. 35; cf. p. 54).

19.   See Cherniss, "Biographical Fashion," pp. 281, 289–91.

20.   See Cherniss, "Biographical Fashion."

21.   That the *eidos* of something is its essence (or what it is to be that thing) is a criterion by which to test definitions and so figures very much in Socratic elenchus; cf. A. Nehamas, "Self-Predication and Plato's Theory of Forms," *American Philosophical Quarterly* 16 (1979): 93–103.

22.   On the example, cf. P. Shorey, "The Idea of Good in Plato's Republic: A Study in the Logic of Speculative Ethics," *University of Chicago Studies in Classical Philology* 1 (1895): 188–239.

23.   Burnyeat (rev. Strauss, *Studies*) rightly objects to Strauss's requirement that the reader of the dialogues first suspend his critical impulses and endeavor instead to understand Plato *as he understood himself*: as I have maintained, it is not our purpose to try to understand Plato's philosophical thought, since this is not possible given the nature of his writings; our aim as philologists is to interpret the Platonic text or as philosophers to think for ourselves, using this text as a guide. But there is criticism and there is criticism. Burnyeat's brief remarks about the alternative to Strauss's proposal risk encouraging the sort of hypercriticism of the intellectual drama that I mentioned above; the danger here is that the reader will become satisfied with "refutation" based on assumptions that remain unexamined and stand as dogma because they are more commonly held and so seem more obvious and cogent. To avoid this recourse to dogma in the face of a challenge to think, one must repudiate such dogmatizing and allow only that criticism which is based on what is already thought through and understood. And, in the philosophical study of Plato, this necessitates paying hard attention to the dialogue and trying to find not a doctrine but those questions one should answer in order to reach his own decision about the topic at issue.

24.   Cornford ("Plato's *Euthyphro*"), in developing the notion of a masked conclusion, presents a worthwhile example of how to interpret the argument of the *Laches* and the *Euthyphro*, although I disagree with the claim that what is masked constitutes doctrine Plato held; cf. F. M. Cornford, *The Laws of Motion in Ancient Thought* (an inaugural lecture read at Cambridge University, 1931) (Cambridge: Cambridge University Press, 1931), p. 9, which describes the interpreter's task as one of finding out what went on in the minds of men long dead.

25.   It may be thought that by discrediting the modern version of the question "What did Plato think?" I have put in doubt the worth of the question itself. This is not the case. There are, for instance, many moderns who identify Plato with the text and take the question "What did Plato think?" to mean "What is the argument in the text?"; when they speak of Plato's thought, they talk of the text and not about something of which the text is a dependent product. Although I endorse this practice, I have avoided speaking this way for the sake of clarity. For one must be careful to distinguish such usage of "Plato" and "Plato's thought" from that more commonly found in the scholarly literature. The former is a shorthand for referring to the argument in what is written and the hints for reflection; it entails no notion of a doctrine of philosophy that the text manifests. These modern interpreters, by the way, are termed philologists here.

4. The Theater of Myth in Plato

1.   S. Rosen, *Plato's Sophist: The Drama of Original and Image* (New Haven: Yale University Press, 1983).

2.   Cf. Marsilio Ficino, *Commentaire sur le Banquet de Platon* (*De Amore*), trans. R. Marcel (Paris: Les Belles Lettres, 1956).

3.   L. Couturat, *De Platonis mythis* (Paris: Alcan, 1896).

4.   V. Brochard, "Les mythes dans la philosophie de Platon," *Année philosophique* (1901), reprinted in *Etudes de philosophie ancienne et de philosophie moderne* (Paris: Alcan, 1912), p. 53.

5.   L. Brisson, *Platon: les mots et les mythes* (Paris: Maspéro, 1982), p. 10.

6.   Besides Critias, who is an Athenian, we can also list outsiders such as the Eleatic Stranger, the Athenian Stranger, Diotima the Stranger from Mantinea, Timaeus from Locri, and Protagoras from Abdera. If we bear in mind that Socrates himself is "a stranger in his own city" (*Phr.*, 230c–d) in the very eyes of his fellow citizens, and that Critias quoting Solon repeats the words of an Egyptian Priest, we must admit that Platonic myth is always related to some foreign source.

7.   Hegel, *Lectures on the History of Philosophy*, trans. E. S. Haldane and F. H. Simson, 3 vols. (Atlantic Highlands, N.J.: Humanities Press, 1983), 2:20.

8.   *Procli Diadochi. In Platonis Rem publicam Commentarii*, ed. W. Kroll, 2 vols. (Leipzig: Teubner, 1899–1901), vol. 2, p. 133, 1. 8–10.

9.   *Procli Diadochi. In Platonis Timaeum Commentaria*, ed. E. Diehl, 3 vols. (Leipzig: Teubner, 1903–6), vol. 2, p. 247, 1. 18–20.

10.   J.-F. Mattéi, *L'Etranger et le Simulacre: Essai sur la fondation de l'ontologie platonicienne* (Paris: Presses Universitaires de France, 1983), pp. 401–9. Cf. J.-F. Mattéi, "Le chiasme heideggerien ou la mise à *l'écart* de la philosophie," in D. Janicaud and J.-F. Mattéi *La métaphysique à la limite* (Paris: Presses Universitaires de France, 1983), pp. 110–5.

11.   J.-F. Mattéi, *L'Etranger et le Simulacre*, passim, and esp. IV, 2, 5, pp. 353–409. For the comprehensive list of the various occurrences of the number five, see pp. 388–89 and 549–51.

12.   Proclus repeatedly insists in his *Comment. Tim.* on the "spheric" property of the pentad which ends with the same number whenever it progresses (vol. 2, p. 454, 1. 27–29). Cf. vol. 2, p. 236, 1. 8–15: "The total number of the soul . . . has progressed according to the pentad so that the soul is turned toward itself, for the pentad has a conversive power toward itself." Cf. also *Comm. Rep.*, ed. Kroll, vol. 2, p. 53, 1. 26–29. Damascius says the same thing again in the *Dubitationes et Solutiones de Primis Principiis, in Platonis Parmenidem*, ed. C. E. Ruelle (Paris: Klincksieck, 1889). "The pentad fits in with the diacosm, since it holds together and contains in a circle the whole peripheral movement of this world (cosmos), and because it is the tetrad returning to the monad" (p. 132, 1. 16–18; para. 265).

13.   R. S. Brumbaugh, *Plato's Mathematical Imagination* (Bloomington: Indiana University Press, 1954) has rightfully established that all the measures of the island are related to numbers five and six (p. 49). Cf. Mattéi, *L'Etranger et le Simulacre*, pp. 405–9.

14.   Heraclitus the rhetor, *Allégories d'Homère*, trans. F. Buffière (Paris: les Belles Lettres, 1962).

15.   The manuscripts give us the words *Dios* or *Dionusou*. The second reading certainly prevails since Zeus has already been mentioned and the new pageant is followed by the Bacchants (*hai bacchai*; 253a6).

16. Mattéi, *L'Etranger et le Simulacre*, pp. 195–203, and "La symphonie de l'être dans le *Sophiste* de Platon," *Dialogue: Canadian Philosophical Review* 24, no. 2 (1985), pp. 237–56.

17. Cf. the sixth book of Proclus' *Commentary on the Parmenides*, and also his *Platonic Theology*, trans. into French by H. D. Saffrey and L. G. Westerink, 4 vols. (Paris: Les Belles Lettres, 1968–81), vol. 1, pp. 57–58, para. 12; Damascius, *Dubitationes*, ed. Ruelle, pp. 287–288, para. 431. Cf. also J. Trouillard, "La notion de *dunamis* chez Damascios," *Revue des Etudes Grecques* 85 (1972): 353–63; J. Combès, "Damascius, lecteur du *Parménide*," *Archives de Philosophie* 38 (1975): 33–60.

18. The author is grateful to Anne Mattéi, and particularly to Charles Griswold, for their translation of this essay from the French.

5. Digression and Dialogue: The *Seventh Letter* and Plato's Literary Form

1. For text and discussion, the following are interesting: J. Souilhé, ed., *Platon: Lettres* (Paris: Edition les Belles Lettres, 1926), vol. 13, pt. 1, of the Budé edition; G. Morrow, *Plato: Epistles* (New York: Bobbs Merrill, 1962); W. K. C. Guthrie, *History of Greek Philosophy* (Cambridge: Cambridge University Press, 1978), 5:399–418; L. Edelstein, *Plato's Seventh Letter* (Leiden: Brill, 1966); R. G. Bury, ed., *Plato: Letters* (text and translation) (New York and London: Loeb Classical Library, 1929). For a demonstration that the method discussed in the digression in this work is philosophically usable, whether the passage is Plato's or not, see my *Rôle of Mathematics in Plato's Dialectic* (Ph.D. Diss., University of Chicago, 1942).

2. I first wrote about this self-illustrating character of the philosophical digression in 1940 in a course syllabus that was never used. I have been a little slow in further treatment of the point.

3. Parmenides, Fr. 6 (*palintropos*).

4. The *Theae.* tries out the "blank tablet," later Locke's psychological model, and the "impressions in the mind" of seals and signet rings, later Hume's psychological model. But both are superseded by the "mad aviary" improvement, which I do not think later psychology has adopted.

5. Socrates introduces and refers back to his comments contrasting the lawyer's life and the philosopher's as digressions.

6. See Egil Wyller, *Der Späte Platon* (Hamburg: Meiner, 1970); my review of the book in *Classical World* 64 (1971): 160; and J. Klein's unpublished "Lecture on the *Statesman*," dated November 21, 1969.

7. The "longer route" in the *Rep.* (Books 5 through 7); the "longer path" for division in the *Pol.* (265a3).

8. This parallel of the *Theaetetus*' and *Seventh Letter*'s digressions deserves more exploration. In the former, it is the philosopher who introduces the central digression, contrasting his philosophy to the narrow view of the lawyer (and in the *Soph.* the ghost of Protagoras is just below stage). In the present *Letter*, Plato introduces a philosopher's reflections on ethics reminiscent of Socrates' digression; the small-minded vanity of Dionysius II certainly sounds like the description of the nonphilosophic lawyer in the *Theae.*

9. For two discussions of this self-instantiating effect, see H. J. Sinaiko's *Love, Knowledge, and Discourse in Plato* (Chicago: University of Chicago Press, 1965), and R. H. Weingartner's *The Unity of the Platonic Dialogue* (Indianapolis: Bobbs-Merrill, 1973).

10. R. S. Brumbaugh, "A New Interpretation of Plato's *Republic*," *Journal of Philosophy* 64 (1967): 661–70.

11. *Pol.* 286d6.

12. R. P. McKeon discusses this characteristic of Platonism in his *Freedom and History* (New York: Noonday Press, 1952).

13. For example, the *Epin.* looks like an incomplete start at adapting two sections of a draft designed for the *Philosopher*.

14. R. S. Brumbaugh, "Plato's *Meno* as Form and as Content of Secondary School Courses in Philosophy," *Teaching Philosophy* 1 (1975): 107–14. For the parallel structure of the *Meno* and the *Theue.*, see E. S. Thompson's edition of the *Meno* (London: Macmillan, 1901), pp. lv–lvii.

15. For example, *H. Min.* 364a: "Makarion, o Ippia."

16. *Seventh Letter*, 343b9.

17. *Seventh Letter*, 342e2; one earlier occurrence of this true logos is presumably *Laws*, X, where the soul is discussed.

18. *Seventh Letter*, 344d5: "peri phuseos akron kai proton" (which is what the forger of the *Second Letter* makes Dionysius II question Plato about).

19. This echoes the criticism of the written word that ends the *Phaedrus*. There is, however, a place for memoranda such as the old men in the *Laws* are supposed to note down.

20. *Laws*, X 895d1–896c1.

21. *Phr.* 275b5–276a1.

22. Cf. *Eighth Letter*.

23. Cf. Weingartner, *Unity of the Platonic Dialogue*.

24. Protagoras Fr. 7 in Diels-Kranz's *Fragments*, 10th ed. (Berlin: Weidmannische Buchhandlung, 1960), 2:266.

6. Plato's Dialogues in Light of the *Seventh Letter*

1. In the view of Konrad Gaiser, for instance, Plato proclaimed to the inner circle an oral doctrine consisting of "a coherent and mature theory of first principles," which could not be treated in the dialogues for "hermeneutic reasons given by Plato himself in the *Phaedrus* and Seventh Letter." See K. Gaiser, "Plato's Enigmatic Lecture 'On the Good,' " *Phronesis* 25 (1980): 5–37; cf. p. 27.

2. An interpretive thesis that has received considerable discussion recently is that Plato was laboring with a perceptual model of knowledge in the early and middle dialogues, but had progressed to a discursive model by the time of the *Sophist*. See, for example, W. G. Runciman's *Plato's Later Epistemology* (Cambridge: Cambridge University Press, 1962), J. Gosling's *Plato* (New York: Routledge & Kegan Paul, 1973), and H. Teloh's *The Development of Plato's Metaphysics* (State College: Pennsylvania State University Press, 1981). The present essay has nothing to say regarding the relative prominence of visual images for knowledge in the earlier and later dialogues, and little to say about changes in Plato's conception of Forms that are alleged to have accompanied the change in models. It is argued later in this essay, however, that Plato retained a nondiscursive model of philosophic knowledge in the *Sophist* and beyond.

3. This is the view that philosophy aims at the formulation of statements (however conceived) that express philosophic truths, or of sentences that represent true propositions (however conceived) about philosophic topics. A nondiscursive view of philosophy is developed in Ludwig Wittgenstein's *Tractatus*, according to which "philosophy does not result in 'philosophical propositions,' but rather in the clarification of propositions" (4.112). Among studies attributing a discursive view of philosophy to Plato are R. Robinson's *Plato's Earlier Dialectic* (Oxford: Oxford University Press, 1953), and my *Plato's Analytic Method* (Chicago: University of Chicago Press, 1969). By suggesting that Plato instead held a nondiscursive view of philosophy, this essay, of course, is not suggesting that Plato's view of philosophy was identical to that of the early Wittgenstein.

4. The term *logos* used at 99e5 is the only word used regularly in Plato's corpus with a meaning approximated by the English "proposition."

5. See n. 4. Two other occurrences of *logos* in the Divided Line passage at 509d9 and 511e3 carry the sense of ratio or proportion.

6. This is discussed in appendix A of my book *Plato's Late Ontology: A Riddle Resolved* (Princeton: Princeton University Press, 1983).

7. This is explicated and defended in *Plato's Analytic Method*.

8. Details are discussed in appendix A of *Plato's Late Ontology*, along with similarities to Aristotle's definition of truth and falsehood at *Metaphysics*, 1011b26–67.

9. Not even at 210b1–2. E. S. Haring's "The *Theaetetus* Ends Well," *Review of Metaphysics* 35 (1982): 509–28, contains a useful discussion of this matter.

10. *Logos* bears the meaning "reason" and "power of mind" at *Phaedo*, 73a5, and that of "evaluation" at *Republic*, 550a4.

11. See *Plato's Late Ontology*, chapter 3, for discussion of meaning.

12. Among recent commentaries that exhibit critical sensitivity to factors of this sort are M. Miller's *The Philosopher in Plato's Statesman* (The Hague: Martinus Nijhoff, 1980), S. Rosen's *Plato's Symposium* (New Haven: Yale University Press, 1968) and *Plato's Sophist* (New Haven: Yale University Press, 1983), and C. Griswold's *Self-Knowledge in Plato's Phaedrus* (New Haven: Yale University Press, 1986).

7. Why Dialogues? Plato's Serious Play

1. This problem of Plato's *using* philosophical writing as a vehicle for *criticizing* philosophical writing has been addressed from a somewhat different angle in Charles Griswold's "Style and Philosophy: The Case of Plato's Dialogues," *Monist* 63 (1980): 530–46. See also his chapter in this volume.

2. See Dionysius of Halicarnassus, *On Literary Composition*, ed. Rhys Roberts (London: Macmillan, 1910), pp. 264–65.

3. The text used is that of John Burnet, 5 vols. (Oxford: Clarendon Press, 1903; reprinted, 1968). Translations are my own (often following Loeb translators).

4. Here I am clearly departing from the familiar supposition—of which Derrida's criticism of "logocentrism" would be a recent example—that *spoken* language escapes Plato's critique.

5. In this chapter I am referring only to the Platonic "Socrates" as we know him through the dialogues.

6. This disagreement is analogous to the one drawn in the *Euthyphro* in the context of practical judgment. As the *Phaedrus* points up the fact that consensus is easily achieved about words to which determinate meaning has been assigned—leaving the way open to disagreement about the meaning of other words, like *justice* and *goodness* (263a2–10)—so the *Euthyphro* points up the fact that consensus is easily achieved about matters of determinate measurement—leaving the way open to disagreement in other matters such as those involving justice and injustice, good and evil (7b6–d5).

7. Compare the report that Heracleitus was supposed to have "deliberately made his book the more obscure in order that none but the adepts would approach it" (Diogenes Laertius, *Lives of the Philosophers*, IX, 6).

8. One recalls that the introduction of censorship in the *Republic* was not unrelated to problems of interpretation. It was in part the discrepancy between what he saw as literal surface meaning and a deeper level meaning in the epic and mythological tales of gods and heroes that prompted Plato to exclude Homer and Hesiod from the education program—"for the young are not able to distinguish what is and is not the real meaning [*ho gar neos ouch hoios te krinein hoti te hyponoia kai ho me*]" (*Rep.*, 2, 378d5–8. An analogous distinction is implied in *Euth.*, 5e5–6c4.

9. Diog. Laer., *Lives*, IX, 16.

10. The traditional injunction to "mind one's own business" (*ta heautou prattein*; for example, *Charm.*, 161b6, 163a7) is picked up by Socrates in the *Republic* (4, 441d2–e2)—and then incorporated into the final account of justice (4, 443c9–d1).

11. Contrast the inadequate interpretation of Anaxagoras' dictum, "nous orders and causes all," of which Socrates complains in the *Phaedo* (97b8–99c6) with the comprehensive interpretation he proposes within the framework of the *Philebus* (26e2–27a2, 28c6–30d8).

12. Contrast the self-contradictory interpretation of the Heracleitean doctrine that "everything is in motion" (*Theae.*, 181b8–183c3) with the interpretation Socrates proposes as the "more sophisticated" (*kompsoteros*) version (*Theae.* 156a2–157b8).

13. Contrast the version of Protagorean doctrine that is shown to be self-contradictory (*Theae.* 161c7–e3, 170e7–171c7) with the version Socrates defends as "the hidden truth" in Protagoras' "obscure saying" (*Theae.*, 155d10, 152c9–10)—so long as it is restricted to infallibility at the perceptual level (*Theae.*, 171d9–e3; 160c4–d1).

14. The traditional statements about being and nonbeing are, in the *Sophist*, found to be fraught with ambiguity, for as the Eleatic Stranger admits to Theaetetus, "I used to think, when I was younger, that I understood perfectly whenever anyone used this term 'non-being.' . . . But you see what a slough of perplexity we are in about it now. And perhaps our minds are in this same condition as regards 'being' also: we may think that it is plain sailing and that we understand when the word is used, though we are in difficulties about non-being—whereas really we understand equally little of both" (243b7–c5).

15. Self-knowledge is evidently presupposed by justice, insofar as the just man must know "what in the true sense concerns one's self, and the things of one's self . . . and must dispose well of what in the true sense of the word is properly his own" (*Rep.*, 4, 443c10–d4).

16. Since Plato does not, in the dialogues, speak in his own name but—if at all—only through the persona of his characters, there might well be questions raised about this suggestion that there are nevertheless to be found in the dialogues philosophical statements or doctrines attributable to Plato himself. Two observations seem to be in order here by way

of justification for this claim. First—according to the thesis being defended here—it becomes clear that the opinions expressed by the various participants do very often contain true insights; the problem is that (in the words of the *Sophist*) they need to be subjected to the purification of cross-examination in order to discard the worse and retain the better interpretations (226d5–10). When these purified insights are seen to be not only consistent across the dialogues but even sustained as mutually complementary, so that their integration yields a coherent philosophical position, then we can seriously entertain the hypothesis that this represents Plato's own thought. Second, when such philosophical doctrines do, moreover, find independent confirmation from outside the dialogues—as, for example, in the *Seventh Letter* (even if it were not actually Plato's own) or in Aristotle's report (for example, of the Platonic doctrine of ideas and participation)—then there seems to me to be reasonable support for believing that these doctrines do in fact represent Plato's own position.

17.   During the course of the dialogues, elenchus produces a wide variety of responses ranging all the way from an eager desire to cooperate (as, for example, with Laches of Phaedrus) through puzzled confusion (as with Meno or Theodorus) to discomfiture or even annoyance (as with Critias or Polus). In the *Theaetetus*, Socrates even describes some of his respondents as "actually ready to bite me" (151c5–7). This acknowledgment is borne out by the report that "frequently, owing to his vehemence in argument, men set upon him with their fists, or tore his hair out" (Diog. Laer., *Lives*, II, 21).

18.   The complementarity of word and deed, logos and ergon—a familiar theme in the tradition (for example, Aeschylus, *Prometheus Bound*, 338; Sophocles, *Electra*, 358; Euripides, *Alcestis*, 339; cf. Herodotus, *Histories*, 4.8; Thucydides, *History*, 2.65)—surfaces at various points through the dialogues (see, for example, *Prot.*, 325d2; *Rep.*, 382a1–2, 382e8–9, 492d5–6, 498e3–4, 563a6–7; *Tim.*, 19e5–8; *Laws*, 769e5–7, 885b2–3; and especially the famous passage at *La.*, 188d1–6; cf. 185e9–11).

19.   Following Plato's terminology, an accurate term for this process of reasoning would seem to be *dianoia*. In both his epistemological theory (where he identifies it as a third phase in his model of a Divided Line) and in the practice of the dialogues themselves, it consists of clarifying and testing the network of hypotheses that constitute our conceptual structure. We do this by moving between two operations: in the first we formulate hypotheses that offer definitions of concepts in implicit or explicit relation to other concepts (for example, via collection into classes and division into subclasses); in the second, we test those hypotheses via deduction—both for coherence with the rest of the conceptual scheme and for consistency with empirical experience. (*Meno*, 86e2–87c12; *Pho.*, 99e4–100b3, 101d3–e1; *Rep.*, 510b4–511a8).

20.   For detailed argument defending this interpretation of Theaetetus' final definition, see my "The Horns of Dilemma: Dreaming and Waking Vision in the *Theaetetus*," *Ancient Philosophy* 1 (1981): 109–26.

21.   Although a modern version of this claim is to be found in Julius Stenzel's 1916 essay on "The Literary Form and Philosophical Content of the Platonic Dialogue" (in *Plato's Method of Dialectic*, trans. and ed. D. J. Allan [Oxford: Clarendon Press, 1940]), the approach has more recently found substantial support in detailed work such as Jacob Klein's *A Commentary on Plato's Meno* (Chapel Hill: University of North Carolina Press, 1965); Hans-Georg Gadamer's *Dialogue and Dialectic: Eight Hermeneutical Studies on Plato*, trans. and with an introduction by P. C. Smith (New Haven: Yale University Press, 1980); Drew Hyland's *The Virtue of Philosophy: An Interpretation of Plato's Charmides* (Athens: Ohio University Press, 1981); Laszlo Versényi's *Holiness and Justice: An Interpretation of Plato's Euthyphro* (Washington: University Press of America, 1982); Stanley Rosen's *Plato's Sophist: The Drama of Original and Image* (New Haven: Yale University Press, 1983); Kenneth M. Sayre's *Plato's*

Late Ontology (Princeton: Princeton University Press, 1983); and Charles Griswold's *Self-Knowledge in Plato's Phaedrus* (New Haven: Yale University Press, 1986).

22.   This enables us to understand how the Socrates who was condemned for *impiety* could, on the contrary, justifiably claim that his life exemplified the kind of true piety that consists of "service to the god" (*he ten emen to theo hyperesian; Apol.*, 30a6–7)—the very definition for which Euthyphro failed to offer any adequate interpretation (*hyperetike tis; Euth.*, 13d7–15b10).

23.   Plato was, of course, not the first to write dialogues: "They say that Zeno the Eleatic was the first to write dialogues. But, according to Favorinus in his *Memorabilia*, Aristotle in the first book of his dialogue *On Poetry* asserts that it was Alexamenus of Styra or Teos. In my opinion Plato, who brought this form of writing to perfection, ought to be adjudged the prize for its invention, as well as for its embellishment" (Diog. Laer. *Lives*, II, 48).

24.   Although, strictly speaking, any statement whatever can pose problems of interpretation, it is not (as the *Phaedrus* points out) ordinary terms like *iron* or *silver* that prove to be seriously problematic but rather the terms that define the values of a culture—like *justice* or *goodness* (*Phr.*, 263a2–b5). For this reason Plato will focus especially on expressions of the tradition. But there is a further dimension involved here. Precisely because we are by nature social—in the sense that it is only by being born into and being nurtured within a particular language, culture, and tradition that we can become fully human—it follows that self-knowledge will require understanding of one's cultural tradition precisely because who and what we are is inevitably bound up with that tradition. Like the laws that shape us, so the tradition is truly parent and author of our being who we are (see *Crito*, 50d5–e1, 51c8–d1).

25.   Although long familiar in the biblical context, these distinctions are reflected in the hermeneutical approach of Friedrich Schleiermacher (*Hermeneutics: The Handwritten Manuscripts*, ed. H. Kimmerle, trans. J. Duke and J. Forstman [Missoula, Mont.: Scholars Press, 1977], esp. pp. 98–99, 108–12, 194, 204), and Wilhelm Dilthey ("The Development of Hermeneutics," in H. P. Rickman, ed. and trans., *Selected Writings* [Cambridge: Cambridge University Press, 1976], pp. 247–63). They are distinctions played on in the contemporary context by thinkers as different as Jacques Derrida and Hans-Georg Gadamer (see below).

26.   The contrast I am pointing to might perhaps be seen as a specification of Richard Bernstein's larger contrast in his *Beyond Objectivism and Relativism: Science, Hermeneutics, and Praxis* (Philadelphia: University of Pennsylvania Press, 1983), see esp. his overview, pp. 8–20.

27.   My point here is to register awareness of the ongoing character of tradition; thus Plato's own reflections *on* tradition become in turn part *of* the tradition—rather as Mencius' commentary on Confucian texts becomes part and parcel of the Confucian tradition, and the rabbinical or patristic fathers' commentaries on Scripture become part and parcel of the Jewish or Christian tradition.

28.   Hans-Georg Gadamer, *Truth and Method* (New York: Seabury Press, 1975); hereafter cited in the text as *TM*.

8. On Socratic Dialogue

1   K. Lorenz, *Elemente der Sprachkritik: Eine Alternative zum Dogmatismus und Skeptizismus in der Analytischen Philosophie* (Frankfurt: Suhrkamp, 1970), p. 13. On the introductory remarks concerning the nature of (philosophical) dialogue, see K. Lorenz, "Dialog,"

in J. Mittelstrass, ed., *Enzyklopädie Philosophie und Wissenschaftstheorie*, vol. I (Mannheim, Zurich and Vienna: Bibliographisches Institut, 1980), pp. 471–72.

2.   *VS*, 22 B 53. H. Diels & Kranz, *Die Fragmente der Vorsokratiker: Griechisch und Deutsch*, 6th ed. (Berlin: Weidmann, 1951), vol. I:162.

3.   *Memorabilia*, IV 5, 12. See L. Sichirollo, Διαλέγεσθαι—*Dialektik: Von Homer bis Aristoteles* (Hildesheim: Olms, 1966), pp. 18ff.

4.   See *Euthyd.*, 271c–272a.

5.   Δισσοὶ λόγοι, *VS*, 90 A 8, 3–5 (Diels, *Die Fragmente der Vorsokratiker*, 2:415).

6.   See *Theae.*, 167d–e.

7.   See *Analytica Priora*, 24a25.

8.   For this, see J. Mittelstrass, "Platon," in O. Höffe, ed., *Klassiker der Philosophie*, vol. 1, *Von den Vorsokratikern bis David Hume* (Munich: C. H. Beck, 1981), pp. 38–62, here pp. 45ff.

9.   See *Meno*, 81c–d; *Pho.*, 74aff.

10.   *Phr.*, 275d–e (trans. R. Hackforth, *Plato's Phaedrus*, [Cambridge: Cambridge University Press, 1972]).

11.   See in this context the relevant analysis in W. Wieland, *Platon und die Formen des Wissens* (Göttingen: Vandenhoeck & Ruprecht, 1982).

12.   See H. J. Krämer, *Arete bei Platon und Aristoteles: Zum Wesen und zur Geschichte der Platonischen Ontologie* (Heidelberg: C. Winter, 1959). (*Abhandlungen der Heidelberger Akademie der Wissenschaften, philos.-hist. Kl.* 6th fasc.), pp. 24ff., 400ff.; H. J. Krämer, "Retraktationen zum Problem des esoterischen Platon," *Museum Helveticum* 21 (1964): 137–67(esp. p. 143ff.); K. Gaiser, *Platons ungeschriebene Lehre: Studien zur systematischen und geschichtlichen Begründung der Wissenschaften in der Platonischen Schule*, 2nd ed. (Stuttgart: E. Klett, 1968), pp. 3, 588. For a critique of these positions, see K. v. Fritz, "Die philosophische Stelle im siebten platonischen Brief und die Frage der 'esoterischen' Philosophie Platons," *Phronesis* 11 (1966): 117–53 (esp. pp. 144ff.); see further, in the context of an extensive documentation of the relevant texts and their interpretation, W. K. C. Guthrie, *A History of Greek Philosophy*, vol. 4, *Plato: The Man and His Dialogues; Earlier Period* (Cambridge: Cambridge University Press, 1975), pp. 56 ff.; and vol. 5, *The Later Plato and the Academy* (Cambridge: Cambridge University Press, 1978), pp. 418ff.

13.   See J. Mittelstrass, "Die Entdeckung der Möglichkeit von Wissenschaft," *Archive for History of Exact Sciences* 2 (1962–66): 410–35, esp. pp. 425ff. The piece is reprinted in J. Mittelstrass, *Die Möglichkeit von Wissenschaft* (Frankfurt: Suhrkamp, 1974), pp. 29–55, 209–21, esp. pp. 43ff. For a more detailed explication of the relationship between mathematics and philosophy in the *Republic*, particularly with respect to the concept of the hypothetical method, see R. C. Cross and A. D. Woozley, *Plato's Republic: A Philosophical Commentary* (London and New York: Macmillan, 1964), pp. 231ff.

14.   For this, see F. Kambartel, "Wie ist praktische Philosophie konstruktiv möglich? Über einige Missverständnisse eines methodischen Verständnisses praktischer Diskurse," in F. Kambartel, ed., *Praktische Philosophie und konstruktive Wissenschaftstheorie* (Frankfurt: Suhrkamp, 1974), pp. 10ff.

15.   I. Lakatos, *Proofs and Refutations: The Logic of Mathematical Discovery*, ed. J Worrall and E. Zahar (Cambridge: Cambridge University Press, 1976). On the distinction between internal and external history, see I. Lakatos, "History of Science and Its Rational Reconstructions," in R. C. Buck and R. S. Cohen, eds., *PSA 1970: In Memory of Rudolf Carnap (Proceedings of the 1970 Biennial Meeting of the Philosophy of Science Association)*,

Boston Studies in the Philosophy of Science, vol. 7, (Dordrecht: D. Reidel, 1971), pp. 105ff; also in I. Lakatos, *Philosophical Papers*, 2 vols, ed. J. Worrall and G. Currie (Cambridge: Cambridge University Press, 1978), 1: 118ff.

16.   Lakatos, *Proofs and Refutations*, p. 5.

17.   "Plato," in P. Edwards, ed., *The Encyclopedia of Philosophy*, (London and New York: Macmillan, 1967), 6: 333.

9.   Plato's Metaphilosophy: Why Plato Wrote Dialogues

1.   The quotation is from Morris Lazerowitz' "A Note on 'Metaphilosophy,' " *Metaphilosophy* 1 (1970): 91. It seems, according to this definition, that "metaphilosophy" is to analyze the causes of philosophical disagreement, with the aim of discrediting these causes and showing that the entire disagreement is a mistake. This strategy obviously has a precedent in Kant's treatment of the "dialectic" of reason. For this and other reasons I will propose that "metaphilosophy" should be understood, in its primary sense, in terms of the Kantian framework. This is the sense in which I will be using the term in the body of this chapter. However, I have no objection to a looser, secondary, sense of the term, such that any reflection from any standpoint about the nature of philosophy can be called "metaphilosophy." In this secondary sense one might speak of "metaphilosophical" objections to the Kantian framework. For a helpful discussion of the whole issue of metaphilosophy, see R. Pippin's "Critical Methodology and Comprehensiveness in Philosophy," *Metaphilosophy* 9 (1978): 197–211.

2.   For the reference, see L. W. Beck's excellent "Toward a Meta-Critique of Pure Reason," in *Essays on Kant and Hume* (New Haven: Yale University Press, 1978), p. 25.

3.   I do not want to claim that every modern philosophy fits this description. Heidegger, for example, would seem to represent an exception. But even the "fundamental ontology" of Heidegger's *Sein und Zeit* has a strongly Kantian bent, a fact that has been noted often enough.

4.   Consider, for example, Kant's criticism of Aristotle for having discovered the forms of judgment in a wholly empirical way, whereas what is required is a "deduction" of these categories (*KRV*, A81 = B107). Fichte turned around and made a similar criticism of Kant. See Fichte's "Second Introduction to the *Science of Knowledge*," in *Fichte: Science of Knowledge (Wissenschaftslehre), with First and Second Introductions*, trans. P. Heath and J. Lachs (New York: Appleton-Century-Crofts, 1970), p. 51. Hegel then accused both Kant and Fichte of having failed on the same score. *Science of Logic*, trans. W. H. Johnston and L. G. Struthers, 2 vols. (New York: Humanities Press, 1966), 1:87–91; and the *Logic* in the *Encyclopaedia*, par. 41–42. See also the comments about Kant, and the general demand for an "unconditioned" starting point for philosophy, in Schelling's 1794 essay "On the Possibility of a Form for All Philosophy," trans. F. Marti, *Metaphilosophy* 6 (1975): 1–24. Certainly the first, "epistemological," part of Hegel's *Phenomenology* is an indirect criticism of non-reflexive pre-Hegelian epistemologies. For an interpretation of Hegel's "metaphilosophy" that is consistent with my remarks about Hegel, see Terry Pinkard's "The Logic of Hegel's *Logic*," *Journal of the History of Philosophy* 17 (1979): 417–35, and the articles by Pippin cited in nn. 1 and 13 of this chapter.

5.   As Beck notes, Kant "compares his procedure to that of the grammarian 'who studies a language in order to detect the rules for the actual use of words and to collect elements for a grammar.' " What Kant calls "transcendental grammar" is the doctrine of the elements of this grammar, elements thanks to which we can "spell" knowledge and experience ("Toward a Meta-Critique," p. 26). A letter/syllable metaphor is used in several of Plato's

dialogues, but with the intent of illustrating the necessity of knowing the "forms" or "elements" in an ontological, not an epistemological sense. See *Pol.*, 277e ff., *Phil.*, 17b, 18b–d and context; consider also *Soph.*, 253a ff. and *Theae.*, 201e ff. Whether or not knowledge of Plato's letterlike forms yields a grammar (the rules) for the correct "spelling" of appearances is a matter of some controversy. Still, both Plato and Kant seem to demand some sort of ascent from the "book" of nature to its more intelligible and "prior" founding principles.

6.   This "intensification" would also have to be interpreted as a *narrowing* of the notion of "philosophy" to "theory of knowledge," that is, to a *foundation* specifying science. For a good account of this narrowing as well as of the rise of "histories of philosophy" which proceed along the lines just adumbrated (the ancients-as-primitive-epistemologists story), see Rorty's *Philosophy and the Mirror of Nature* (Princeton: Princeton University Press, 1979), pp. 131ff. As Rorty points out, the terms "theory of knowledge" and "epistemology" (*Erkenntnis Theorie, Erkenntnislehre*) were invented in the early nineteenth century, along with the whole notion of philosophy as a professional academic discipline.

7.   Philosophical disputes (such as those portrayed in Plato's dialogues) do frequently seem to assume too *much*, and do seem fruitless because the disputants have not clearly seen their own, and each other's, assumptions and because they have not agreed on a decision procedure to settle their disputes. Earlier philosophers (so the charge goes) just did philosophy naively, without sufficient self-reflection; they philosophized dogmatically, and were therefore unable to locate the common a priori structure of reason that could serve as a "tribunal" (see *KRV*, Axi). They disputed about topics whose solution transcends the power of reason, and thus "wrestle with their own shadows," as Kant puts it (*KRV*, A756 = B784). Hume presents a similar argument in the Introduction to the *Treatise*.

8.   That is, it seems that an object level knowledge claim cannot serve as a basis for ranking claims, since it itself has to be evaluated in the manner described above. The alternative to such evaluation would seem to just be dogmatism. For example, someone who claims that his conception of God is the only true one cannot dismiss other claims merely by asserting that his conception is the true one; for that just amounts to asserting that it is true because he says it is. Since the reasons he offers in favor of his conception are not accepted by his opponents, the dispute is undecidable unless we ascend to a higher plateau on which references to God are replaced by discussion of the possibility of referring meaningfully to the divine. This is precisely what Kant, for example, does in the *Transcendental Dialectic* of the *KRV*.

9.   The epistemological formulation of the self-knowledge issue by some modern philosophers is thought to answer dogmatic skepticism (the view that nothing can be known) by clearly delineating what can, and cannot, be known. The answer, that is, is twofold: our metaphilosophers grant the skeptic that certain things cannot be demonstrated satisfactorily (in Kant's case, these would be the "transcendental Ideas," such as those of the existence of God, Freedom, Immortality); but they insist that within well-defined boundaries scientific knowledge does exist. So long as we are unclear about our metaphilosophy, they argue, a convincing response to the skeptic is impossible. The skeptic may question the very framework within which we adjudicate claims to know, and this a priori framework must first be established. For an excellent discussion of Kant's reply along these lines to Hume, see Beck's "Kant's Strategy," in *Essays*, pp. 3–19.

10.   Hegel, *Lectures on the History of Philosophy*, trans. Haldane and Simson, 3 vols. (Atlantic Highlands: Humanities Press, 1974), 2:9, 14, 17.

11.   While Socrates' conversation with Protagoras looks like a conversation between mature philosophers, I do not count it as such since everyone in the dialogue, including Socrates and Protagoras, classifies the one as a philosopher and the other as a sophist.

12.   For an extended argument for the view that Plato does not offer a "theory" of

Ideas, see W. Wieland, *Platon und die Formen des Wissens* (Göttingen: Vandenhoeck & Ruprecht, 1982), pp. 125–50.

13.   Hegel, *The Logic*, pt. 1 of *The Encyclopaedia of the Philosophical Sciences*, trans. W. Wallace (Oxford: Clarendon Press, 1975), par. 10. The criticism is also accepted as definitive by Habermas, *Knowledge and Human Interests*, trans. J. J. Shapiro (Boston: Beacon Press, 1971), pp. 7–8. A similar criticism of Kant is accepted by Beck in "Toward a Meta-Critique." For example, Beck argues that Kant did not and could not demonstrate (given the *KRV*'s own doctrine of judgment) that all intuition is sensible (p. 24) or that time and space are the only two forms of intuition (p. 25), and still more fundamentally that Kant "has no explicit theory of how we come to know of the operations and faculties or abilities of the mind" (p. 33; italicized in the original). As Beck also remarks here: "It is regrettable that Kant did not say more about the peculiarities of self-knowledge"; in order to do so, Kant would have had to say more about "rational psychology." In order to construct a metacritique of Kant's philosophy it is necessary to use non-Kantian terms (p. 26). That self-knowledge cannot dispense with this "empirical" dimension is a very Platonic claim. For some criticism of Beck's suggestion that the "transcendental physiology" discussed in the "Architectonic of Pure Reason" chapter of the *KRV* might supply Kant with a viable "metacritique," see G. V. Agich, "L. W. Beck's Proposal of Meta-Critique and the *Critique of Judgment*," *Kant-Studien* 74 (1983): 261–70. Agich suggests that Kant's treatment of the metacritical problem is to be found in the notion of aesthetic judgment in the *Critique of Judgment*. For an excellent discussion of Hegel's dialectical efforts to avoid the self-reflexive problem he attributes to Kant, see R. Pippin's "Hegel's Phenomenological Criticism," *Man and World* 8 (1975): 296–314. Of course, the problem of demonstrating "first principles" has a long history in philosophy. See Aristotle's discussion of the matter in the *Anal. Post.*, bk. I, ch. iii.

14.   For a comprehensive interpretation of the *Charm.* which supports my remarks about the dialogue, see D. Hyland, *The Virtue of Philosophy* (Athens: Ohio University Press, 1981).

15.   See my "Self-knowledge and the Idea of the Soul in Plato's *Phaedrus*," *Revue de Métaphysique et de Morale* 86 (1981): 477–94.

16.   N. Rescher, *Dialectics—a Controversy-Oriented Approach to the Theory of Knowledge* (Albany: State University of New York Press, 1977), p. 56.

17.   That is, although there are vast differences between the poets, skeptics, sophists, and others in terms of the radical disagreement at issue, they can all be said to share a hostility or indifference to philosophy. Consider *Grg.*, 502c–d (poetry as a *kind* of rhetoric which flatters the crowds); *Rep.*, 596c–e and context (the sophists, painters, poets have the ability to produce imitations of all things); *Theae.*, 160d and context (Homer, Heraclitus, and Protagoras belong in the same camp); see too *Prot.*, 316d–e (with which *Theae.*, 180d should be compared), *Phr.*, 278c, *Rep.*, 492b–e and context. The crucial diairesis of the human race seems to be, for Plato, that between the philosophers and everyone else. Similarly, the Platonic dialogues everywhere present us with a conflict between philosophy (Socrates) and the polis (Athens) as such. I do not mean to simply identify the modern critics of philosophy (such as Nietzsche and Rorty) with the ancient critics. I am not making the argument that the anti-philosophers in Plato's dialogues have Rorty's strategy in mind. But I am suggesting that the Platonic dialogue form makes sense if one supposes that Plato treated them as though they did have something like it in mind, and so treated them with an awareness of what is required to attack them successfully. Moreover, there *are* connections between modern and ancient critics of philosophy. For example, on p. 157 of *Philosophy* Rorty says that if his recommendations are followed out, "We shall, in short, be where the Sophists were before Plato brought his principle to bear and invented 'philosophical thinking.' " Throughout the book Rorty opposes himself explicitly to the "Platonic Principle." Thus on pp. 392 and 394 Rorty

explicitly criticizes the philosopher's "quaestiones juris." Nietzsche's debt to Heraclitus, moreover, is well known. Much more can and should, of course, be said about these connections.

18.   See "The Problem of Socrates," in *Twilight of the Idols*; also the *Birth of Tragedy*, trans. W. Kaufmann (New York: Random House, 1967), sections 14 and 15. On p. 106 of *Birth* Nietzsche writes: "In this contrast [between the theoretic and tragic world view] I understand by the spirit of science the faith that first came to light in the person of Socrates—the faith in the explicability of nature and in knowledge as a panacea." On p. 377 of *Philosophy*, Rorty declares that for the edifying philosophy "the Platonic notion of Truth itself is absurd."

19.   *Birth of Tragedy*, pp. 22, 52, 141. Of course, I am quoting here from Nietzsche's first publication, one which he himself criticized subsequently. Though I cannot prove it here, the critical importance of art understood as an "aesthetic justification" is developed but not abandoned in Nietzsche's later thought. "Justification" does not, in any event, here mean what philosophers mean by it—else the phrase would express the very opposite of Nietzsche's thought on the matter (and does express with less ambiguity in later writings). Cf. *The Gay Science*, trans. W. Kaufmann, (New York: Random House, 1974), bk. II, section 107: "As an aesthetic phenomenon existence is still *bearable* for us, and art furnishes us with eyes and hands and above all the good conscience to be *able* to turn ourselves into such a phenomenon."

20.   For discussion of the *Rep.* passage, see my "The Ideas and the Criticism of Poetry in Plato's *Republic*, Book 10," *Journal of the History of Philosophy* 19 (1981): 135–150.

21.   I do not wish to minimize the heterogeneity of the interlocutors in the Platonic dialogues. Some are outright antiphilosophers (Callicles); others are untried in philosophy but prominent in another field of intellectual activity (Theaetetus) or in political matters (Laches, Nicias). Still others are too young to have been tried in any field (Lysis). But the fact remains that none of those with whom the mature Socrates talks philosophically is a philosopher. I am far from denying that there is constructive philosophizing in the dialogues, or that the epistemological and metaphysical discussions (though fragmentary) are important and interesting. I shall in fact argue below (section VII) that when properly understood the dialogue form leads to, indeed requires, consideration of several metaphysical theses.

22.   For an interesting discussion, with reference to Hegel, of the issue of prefaces, see J. Derrida, "Hors Livre," in *La Dissémination* (Paris: Seuil, 1972), pp. 9–67. The problem of the status of the introductions to Hegel's works has, of course, been extensively discussed in the literature.

23.   The best discussions of Socrates' near complete silence in the presence of the Eleatic Stranger are to be found in M. Miller's *The Philosopher in Plato's Statesman* (The Hague: Nijhoff, 1980), and S. Rosen's *Plato's Sophist: The Drama of Original and Image* (New Haven: Yale University Press, 1983). For some further discussion of the reasons for the absence in Plato's texts of a dialogue between mature philosophers, see my "Reflections on 'Dialectic' in Plato and Hegel," *International Philosophical Quarterly* 22 (1982): 126–29.

24.   *Philosophy*, pp. 366, 369, 377. On p. 317 Rorty compares his position to that of "the informed dilettante, the polygramatic, Socratic intermediary between various discourses."

25.   For an excellent discussion of Derrida and dissemblance, see V. Descombes, *Modern French Philosophy*, trans. Scott-Fox and Harding (Cambridge: Cambridge University Press, 1980), chap. 5. Similarly, N. Garver concludes his "Derrida on Rousseau on Writing" by remarking that "In the end, when we survey the ground that Derrida would have cleared by his call for us to recognize the full honor and priority of writing, we find no metaphysics, no logic, no linguistics, no semantics, and no grammatology left to carry on, but only the

290 Notes to Chapter 9

brilliant scholarly mischievousness" (*Journal of Philosophy* 74 [1977]: 673). Cf. the strikingly similar terms with which Feyerabend characterizes his own rhetoric: "Always remember that the demonstrations and the rhetorics used [in this book] do not express any 'deep convictions' of mine. They merely show how easy it is to lead people by the nose in a rational way. An anarchist [Feyerabend] is like an undercover agent who plays the game of Reason in order to undercut the authority of Reason (Truth, Honesty, Justice, and so on)" (*Against Method: Outline of an Anarchistic Theory of Knowledge* [London: New Left Books, 1975], pp. 32–33). In the footnote to this passage, Feyerabend suggests a comparison between his strategy and Dadaism (see also p. 21, n. 12).

26. On the point in the context of the classical skeptics, see M. Frede's "The Sceptic's Two Kinds of Assent and the Question of the Possibility of Knowledge," a paper delivered to the Princeton colloquium on ancient Greek philosophy (Dec. 1982). Frede distinguishes between two kinds of skeptical assent, that·of the dogmatic skeptic and that of the classical skeptic. The former defends the view that nothing is or can be known, thereby making an implicit knowledge claim and contradicting himself. The latter (Arcesilaus and followers, Sextus Empiricus) does not make this claim, so avoiding the reflexive problem, and limits himself to showing on his opponent's ground that his opponent's claims fail. This is precisely the strategy of Rorty and Derrida. Frede also argues that the classical skeptics believed themselves to be following in Socrates' footsteps here. The "assent" given by the classical skeptic to the view that nothing is or can be known is not, according to Frede, a claim but an "impression," an "acquiescence." It is just this sort of feeling that Rorteans and Derrideans want to generate in dogmatic philosophers so as to turn them away from the search for "Truth." Rorteans and Derrideans want to do this in such a way as to escape the "having a view about not having views" paradox.

27. Rorty, *Philosophy*, p. 371. Rorty continues a few lines later: "Perhaps saying things is not always saying how things are. Perhaps saying *that* is itself not a case of saying how things are." The "perhaps" is the nub of the matter. Rorty wants to affirm these propositions, and Plato and Hegel to deny them.

28. Derrida, *De la Grammatologie* (Paris: Minuit, 1967), pp. 73, 102–3, passim. On p. 38 and context Derrida comments on the Heideggerean origins of the "sous rature" strategy. Even the translator of this book indicates that her comments too about Derrida deconstruct themselves. See the closing remarks of G. C. Spivak's Translator's Preface to *Of Grammatology* (Baltimore: Johns Hopkins Press, 1974). For Rorty's evaluation of Derrida (who is referred to only in passing in *Philosophy*), see his "Philosophy as a Kind of Writing: An Essay on Derrida," in *Consequences of Pragmatism* (Minneapolis: University of Minnesota Press, 1982), pp. 90–109; and "Derrida on Language, Being, and Abnormal Philosophy," *Journal of Philosophy* 57 (1977): 673–81. Rorty clearly endorses Derrida's project, though in the former essay he sounds the alarm against the vaguely "luminous, constructive" aspects of *De la Grammatologie*. On p. 390 of *Philosophy*, Rorty refers to his own book as an effort to "deconstruct the image of the Mirror of Nature" (cf. p. 192).

29. It is true that Socrates sometimes remarks that what counts is the logos, not who holds it, and that what is important is the truth regardless of whether anyone else cares about it. And the *Phil.* presents us with a rather formalized-looking debate in which "positions" confront each other (see the very start of the *Phil.*). Nevertheless, Socrates always investigates a position dialogically.

30. For a fascinating discussion of this point, see A. Kojève's "Philosophie et Sagesse" (pt. I) in *Introduction à la lecture de Hegel* (Paris: Gallimard, 1947), pp. 271–82.

31. I am not arguing that I have specified the only reasons Plato wrote *dialogues*. A fuller treatment of the matter would have to consider, among other things, Socrates' criticisms

of writing at the end of the *Phr.* For some discussion of these criticisms, see my *Self-Knowledge in Plato's Phaedrus* (New Haven: Yale University Press, 1986), chap. 6.

32.   *Truth and Method*, trans. Sheed and Ward, Ltd. (New York: Seabury Press, 1975), p. 329. For a very strong statement of the view that for Plato philosophical knowledge cannot be stated in "propositional" form, see W. Wieland's *Platon und die Formen des Wissens*.

33.   Indeed, thanks to its nontechnical nature, Plato's dialectical poetry may escape the charge frequently brought against Hegel's ostensibly "descriptive" phenomenology, namely, that it is structured in such a way as to prejudice the process in favor of the author's position. Plato does not construct *doxa* (opinion), he "imitates" it; although, admittedly, this is not the same as just copying or mirroring it. For further discussion of the Hegel-Plato relationship, see R. Bubner, "Dialog und Dialektik oder Plato und Hegel," in *Zur Sache der Dialektik* (Ditzingen: Reclam, 1980), pp. 124–60.

34.   I am putting aside here the complicated question of the *Letters*. As Gadamer argues in his "Dialectic and Sophism in Plato's *Seventh Letter*," chap. 5 of *Dialogue and Dialectic: Eight Hermeneutical Studies on Plato*, trans. P. C. Smith (New Haven: Yale University Press, 1980), even the *Seventh Letter* (which may well be genuine) presents certain hermeneutical problems to the interpreter.

35.   For further discussion, see my *Self-Knowledge in Plato's Phaedrus*, chap. 6.

36.   There's a good deal more to be said about Platonic irony, and its difference from Socratic irony, than I have said here. For some discussion of the issue, see W. Boder, *Die sokratische Ironie in den platonischen Frühdialogen* (Amsterdam: B. R. Grüner, 1973); R. Schaerer, "Le mécanisme de l'ironie dans ses rapports avec la dialectique," *Revue de Métaphysique et de Morale* 48 (1941): 181–209; and my "Irony and Aesthetic Language in Plato's Dialogues," in *Literature as Art*, ed. D. Bolling (New York: Haven Press, 1987).

37.   "Dialectic and Sophism," pp. 119, 117. A similar view is argued at length by Wieland, *Platon*, pp. 125–50. Consider also *Parm.*, 135b5–c3.

38.   The translation is W. C. Helmbold's, slightly amended (*Plato's Gorgias* [Indianapolis: Bobbs-Merrill, 1952], p. 83).

39.   That is, however "subjective" or "relativist" a position may be, Socrates seeks to show that it ultimately must know itself as "true" in a sense that is not just subjective or relativist. For an excellent discussion of Socrates' criticism in the *Theae.* of Protagoras along these lines, see M. F. Burnyeat's "Protagoras and Self-Refutation in Plato's *Theaetetus*," *Philosophical Review* 85 (1976): 172–95. Burnyeat concludes that "no amount of maneuvering with his relativizing qualifiers will extricate Protagoras from the commitment to truth absolute which is bound up with the very act of assertion. To assert is to assert that p—as Passmore puts it, that something is the case—and if p, indeed if and only if p, then p is true (period). This principle, which relativism attempts to circumvent, must be acknowledged by any speaker" (p. 195).

40.   *Theae.*, 161e; if Protagoras' position is right, then Socrates' "maieutic art" is "laughable," as is "the whole business of dialectic (*dialegesthai*)."

41.   It is fairly clear, for example, that Rortean "conversation" between an advocate of normal discourse (discourse governed by an agreed upon set of neutral commensurating principles which tell us how to settle a debate; examples of such discussion being systematic philosophy and epistemology) and an advocate of a certain species of abnormal discourse (the "edifying" philosopher who violates the metarule that all changes in normal discourse should be warranted by the discovery of a new set of commensurating rules) is impossible. Rorty initially sets up "hermeneutics" as "the study of an abnormal discourse from the point of view of some normal discourse" (*Philosophy*, p. 320) in the hope of generating a "con-

versation" between the two (p. 318). But hermeneutics soon collapses into edifying philosophy, the point of which is to keep the conversation going (p. 372, 77; cf. p. 366). The reason for this collapse is surely that Rorty understands hermeneutics from the start as generating a conversation that does *not* reach for Truth or Agreement in the sense assumed by the advocates of normal discourse (pp. 315, 318, 372). When he says that this conversation is "hermeneutics with polemical intent" (p. 365) he is simply conceding what he says throughout: there is no argument or genuine exchange possible between normal and edifying philosophers (pp. 181, 364–65; *Consequences*, pp. xliii, 98). The two sides are not playing by the same rules or even the same metarule (the one that stipulates that we both want to learn the Truth). Since the conversation between normal philosophers is of no interest (for it would not be sufficiently radical), Rorty is presumably promising us conversation between edifying philosophers. But such a conversation seems impossible, since edifying philosophers are "reactive" and "parasitic," and so "having sense *only* as a protest against attempts to close off conversation by proposals for universal commensuration" (p. 377; emphasis added). Edificationists cannot react to each other. Indeed Rorty warns that to introduce "abnormal discourse *de novo*, without being able to recognize our own abnormality, is madness in the most literal and terrible sense" (p. 366). Moreover, the normal/abnormal dualism is permanent; though the future of philosophy cannot be predicted, this dualism will necessarily be present.

42.   I do not mean to imply, of course, that Aristotle uses the insult without argumentation. It is worth noting that even Rorty wants to distinguish between the sane, on the one hand, and the "stupid," "psychotic," and "moronic," on the other. Conversation is worthwhile only with the sane (*Philosophy*, pp. 190, 349; cf. the reference on p. 366 to "madness in the most literal and terrible sense.") Presumably Rorty does not think that the sane/insane distinction boils down to the normal/abnormal discourse distinction. But then how does he account for it?

43.   On shame, see *Symp.*, 216b, *Phr.* 243c, *Grg.*, 461b, 482d, *Prot.*, 248c; and R. McKim's "Shame and Truth in Plato's *Gorgias*" in this volume.

44.   Rorty says that there are human rights "worth dying for" (*Philosophy*, p. 177); but do people die while self-consciously holding that these rights "have been granted or denied, in the way in which social and intellectual historians understand this" (p. 178)? Not even intellectuals would die for rights so understood; even they revert to the naive realism of common sense, a realism with which Plato is much more sympathetic. That is, there is something terribly "theoretical" about the sort of position Rorty wants to advocate. Just as Rorty does not want to either affirm or deny the existence of God, and hopes to just set aside the "vocabulary of theology" since he does not see the point in using it (*Consequences*, p. xiv), so too he would presumably want to set aside the political rhetoric (which is usually contaminated by religious rhetoric) with which nations everywhere define themselves. But then Rorty is fairly clear in his view that the whole "mirror of nature" image, along with the notion that our ideas correspond to some reality out there, do not express a "pre-analytic intuition" (*Philosophy*, pp. 34, 158–59; yet see pp. 22, 286). I find this very doubtful. On "intuitive realism," see Rorty's response in the Introduction to *Consequences*.

45.   Rorty's quasi-Sartrean talk about the "burden of choice" (*Philosophy*, p. 376) imposed on us by the absence of commensurating discourse is presumably the basis for his criticisms of "totalitarianism" and the "secret police" (pp. 333, 351, 389), for the latter tend to extirpate conversation. To make sure that the conversation continues and the burden is not lifted is the "moral concern" of the philosopher (pp. 383, 394). Presumably giving up the burden of choice is bad because it leads to "dehumanization" (p. 377), "bad faith" (p. 383), "self-objectification" (pp. 378, 389; cf. 349). But why is all that so bad? What if dehumanization becomes, at some point, a self-description which people find "interesting"

and "new" (pp. 321, 359)? And if their "present moral intuitions" (p. 306) were totalitarian? Rorty must say that there would be something wrong with this. But here Rorty reaches a point that cannot be relativized further without destroying the force he wants to attribute to his own words. Rorty must have some description of human nature, and of its debasement, which is not just true for his "linguistic conventions" or "social practices." As always in coherent statements of liberalism, there is a hidden metarule that all views must be tolerated except the view that tolerance cannot be tolerated. Otherwise we fall prey to what K. Popper calls the "paradox of tolerance"—the fact that "unlimited tolerance must lead to the disappearance of tolerance" (*The Open Society and Its Enemies*, 5th ed. [Princeton: Princeton University Press, 1966], 1:265).

46. The remark is S. Rosen's, in his review in *Review of Metaphysics* 33 (1980): 801. Rosen also takes note of other important defects in Rorty's interpretation of Plato.

10. Liberalizing the *Crito*

1. Richard Kraut, *Socrates and the State* (Princeton: Princeton University Press, 1984).

2. *Four Texts on Socrates*, trans. T. G. West and G. S. West (Ithaca: Cornell University Press, 1984).

3. For studies of the *Crito* that seek to do justice to the problem of Socratic irony, see Drew Hyland, "Why Plato Wrote Dialogues," *Philosophy and Rhetoric* 1 (1968): 38–50; Frederick Rosen, "Obligation and Friendship in Plato's *Crito*," *Political Theory* 1 (1973): 307–16; Ann Congleton, "Two Kinds of Lawlessness," ibid. 2 (1974): 432–46; Leo Strauss, "On Plato's *Apology of Socrates* and *Crito*," in *Essays in Honor of Jacob Klein* (Annapolis: St. John's College Press, 1976), reprinted in Strauss, *Studies in Platonic Political Philosophy* (Chicago: University of Chicago Press, 1984); Ernest F. Weinrib, "Obedience to the Law in Plato's *Crito*," *American Journal of Jurisprudence* 27 (1982): 85–108; Martin D. Yaffe, "Civil Disobedience and the Opinion of the Many," *Modern Schoolman* 54 (1977): 123–36. Kraut's bibliography lists none of these.

11. Terence Irwin's Reading of Plato

1. Malcolm Schofield, "Review of Terence Irwin's *PMT*," *Classical Review* 28 (1978): 246. The full reference to the book under discussion here is *Plato's Moral Theory: The Early and Middle Dialogues* (Oxford: Clarendon Press, 1977).

2. C. C. W. Taylor, "Review of *PMT*," *Mind* 88 (1979): 597.

3. Gregory Vlastos, "The Virtuous and the Happy," *TLS*, February 24, 1978, p. 232.

4. Ibid.; Miles Burnyeat, review of *PMT*, *New York Review of Books*, September 27, 1979, pp. 56–60. Of course, the *TLS* often reviews philosophical works.

5. This may seem unfair to Burnyeat. After stating that "the dialogues are a miraculous blend of philosophical imagination and logic" he does criticize Irwin for being too one-sided, for "being all argument with no vision" (p. 56). However, the only alternative Burnyeat offers to *PMT* is the work of John Findlay, also the subject of his review. Findlay gets lambasted for being too visionary, whereas *PMT* is praised for its "skillful marshalling of evidence" and for being "a tour de force of philosophical scholarship" (p. 57). This review

is terribly misleading because it fosters the impression that the only alternative to "analytic" Platonism is the careless speculation of John Findlay.

6. Schofield, p. 246. My critique of Irwin obviously does not address all practitioners of "analytic Platonism," many of whom would deny that *PMT* is a paradigm of their interpretive method. For example, Vlastos, in spite of his admiration for Irwin, does think that *PMT* is totally wrong.

7. See E. N. Tigerstedt's *Interpreting Plato* (Stockholm: Almquist, 1977), pp. 26–51, for a good summary of this tradition.

8. All page numbers in the text refer to *PMT*.

9. George Klosko, "The Technical Conception of Virtue," *Journal of the History of Philosophy* 18 (1981): 101.

10. This has led some reviewers to complain of *PMT*'s style. Vlastos calls it "flat, bookish, repetitious" ("The Virtuous and the Happy," p. 230). The issue, however, is not merely a stylistic one, as will be seen below.

11. Leo Strauss, *The City and Man* (Chicago: University of Chicago Press, 1978), p. 60.

12. Tigerstedt, *Interpreting Plato*, p. 22.

13. Throughout this chapter I am assuming that something like an accurate interpretation of a text is possible. Given the current popularity of deconstructive criticism, this assumption requires defense, a task I postpone for a later work.

14. Burnyeat, review of *PMT*, p. 59.

15. I refer to Strauss, *The City and Man*; Stanley Rosen, *Plato's Sophist* (New Haven: Yale University Press, 1984); Jacob Klein, *A Commentary on Plato's Meno* (Chapel Hill: University of North Carolina Press, 1967); Drew A. Hyland, *The Virtue of Philosophy* (Athens: Ohio University Press, 1981).

16. This is not to imply that an interpretation must absolutely restrict its comments to a single dialogue. Klein, for one, relies heavily on the *Republic* to explicate the *Meno*. The point is that the basic unit with which the interpreter is concerned is neither the corpus nor Plato's developing psyche but the self-contained literary work that is the dialogue. Also, I do not imply that the only two methods of interpretation are the "Straussian" and the "analytic." I do, however, suggest that a successful interpretation must be informed by the "hermeneutical prudence" Strauss championed.

17. Strauss, *The City and Man*, p. 59.

18. Irwin does not comment on this passage, but I am confident that he would agree with my presentation of it.

19. I believe Irwin is mistaken on this point. There is ample evidence that throughout his career Plato conceived of two distinct modalities of techne, namely, the productive and the theoretical. See *Charm.* 166a5–b3; *Grg.* 450c–d; *Soph.* 219a–c; *Pol.* 258d–e; and *Phil.* 55d–56d. Theoretical techne is consistently exemplified by mathematics. On p. 298 of *PMT*, Irwin argues (unconvincingly) that a mathematical techne is productive in nature.

20. I refer to the letters that appeared in *TLS* on 3/17/78, 4/21/78, 6/16/78, 7/14/78, and 8/14/78. This exchange is instructive because it demonstrates that Irwin's primary commitment in *PMT* is not explication of the text. For example, on 3/17 he states, "I do not claim that there is clear textual evidence that Socrates accepts the instrumentalist thesis—though I think he accepts doctrines that logically commit him to it" (p. 321). Vlastos responds not by demanding that Irwin return to the text but by saying that the issue is "not the logical coherence of the doctrine that is being ascribed to Socrates in Irwin's letter, but its sanity" (p. 445).

The debate then focuses on the coherence and sanity of the instrumentalist thesis, and Plato is left behind.

21. Gregory Vlastos, Introduction to *Plato's Protagoras* (New York: Bobbs-Merrill, 1956), p. xi.

22. A. E. Taylor, *Plato* (London: Methuen, 1926), p. 260; J. P. Sullivan, "The Hedonism in Plato's *Protagoras*," *Phronesis* 6 (1961): 10–29; G. M. A. Grube, "The Unity of Plato's *Protagoras*," *Classical Quarterly* 21 (1933): 203–9.

23. I base this on the prologue, particularly lines 310c2–d2, where I believe it can be established that Hippocrates had been out drinking the previous night and demonstrated behavior that appears to be, but actually is not, incontinent. In other words, I would argue that his erga foreshadow the logoi that are to follow.

24. Klosko, in the appendix to "The Technical Conception of Virtue," discusses several of the passages Irwin uses as evidence for his reading of the CA.

25. Hyland, *The Virtue of Philosophy*, pp. 96ff. Although I agree with his interpretation, it must be admitted that *ē ou* regularly meets with an affirmative response in Plato.

26. Klosko, "The Technical Conception of Virtue," p. 102.

27. See Klein, *A Commentary on Plato's Meno*, for a thorough discussion of Meno's character.

28. See Hyland, *The Virtue of Philosophy*, pp. 97ff., for an elaboration of this thesis. The interpretation of the CA I suggest can be called the "dramatic" or "rhetorical," as opposed to Irwin's "theoretical," reading. I would argue that refutation is the principal rhetorical function for which Socrates applies to CA. In addition, he uses it to exhort his interlocutors to seek moral knowledge. See, for example, *Crito* 46c–47d, and *La.* 184e–185e. Irwin reads both these passages "theoretically" (see p. 71). I would argue that the analogy in both passages is meant to encourage Socrates' interlocutors, Crito and Lysimachus, not to submit to mere doxa but to seek knowledge. Both passages commit Socrates only to the proposition that moral knowledge is desirable and should be sought; they do not commit him to a theoretical conception of that knowledge.

12. Reading Plato: Paul Woodruff and the *Hippias Major*

1. Paul Woodruff, *Plato: Hippias Major* (Indianapolis: Hackett, 1982); hereafter cited in the text by page number.

2. See esp. p. 150. These requirements seem similar to R. E. Allen's characterization of forms as paradigms, essences, and universals. See, for example, *Plato's "Euthyphro" and the Earlier Theory of Forms* (New York: Humanities Press, 1970), pp. 67–79.

3. I must forgo discussing two intriguing points in Woodruff's interpretation: the *Hippias Major* as an instance of the genre of comedy and the beneficial as coextensive with the fine without being its definition.

4. I am enthusiastic about Woodruff's recognition that Hippias himself is a metaphor for the fine, but disappointed that it was not utilized more in the interpretation. Another author commenting upon Woodruff's book thinks the notion quite dubious (Charles Kahn in "The Beautiful and the Genuine," *Oxford Studies in Ancient Philosophy* 3 [1985]: 272), so there is need to give more evidence for the insight—evidence that is definitely available—as well as to pursue it further.

5. On pp. xii–xiii, Woodruff states about the fine: "Plato's subject is as alarmingly

slippery as Hippias himself. It is the important thing Socrates' other objects of search have in common: the *kalon*. Variously translated 'beautiful,' 'noble,' 'admirable,' and 'fine,' *kalon* is a general term of commendation. The virtues Socrates wants to know about elsewhere are each of them *kalon*. So are the lovely boys and young men with whom he spends his days. So are sound laws and good habits, fast horses and fierce fighting birds. So are true sentences and morally improving speeches. And so, surprisingly, is ugly old Socrates himself."

6. Note the references to things "in truth" as opposed to mere seeming (281b5 and 284e). Woodruff suggests that the fine is crucial for commendation and is intimately tied to virtue. He might have proceeded to trace its peculiar connection with wisdom, which is the leitmotif of the dialogue. See, especially, 281a1, 281c5, 281d, 283a–b, 283c, 284a1–4, 284e, 286d, 287b, 287c5, 288a3–5, 289b4–5, 291a7–8, 294c8 d4, 296a, 296e3, 300d1–2, and 304e. The importance of this point is that the distinction between apparent and real fine things exists because the many lack the wisdom to discern the one from the other (see 294c8–d4). See also my comments in n. 11 below.

7. Cf. p. 36, "We can have no doubt that the subject of the dialogue is not Hippias but the fine."

8. See *The Hippias Major Attributed to Plato* (Cambridge: Cambridge University Press, 1928), p. xxxv.

9. In the case of the *Euthyphro*, Woodruff himself notes that it is Euthyphro who needs to show that his action of trying his father is completely and exclusively pious and that Socrates does not necessarily accept this at all (p. 178). Woodruff does not, however, give this consideration the weight it deserves nor does he recognize generally that all Socrates' lines of argument receive direction from his particular respondents.

10. If, broadly speaking, there might be four factors to account for what appears in a Platonic dialogue—(1) Plato's views, (2) Socrates' views, (3) the views of Socrates' interlocutors, and (4) the truth about the matters at issue—then I think we must concentrate upon (3) and (4).

11. In brief, my analysis of the interaction of the characters in the *Hippias Major* is as follows. Evidently, Hippias, just as most of us, has great difficulty with the distinction between the apparent and the truly fine. The early discussion of law seems to be Socrates' model of how the distinction between the apparent and the real may apply to the fine (see esp. 284e). Hippias, uncomfortable with the distinction made in Socrates' way, nonetheless aims in his answers for what seems to him to be the truly fine. What is truly fine for him is what everybody will agree to be so. Rather than confusing universal and particular in his answers, Hippias denies there is any universal and takes Socrates' request for *the* fine to be a demand that he name what he and everybody else thinks is truly fine. Hence, he insists he understands what Socrates wants. When Hippias says in 287e4, "if one ought to state the truth, a fine girl is a fine thing," what needs to be accentuated is the claim to truth. The standard for truth, according to Hippias, is what everyone will accept (see, for example, 288a3–5 and 292e4–5), for to his mind, where there is universal agreement there can be no refutation. As I have suggested, Hippias' first three answers are his attempts to say what is really fine, where the really fine is that which all men will readily agree is fine. Socrates, being unable to believe that all men will agree on the truly commendable (294c–d; cf. 284e), comes at the fine another way. He attempts to link the fine with the truly good. When the Socratic definitions also get into trouble, Socrates, in his last attempt, tries to synthesize the tendencies of Hippias and himself in his answer about the pleasant through sight and hearing. This synthesis of the apparent and the truly fine also runs into difficulty, but perhaps primarily because Hippias comprehends it poorly: note his inability to include law under it (298b) and his problems with both and each. I conclude that we must take very seriously Socrates' final comment that

he has been benefited by conversation both with Hippias and with the questioner and that from it he has gained knowledge that fine things are hard (304e).

Reply to Ronald Polansky

1. To evaluate the example, Socrates would want to appeal to the account (286c5–d2, 304d4–e3); see my *Plato: Hippias Major* (Indianapolis: Hackett, 1982), pp. 138ff.

2. Polansky's view that "all Socrates' lines of argument receive direction from his particular respondents" (n. 9) is seriously overstated.

3. I treated this issue in only one chapter; that one was added to the manuscript late at the insistence of the publisher's readers and is plainly tangential to my positive reading of the dialogue. In his emphasis on this material, Polansky overlooks the attention I give to the the dialogue's positive contribution to value theory in chapter 8.

4. I am particularly dissatisfied with the usual views about Plato's middle dialogues, which do not in my view present a complete ontological theory. For this reason I share Polansky's reservations about my placement of the *Hippias Major* between *Euthyphro* and *Republic*. I do not agree with Polansky, however, that the ontological naïveté I find in the early dialogues is immaturity; indeed, I think the greater part of Plato's mature work shows traces of an admirable naïveté toward ontological issues.

5. Although it belongs to the *Euthyphro* group, I think the *Hippias Major* shows several signs of having been written later (*Plato: Hippias Major*, p. 177). Polansky cites critically an argument for this view that I borrow from M. Soreth (*Der platonische Dialoge Hippias Maior*, Zetemata 6 [Munich: Beck'sche, 1953], pp. 19–25; *Plato: Hippias Major*, p. 177): the *Hippias Major* uses a principle that undercuts an argument in the *Euthyphro*. Had Plato been thinking of the principle when he wrote the *Euthyphro*, he would not have made Socrates argue as he did in that dialogue. Polansky evidently thinks Socrates would consciously use a fallacy against Euthyphro if Euthyphro walked into it. But this would not serve Socrates' aim, which is to demonstrate (and not merely show dialectically to Euthyphro) the failure of Euthyphro's answers as evidence for his claim to expert knowledge. On the demonstrative role of Socrates' definition-testing arguments, see my forthcoming paper, "What a General Needs to Know: Priority of Definition in the *Laches* and *Apology*," *Boston Studies in Ancient Philosophy* (1987).

6. I do not see how these can be considered components in the strict sense, as any presentation of philosophy in a text will be literary.

7. Polansky considers some of my reasons for interpreting Hippias' character as I do, but overlooks the one that underlies all the others: that of charity. The form of the *Hippias Major* is that of a confrontation between a boaster and a clever fellow who will humble him. The effect would be lost if the booster were such a fool as to humble himself at every turn. In fact, Plato's use of this form here is original, sophisticated, and (in my view) highly effective.

13. Kenneth Dorter's Interpretation of the *Phaedo*

1. *Plato's Phaedo: An Interpretation* (Toronto: University of Toronto Press, 1982).

2. About this structure of dialogue and about Plato's conception of philosophy, I have tried to say something in earlier essays, such as "Die philosophische Aussage der künstler-

ischen Gestaltung platonischer Dialoge," in *Gegenwart der Antike* (Munich: F. Hörmann, 1974), pp. 5ff; and "Gedanken zur Lektüre platonischer Dialoge," *Zeitschrift für philosophische Forschung* 29 (1975): 169ff.

14. Recollection, Dialectic, and Ontology

1. Kenneth M. Sayre, *Plato's Late Ontology* (Princeton: Princeton University Press, 1983); hereafter cited in the text by page number.

2. In my own view it is not elenchus that Plato saw as sufficient for episteme but rather a sturdy, well-tested logos of the sort he depicts Socrates as looking for, a logos that Socrates could not refute. See my *Plato's Theory of Understanding* (Madison: University of Wisconsin Press, 1981), pp. 43–51; hereafter abbreviated as *PTU*.

3. The tentativeness is very apparent at *Meno* 84b. It is possible that the recollection story expressed not a Platonic doctrine but a mere epode designed to get a balky interlocutor to continue the inquiry. On epodai (charms) see *PTU*, pp. 66–69.

4. One of Sayre's reasons is that "the realm of the Forms is atemporal. To be in the immediate presence of the Forms, accordingly, the Mind itself must exist atemporally. And there is no intelligible way the Mind can exist atemporally *before* entering the body, since what is atemporal does not enter into temporal relationships" (p. 191). The argument is valid but not sound, for there is no good evidence that Plato believed Forms atemporal, and good evidence that he conceived of Forms as everlasting, not atemporal (see *Pho.* 79a, d, 103e; *Rep.* 484b, 486a). *Tim.* 37e–38c cannot be good evidence for forms as atemporal, in Sayre's view, because of the mythical, noncommittal character of the entire dialogue as he interprets it.

5. I have suggested a somewhat different treatment of the separation metaphor and of related metaphors in *PTU*, pp. 95, 97, 100–105, 117–18.

6. It is not clear to what ontological category unity (limit) and the great and the small (unlimited) belong, in Sayre's interpretation. Plato calls them *eidē* at *Phil.* 23c–d, but Sayre balks at translating this as "Form" for reasons having to do with his interpretation of Forms as "separate."

7. Gilbert Ryle, "Teaching and Training," in R. S. Peters, ed., *The Concept of Education* (New York: Macmillan, 1967).

8. See *PTU*, chap. 3.

9. See *Laws* 644c–645c.

15. Observations and Questions about Hans-Georg Gadamer's Interpretation of Plato

1. I confine myself to the views in his collection, *Dialogue and Dialectic* (New Haven: Yale University Press, 1980), especially chaps. 5–8; hereafter cited in the text by page number.

2. On this theme, see also Charles Griswold, "Style and Philosophy: The Case of Plato's Dialogues," *Monist* 63 (1980): 530–46, esp. 535, and n. 12. I am indebted to Professor Griswold for comments on this chapter.

3. The general outlook presented here is largely the same as that in my book, *Plato*

on Knowledge and Reality (Indianapolis: Hackett, 1976), although on particular issues, especially pertaining to the *Seventh Letter* and to the notion of direct apprehension or intuition, I go beyond what I said there.

4. See pp. 110, 203–4, although I am not completely confident that I am interpreting him correctly.

5. I take myself to be in agreement with Gadamer that in a certain sense the *Seventh Letter* does not present "the specific consent of Plato's philosophy" (p. 98)—at least, I do not think that I interpret it as having any more specific content than Gadamer does.

6. In n. 20 on p. 105, Gadamer seems to discard the connection of Plato's point about language with the issue about *ti* and *poion*, which seems to me firmly present in the text, and replaces it on p. 105 with another explanation of the point about language of which I myself can find nothing in the text.

7. I have tried in my book, *Plato on Knowledge and Reality*, to bring out the importance in Plato of the notion of confusing one form with another.

8. For the two possibilities joined together, see *Phil.* 39c4–5. Nothing in the dialogues seems to me to indicate that Plato ever believed that all cognition is formulated in language, although what he calls dianoia apparently is (see *Theae.* 189e–190b, 206d; *Soph.* 263e–264a; *Phil.* 38d, 39a). *Tim.* 37b–c needs more discussion than I can give it here, but the main point is that whereas it says that logos of a certain sort necessarily engenders nous and episteme, it does not say that all nous or episteme involves logos.

9. See Bertrand Russell, "Knowledge by Acquaintance and Knowledge by Description," originally published in 1911, and reprinted in *Mysticism and Logic* (London: Allen & Unwin, 1917), and also "On the Nature of Acquaintance," originally published in 1914, and reprinted in R. C. Marsh, ed., *Logic and Knowledge* (London: Allen & Unwin, 1956), esp. pp. 150–51.

10. See, for example, Hartry H. Field, "Mental Representation," *Erkenntnis* 13 (1978): 9–61, and Gilbert Harman, "Is There Mental Representation?" in *Minnesota Studies in the Philosophy of Science*, vol. 9 (Minneapolis: University of Minnesota Press, 1978), 57–64.

11. Gadamer identifies recognition with "knowing again." The qualification must be that a case of knowing again is not recognition unless one recognizes the thing as what one knew before, at least in some sense. See my *Plato on Knowledge and Reality*, p. 101.

12. See E. N. Lee, in W. H. Werkmeister, ed., *Patterns in Plato's Thought* (Assen: Van Gorcum, 1976), and my paper, "*The Rulers' Choice*," forthcoming in the *Archiv für Geschichte der Philosophie* (see esp. pt. IV). I am thus there suggesting a different treatment of the same problem that is treated by Griswold, "Style and Philosophy," p. 535.

Reply to Nicholas White

1. *The Idea of the Good in Platonic-Aristotelian Philosophy*, trans. and with an introduction by P. C. Smith (New Haven: Yale University Press, 1986).

2. In *Dialogue and Dialectic: Eight Hermeneutical Studies on Plato*, trans. and with an introduction by P. C. Smith (New Haven: Yale University Press, 1980), pp. 93–123.

3. N. P. White, *Plato on Knowledge and Reality* (Indianapolis: Hackett, 1976).

4. See my essay "Mathematik und Dialektik bei Plato," in *Physik, Philosophie und Politik*, Festschrift für C. F. von Weizsaecker, ed. K. M. Meyer-Abich (Munich: Hanser,

1982), pp. 229–44. To be reprinted in my *Gesammelte Werke*, vol. 7, *Griechische Philosophie 3*.

5. H. Langerbeck, *DOXIS EPIRYSMIH*. Studien zu Demokrits Ethik und Erkenntnislehre (Berlin: Gräfenhainichen, 1934). See my critique in *Zeitschrift für die gesamte Naturwissenschaft* 2 (1936–37): 243–45, reprinted in my *Gesammelte Werke*, vol. 5, *Griechische Philosophie* 1 (Tübingen: J. C. B. Mohr, 1985), pp. 341–43.

Selected Bibliography

This bibliography consists of works that discuss in some detail one or both of the themes that guide the present volume, namely, why Plato wrote dialogues (included under this heading are works focusing on esotericism, Plato's critique of writing, and the difference between writing and orality), and how one ought to interpret the dialogues (including their literary characteristics, such as the use of irony, myth, imagery). Where a section or a chapter of one of the books listed is particularly relevant to one or both of these themes, for the convenience of the reader I have noted it as such. Although this is the most extensive bibliography of its kind that I know of, it is not intended to be exhaustive. A number of pertinent works, for example, are cited and discussed by Krämer, Thesleff, and Tigerstedt (see below), and I have omitted them from the present list. For a helpful review of bibliographies on the secondary literature on Plato, see Y. Lafrance's "L'Avenir de la Recherche Platonicienne" (cited below).

Charles L. Griswold, Jr.

Ambrosio, F. J. "Gadamer, Plato, and the Discipline of Dialogue." *International Philosophical Quarterly* 27 (1987): 17–32.

Anderson, J. M. "On the Platonic Dialogue." In *Essays in Metaphysics*. Ed. C. G. Vaught. University Park: Pennsylvania State University Press, 1970, pp. 5–17.

Andrieu, J. *Le dialogue antique: Structure et présentation*. Paris: Société d'édition les 'Belles Lettres', 1954.

Aubenque, P., and Solignac, A. "Une nouvelle dimension du platonisme: La doctrine 'non écrite' de Platon." *Archives de philosophie* 28 (1965): 251–65. [An article review focusing on works by K. Gaiser and H. J. Krämer.]

Bambrough, R. "The Disunity of Plato's Thought: Or, What Plato Did Not Say." *Philosophy* 47 (1972): 295–307.

Baumgartner, H. M. "Von der Möglichkeit, das Agathon als Prinzip zu denken: Versuch einer tranzendentalen Interpretation zu Politeia 509b." In *Parusia: Studien zur Philosophie Platons und zur Problemgeschichte des Platonismus. Festgabe für J. Hirschberger.* Ed. K. Flasch. Frankfurt am Main: Minerva, 1965, pp. 89–101.

Bergson, L. "Eiron und Eironeia." *Hermes* 99 (1971): 409–22.

Berti, E. "Über das Verhältnis von literarischem Werk und ungeschriebener Lehre bei Platon in der Sicht der neueren Forschung." In *Das Problem der ungeschriebenen Lehre Platons: Beiträge zum Verständnis der platonischen Prinzipienphilosophie.* Ed. J. Wippern. Darmstadt: Wissenschaftliche Buchgesellschaft, 1972, pp. 88–94.

Boas, G. "Ancient Testimony to Secret Doctrines." *Philosophical Review* 62 (1953): 79–92.

Boder, W. *Die sokratische Ironie in den platonischen Frühdialogen.* Amsterdam: B. R. Grüner, 1973.

Bolotin, D. "Review of T. Irwin's *Plato's Moral Theory.*" *St. John's Review* 32 (1981): 95–97.

Brague, R. *Le restant: Supplément aux commentaires du Ménon de Platon.* Paris: Vrin, 1978. [See esp. the introduction for comments on the interpretation issue.]

Brownstein, O. L. "Plato's *Phaedrus*: Dialectic as the Genuine Art of Speaking." *Quarterly Journal of Speech* 51 (1965): 392–98.

Brumbaugh, R. S. "Doctrine and Dramatic Dates of Plato's Dialogues." In *Essays in Ancient Greek Philosophy.* Vol. 2. Ed. J. P. Anton and A. Preus. Albany: State University of New York Press, 1983, pp. 174–85.

Bubner, R. "Dialog und Dialektik oder Plato und Hegel." In *Zur Sache der Dialektik.* Ditzingen: Reclam, 1980, pp. 124–60.

Burge, E. L. "The Irony of Socrates." *Antichthon* 3 (1969): 5–17.

Burger, R. *Plato's Phaedrus: A Defense of a Philosophic Art of Writing.* University: University of Alabama Press, 1980.

Burnyeat, M. F. "Review of L. Strauss' *Studies in Platonic Political Philosophy.*" *New York Review of Books*, May 30, 1985, pp. 30–36. [See also the replies to Burnyeat, and Burnyeat's rejoinders, in *NYRB* October 10, 1985, pp. 41–44; October 24, 1985, p. 57; April 24, 1986, p. 51–53.]

Caton, H. "Speech and Writing as Artifacts." *Philosophy and Rhetoric* 2 (1969): 19–36.

Cherniss, H. "Ancient Forms of Philosophic Discourse." In *Harold Cherniss: Selected Papers.* Ed. L. Tarán. Leiden: Brill, 1977, pp. 14–35.

———. *The Riddle of the Early Academy.* Berkeley: University of California Press, 1945.

Clay, D. "Platonic Studies and the Study of Plato." *Arion*, n.s. 2 (1975): 116–32.

Cornford, F. M. "Plato's *Euthyphro* or How to Read a Socratic Dialogue." In *F. M. Cornford: Selected Papers.* Ed. A. C. Bowen. New York: Garland Press, 1987, pp. 221–38.

———. *The Unwritten Philosophy and Other Essays.* Ed. with an introductory memoir by W. K. C. Guthrie. Cambridge: Cambridge University Press, 1950.

Coulter, J. A. *The Literary Microcosm: Theories of Interpretation of the Later Neoplatonists.* Columbia Studies in the Classical Tradition, 2. Leiden: Brill, 1976.

Cropsey, J. "The Dramatic End of Plato's Socrates." *Interpretation* 14 (1986): 155–75.

Dalfen, J. "Gedanken zur Lektüre platonischer Dialoge." *Zeitschrift für philosophische Forschung* 29 (1975): 169–94.

Derbolav, J. "Der Entlastungs—bzw. Entfremdungscharakter der Schrift; Kritik und Rechtfertigung der philosophischen Schriftstellerei im *Phaidros.*" In *Platons Sprachphilosophie im Kratylos und in den späteren Schriften.* Darmstadt: Wissenschaftliche Buchgesellschaft, 1972, pp. 199–205.

———. "Was Plato 'sagte' und was er 'gemeint hat': Erörterung einer hermeneutisch bedeutsamen Differenz." In *Beispiele: Festschrift für E. Fink zum 60. Geburtstag.* Ed. L. Landgrebe. The Hague: Nijhoff, 1965, pp. 161–87.

Derrida, J. "La pharmacie de Platon." In *La dissémination.* Paris: Seuil, 1972, pp. 69–198.

Detel, W. "Bemerkungen zum Einleitungsteil einiger platonischer Frühdialoge." *Gymnasium* 82 (1975): 308–14.

Dionysius of Halicarnassus. *De Compositione Verborum.* Ed. and trans. W. R. Roberts. London: Macmillan & Co., 1910.

Dorter, K. *Plato's Phaedo: An Interpretation.* Toronto: University of Toronto Press, 1982.

Ebert, T. *Meinung und Wissen in der Philosophie Platons.* Berlin: W. de Gruyter, 1974.

Eckstein, J. *The Platonic Method: An Interpretation of the Dramatic-Philosophic Aspects of the Meno.* New York: Greenwood, 1968.

Edelstein, L. "Platonic Anonymity." *American Journal of Philology* 83 (1962): 1–22.

———. "The Function of the Myth in Plato's Philosophy." *Journal of the History of Ideas* 10 (1949): 463–81.

Erler, M. *Der Sinn der Aporien in den Dialogen Platons. Übungsstücke zur Anleitung im philosophischen Denken.* Berlin: W. de Gruyter, 1987.

Festugière, A. J. "L'ordre de lecture des dialogues de Platon aux Ve/VIe siècles." *Museum Helveticum* 26 (1969): 281–96.

Findlay, J. N. *Plato: The Written and Unwritten Doctrines.* London: Routledge & Kegan Paul, 1974.

Fisher, J. "Plato on Writing and Doing Philosophy." *Journal of the History of Ideas* 27 (1966): 163–72.

Flashar, H., ed. (with K. Gründer and A. Horstmann). *Philologie und Hermeneutik im 19. Jahrhundert.* Göttingen: Vandenhoeck & Ruprecht, 1979.

Friedländer, P. "Phaedrus." In vol. 3 of *Plato.* Trans. H. Meyerhoff. Princeton: Princeton University Press, 1969, pp. 219–42.

———. *Plato: An Introduction.* Vol. 1 of *Plato.* Trans. H. Meyerhoff. 2nd ed. 1958. Reprint. Princeton: Princeton University Press, 1973.

Fritz, K. von. "The Philosophical Passage in the Seventh Platonic Letter and the Problem of Plato's 'Esoteric' Philosophy." In *Essays in Ancient Greek Philosophy.* Ed. J. P. Anton and G. L. Kustas. Albany: State University of New York Press, 1971, pp. 408–47.

———. "Zur Frage der 'esoterischen' Philosophie Platons." *Archiv für Geschichte der Philosophie* 49 (1967): 255–68.

Frutiger, P. *Les mythes de Platon: Etude philosophique et littéraire.* Paris: F. Alcan, 1930. [See esp. pt. II, "L'interprétation philosophique des mythes."]

Gadamer, H.-G. "Correspondence Concerning *Wahrheit und Methode.*" *Independent Journal of Philosophy* 2 (1978): 5–12.

———. *Dialogue and Dialectic: Eight Hermeneutical Studies on Plato.* Trans. P. C. Smith. New Haven: Yale University Press, 1980.

———. "Hermeneutics and Historicism." Supplement I of *Truth and Method.* Trans. Sheed and Ward Ltd. New York: Seabury Press, 1975. [See esp. pp. 482–91 on questions of interpretation.]

———. *Platos dialektische Ethik: Phänomenologische Interpretationen zum Philebos*. Rev. ed. Hamburg: Meiner, 1983.

Gadamer, H.-G., and W. Schadewaldt, eds. *Idee und Zahl: Studien zur platonischen Philosophie*. Heidelberg: C. Winter, 1968. [Includes essays by H.-G. Gadamer, K. Gaiser, H. Gundert, H. J. Krämer, and H. Kuhn.]

Gaiser, K. *Platone come scrittore filosofico: Saggi sull' ermeneutica dei dialoghi platonici*. Con una premessa di M. Gigante. Naples: Bibliopolis, 1984.

———. *Platons ungeschriebene Lehre*. 2nd ed. Stuttgart: E. Klett, 1968.

———. "Plato's Enigmatic Lecture 'On The Good.' " *Phronesis* 25 (1980): 5–37.

———. *Protreptik und Paränese bei Platon: Untersuchungen zur Form des platonischen Dialogs*. Stuttgart: Tübinger Beiträge zur Altertumswissenschaft, bd. 40. Stuttgart: Kohlhammer, 1959.

Gaiser, K., ed. *Das Platonbild: Zehn Beiträge zum Platonverständnis*. Hildesheim: G. Olms, 1969. [Includes essays by H. Gundert, N. Hartmann, K. F. Hermann, W. Jaeger, H. J. Krämer, H. Kuhn, P. Natorp, F. Schleiermacher, F. Solmsen, and J. Stenzel.]

Gerstmeyer, T. "Konrad Gaiser, *Platons ungeschriebene Lehre; Studien zur systematischen und geschichtlichen Begrundung der Wissenschaft in der platonischen Schule*" (review). Trans. D. J. Schmidt. *Contemporary German Philosophy* 4 (1984): 312–319.

Goldschmidt, V. *Les dialogues de Platon: Structure et méthode dialectique*. Paris: Presses Universitaires de France, 1947.

———. *Questions platoniciennes*. Paris: J. Vrin, 1970.

Gould, J. "Klein on Ethological Mimes, for Example, the *Meno*." *Journal of Philosophy* 66 (1969): 253–65.

Graeser, A. "Kritische Retraktationen zur esoterischen Platon-Interpretation." *Archiv für Geschichte der Philosophie* 56 (1974): 71–87.

Griswold, C. "Gadamer and the Interpretation of Plato." *Ancient Philosophy* 1 (1981): 171–78.

———. "Irony and Aesthetic Language in Plato's Dialogues." In *Philosophy and Literature*. Ed. D. Bolling. New York: Haven Press, 1987, pp. 71–99.

———. "R. Burger's *Plato's Phaedrus: A Defense of a Philosophic Art of Writing*" (review). *Independent Journal of Philosophy* 4 (1983): 158–60.

———. "Reflections on 'Dialectic' in Plato and Hegel." *International Philosophical Quarterly* 22 (1982): 115–30.

———. *Self-Knowledge in Plato's Phaedrus*. New Haven: Yale University Press, 1986. [See esp. the introduction on issues of interpretation, and chap. 6 on why Plato wrote dialogues.]

———. "Style and Philosophy: The Case of Plato's Dialogues." *Monist* 63 (1980): 530–46.

———. "The Ideas and the Criticism of Poetry in Plato's *Republic*, Book 10." *Journal of the History of Philosophy* 19 (1981): 135–50.

Gründer, K. See Flashar, H.

Gundert, H. *Der platonische Dialog*. Heidelberg: C. Winter, 1968.

————. *Dialog und Dialektik; zur Struktur des platonischen Dialogs*. Amsterdam: B. R. Grüner, 1971.

Guthrie, W. K. C. *A History of Greek Philosophy*. 6 vols. Cambridge: Cambridge University Press, 1962–81. [See esp. vol. 4 (1975), chap. 3, "The Dialogues"; and vol. 5 (1978), chap. 8, "Plato's 'Unwritten' Metaphysics."]

Hager, F. P. "Zur philosophischen Problematik der sogenannten ungeschriebenen Lehre Platons." *Studia Philosophica* 24 (1964): 90–117.

Hartland-Swann, J. "Plato as Poet: A Critical Interpretation." *Philosophy* 26 (1951): pt. I, 3–18; pt. II, 131–41.

Haslam, M. "Plato, Sophron, and the Dramatic Dialogue." *Bulletin of Classical Studies* (University of London) 19 (1972): 17–38.

Hathaway, R. "Sceptical Maxims about the 'Publication' of Plato's Dialogues." *Agon*, Supp. 2 (1969): 28–42.

Havelock, E. A. *The Muse Learns to Write*. New Haven: Yale University Press, 1986.

————. "The Socratic Problem: Some Second Thoughts." In *Essays in Ancient Greek Philosophy*. Vol. 2. Ed. J. P. Anton and A. P. Preuss. Albany: State University of New York Press, 1983, pp. 147–73.

Hegel, G. W. F. *Lectures on the History of Philosophy*. Trans. E. S. Haldane and F. H. Simson. 3 vols. 1892. Reprint. Atlantic Highlands: Humanities Press, 1974. [See esp. vol. 2, chap. 3.A, "The Philosophy of Plato."]

————. "Solgers nachgelassene Schriften und Briefwechsel" (review). In *Werke*. 20 vols. Frankfurt: Suhrkamp, 1970. [See esp. vol. 11, pp. 205–74. This is Hegel's 1828 discussion of an 1826 posthumous edition of Solger's writings. As irony and the dialogue form were central topics for Solger, Hegel discusses them both, with significant reference to Plato.]

Hermann, K. F. "Über Platos schriftstellerische Motive." In *Das Platonbild: Zehn Beiträge zum Platonverständnis*. Ed. K. Gaiser. Olms: Hildesheim, 1969, pp. 33–57.

Hirzel, R. *Der Dialog: Ein Literarhistorischer Versuch*. 2 vols. Leipzig: S. Hirzel, 1895.

Hoffmann, E. "Die literarischen Voraussetzungen des Platonverständnisses." *Zeitschrift für philosophische Forschung* 2 (1947): 465–80.

Holzhey, H., and W. C. Zimmerli, eds. *Esoterik und Exoterik der Philosophie: Beiträge zu Geschichte und Sinn philosophischer Selbstbestimmung*. Basel and Stuttgart: Schwabe, 1977.

Horstmann, A. See Flashar, H.

Hyland, D. *The Virtue of Philosophy: an Interpretation of Plato's Charmides*. Athens: Ohio University Press, 1981.

————. "Why Plato Wrote Dialogues." *Philosophy and Rhetoric* 1 (1968): 38–50.

Ilting, K. H. "Platons 'Ungeschriebene Lehren': Der Vortrag über das Gute." *Phronesis* 13 (1968): 1–31.

Irwin, T. *Plato's Moral Theory: The Early and Middle Dialogues*. Oxford: Clarendon Press, 1977.

Jacques, F. *Dialogiques: Recherches logiques sur le dialogue*. Paris: Presses Universitaires de France, 1979.

Jaeger, W. "Der Wandel des Platobildes im neunzehnten Jahrhundert." In *Humanistische Reden und Vorträge*. Berlin and Leipzig: W. de Gruyter, 1937, pp. 138–52.

Kahn, C. H. "Did Plato Write Socratic Dialogues?" *Classical Quarterly* 31 (1981): 305–20.

306   Bibliography

Kayser, J. R. "Noble Lies and Justice: On Reading Plato." *Polity* 5 (1973): 489–515.

Kierkegaard, S. *The Concept of Irony.* Trans. L. M. Capel. New York: Harper & Row, 1965.

Kimmerle, H. "Die Widersprüche des Verhältnisses von esoterischer und exoterischer Philosophie in Hegels Systemkonzeptionen." In *Esoterik und Exoterik der Philosophie*, ed. H. Holzhey and W. C. Zimmerli. Basel and Stuttgart: Schwabe, 1977, pp. 139–57.

Klein, J. *A Commentary on Plato's Meno.* Chapel Hill: University of North Carolina Press, 1965. [See esp. the introduction on issues of interpretation.]

Klosko, G. "Criteria of Fallacy and Sophistry for Use in the Analysis of Platonic Dialogues." *Classical Quarterly* 33 (1983): 363–74.

Krämer, H. J. *Arete bei Platon und Aristoteles: zum Wesen und zur Geschichte der platonischen Ontologie.* Heidelberg: C. Winter, 1959.

———. *La nuova immagine di Platone.* Premessa di M. Gigante. Naples: Bibliopolis, 1986.

———. "Neues zum Streit um Platons Prinzipientheorie." *Philosophische Rundschau* 27 (1980): 1–38. [An article review of books by E. Tigerstedt and J. Findlay, among others.]

———. *Platone e i fondamenti della metafisica: Saggio sulla teoria dei principi e sulle dottrine non scritte di Platone con una raccolta dei documenti fondamentali in edizione bilingue e bibliografia.* Trans. and with introduction by G. Reale. Milan: Vita e Pensiero, 1982. [Presently available only in Italian, this work includes a detailed discussion of Schleiermacher's interpretation of Plato, as well as a helpful bibliography of works about the "unwritten" doctrines.]

———. "Retraktationen zum Problem des esoterischen Platon." *Museum Helveticum* 21 (1964): 137–67.

Krentz, A. A. "Dramatic Form and Philosophical Content in Plato's Dialogues." *Philosophy and Literature* 7 (1983): 32–47.

Krüger, G. *Einsicht und Leidenschaft; Das Wesen des platonischen Denkens.* Frankfurt: Klostermann, 1973.

Kuhn, H. "Platon und die Grenze philosophischer Mitteilung." In *Idee und Zahl: Studien zur platonischen Philosophie.* Ed. H.-G. Gadamer and W. Schadewaldt. Heidelberg: C. Winter, 1968, pp. 151–73.

Laborderie, J. *Le dialogue Platonicien de la maturité.* Paris: Société d'édition 'Les Belles Lettres', 1978. [This book is helpful on all aspects of the platonic dialogue form, including the question of interpretation and the history of debate about it, the reasons for which Plato wrote dialogues, the use of myth and irony, and the precursors to the Platonic dialogue form.]

Lachterman, D. "Review of J. Klein's *Plato's Trilogy.*" *Nous* 13 (1979): 106–12.

Lacoue-Labarthe, P. "Typographie," *Mimésis des articulations.* Paris: Aubier Flammarion, 1975, pp. 165–270. [A section of this work is translated in *Diacritics* 8 (1978): 10–23.]

Lafrance, Y. "Autour de Platon: Continentaux et analystes." *Dionysius* 3 (1979): 17–37.

———. "L'avenir de la recherche Platonicienne." *Revue des Etudes Grecques* 99 (1986): 271–92.

Lang, B. "Presentation and Representation in Plato's Dialogues." *Philosophical Forum* 4 (1972–73): 224–40.

Lasso de la Vega, J. S. "El diálogo y la Filosofía Platónica del Arte." *Estudios Clásicos* 54 (1968): 311–74. [Especially helpful on the question of interpretation. The notes contain valuable references to other discussions of interpretation and of the literary dimension of Plato's dialogues.]

Lesser, H. "Style and Pedagogy in Plato and Aristotle." *Philosophy* 57 (1982): 388–94.

Levi, A. "Questioni Platoniche." *Revue de Philologie* 14 (1940): 110–26. [This article focuses on Plato's reasons for writing dialogues.]

Levi, A. W. "Philosophy as Literature: The Dialogue." *Philosophy and Rhetoric* 9 (1976): 1–20.

Levinson, R. B. "Plato's *Phaedrus* and the New Criticism." *Archiv für Geschichte der Philosophie* 46 (1964): 293–309.

Luther, W. "Die Schwäche des geschriebenen Logos." *Gymnasium* 68 (1961): 526–48.

Marten, R. " 'Esoterik und Exoterik,' oder 'Die philosophische Bestimmung wahrheitsfähiger Öffentlichkeit,' demonstriert an Platon und Aristoteles." In *Esoterik und Exoterik der Philosophie*, ed. H. Holzhey and W. C. Zimmerli. Basel and Stuttgart: Schwabe, 1977, pp. 13–31.

Mattéi, J.-F. *L'etranger et le simulacre: Essai sur la fondation de l'ontologie Platonicienne.* Paris: Presses Universitaires de France, 1983. [See esp. part 1 for issues of interpretation.]

McKeon, R. "Literary Criticism and the Concept of Imitation in Antiquity." In *Critics and Criticism*. Ed. R. C. Crane. Chicago: Chicago University Press, 1952, pp. 147–75.

Merlan, P. "Form and Content in Plato's Philosophy." *Journal of the History of Ideas* 8 (1947): 406–30.

Meyer, M. "Dialectic and Questioning: Socrates and Plato." *American Philosophical Quarterly* 17 (1980): 281–89.

Miller, M. H. *Plato's Parmenides.* Princeton: Princeton University Press, 1986.

———. *The Philosopher in Plato's Statesman.* The Hague: Nijhoff, 1980. [See esp. the introductions to both books for issues of interpretation.]

Mittelstrass, J. "Ontologia More Geometrico Demonstrata." *Philosophische Rundschau* 14 (1966): 27–40. [An article review of K. Gaiser's *Platons ungeschriebene Lehre.*]

Moors, K. F. *Platonic Myth: An Introductory Study.* Washington, D.C.: University Press of America, 1982.

———. "Plato's Use of Dialogue." *Classical World* 72 (1978): 77–93.

Muecke, D. C. *The Compass of Irony.* London: Methuen & Co., 1969.

Mulhern, J. J. "Treatises, Dialogues, and Interpretation." *Monist* 53 (1969): 631–41.

———. "Two Interpretative Fallacies." *Systematics* 9 (1971): 168–72.

Nussbaum, M. C. *The Fragility of Goodness: Luck and Ethics in Greek Tragedy and Philosophy.* Cambridge: Cambridge University Press, 1986.

Oehler, K. "Der entmythologisierte Platon: Zur Lage der Platonforschung." In *Das Problem der ungeschriebenen Lehre Platons: Beiträge zum Verständnis der platonischen Prinzipienphilosophie.* Ed. J. Wippern. Darmstadt: Wissenschaftiche Buchgesellschaft, 1972, pp. 95–129.

———. "Neue Fragmente zum esoterischen Platon." *Hermes* 93 (1965): 397–405.

Ogilvy, J. A. "Socratic Method, Platonic Method, and Authority." *Educational Theory* 21 (1971): 3–16.

Palante, G. "L'ironie: Étude psychologique." *Revue Philosophique de la France et de l'Etranger* 61 (1906): 147–63.

Partee, M. H. *Plato's Poetics: The Authority of Beauty*. Salt Lake City: University of Utah Press, 1981.

Perelman, C., ed. *Dialectics*. The Hague: Nijhoff, 1975.

———. "La méthode dialectique et le rôle de l'interlocuteur dans le dialogue." *Revue de Métaphysique et de Morale* 60 (1955): 26–31.

Pieper, J. "Über die Wahrheit der platonischen Mythen." In *Einsichten: Gerhard Krüger zum 60. Geburtstag*. Ed. K. Oehler and R. Schaeffler. Frankfurt: Klostermann, 1962, pp. 289–96.

Plass, P. "Philosophic Anonymity and Irony in the Platonic Dialogues." *American Journal of Philology* 85 (1964): 254–78.

———. " 'Play' and Philosophic Detachment in Plato." *Transactions and Proceedings of the American Philological Association* 98 (1967): 343–64.

Poser, H., ed. *Philosophie und Mythos: Ein Kolloquium*. Berlin: W. de Gruyter, 1979.

Randall, J. H., Jr. *Plato: Dramatist of the Life of Reason*. New York: Columbia University Press, 1970.

Reale, G. *Per una nuova interpretazione di Platone: Relettura della metafisica dei grandi dialoghi alle luce delle 'Dottrine non scritte.' "* 4th ed. Milan: Cooperativa Universitaria Studio e Lavoro, 1986.

Richard, M.-D. *L'enseignement oral de Platon: Une nouvelle interprétation du platonisme*. Paris: Cerf, 1986.

Robinson, R. "Plato's Consciousness of Fallacy." *Mind* 51 (1942): 97–114.

———. *Plato's Earlier Dialectic*. Ithaca: Cornell University Press, 1941.

Roochnik, D. L. "The Impossibility of Philosophical Dialogue." *Philosophy and Rhetoric* 19 (1986): 147–65.

Rosen, S. *Plato's Sophist*. New Haven: Yale University Press, 1983.

———. *Plato's Symposium*. 2nd ed. New Haven: Yale University Press, 1987. [See esp. the introductions of both books for issues of interpretation.]

Rowe, C. J. *Plato*. Brighton, U.K.: Harvester Press, 1984.

———. "The Argument and Structure of Plato's *Phaedrus*." *Proceedings of the Cambridge Philological Society* 212, n.s. 32 (1986): 106–25.

Rudberg, G. "Das dramatische Element bei Platon." *Symbolae Osloenses Fasc.* 19 (1939): 1–13.

Sabine, G. H. "Review of Strauss' *Persecution and the Art of Writing*." *Ethics* 63 (1953): 220–22.

Sallis, J. *Being and Logos: The Way of Platonic Dialogue*. Pittsburgh: Duquesne University Press, 1975. [See esp. the introduction for issues of interpretation.]

Sayre, K. M. *Plato's Late Ontology: A Riddle Resolved*. Princeton: Princeton University Press, 1983.

Schadewaldt, W. See H.-G. Gadamer.

Schaerer, R. *La question Platonicienne: Etude sur les rapports de la pensée et de l'expression dans les dialogues*. 2nd ed. Paris: Vrin, 1969.

———. "Le mécanisme de l'ironie dans ses rapports avec la dialectique." *Revue de Métaphysique et de Morale* 48 (1941): 181–209.

Schleiermacher, F. E. D. *Introductions to the Dialogues of Plato.* Trans. W. Dobson. 1836. Reprint. New York: Arno Press, 1973.

Schmalzriedt, E. *Platon: Der Schriftsteller und die Wahrheit.* Munich: R. Piper, 1969. [On issues of interpretation, see esp. the preface, "Literarische Form und philosophische Wahrheit."]

Scholtz, G. "Zur Darstellung der griechischen Philosophie bei den Schülern Hegels und Schleiermachers." In *Philologie und Hermeneutik im 19. Jahrhundert.* Ed. H. Flashar (with K. Gründer and A. Horstmann). Göttingen: Vandenhoeck & Ruprecht, 1979, pp. 289–311.

Seeskin, K. *Dialogue and Discovery: A Study in Socratic Method.* Albany: State University of New York Press, 1987.

———. "Formalization in Platonic Scholarship." *Metaphilosophy* 9 (1978): 242–51.

———. "Socratic Philosophy and the Dialogue Form." *Philosophy and Literature* 8 (1984): 181–94.

Sesonske, A. "Ryle on the *Republic.*" *Agon,* supp. 2 (1969): 63–71.

Shorey, P. *The Unity of Plato's Thought.* 1903. Reprint. Chicago: University of Chicago Press, 1968.

Sichirollo, L. *Dialegesthai-Dialektik.* Hildesheim: Olms, 1966.

Sicking, C. M. J. "Organische Komposition und Verwandtes." *Mnemosyne* 16 (1963): 225–42.

Sinaiko, H. L. *Love, Knowledge, and Discourse in Plato: Dialogue and Dialectic in Phaedrus, Republic, Parmenides.* Chicago: University of Chicago Press, 1965. [See esp. chap. 1 for issues of interpretation and on why Plato wrote dialogues.]

Solignac, A. See Aubenque, P.

Sparshott, F. E. "Socrates and Thrasymachus." *Monist* 50 (1966): 421–59.

Sprague, R. K. "Logic and Literary Form in Plato." *Personalist* 48 (1967): 560–72.

———. *Plato's Use of Fallacy: A Study of the Euthydemus and Some Other Dialogues.* New York: Barnes & Noble, 1962.

Stenzel, J. *Plato's Method of Dialectic.* Trans. D. J. Allan. Oxford: Clarendon Press, 1940.

———. *Zum Aufbau des platonischen Dialoges.* Festschrift für Karl Joël. Basel: Helbing & Lichtenhahn, 1934.

Stewart, J. A. *The Myths of Plato.* Ed. G. R. Levy. 1905. Reprint. Carbondale: Southern Illinois University Press, 1960.

Stöcklein, P. "Über die philosophische Bedeutung von Platons Mythen." *Philologus,* supp. 30 (1937): 1–58.

Stokes, M. C. *Plato's Socratic Conversations: Drama and Dialectic in Three Dialogues.* Baltimore: Johns Hopkins University Press, 1986. [See esp. the introduction and epilogue on issues of interpretation.]

Strauss, L. "Correspondence concerning *Wahrheit und Methode.*" *Independent Journal of Philosophy* 2 (1978): 5–12.

———. "On a Forgotten Kind of Writing." *Independent Journal of Philosophy* 2 (1978): 27–31.

———. *Persecution and the Art of Writing.* 1952. Reprint. Westport, Conn.: Greenwood Press, 1973.

————. *The City and Man.* Chicago: University of Chicago Press, 1964. [See esp. pp. 50–62 on issues of irony and interpretation.]

Sulliger, J. "Platon et le problème de la communication de la philosophie." *Studia Philosophica* 11 (1951): 155–75.

Szlezák, T. A. "Dialogform und Esoterik: Zur Deutung des platonischen Dialogs 'Phaidros.' " *Museum Helveticum* 35 (1978): 18–32.

————. *Platon und die Schriftlichkeit der Philosophie.* Berlin: W. de Gruyter, 1985. [See esp. the first appendix, "Die moderne Theorie der Dialogform."]

————. "Probleme der Platoninterpretation." *Göttingische Gelehrte Anzeigen* 230 (1978): 1–37. [Article review of books by J. N. Findlay, T. Ebert, G. Watson, L. Tarán, and E. N. Tigerstedt that discuss Platonic esotericism.]

————. "The Acquiring of Philosophical Knowledge according to Plato's Seventh Letter." In *Arktouros: Hellenic Studies Presented to B. M. W. Knox.* Ed. G. W. Bowersock, W. Burkert, and M. C. J. Putnam. Berlin: W. de Gruyter, 1979, pp. 354–63.

Tarrant, D. "Plato as Dramatist." *Journal of Hellenic Studies* 75 (1955): 82–89.

Tejera, V. *Plato's Dialogues One by One.* New York: Irvington Publishers, 1984. [See esp. the "Interdialogical Interlude I" on the issue of irony.]

Thesleff, H. *Studies in Platonic Chronology.* Helsinki: Societas Scientiarum Fennica, 1982.

————. *Studies in the Styles of Plato.* Helsinki: Societas Philosophica Fennica, 1967.

Tigerstedt, E. N. *Interpreting Plato.* Uppsala: Almquist & Wiksell, 1977.

————. *The Decline and Fall of the Neoplatonic Interpretation of Plato.* Helsinki: Societas Scientiarum Fennica, 1974.

Vicaire, P. *Platon: Critique littéraire.* Paris: C. Klincksieck, 1960.

Vlastos, G. "On Plato's Oral Doctrine." In *Platonic Studies.* 2nd ed. Princeton: Princeton University Press, 1981, pp. 379–403. [A review of H. J. Krämer's *Arete*, accompanied by an appendix entitled "Does Ti. 53C8–D7 Give Support to the Esotericist Thesis?" The review was originally published in *Gnomon* 41 (1963): 641–55.]

Watson, G. *Plato's Unwritten Teaching.* Dublin: Talbot Press, 1973.

Weingartner, R. W. *The Unity of the Platonic Dialogue.* Indianapolis: Bobbs-Merrill, 1973. [See esp. the introduction on the issue of interpretation.]

Westerink, L. G., ed. & trans. *Anonymous Prolegomena to Platonic Philosophy.* Amsterdam: North-Holland Publishing Co., 1962.

White, N. *Plato on Knowledge and Reality.* Indianapolis: Hackett, 1976. [See esp. chaps. 5 and 8 on esotericism and writing.]

Wiehl, R. "Schleiermachers Hermeneutik—Ihre Bedeutung für die Philologie in Theorie und Praxis." In *Philologie und Hermeneutik im 19. Jahrhundert.* Ed. H. Flashar (with K. Gründer and A. Horstmann). Göttingen: Vandenhoeck & Ruprecht, 1979, pp. 32–67.

Wieland, W. *Platon und die Formen des Wissens.* Göttingen: Vandenhoeck & Ruprecht, 1982.

Wippern, J., ed. *Das Problem der ungeschriebenen Lehre Platons: Beiträge zum Verständnis der platonischen Prinzipienphilosophie.* Darmstadt: Wissenschaftliche Buchgesellschaft, 1972. [Includes essays by E. Berti, W. Bröcker, H. Cherniss, K. Gaiser, H. Gomperz, H. J. Krämer, H. Leisegang, K. Oehler, L. Robin, J. Stenzel, C. J. de Vogel, and P. Wilpert.]

Wolz, H. G. "Philosophy as Drama: An Approach to Plato's Dialogues." *International Philosophical Quarterly* 3 (1963): 236-70.

Woodruff, P. *Plato: Hippias Major.* Indianapolis: Hackett, 1982.

Wyller, E. A. "The Architectonic of Plato's Later Dialogues." *Classica et Mediaevalia* 27 (1966): 101-15.

Zaslavsky, R. *Platonic Myth and Platonic Writing.* Washington, D.C.: University Press of America, 1981.

Zimmerli, W. C. See Holzhey, H.

Index of Proper Names

The Index of Proper Names includes ancient and modern authors, as well as the names of characters, figures, and places mentioned in this book. Names cited continuously throughout the book (such as "Plato" and "Socrates") are not indexed.

273nn8, 11, 17, 18, 21, 22, 274nn24, 33, 289n21
Campbell, L., 52
Cappon, L. J., 268n11
Careggi, 66
Cebes, 218, 269n4
Cephalus, 22, 23, 32, 270n13, 274n33
Chaignet, A.-Ed., 279n17
Charmides, 114, 120, 192, 194, 197, 236
Charybdis, 122
Cherniss, H. F., 49, 54, 61, 93, 275n1, 276nn12, 15, 16, 277nn19, 20
Clay, D., 5, 6
Clotho, 72
Cocytus, 74
Cohen, R. S., 285n15
Combès, J., 82, 279n17
Congleton, A., 293n3
Cornford, F. M., 276nn12, 15, 16, 277n24
Coulter, J. A., 276n17
Couturat, L., 67, 68, 278n3
Crete, 20, 181, 220
Critias, 67, 69, 80, 114, 115, 118, 120, 192, 194, 197, 278n6, 283n17
Crito, 172, 175, 176, 179, 180, 295n28
Croesus, 218, 230
Cronos, 80
Cross, R. C., 285n13
Currie, G., 286n15
Cusanus, 133

Daedalus, 113, 118
Dalfen, J., 13, 225, 228, 229, 230, 231, 232
Damascius, 82, 278n12, 279n17
Delium, 120
Derrida, J., 12, 14, 144, 149, 155, 157, 164, 166, 269n14, 281n4, 284n25, 289nn22, 25, 290nn26, 28
Descartes, R., 15, 145
Descombes, V., 289n25
Desjardins, R., 9, 10, 14
Diehl, E., 278n9
Diels, H., 280n24, 285nn2, 5
Dilthey, W., 284n25
Diogenes Laertius, 3, 83, 267n4, 282nn7, 9, 283n17, 284n23
Dion, 88, 102
Dionysius II, 86, 87, 88, 91, 96, 115, 259, 279n8, 280n18
Dionysius of Halicarnassus, 281n2
Dionysus, 77, 81
Diotima, 75, 76, 98, 261, 278n6

Dodds, E. R., 39, 40, 272n1, 273nn10, 11, 12, 13, 14, 17, 19, 20, 274nn27, 34
Dorter, K., 13, 215, 216, 217, 218, 219, 220, 221, 222, 223, 224
Duke, J., 284n25
Dümmler, F., 21

Edelstein, L., 279n1
Eden, 26
Edwards, P., 286n17
Ehrenberg, V., 32, 271n20, 272n27
Eleatic Stranger, 82, 105, 147, 154, 227, 278n6, 282n14, 289n23
Er, 32, 69, 72, 74, 77, 133, 271n15
Eros, 67, 70, 75, 79
Euclid, 263
Euripides, 60, 61, 283n18
Europe, 73
Euthyphro, 113, 114, 235, 284n22, 296n9, 297n5
Evenus of Paros, 189

Favorinus, 284n23
Feyerabend, P., 144, 290n25
Fichte, J. G., 142, 151, 286n4
Ficino, M., 278n2
Field, H. H., 299n10
Findlay, J., 14, 268n13, 293n5
Flashar, H., 267n6
Forstman, J., 284n25
Foucault, M., 144
Frede, M., 275n6, 276n16, 290n26
Friedländer, P., 270nn12, 14
Fritz, K. von, 285n12

Gadamer, H.-G., 10, 14, 125, 144, 149, 160, 162, 184, 247, 248, 249, 250, 251, 252, 253, 254, 255, 256, 257, 283n21, 284n25, 284n28, 291n34, 299nn5, 6, 11
Gaiser, K., 14, 53, 54, 93, 267n6, 268n13, 269n14, 280n1, 285n12
Garver, N., 289n25
George, S., 53, 276n12
Germany, 21, 50, 53
Gillies, S., 126
Glaucon, 21, 22, 23, 24, 25, 26, 27, 28, 29, 31, 68, 69, 78, 79, 178, 272n24
Gomperz, H., 54
Goodman, N., 149, 153
Gorgias, 38–43 passim, 70, 89, 263, 273n11, 274n33
Gorgon, 70

314   Index

Gosling, J., 196, 280n2
Graham, A. J., 272n24
Greece, 270n10
Griffin, D. R., 267n1
Griswold, C., 110, 183, 277n18, 279n18, 281n12, 281n1, 284n21, 298n2, 299n12
Grote, G., 54
Grube, G. M. A., 191, 295n22
Gründer, K., 267n6
Gulley, N., 244
Guthrie, W. K. C., 194, 230, 273n21, 274n27, 279n1, 285n12

Habermas, J., 144, 288n13
Hackforth, R., 285n10
Hades, 69, 74, 79, 80, 219, 220, 223
Haldane, E. S., 278n7, 287n10
Hall, R. M., 271n16
Harding, J. M., 289n25
Haring, E. S., 281n9
Harman, G., 299n10
Haslam, M. W., 267n5
Heath, P., 286n4
Hegel, G. W. F., 12, 15, 52, 71, 142, 144, 147, 149–156 passim, 160, 161, 267n6, 269n15, 278n7, 286n4, 287n10, 288n13, 289nn22, 23, 290n27, 291n33
Heidegger, M., 144, 149, 154, 158, 166, 286n3
Helmbold, W. C., 291n38
Hera, 81
Heraclitus, 80, 85, 113, 129, 131, 137, 278n14, 282n7, 288n17
Herder, J. G., 145
Hermann, K. F., 50, 53, 54, 58, 275n10
Herodotus, 283n18
Herring, H., 269n1
Hesiod, 282n8
Hestia, 77
Heyting, A., 251
Hippias, 87, 200, 201, 202, 203, 204, 205, 206, 207, 208, 209, 210, 295n4, 296nn5, 7, 11, 297n7
Hippocrates, 191, 295n23
Hobbes, T., 173
Höffe, O., 285n8
Hoffmann, E., 50, 52
Hölderlin, F., 126
Holzhey, H., 269n15
Homer, 21, 80, 271n19, 282n8, 288n17
Horstmann, A., 267n6
Hume, D., 195, 279n4, 287nn7, 9

Hyland, D., 188, 192, 283n21, 288n14, 293n3, 294n15, 295nn25, 28
Irwin, T., 13, 35, 183, 184, 185, 186, 187, 188, 189, 190, 191, 192, 193, 272nn1, 3, 273nn6, 9, 10, 22, 274nn24, 27, 29, 34, 35, 36, 294nn6, 18, 19, 20, 295nn24, 28
Isles of the Blessed, 73
Ismenias of Thebes, 30

Jaeger, W., 50, 268n6
Janicaud, D., 278n10
Jefferson, T., 4, 268n11
Johnston, W. H., 286n4

Kahn, C., 272n1, 273nn10, 11, 18, 274nn25, 27, 28, 29, 295n4
Kallipolis, 19–33 passim, 270nn6, 8, 271n16
Kambartel, F., 285n14
Kant, I., 12, 142, 145, 146, 149, 150, 151, 155, 161, 195, 259, 264, 265, 286nn1, 4, 5, 287nn7, 8, 9, 288n13
Kaufmann, W., 289nn18, 19
Kelsen, H., 53
Kimmerle, H., 269n15, 284n25
Klein, J., 85, 184, 188, 279n6, 283n21, 294nn15, 16, 295n27
Kleinias, 28, 29
Klosko, G., 185, 186, 192, 294n9, 295nn24, 26
Kojève, A., 290n30
Krämer, H. J., 14, 53, 54, 93, 268n13, 269n14, 285n12
Kranz, W., 280n24, 285n2
Kraut, R., 13, 171, 172, 173, 174, 175, 176, 293nn1, 3
Kroll, W., 270n11, 278n8
Kuhn, T., 144

Laches, 283n17, 289n21
Lachesis, 72
Lachs, J., 286n4
Lacoue-Labarthe, P., 269n14
Lakatos, I., 141, 285n15, 286n16
Langerbeck, H., 265, 299n4
Lazerowitz, M., 286n1
Lee, E. N., 299n12
Leibniz, G. W., 19, 269n1
Levinson, R. B., 269n4, 270n10
Locke, J., 145, 279n4
Lorenz, K., 284n1
Lysias, 70, 97, 98, 118, 120, 121

NOTES ON THE CONTRIBUTORS

Alan C. Bowen received his Ph.D. in 1977 from the University of Toronto. He is currently director of the Institute for Research in Classical Philosophy and Science (Pittsburgh) as well as research associate in the Department of Classics at the University of Pittsburgh and co-editor of *Ancient Philosophy*. His publications and research concern philosophy and the exact sciences in antiquity.

Robert S. Brumbaugh is professor of philosophy at Yale University. He is author of numerous articles on the history of philosophy, as well as of *Plato's Mathematical Imagination* (Bloomington: Indiana University Press, 1954), *Plato on the One* (New Haven: Yale University Press, 1962), *Plato for the Modern Age* (New York: Crowell-Collier Press, 1962), *The Philosophers of Greece* (New York: T. Y. Crowell, 1964), and *Whitehead, Process Philosophy, and Education* (Albany: State University of New York Press, 1982).

Diskin Clay is Francis White Professor of Greek at the Johns Hopkins University (Baltimore, Maryland). He is author (with Stephen Berg) of *Sophocles' Oedipus* (Oxford: Oxford University Press, 1978), *Lucretius and Epicurus* (Ithaca: Cornell University Press, 1983), and a monograph on the philosophical inscription of Diogenes of Oenoanda (to appear in the *Aufstieg und Niedergang der römischen Welt*, Part II, vol. 36). Clay is also an editor (with J. Clay and R. Horwitz) of *John Locke: Questions Concerning the Law of Nature* (Charlottesville: University Press of Virginia, 1988). He is now at work on a book on Plato for the Yale Hermes Guides to Classical Authors series.

Joachim Dalfen is professor at the Institut für klassische Philologie at the University of Salzburg. He is author of *Polis und Poiesis: Die Ausein-*

andersetzung mit der Dichtung bei Platon und seinen Zeitgenossen (Munich: Fink, 1974), as well as of works on Marcus Aurelius and on Greek philosophy and literature. Since 1985 he has also served as rector of the university.

Rosemary Desjardins has taught philosophy at Swarthmore, Bryn Mawr, and Haverford colleges, as well as at the University of Pennsylvania. She is author of *The Rational Enterprise: Logos in Plato's Theaetetus* (Albany: State University of New York Press, 1988), as well as of articles in ancient philosophy.

Kenneth Dorter is professor of philosophy at the University of Guelph, Ontario. He is author of articles on the history of philosophy, aesthetics, and metaphysics. He wrote *Plato's Phaedo: An Interpretation* (Toronto: University of Toronto Press, 1982), and is at present completing a book tentatively entitled *Truth and Perspective*.

Hans-Georg Gadamer is professor emeritus at the University of Heidelberg. One of the most influential philosophers of the twentieth century, Professor Gadamer is best known for his work in philosophical hermeneutics and for his interpretations of Greek literature and philosophy. His major works include *Wahrheit und Methode* (Tübingen: J. C. B. Mohr, 1960), *Platos dialektische Ethik* (Hamburg: Meiner, 1931), *Vernunft im Zeitalter der Wissenschaft* (Frankfurt: Suhrkamp, 1976), *Philosophische Lehrjahre* (Frankfurt: Klostermann, 1977), *Die Idee des Guten zwischen Plato und Aristoteles* (Heidelberg: C. Winter, 1978), *Heideggers Wege* (Tübingen: J. C. B. Mohr, 1983), *Lob der Theorie* (Frankfurt: Suhrkamp, 1983).

Charles L. Griswold, Jr., is associate professor of philosophy at Howard University. He is author of *Self-Knowledge in Plato's Phaedrus* (New Haven: Yale University Press, 1986), as well as of numerous articles on Greek philosophy, philosophy of art, and political philosophy. With the support of a research fellowship from the National Endowment for the Humanities, he has recently worked on the thought of Adam Smith and its connection with the American Founding.

Terence Irwin is professor of philosophy at Cornell University. He is author of *Plato's Moral Theory* (Oxford: Clarendon Press, 1977), *Plato's Gorgias* (Oxford: Clarendon Press, 1979; a translation with notes), *Aristotle: Nicomachean Ethics* (Indianapolis: Hackett, 1985; a translation with notes), as well as of numerous articles in ancient philosophy.

Richard Kraut is professor of philosophy at the University of Illinois, Chicago. In addition to *Socrates and the State* (Princeton: Princeton University Press, 1984), he is author of several articles on the moral philosophy of Plato and Aristotle. Currently he is writing a book on Aristotle's ethics.

Jean-François Mattéi is chairman of the department of philosophy at the Université de Nice, France. He received his Doctorat des Lettres from the Sorbonne in 1979 and is author of, among other works, *L'Etranger et le Simulacre: Essai sur la fondation de l'ontologie Platonicienne* (Paris: P.U.F., 1983) and with D. Janicaud of *La métaphysique à la limite* (Paris: P.U.F., 1983). Mattéi is also editor of the third volume (entitled *Dictionary of Philosophical Works*) of the *Encyclopédie philosophique universelle* (Paris: P.U.F., 1988).

Richard McKim received his Ph.D. from Princeton University and wrote his dissertation on Plato. Since then, he has taught classics and ancient philosophy at the University of Texas at Austin and has published on Greek philosophy. During the 1985–86 year he was a Junior Fellow at the Center for Hellenic Studies in Washington, D.C.

Jürgen Mittelstrass is professor of philosophy at the University of Konstanz, West Germany. He is author of *Die Rettung der Phänomene: Ursprung und Geschichte eines antiken Forschungsprinzips* (Berlin: de Gruyter, 1961), *Neuzeit und Aufklärung: Studien zur Entstehung der neuzeitlichen Wissenschaft und Philosophie* (Berlin: de Gruyter, 1970), *Die Möglichkeit von Wissenschaft* (Frankfurt: Suhrkamp, 1974), *Wissenschaft als Lebensform: Reden über philosophische Orientierungen in Wissenschaft und Universität* (Frankfurt: Suhrkamp, 1982).

Jon Moline is professor of philosophy, dean, and vice president of academic affairs at St. Olaf's College, Minnesota. He is the author of numerous articles on Greek philosophy, as well as of *Plato's Theory of Understanding* (Madison: University of Wisconsin Press, 1981).

Clifford Orwin teaches political science at the University of Toronto. His numerous articles on both ancient and modern political philosophy include a translation and interpretation of Plato's *Cleitophon*, and he has recently completed a book on the problem of justice in Thucydides.

Ronald Polansky is professor of philosophy at Duquesne University. He is the editor of *Ancient Philosophy* and has published articles on Plato and Aristotle in journals such as *Oxford Studies in Ancient Philosophy, Southern Journal of Philosophy*, and *Ancient Philosophy*. Polansky recently completed a book on Plato's *Theaetetus*.

David Roochnik is an associate professor of philosophy and classical studies at Iowa State University. He has published a number of articles on a variety of subjects in Greek philosophy and literature and is currently writing a book on Greek tragedy and Plato.

Kenneth M. Sayre is author or editor of thirteen books, including *Plato's Analytic Method* (Chicago: University of Chicago Press, 1969), and *Plato's Late Ontology: A Riddle Resolved* (Princeton: Princeton University

Press, 1983), as well as of several dozen articles. Currently he is professor of philosophy and director of the Philosophic Institute at the University of Notre Dame, Indiana.

Nicholas P. White is professor of philosophy at the University of Michigan. He is author of *Plato on Knowledge and Reality* (Indianapolis: Hackett, 1976), and of *A Companion to Plato's Republic* (Indianapolis: Hackett, 1979). He has also written articles on the ethics and metaphysics of Plato and Aristotle, on Stoic ethics, and on contemporary metaphysics.

Paul Woodruff teaches at the University of Texas at Austin and publishes in ancient philosophy, ethics, and aesthetics. He has translated Plato's *Hippias Major* (Indianapolis: Hackett, 1982) as well as the *Ion* (Indianapolis: Hackett, 1983), and is now working on a book about Plato's representation of Protagoras.